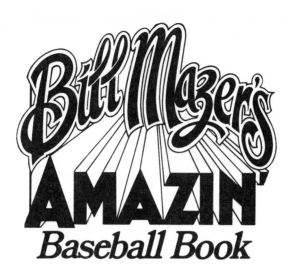

Bill Mazer's AMAZIN' Baseball Book

Bill Mazer's AMAZIN' Baseball Book

By BILL MAZER
With Stan and Shirley Fischler

ZEBRA BOOKS
KENSINGTON PUBLISHING CORP.

ZEBRA BOOKS

are published by

Kensington Publishing Corp.
475 Park Avenue South
New York, NY 10016

First trade paperback edition: April, 1991

Printed in the United States of America

To Dutch: to whom I will always be indebted for her understanding and tolerance while I devoted so much time to the world of sports; and to Arnie, who not only contributed mightily to the book but also served as a key motivating force when I needed it most.

CONTENTS

ACKNOWLEDGMENTS

It takes two to tango, usually three to make a double play, and Heaven knows how many to put a book like this together.

I was lucky. My wife, Dutch, was, as always, an inspiration, and I say ditto for my son, Arnie, who also contributed ideas and illustrations that helped immeasurably.

Of course there never would have been a book had it not been for my pal, publisher Walter Zacharius, who prodded me to the plate when I had serious doubts about handling his pitch.

Considerable help was provided in unearthing what had been deemed unattainable material. For that I am eternally grateful to Barry Halper, baseball historian and collector *par excellence.* Among other good things, Barry delivered the majority of photos that appear herein.

And when it was necessary to verify certain facts, I knew I'd get the authentic answer from Seymour Siwoff and his able staff at the Elias Sports Bureau.

Every batting order requires a reliable cleanup hitter and, in our case, we couldn't have topped Wallace Exman, our scrupulous and indefatigable editor at Zebra Books.

In the last-but-not-least department, I am deeply indebted to my friends Shirley and Stan Fischler, who did so much in coauthoring the book. To one and all, THANKS!

Bill Mazer
New York City, 1990

We would like to acknowledge the exceptional efforts of our research editors, Arnie Mazer, Dennis Nolan, and Victor Lavella, and would also like to thank Bruce Myerson, Mark Malinowski, Linda Lundgren, Jeff Resnick, Kay Ohara, David Katz, Steve Haft, Neal Dorosin, Mitchell Polo, Jeff Diamant, Chris Botta, Keven Friedman, Adam Reich, Teresa Faella, Josh Sipkin, Rich Calder, Greg Goldstein, Nick Lanteri, Jean Snyder, Michael Burton, Nadia Moszkowicz, and Stuart Kliternick. In addition, special thanks and a Standing O to our artist Andrew Knipe and copy editors Jane Cee Redbord and David Gilbert, and Zebra's Associate Production Manager, Laura Langlie.

Stan and Shirley Fischler
New York City, 1990

INTRODUCTION

God, I wish my *zayde* were still alive—a strange thought as I sit in this picture window at Mickey Mantle's restaurant in mid-Manhattan where I do a daily two-hour radio program on WFAN, New York's all-sports station. A strange thought because I'm a grandfather myself now, with a grandson who calls me *zayde*. What's a *zayde?* Yiddish for *grandfather*. But you would never have called my *zayde*, Jacob, "grandfather." He was definitely a *zayde*, as I am to my grandson Jacob.

What makes me think of my *zayde?* Well, on this day Mickey Mantle is in. Donald Trump has just dropped by, Keith Hernandez will be in soon, as will the comic, Richard Lewis. I've grown into a name-dropper, but that's the point: my *zayde* would have loved it! Just as he loved me and I him. Sounds schmaltzy, I know, but it wasn't back then when I was a young boy growing up in Brooklyn.

I represented something important to my *zayde:* he thought I was the reincarnation of my great, great *zayde*, a man named Lebenyou Muhte, who was the rabbi of a village called Soslov, near the city of Kiev in the Ukraine. He was the man with the great memory—of the town, for the town, and mostly of the Talmud.

My *zayde* used to speak of this man, Lebenyou Muhte, with such reverence that to this day I can remember the litany of his life as the older generation used to relate it to me. He drank two samovars of tea each day, while keeping his head buried in the Talmud. He was a man of great learning and—most important to the life of yours truly—a man of incredible memory.

When I first showed signs of having both a copious memory and an interest in books, I remember the nods and knowing looks that passed between my *zayde* and my father and mother. You could almost hear them saying to each other: "It's Lebenyou Muhte." He'll be a scholar, a Talmud *chuchum* . . ." So it was way back in my childhood when remarks about my memory began.

Who knew it would end up centering around sports?

Now, many years later, I sit at Mickey Mantle's and at Fox Five, the TV station in New York City where I anchor the evening sports news and do a weekend half-hour show called *Sports Extra.* And the trivia questions pour in.

Did I get my memory from this village sage, Lebenyou Muhte? I never knew the man and I rather doubt he knew the batting averages of the various czars of Russia. But I can tell you this: When my mother passed away, I went out to Milwaukee for the funeral and while the prayers were being said, I noticed this little boy standing nearby. He was saying the prayers without benefit of a prayer book. He obviously had the prayers committed to memory, and it was not just one prayer; it was a sequence of many, many prayers over many, many pages.

I looked at this kid and thought: My God, I'm looking at myself, because that's what I was like as a little boy.

When the service was over, I asked my niece about the boy and learned that he was her son, Benjy. She said, "We named him after your father, Ben."

"What kind of memory does he have?" I asked.

"Really terrific," she replied.

A little later the boy got up enough courage to come to me and say, "Uncle Bill, can I ask you a question?"

"Sure, Benjy," I answered.

"Do you really know Mickey Mantle?" he queried, to my shock.

I thought, The combination is here all over again. Here's a kid with a memory and with an interest in and love of sports. It felt as though I was the clone of Lebenyou Muhte and this little boy, Benjy, was my clone.

Another tale . . .

Even though sports has occupied the center of my professional life for dogs' years now, I have never entirely given up being just a bit of a scholar. In particular, I follow Biblical studies and archaeology with interest. After the Dead Sea Scrolls were discovered, I read almost every word published about them for some years, including a particular tome called *The Sacred Mushroom and the Cross,* by John Allegro. The author concluded, through studies of ancient Hebrew and a dead language called Acadian, that the Old Testament prophets had used hallucinogenic mushrooms to write most of the Talmud!

I was as shocked, horrified and just plain mad about his findings as I had been about Walter O'Malley's moving the Dodgers out of Brooklyn. But instead of writing an irate letter to the author, I decided to find an expert of my own, a biblical scholar who was also a linguist, and I finally found one in the person of a professor at Columbia University. I called this erudite gentleman at his home, and basically the following conversation took place:

"Professor, my name is Bill Mazer and I'd like to ask you a question if you have the time."

"What is it you want?" the gentleman asked with quite a pronounced accent.

"Would you please tell me what you think about John Allegro?"

The learned professor burst into an unbelievably heated diatribe: "How dare you call me about that man who has disgraced the academic community!" he began, and went on like this for several minutes. Then suddenly he stopped.

"Are you Bill Mazer? Is that what you said your name was?"

"Yeah," I responded, somewhat nervously.

"The sports announcer?"

Again I responded in the affirmative, and suddenly he blurted, "Well, tell me, what's wrong with the Knicks?"

I laughed so hard, I nearly went into convulsions.

Lastly . . .

I was at the television station where I do *Sports Extra* one night, and ended up in a heated discussion about soccer players with several of my colleagues. Ironically, I could not, for the life of me, remember the name of the great Soviet athlete who had played in the World Cup in 1982.

It just so happens that the Soviet Embassy is almost directly across the street from the Channel Five studio, so I blithely said, "No problem, I'll just walk across the street to the embassy. Somebody there will know the name I'm trying to remember."

There is always a New York City cop standing guard in front of the Soviet Embassy, and as I walked up, that evening's representative of New York's finest asked me, "What do you want, Bill?"

"I want to find out the name of one of their soccer players."

"Okay," he said, "go right in there to the foyer."

I walked into what seemed like a typical New York City apartment building foyer, but there wasn't a soul in sight. I stood there trying to find a bell to push when suddenly a voice came out of nowhere: "What do you want?"

"I want to find out something about a Soviet soccer player . . ." I began.

"Just one moment."

A door opened and a woman looked at me and said, "Oh, it's *you!*"

"What do you mean, Oh it's me?"

"I know you. You're the 'Amazin'' (the nickname given me by my Fox Five anchor, John Roland, in reference to my ability to answer trivia questions). What do you want?"

"I have a trivia question for you," I said a bit sheepishly. "What was the name of the player on your soccer team in 1982 —the star from the Ukraine?"

"I don't know," she said, "but"—and she called out another young woman, a lovely blonde—"she's from the Ukraine. She'll tell you."

I repeated my question and the young blonde instantly replied, "Oleg Blokhin."

"That's right!" I yelled, just as surprised as some of my questioners are each night.

"Hah! We stumped you!" the blonde exclaimed, and the two went triumphantly back inside the embassy.

These tales are my way of pointing out that the love of sports transcends all boundaries, whether it's generations, countries, classes, sexes, or races. And the so-called trivia surrounding sports is really the thread, the history, if you will, of sports itself.

Frankly, I had covered the trivia aspect of baseball in previous books and had no intention of writing any more *if* it was going to be trivial, but when Walter Zacharius, Chairman of the Board at Zebra Books, suggested that I combine a genuine history of the game through trivia with significant autobiographical remembrances along the base paths, I went for his pitch.

Needless to say, I believe that baseball trivia has its place in a book of this kind, but I must add that I take the game too seriously to simply settle for a shallow question-and-answer volume about a sport that deserves much more. Therefore what I have tried to do is present as wide a spectrum of baseball history as possible and deliver it in several forms. Hopefully, all will be palatable.

I strongly believe that the personal side—my firsthand experiences in the baseball business—is as vital as the other elements and I do hope you find it as enjoyable in the reading as I have in the writing.

After all, baseball has been a part of my life since I was old enough to take a five-cent trolley-car ride to Ebbets Field when I was still wearing knickers, and my love affair with the game has endured over the years. If you'll forgive the bromide, I've seen 'em all. Now I'll try to tell all to you. I do hope you enjoy it.

PART ONE

BASEBALL FROM BIRTH TO "THE BABE"

NINETEENTH-CENTURY BASEBALL

(1845–1900)

The historian Jacques Barzun noted, upon observing the customs and practices of the burgeoning young United States, "Whoever wants to know the heart and mind of America had better learn baseball."

Even though it all began less than two hundred years ago, in an era when there were newspapers in virtually every little burg in the country, the origins of The Game are still a matter of controversy and endless argument.

Talk about the beginnings of baseball and three things usually come to mind: Abner Doubleday, Cooperstown, New York, and the year 1839. The popular story is that a young man named Abner Doubleday wrote down the rules of baseball and laid out the baseball diamond in Cooperstown in 1839 when he was a West Point cadet. The only fact known for certain about Doubleday is that he was the man who ordered the first shot fired at Fort Sumter, driving the Union into the Civil War. As for the popular myth of his inventing baseball, it's a moot point whether Doubleday ever played the game in his life. And Cooperstown was just a nice village in upstate New York where they played a game commonly known as "town ball."

Baseball—"The Great American Pastime"—almost certainly evolved from two British games, rounders and cricket. Cricket was introduced to the American Colonies in the mid-1700's, and there is some evidence that rounders actually may have preceded cricket.

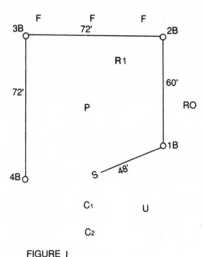

FIGURE I

Fig. 1: This is a diagram of a baseball playing field in the early 1840's, shortly after bases had replaced stakes, and the game was actually being called "baseball." Modeled almost exactly after the British game of rounders, the game required 12 players: two catchers, a thrower or pitcher, four basemen, three outfielders, a roving outfielder, and a roving infielder. *(from the collection of Barry Halper)*

While there probably wasn't a great deal of time for our country's forefathers to play games—they were immigrants with more important events to handle, like the American Revolution and such—the rudiments of rounders and cricket, including a ball, a bat, and a playing field with stakes or "bases," were there and were passed down from generation to generation.

The game that would become baseball was called town ball because people congregated on the village green to play it, and it usually took the form of a modern rounders field: four bases with a "thrower's" area and a "striker's" or hitter's area.

In New York a variation closer to cricket, often called "one-eyed cat"—if you can discover the derivation of that name, you're a better trivia buff than I—was played, with only one base to which the hitter ran and then ran home. In other words, the rules of the early game were unique to the area of the country in which it was played: Improvisation was the rule of thumb. For example, if wooden stakes weren't available, trees, rocks, anything could be used to make a base. Still, even as late as the end of the nineteenth century, players would still yell, "Run to your stake!"

In early baseball, the practice of "plugging" was common, and it was because of the lack of rules, or uniformity, that this practice was eventually eliminated. Plugging was when a fielder threw the ball directly at a base runner to get an out. With no set rules, the kind of ball used varied widely, and some balls were harder than others, so it's easy to imagine the number of injuries caused by plugging. By the early 1840's plugging was passé everywhere except, we are told, in Boston, and you'll have to ask them in Boston why they continued to lambaste the runners to get an out.

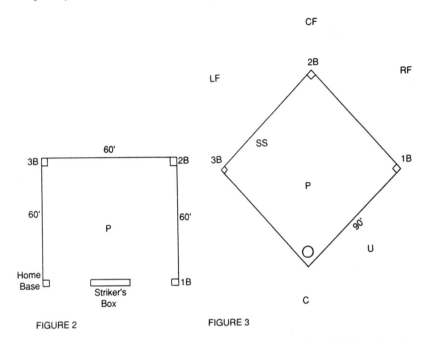

FIGURE 2

FIGURE 3

Fig. 2: This was the basic layout of the field for "town ball," which is believed to have appeared in the late 1830's in the city of Boston. Town ball existed until the 1860's, and had no set rules as to the number of players on a side. It varied from 11 to 16. *(from the collection of Barry Halper)*

Fig. 3: This is a replica of the baseball playing field designed by Alexander Cartwright in the spring of 1846. Cartwright's team, the Knickerbocker Baseball Club (of New York City), voted to accept this scheme, and the first game between organized clubs was played on this field, with the distance between the pitcher and home plate being 45 feet. The only changes in this diagram in over 100 years are that the shortstop now plays behind the baseline, home plate has been moved back to the corner of the diamond, and the distance from pitcher to home is 60 feet, 6 inches. *(from the collection of Barry Halper)*

Town ball had become standardized in Boston and Philadelphia by the late 1830's. The game had a box—or diamond—shape to it, with the striker facing the thrower. Each team carried 11 to 16 players. But it would be in New York City that what we call base-

Abner Doubleday was, for many years, credited with "inventing baseball," when it is now known that a young bank teller and surveyor named Alexander Cartwright (shown here) actually designed the modern baseball diamond. *(National Baseball Hall of Fame)*

ball would finally be designed and delineated, by a young bank teller, surveyor, volunteer fireman and member of the Knickerbockers Base Ball Club named Alexander Joy Cartwright.

Cartwright studied the fields used for town ball and "the New York game"—the one that was also called one-eyed cat—and rejected them both. During the winter of 1845–46 Cartwright designed the "baseball square," which we now call the baseball diamond. The field had 90 feet to a side, with a base on each corner. More importantly, a whole new set of rules went along with the playing field. Instead of two catchers, a pitcher, four basemen, three outfielders and two rovers, a side, or team, would now field only nine players.

The game, as drafted by Cartwright and his colleagues, was almost baseball as we know it today: nine innings, three strikes constituted an out, and there would be three outs a side per inning. Fielders produced outs by catching a batted ball on the first bounce, catching a ball on the fly in the air, tossing the ball to a base ahead of the runner—no more plugging—or tagging a runner out between bases.

Cartwright and the Knickerbockers then publicly challenged any team with the nerve to test them. It was another group of gentlemen, calling themselves "The New York Nine," who dared the Knickerbockers. Ironically, the only place the two clubs could find to accommodate Cartwright's new design was an old cricket field, called Elysian Field, in Hoboken, New Jersey. It was there that the first recorded "public" game of baseball took place, on June 19, 1846. The Knickerbockers had to make do without the services of their genius, Cartwright—he was named the game's umpire—and they were roundly trounced by the New York Nine, 23–1. Cartwright, as umpire, recorded another first—he fined player James Whyte Davis for swearing!

While Cartwright eventually disappeared from the New York scene to follow the gold rush craze to California and finally to Hawaii where he died in 1892, baseball remained, and grew. In 1858, the National Association of Base Ball Players (NABBP) was organized, with some 50 teams from the East. Unfortunately, one of the basic reasons for the formation of the NABBP was to bar players who were not considered gentlemen. Baseball, as opposed to town ball, was originally played by men of "the right social standing," which, of course, meant excluding anyone who might be tarred with the brush called "professionalism."

Brooklyn sported the first club to "go on the road," when the Excelsiors clobbered clubs in Baltimore, Wilmington, and Philadelphia in 1860. At times there were as many as 3,000 fans—they were called "cranks" then—at the games.

Enter the Civil War, and it might be assumed that baseball would be forgotten in the midst of this nightmare that tore the country literally into pieces. But no, on Christmas Day, 1862, forty thousand troops watched baseball games. In prison camps Union prisoners challenged their Confederate captors to baseball games, and the game spread south.

Cricket had been too slow for Americans, true children of the Industrial Revolution. But, as Mark Twain once said, baseball was "the very symbol, the outward and visible expression of the drive and push and rush and struggle of the raging, tearing, booming nineteenth century."

WHICH PITCHER IS CREDITED WITH INVENTING THE CURVE BALL?

William Arthur "Candy" Cummings, a slight, five-feet-nine-inch, 120-pounder for the New York Excelsior Club, is regarded as the originator of the curve.

Cummings got the idea in 1863 when he was throwing clam shells with his friends and became interested when the projectiles turned to the right and left. He decided to try it out on a baseball.

He toyed with his posture, thinking that controlled the flight. He also tried gripping the ball in different ways. Finally, in 1867, his team traveled to Boston for a series of games. In a game against a Harvard team, his curve began to show. Unfortunately for Cummings, for years many men would refuse to accept the fact that the ball actually moved.

WHO IS BELIEVED TO BE THE FIRST SALARIED BASEBALL PLAYER?

Lipman Pike, who played with the Athletic Club of Philadelphia in 1866. Pike is considered number one, although for many years Al Reach, second baseman of the New York Eckfords, bragged that he was the first pro of the game. However the printed records of the day (*The Sporting Life* of Philadelphia and *The Sporting News* of St. Louis) agree that Pike was the first to sign.

Pike, who was Jewish, was also the first star of the game. He once hit six home runs in a game and was baseball's first long-ball threat.

Lipman Pike, one of the earliest stars of baseball, is recorded as being the first salaried player. *(from the collection of Barry Halper)*

WHICH PROFESSIONAL TEAM HAS THE RECORD FOR MOST CONSECUTIVE GAMES WITHOUT A LOSS?

The Cincinnati Red Stockings became an all-professional team in 1869. Managed by Harry Wright, the Red Stockings met the likes of the New York Mutuals in Brooklyn. They played a game before then-President Ulysses S. Grant. The club traveled almost 12,000 miles from coast to coast, using trains, stagecoaches, and boats. Over 200,000 people saw them play. They finished the 1869 season with 65 victories (no losses and one tie). In 1870, the Red Stockings won 26 and tied one before losing to the Brooklyn Atlantics on June 14, 1870. The record of 92 straight games without a loss still stands today and will never be broken.

WHEN WAS THE OLD NATIONAL ASSOCIATION FORMED AND WHICH TEAMS WERE ORIGINAL MEMBERS?

On St. Patrick's Day, March 17, 1871, at Collier's Cafe on Broadway and 13th Street in New York City, the National Association was formed. The charter member teams were: Boston Red Stockings (run by the Wright Brothers who had founded the Cincinnati Red Stockings), the Chicago White Stockings, the Cleveland Forest Citys, the Fort Wayne Kekiongas (not actually present at the meeting), the New York Mutuals, the Philadelphia Athletics, the Rockford Forest Citys, the Washington Nationals, the Washington Olympics, and the Troy Haymakers. The Washington Nationals never actually fielded a team and the Brooklyn Eckfords chose not to participate that first season, but when the Kekiongas dropped out midway, the Eckfords joined. The Philadelphia A's won the first National Association championship.

WHAT BECAME OF THE OLD NATIONAL ASSOCIATION?

The National Association brought about its own demise largely because the loosely knit federation was led by bunglers, was rife with player-drunks, and manipulated throughout by gamblers. To illustrate the sorry state of the National Association in 1875, the champion Boston Red Stockings finished with an .899 winning percentage, while at the same time five of the Association's 13 teams finished with percentages below .200. In fact, almost half the teams didn't even play a complete schedule!

A number of corporate types saw this shambles as an opportunity to: 1) put the old National Association to its final rest and 2) make a hefty profit while doing so. On February 2, 1876, at the Grand Central Hotel in New York City, these businessmen met, drafted a constitution for a new organization and decided to call it the National League. The league's new president would be Morgan Bulkeley, but it was generally acknowledged that William Hulbert, owner of the Chicago White Stockings, actually ran the National League. After the inaugural season Bulkeley resigned and Hulbert was named president, the office he held until his demise in 1882. Hulbert was known as a tyrant who maintained almost absolute control of the National League, despite many of the same kinds of problems that had plagued the old National Association, to wit, scandals, bankruptcies, and corruption.

The original cities that comprised the National League were Boston, Chicago, St. Louis, Hartford, New York, Philadelphia, and Louisville. The new federation presented its opening game on April 22, 1876, at Philadelphia, with Boston taking the game 6–5, before 3,000 fans.

WHAT MAN COINED MANY WELL-KNOWN BASEBALL TERMS AND EXPRESSIONS IN THE 1870's?

While on tour in England in 1874, Henry Chadwick created a dictionary of baseball terminology for the benefit of British writers, including assists, passed balls, balls, fungoes, grounders, pop-ups, double plays, and overthrows. He also used the term "line balls," which later became known as line drives.

WHERE WERE THE FIRST FOREIGN EXHIBITIONS HELD AND WHEN?

Called barnstorming, the first foreign tour dates back to 1874, when members of the Boston and Philadelphia teams of the National

Association went to Ireland and England to play fourteen baseball games and seven cricket matches. In 1888, A. G. Spalding gathered a group of twenty players, mostly from the Chicago National League team, and made the first around-the-world baseball tour, playing in such areas as New Zealand, Australia, Ceylon, Egypt, Italy, France, England, and Ireland.

WHAT PITCHER GAVE UP THE PROMISE OF A RECORD-BREAKING CAREER TO RUN A SPORTING GOODS BUSINESS?

Al Spalding, whose name graces the popular rubber balls, had the talent to be one of the greatest pitchers of all time. He first pitched at the age of 17, leading the Forest City team of Rockford, Illinois, to a victory over the Washington Nationals. That victory, at such a young age, made him a national hero. He began his major league

career in the National Association with the Boston Red Stockings, going 207–56 in his first five years. He mastered an unorthodox underhand delivery that led him to a remarkable fastball and a fantastic 57–5 record in 1875, a year that saw the Red Sox go 71–8 and completely dominate the inferior opposition.

A. G. Spalding gave up a promising pitching career to run a sporting goods business. *(National Baseball Hall of Fame)*

Spalding had an ambitious streak in him, however, and a very keen eye for business. When new Chicago White Stockings owner, William Hulbert, offered him $4,000 and the position of manager and team captain to come pitch in his hometown of Chicago, Spalding jumped at the chance. He even brought three of his fellow Red Sox stars with him, breaking up the Boston dynasty. Spalding became the first player to truly appreciate the business side of baseball, and assisted Hulbert in the creation of baseball's "first corporation," the National League. Nowhere was the concept of the new league as big a hit as in Chicago, where Hulbert and Spalding resided.

Spalding capitalized on his position as player-manager of the White Sox by also opening, as the *Chicago Tribune* reported, "a large emporium in Chicago where he sold all kinds of baseball goods and his place became the headquarters for the western ball clubs." Spalding clothed the players of his team in uniforms his shop produced, along with different-colored hats for each position. He was also granted a monopoly by the league to produce the official baseballs for the league, as well as its official guide. Spalding was on cloud nine.

Upon William Hulbert's death, Spalding assumed complete control of the club, becoming president and principal owner in 1882. By that time, Spalding had lost his interest in playing baseball, as his club was still successful without his playing for them, and had slowly withdrawn from active play between 1878 and 1882. Spalding had a brief but dazzling career; had he continued playing, it is entirely possible he could have owned the career mark for wins by a pitcher, now owned by Cy Young.

WHAT WERE THE RULES REGARDING AN INDIVIDUAL AT BAT IN 1876?

The game of baseball in 1876 bore very little resemblance to the game we know and love today. The pitcher, still known to some as the "bowler," stood 45 feet from the plate, and threw underhand. The catcher did not wear a mask, and stood a few feet behind the hitter, trying as hard as he could to catch the ball on its first bounce. A pitcher's success often depended on his ability to change speeds on his pitches.

The batter could tell the pitcher whether he wanted a high pitch or a low pitch. There wasn't a defined strike zone, but called strikes were defined by the umpire on the spot. A strike was a "good pitch" that the batter let go by, and after the third strike, the umpire issued a warning. If the batter then let a fourth "good pitch" or strike go by, he was called out on a called strikeout. If the pitcher threw nine balls that were not where the batter requested, he drew a walk, which was counted as an at bat. By 1882, seven balls constituted a walk, and by 1889, the four-balls-a-walk rule came into play.

WHO WAS THE FIRST BATTER IN NATIONAL LEAGUE HISTORY?

George Wright, brother of Harry and co-founder of the Cincinnati Red Stockings, which became the new National League Boston Red Stockings. Harry designated George the "lead-off" batter, whereupon George made his mark in baseball history on April 22, 1876, when he was retired on a ground ball to the Philadelphia Athletics' shortstop.

George Wright, brother of Harry and co-founder of the Cincinnati Red Stockings, was the lead-off batter for the National League on April 22, 1876. *(National Baseball Hall of Fame)*

WHO PITCHED THE FIRST NO-HITTER IN NATIONAL LEAGUE HISTORY?

George Washington Bradley of St. Louis, against Hartford, 2–0, on July 15, 1876.

WHAT IS THE MEANING OF THE TERM "CHICAGOED," OR "WHITEWASHED"?

In the 1876 season, the Chicago White Stockings won 52 games, many of them by shutouts. "Chicagoed" and "Whitewashed" meant losing, by no runs scored, to the White Stockings.

Chicago won the first-ever National League pennant that year, with Al Spalding on the mound a great deal of the time.

WHAT WAS A "FAIR-FOUL" HIT IN 1876?

If a ball was in fair territory for *any part* of its trajectory, it was a recorded hit. Ross Barnes was a master of the "fair-foul" hit and led the league with .429.

To show how nonspecialized the ballplayers of the last century were, Chicago's first baseman, Cal McVey, recorded a .347 batting average and also pitched five winning games. McVey spelled pitcher Al Spalding, who would rest his pitching arm by playing McVey's position occasionally.

WHAT WAS THE LOUISVILLE SCANDAL OF 1877?

The Louisville Grays of the new National League had a large lead over Boston, and with 15 games to go, the Grays only needed to win seven games to clinch the flag. Boston, on the other hand, needed to take 13 of their remaining 15. Louisville looked to be a cinch.

Suddenly the Grays began dropping games due to strikeouts, pick-offs, and silly errors. Almost impossibly, Louisville lost its lead, finishing second to Boston. What could have been a dramatic pennant chase ended up instead with a foul odor. The *Louisville Courier-Journal* strongly implied that the Grays had taken a dive, reportedly under the direction of catcher Jim Devlin, who suddenly appeared around town mysteriously sporting an array of new finery and jewelry.

A subsequent league investigation agreed with the rumors and resulted in the lifetime expulsion of Devlin, outfielder George Hall, shortstop Bill Craver, and Al Nichols. Nichols, a substitute player, was allegedly the key connection to seedy New York gamblers, and the mastermind behind the Louisville swoon.

WHAT NEW EQUIPMENT BECAME PART OF BASEBALL IN THE 1870s?

The Catcher's mask was adopted in the National League in 1875, as were the first fielding gloves and the chest protector for catchers. Turnstiles were introduced at ball fields in the mid-1870s. Ironically the baseball itself had not yet been standardized.

HOW DID A .400 HITTER HAVE HIS OFFICIAL BATTING AVERAGE REDUCED TO .317?

Cap Anson, the first major-leaguer to get 3,000 hits, originally was credited in 1879 with a .407 average on 90 hits in 221 at bats for the Chicago White Stockings. Some years later, however, National League officials checked published daily box scores and could only find that Anson produced 72 hits in 227 trips to the plate for a .317 average.

It was soon discovered that league official secretary, Nick Young, occasionally had added a few hits when he compiled the statistics. Another time, Young had credited 57 stolen bases to Bug Holliday, who that year (1896) stole only one base for the Cincinnati Reds! The situation was further confused by the practice, in 1879, of counting walks as at bats.

Anson is now credited by the Hall of Fame with 90 hits in 227 at bats during the 1879 campaign, an average of .396.

Cap Anson was the first major-leaguer to get 3,000 hits. *(National Baseball Hall of Fame)*

WHO WAS THE LAST PITCHER TO START EVERY GAME IN WHICH HIS CLUB WAS VICTORIOUS?

In 1879, Will White of the Cincinnati Red Stockings pitched in 76 of his team's 80 games. White compiled a record of 43 wins and 31 losses for a 1.99 earned run average. The Redlegs finished the season with a 43–37 record, and in all 43 wins, White started for them.

WHAT GREAT FIELDING THIRD BASEMAN OF THE 1880's DIDN'T USE A GLOVE?

Until the 1880's players' use of gloves was split about fifty-fifty, with half of the players wearing two-finger gloves on each hand and the other half wearing the predecessor of the modern baseball glove, although unpadded and unwebbed. Some, however, felt that wearing a glove was a sissy way to avoid the pain normally associated with the game. One of these players was star second baseman Fred "Sure Shot" Dunlap, who said he didn't need "the thing." Dunlap went through his entire career not wearing the glove, and he must have been on to something, because he led the National League in fielding four times during the 1880's, playing for Cleveland, St. Louis, Detroit, Pittsburgh, and finally Washington of the old American Association.

WHAT TEAM WAS BANISHED FROM THE NATIONAL LEAGUE IN 1880?

After tumbling into the cellar in 1880, the Cincinnati Red Stockings had to put up with the scorn of the other teams in the league. When the club insisted on selling beer at its home games and leasing its park to teams that played on Sunday, National League President William Hulbert was persuaded to expel the Redlegs from the league.

WHAT WAS THE WORST-ATTENDED GAME IN THE NATIONAL LEAGUE?

On September 27, 1881 at Troy, New York, a game between the

Chicago White Stockings and the host team from Troy drew an audience of twelve fans to the rain-swept field. The White Stockings, who had the pennant clinched, were playing their final game of the season and boasted such stars as Cap Anson, who hit .399 that year, and outfielder Mike "King" Kelly, who batted .323 and, like Anson, was later elected to the Hall of Fame. Despite the rain, umpires ordered the game played since there were, in fact, a dozen paying customers on hand and it was the last game of the regular schedule.

WHAT LEAGUE RIVALED THE NATIONAL LEAGUE, STARTING IN 1882?

In 1882, National League President William Hulbert passed away and the league lost its exclusive monopoly on major league baseball. Cincinnati, Louisville, and St. Louis (note that these three teams were all National League castoffs and, more significant, all in cities in which breweries and the sale of beer were an important part of the city's economy) combined with outfits from Pittsburgh, Philadelphia, and Baltimore to form the rival American Association.

At the outset, the quality of play was inferior to that in the older league, but its flamboyant operation, which included beer in all its parks, baseball on Sunday, and halving the National League's fifty-cent admission price, provided a sharp contrast to the tight-fisted, cadaverous image of the old-guard moguls. Dressing its players in gorgeous silks and showing no qualms about hiring black-listed players or raiding National League rosters for disenchanted stars, the American Association soon attained parity, compelling the National League to keep pace by reinstating New York and Philadelphia and dropping the franchises in Troy and Worcester. The American Association lasted until 1891.

WHO KEPT SCORE FOR THE CHICAGO WHITE STOCKINGS—THE TEAM THAT IS NOW THE CUBS— FROM 1882 TO 1891?

Al Spalding, then president of the White Stockings, felt that the official scorer should not be subjected either to pressures for favors or to criticism. Writer Alex Haas penned that Spalding kept the identity of his official scorer secret for an entire decade. No one, including Cap Anson, the team manager, the league president, who received the scores, or the press, had any idea who the official scorer was. Even the chap who mailed the tallies to the league office was in the dark; he only knew he was mailing something for his dear old mum.

The anonymous postman was the son of Elisa Green Williams, who was the official scorer. While attending every game, Mrs. Williams sat demurely between the wives of Cap Anson and Abner Dalrymple, scoring every play without revealing that her scribbles were official.

WHAT BASEBALL CLUB HOLDS THE DISTINCTION OF HAVING THE LONGEST-RUNNING NICKNAME IN PRO SPORTS?

The Philadelphia Phillies came into the National League in 1883, having moved from Worcester, Massachusetts. In Massachusetts, the baseball club was known as the Brown Stockings; however, the National League club in Philadelphia was immediately dubbed the Phillies and has remained so named from 1883 on.

Although the club was known as the Blue Jays in 1944 and 1945, the nickname was never *officially* changed from the Phillies.

WHO WAS THE BEST HOME-RUN HITTER BEFORE BABE RUTH?

Roger Connor, an outfielder-first baseman who spent eighteen years in the National League before the turn of the century, blasted 136 home runs, in addition to 441 doubles and 233 triples, fifth on the all-time list behind notables Ty Cobb, Honus Wagner, and Sam Crawford. He also compiled a lifetime batting average of .317.

Born on July 1, 1857 in Waterbury, Connecticut, Connor played semipro ball up and down New York's Hudson River Valley and started his major-league career with the Troy Haverstraws, then of the National League. His first year in the bigs, Connor hit .332 with three home runs. Finally, in 1883, the club signed him to a whopping $1,800 contract, which, with bonuses, came to $2,100—this in an era when a steak dinner cost a whole quarter. Connor justified manager John Clapp's faith in him, hitting .357 to lead the club.

Connor played for Troy for 11 years, was released in 1894, and immediately signed with the St. Louis Browns. One year to the day after joining the Browns, Connor found himself back in New York. He celebrated his return by smacking three singles, two doubles, and a triple, as the Browns rolled, 23–2. Each time up to the plate, the fans gave him a standing ovation.

Roger Connor was professional baseball's greatest hitter in the days before Babe Ruth. *(National Baseball Hall of Fame)*

Roger Connor died in Waterbury, Connecticut, on January 4, 1931, forgotten by all, but not before he witnessed a fellow named Ruth perform some Connorian baseball feats.

HOW DID THE "LOUISVILLE SLUGGER" BAT MAKE ITS DEBUT?

The Louisville Slugger, produced by Hillerich & Bradsby, is the best-known trademark in baseball bats, as well as the longest lasting. It traces its heritage back to 1884, when Pete Browning, one of the best hitters of the time, was playing for Louisville. Playing in a crucial series, Browning broke his bat in his final at bat of the first game. Unlike now, when a player always has five personal bats on hand, broken bats were a bigger deal then, and when one did break, it was time to construct another. Usually, the player would sweat out the waiting period while another bat was being made by using a teammate's bat, but because of the importance of the series, and the importance of Browning's hitting to Louisville, Browning convinced the owner of the local wood-turning shop, J. F. Hillerich, to make a bat that was an exact duplicate of the one that he had broken. Hillerich followed his orders very carefully, and had the bat, made from the wood of a wagon tongue, ready the next day. Browning connected for four hits with the bat, and Hillerich's reputation rapidly grew. Eventually his wood-turning shop became the biggest bat manufacturer in the world, with the Louisville Slugger, named after the bat of Pete Browning, the top of the line.

WHAT HALL OF FAMER PERSONALLY POSTPONED THE BREAKING OF BASEBALL'S COLOR BARRIER FOR ABOUT 60 YEARS?

White Sox first baseman Adrian "Cap" Anson.

In 1884, two black players, brothers Moses Fleetwood and Welday Walker, played for the Toledo Mudhens of the American Association, with Moses appearing in 42 games, batting .263, and Welday appearing in five. The American Association had been recognized then by the National League as a major league, but in baseball's "official eyes" today, this record is not a "real" part of the game's history.

Midway through the 1884 season, Anson's Chicago White Stockings played the Mudhens. Anson was recognized as one of the top—if not the top—players of the time, as well as baseball's most outspoken racist among the players. He informed the Mudhens on the day of the game that the White Sox would play the scheduled game only if the Walkers were kept off the field.

No one challenged Anson for three years, until another black, George Stovey, who had been playing with Newark in the International League, was given the opportunity to play in the National League. Unfortunately Anson wasn't ready to change his mind. He openly admitted that he had a "dislike for Negroes," and prevented Stovey from joining the league. Anson's one-man color barrier was not challenged again until long after he died.

WHAT YEAR SAW THE FIRST POSTSEASON COMPETITION (FORERUNNER OF THE WORLD SERIES) BETWEEN THE NATIONAL LEAGUE AND THE AMERICAN ASSOCIATION?

In 1884 the National League pennant winner, the Providence Grays, won a best-of-five game postseason series against the New York Metropolitans of the upstart American Association. This was also the first year ever that the pennant had been decided on a percentage basis rather than simply on Games Won.

WHAT CLEVELAND MINOR-LEAGUER WAS ARRESTED ON MAY 28, 1885, FOR PLAYING BASEBALL ON SUNDAY?

Joseph Andrew Sommers, later a major-league catcher, was arrested in Cleveland and charged with playing ball on a Sunday. During the ensuing jury trial, the team attempted to submit proof that baseball had been played on Sunday in Cleveland for some time without prosecution of the then-existing "blue laws" that prohibited entertainment on the Sabbath. Insisting to the jury that the only legal issue was whether Sommers had played ball on Sunday or not, the judge refused the team's evidence. Since Sommers had already admitted to playing baseball on Sunday, the verdict of guilty was inevitable.

The club appealed the ruling on the grounds that the law was unconstitutional because it ignored anyone whose religion demanded a holy day other than Sunday. A rather complicated addition to the appeal was the argument that Sommers had not been "playing" the game of baseball but adhering to his legal right to an "avocation." The appeal, although inventive, was denied.

WHAT WAS THE MOST UNUSUAL CRITICISM OF AN UMPIRE?

In 1886, an irate baseball fan, enraged over inferior officiating, composed the following poem:

Mother, may I slug the umpire,
May I slug him right away?
So he cannot be here, mother,
When the clubs begin to play?

Let me clasp his throat, dear mother,
In a dear, delightful grip,
With one hand and with the other
Bat him several in the lip.

Let me climb his frame, dear mother,
While the happy people shout,
I'll not kill him, dearest mother,
I will only knock him out.

Let me mop the ground up, mother,
With his person, dearest do,
If the ground can stand it, mother,
I don't see why you can't, too.

WHO INVENTED SPRING TRAINING?

Cap Anson, Chicago White Stockings, 1886. Following the 1885 season, player-manager Anson, a disciplinarian who implicitly believed in the integrity of baseball, became disenchanted with the off-year deportment of some of his players. As their paunches grew, so did Anson's boiling point drop until, finally, he read the riot act to his players.

In an unusual order, Anson instructed the White Stockings to report to him almost two months before the start of the 1886 season. Rather than send them right out to the ballpark, Anson took the players to Hot Springs, Arkansas, on the theory that the famed resort would do wonders for their collective midsections.

Anson organized a rigorous daily training schedule, despite the complaints of his employees. The man who is considered one of the greatest first basemen of all time was undaunted. He had led the White Stockings to five pennants and he was an extremely prideful man.

Although the complaints continued, Anson pursued his unique

preseason training program until just prior to the start of the 1886 campaign. Soon the White Stockings began to perceive the method to his "madness." Their tummies shrank and their muscles tightened. When the 1886 schedule was launched, the White Stockings were in the best shape of any major-league club and breezed to the pennant. Cap Anson, who had startled the baseball world with his innovative spring training order, soon found that others were copying his preseason program until, at last, it became very much *de rigueur* in baseball.

NAME THE EVANGELIST WHO ALSO WAS A TOP-FLIGHT BASEBALL STAR.

Billy Sunday. Before turning to a career on the pulpit as the Reverend Billy Sunday, he was a superb outfielder for the Chicago White Stockings, although his hitting left something to be desired. Sunday debuted on May 22, 1883, and proceeded to set a record by striking out in his first 14 at bats. However, many observers credited Sunday with helping Chicago win the pennant in 1886. It all happened in a crucial game between Detroit and Chicago with the White Stockings holding a slim lead over their opponents.

Detroit had two men on base with two out and catcher Charley Bennett at the plate. The pitch was just where Bennett wanted it and he slammed the ball toward very deep right field. Sunday, who was considered the fastest man in both leagues, turned and ran in the direction of the ball. He leaped over a bench on the lip of the outfield and continued running. As he made his way, Sunday shouted: "Oh, God. If you're going to help me, help me now!" At this point Sunday leaped in the air and threw up his hand, nabbed

Billy Sunday, the man who saved ball games from the Chicago White Stockings' outfield before he took up saving souls from the pulpit. *(National Baseball Hall of Fame)*

the ball, and fell on his back. Thanks to Sunday, Chicago won the game and, eventually, the pennant.

Sunday enjoyed telling friends that he played for two teams, the White Stockings and "God's team." When asked how he got on God's team, Billy would explain: "I walked down a street in Chicago with some ballplayers, and we went into a saloon. It was Sunday afternoon and we got tanked up and then sat down on a curbing. Across the street a company of men and women were playing on instruments—horns, flutes, and slide trombones—and the others were singing the gospel hymns that I used to hear my mother sing back in the log cabin in Iowa and in the old church there where I used to go to Sunday school. I arose and said to the boys, 'I'm through. I am going to Jesus Christ. We've come to the parting of the ways.' "

Although his teammates needled him, Sunday followed the Salvation Army singers into the Pacific Garden Restaurant Mission on Van Buren Street. Billy may not have known it at the time, but he was on his way to the sawdust trail where, as he put it, he would emerge as the scrappiest antagonist that "blazing-eyed, eleven-hoofed, forked-tail old Devil" ever had to go against.

WHO WAS THE "MIGHTY MITE?"

The ace pitcher for the 1886 American Association's pennant-winning St. Louis Browns was Bobby Caruthers, who stood five feet seven inches and weighed 138 pounds—in his shoes, some said! The Mighty Mite had a 30–14 record that season, while also batting .342 and playing the outfield when he wasn't pitching! Caruthers pitched a 218–99 record through nine seasons (1883–1892).

WHAT RULE EXISTED IN THE 1887 SEASON THAT HOISTED BATTING AVERAGES OUT OF SIGHT?

Major-league baseball rules for the 1887 season counted a walk as a hit and that rule, combined with allowing batters four strikes, created a field day for batters, with more than a dozen .400-hitters recorded that year.

If the "walk-hits" were removed from the records, however,

there would have been only three .400-hitters in 1887. For instance, Harry Stovey's average (.402), with his walks removed from his hits, dropped to a lowly .286!

WHEN WAS THE LONGEST POSTSEASON COMPETITION AND WHICH TEAMS PARTICIPATED IN THIS GRUELING BASEBALL MARATHON?

In 1887 the National League pennant winner, Detroit, challenged the American Association champ, St. Louis, to a 15-game series that took place in 10 different cities. While Detroit won 10 of the 15 games against the Browns, a lot of fans didn't show up and the concept was dropped due to disappointing gate receipts.

WHO WAS THE AUTHOR AND WHERE DID HIS POEM, *CASEY AT THE BAT*, FIRST APPEAR?

Ernest Lawrence Thayer's classic baseball poem was published in the *San Francisco Examiner* on June 3, 1888. Who can forget the immortal last lines:

> *Oh, somewhere in this favored land the sun is shining*
> *   bright;*
> *The band is playing somewhere, and somewhere hearts*
> *   are light,*
> *And somewhere men are laughing, and somewhere*
> *   children shout;*
> *But there is no joy in Mudville—mighty Casey has*
> *   struck out.*

WHO WAS THE BEST PITCHER AT FINISHING WHAT HE STARTED?

Denton True "Cy" Young, who pitched for Cleveland, St. Louis, and Boston in the National League, and Cleveland and Boston in the American League, won 511 games, more than anyone in major-league baseball history; and Young completed more than anyone. The right-hander started 816 games and finished 753. A surplus of Cy Youngs could have wiped out the relief pitching industry, which, of course, hardly existed in those days anyway.

HOW DID CY YOUNG ACQUIRE HIS NICKNAME?

Denton True "Cy" Young is regarded as one of the greatest pitchers of all time. He holds the record for most career wins, complete games, innings pitched, as well as losses. During his 22 seasons (1890–1911) in baseball, he threw three no-hitters in his career, and posted twelve 20-win seasons as well as five 30-win seasons.

When he was a youngster trying out for the Cleveland Spiders, he pitched in front of the Cleveland scouts, and they couldn't believe what they saw. The Ohio farm boy was a fantastic pitcher, with a fastball that blurred before the eyes. One scout commented, "He sure gets the ball over the plate quickly," and the other one replied, "Faster even than a cyclone." Thus, Denton True Young became Cy Young, short for Cyclone.

"Cy" Young, winner of 511 major league games. *(from the collection of Barry Halper)*

WHO IS CREDITED WITH BEING THE FIRST PINCH HITTER IN PROFESSIONAL BASEBALL?

Mickey Welch of New York was allegedly the first pinch hitter when he came to bat for pitcher Hank O'Day in 1889.

WHAT HALL OF FAMER TURNED DOWN A $10,000 CONTRACT OFFER FROM THE NATIONAL LEAGUE IN ORDER TO STAY IN THE PLAYERS' LEAGUE?

In 1890, the Players' National League of Baseball Clubs (PNLBC) was formed as competition for the National League and the corporate atmosphere of the Senior Circuit. The Players' League, also known as the Brotherhood League because of its association with the baseball players' first union, the Brotherhood, which had been founded in 1885, was an experiment in owner/player profit sharing, and soon after its founding, 80% of the National Leaguers jumped to the new league. Al Spalding, president and principal owner of the White Sox, was told to hunt for "big game" in order to keep the National League going. His target was Mike "King" Kelly, one of the best players of the 1800's. Spalding offered Kelly a three-year, $10,000 contract, and told Kelly that if $10,000 wasn't enough, the King could write in his own price. Supposedly, Kelly asked Spalding if the contract meant Kelly would have to "quit the Brotherhood." Spalding responded, "That's just what it means." After mulling over the problem, Kelly told Spalding, "I want the ten thousand bad enough, but I've thought the matter over, and I can't go back on the boys. And neither would you. I'm with the Brotherhood." Unfortunately for Kelly, the Players' League folded after the 1890 season.

WHO WAS KNOWN AS "THE HOOSIER THUNDERBOLT"?

Amos Rusie of the New York Giants was the first true sports hero in New York City. Known as "the world's greatest pitcher," Rusie was a big, strong man whose raw speed and accompanying lack of control became legendary. The mystique that surrounded his dominating fastball—which was one of the main reasons for the addition of 10 feet to the distance of the pitching mound from home plate—gave him a presence on the mound unmatched by any other pitcher of his day. Amos also had the dubious honor of leading the National League in walks five times, and is fifth on the all-time list for bases on balls.

Once a fastball thrown by Rusie knocked Baltimore shortstop Hughie Jennings unconscious for almost four days. The next batter smacked a fastball into Rusie's ear, causing him permanent hearing damage. Rusie averaged 20-plus wins from 1890 to 1898, including his career-best season of 1897, when he was 29–8 with the league's best ERA.

Amos Rusie sported the most fearsome fastball of his era but also had the dubious honor of leading the National League in walks five times! *(National Baseball Hall of Fame)*

WHICH TEAM BECAME THE FIRST TO WIN CONSECUTIVE FLAGS WITHOUT A SINGLE HALL OF FAMER ON THE ACTIVE ROSTER?

When Brooklyn won the National League crown in 1890, the team did not have a Hall of Famer on the roster. Oyster Burns led the team in hitting with a .304 average and Bob Caruthers was 40–11 with a 3.13 earned run average in winning the 1889 American-Association flag. In 1890, Burns led the National League in runs batted in with 128 and Caruthers went 23–11 with a 3.09 ERA. The feat also marked the only time a team won a flag in two different leagues in consecutive years.

WHAT WAS THE BEST TRICK PLAY THAT FAILED?

"The safety ball," used by the Baltimore Orioles in 1890. This was a pluralized version of the hidden-ball trick. In this case the Orioles' outfielders would hide a few baseballs in strategic locations near their positions.

The theory was that when a ball was hit in their vicinity, they might occasionally utilize one of the "safety" balls in order to hold the batter to a single. But in practice the ploy failed when an opponent hit a sharp drive to left-center field. Pursuing the legitimate ball, the left fielder suddenly came upon a "safety" ball, picked it up, and hurled the sphere to second base, thereby holding the amazed batter to a single.

Unfortunately for the Orioles, the industrious center fielder had tenaciously pursued the correct baseball, finally trapped it, and heaved his ball back to the infield. At first thinking he was suffering from double vision, the umpire suddenly realized a ruse was afoot and charged Baltimore with a forfeit defeat.

WHEN DID A BALLPARK GO UP IN SMOKE WHILE A FIGHT BROKE OUT ON THE DIAMOND?

During a bitterly fought game between the Baltimore Orioles and the Boston Braves on May 16, 1894, in Boston, the Orioles' truculent third baseman, John H. "Mugsy" McGraw, had antagonized several members of the home team. The hostility multiplied in intensity until finally McGraw became embroiled in a fight with Boston's equally belligerent first baseman, Tommy "Foghorn" Tucker.

As the players bloodied themselves on the field, the frenzied fans worked themselves to fever pitch in the stands. Suddenly a gang of hoodlums watching the game in the bleachers decided to set their seats on fire. What began as a prank degenerated into a disaster. Within a few minutes, the blaze spread to other parts of the stadium,

John "Mugsy" McGraw of the Baltimore Orioles, circa 1894. *(from the collection of Barry Halper)*

eventually burning down not only the ballpark but 170 other buildings as well. According to one estimate, the property damage resulting from the ballpark fire ran into the millions of dollars!

WHAT IS THE ALL-TIME HIGH FOR A SINGLE-SEASON BATTING AVERAGE?

Hall of Famer Hugh Duffy, a five-feet-seven-inch outfielder for the National League Boston Beaneaters, set the all-time high when he hit .438 in 1894. In addition to this feat, Duffy led the league in home runs, hits, doubles, slugging average, and total bases.

WHO RECEIVED THE WORST SALARY RAISE?

Hugh Duffy. After setting the all-time batting mark of .438 in 1894, he was at first refused a raise by the Boston club's management. Duffy continued to argue his case until the start of the 1895 campaign, when he finally scored a Pyrrhic victory—a $12.50-a-month salary increase. However, an amendment to the agreement provided that Duffy was also compelled to become team captain. A clause in the captain's section of his contract stipulated that Duffy, as captain, was responsible for all lost equipment. By the season's end, the club had lost so much equipment that his increased liabilities far outweighed his boost in salary.

Hugh Duffy still holds the all-time high for a single-season batting average, hitting .438 in 1894. *(National Baseball Hall of Fame)*

WHO WAS THE FIRST MAJOR-LEAGUER TO RECORD FOUR HOMERS IN ONE GAME?

Bobby Lowe, teammate of the aforementioned Hugh Duffy, in 1894. Lowe's record was matched in 1896 by "Big Ed" Delahanty, who was awarded four boxes of chewing gum for his accomplishment!

WHAT WAS THE FIRST TEAM TO USE BACKUP PLAYS ON DEFENSE?

The Baltimore Orioles (not the same team currently located in Baltimore) dominated the opposition in the mid-1890's with powerful hitting, but the true key to their success was a fielding strategy that was decades ahead of its time. At the time, the Orioles' style was called "inside baseball," and opposing teams were so stunned by the ease with which the Orioles controlled the game in the field that they claimed it was illegal. The Orioles were the first team ever to set up relay throws and to rotate the defense in order to back up their teammates. On a typical ball hit to left field, the third baseman would swing to the outfield grass to receive a relay throw, while his position would be covered by the shortstop, with the second baseman staying where he belonged. The pitcher and catcher moved into position to back up on overthrows, while the center fielder backed up the left fielder in case he couldn't catch the ball. The Orioles were also the first team to use fake steals as a weapon, but it was their revolutionary fielding techniques that set them apart from the rest of the National League.

HOW DID THE TERM "BLEACHERS" COME INTO USE?

The ballparks of the late 19th century, like the game of baseball itself, had the appearance of being temporary edifices, with the perception being that they would exist only as long as the curious sport with which they were associated. They weren't stadiums, as they are today, but playing fields surrounded by seating for observers. The stands were made out of wood, as were the fences. Some portions of the stands were partially protected by a wooden roof, while others were simple, unsheltered wooden seats made from boards that gradually bleached to a pale gray in the elements. Designated the less expensive seats because they lacked a roof, the "bleacher" tradition lives on to this day.

WHICH TEAM WAS THE WORST IN BASEBALL HISTORY?

The National League Cleveland Spiders, 1899. Unlike the oft-ridiculed 1962 New York Mets, who finished 60½ games out of first place, the Cleveland club was conspicuously worse. They won only 20 while losing 134 for a .130 percentage, and finished 84 games behind the first place Brooklyn team. They lost a record 24 in a row. The Clevelanders scored only 529 runs during the entire season while 1,252 were scored against them.

A NEW CENTURY
AND A NEW LEAGUE

(1900–1918)

It was now the dawn of the twentieth century and the game of baseball would undergo massive changes in the next two decades.

For one thing, the National League (which had absorbed the old American Association in 1891) had become debt- and scandal-ridden as well as unwieldy. The league sported 12 teams once it absorbed the American Association, and had reneged for years on its annual promise to create two six-team divisions.

After the debacle of the pathetic Cleveland Spiders in 1899, the National League went back to its old eight-team format, cutting out Cleveland, Washington, Louisville, and Baltimore. The reorganized league consisted of Boston, Brooklyn, Cincinnati, New York, Philadelphia, Pittsburgh, St. Louis, and Chicago.

But the problems within and without the league still existed. Violent behavior and language were commonplace on the field, umpire-baiting was virtually a way of life, the players hated the $2,400 salary limitation, and the owners were constantly squabbling among themselves. Furthermore, other forms of entertainment—dance halls, theaters, a new industry called silent movies, and other burgeoning sports—were taking a big bite out of the attendance at baseball games.

Competition, that great American way of life, would soon provide the catalyst that would temporarily rejuvenate the game of baseball.

IN 1900, AN ENTERPRISING YOUNG JOURNALIST NAMED BAN JOHNSON HAD ASPIRATIONS OF FORMING A NEW MAJOR LEAGUE THAT WOULD RESEMBLE THE ALREADY-EXISTING NATIONAL LEAGUE. THE NATIONAL LEAGUE OWNERS AGREED TO TALK WITH HIM. WHAT HAPPENED THEN?

The National League owners snubbed Johnson. He waited in a hallway outside the owners' annual meeting for several hours, after which they had agreed to talk with him. But when the meeting was finished, they quickly departed by a side door, leaving Johnson standing in the hall.

Instead of getting mad, Johnson chose to get even. He met with Charles Comiskey, a one-time player and manager after whom Chicago's venerable Comiskey Park is named, and between the two of them, they created the American League. The new league instituted harsh but effective rules for player conduct and raided the team rosters of the National League royally. Of the 182 players in the American League for its first season, 111 had been recruited from the National League.

Furthermore, Johnson and Comiskey chose to ignore the National Agreement, under which all of organized baseball supposedly operated, and placed American League teams in such National League cities as Baltimore/Washington, Boston, Chicago, and Philadelphia.

The winners of the American League pennants in 1900 and 1901 were the Chicago White Sox, featuring then-stars Frank Shugart at shortstop, Hermas McFarland in left field, and pitcher John Katoll.

Ban Johnson, enterprising young journalist, would turn a snub into a windfall. *(National Baseball Hall of Fame)*

BEFORE THE 1900 SEASON, THE CINCINNATI REDS OBTAINED AMOS RUSIE IN A TRADE FROM THE NEW YORK GIANTS. RUSIE HAD BEEN ONE OF THE BEST PITCHERS OF THE 1890's. WHILE IT MAY HAVE SEEMED LIKE THE REDS HAD GOTTEN THE BEST OF THE TRADE AT FIRST, THE GIANTS WOULD SOON EVOLVE AS A CLEAR-CUT WINNER. WHAT PLAYER DID THE GIANTS GET FROM THE REDS?

Christy Mathewson, who won 373 games from 1900 to 1916, was traded to the Giants for Amos Rusie, in what may have been arguably the most one-sided trade in baseball history. During the season of the trade, neither pitcher won any games. For Mathewson, it was onward and upward from there on. Winning thirty games or more in fourteen seasons, Matty won thirty-seven in 1908, a modern National League record that still stands.

MATHEWSON

Christy Mathewson won 30 or more games in 14 seasons, and in 1908 won 37 games, a record that has stood until today. *(from the collection of Barry Halper)*

Besides being a pitcher of epic proportions, Mathewson was also known for his honesty. His word was so respected that umpires often asked him for help on close plays.

Yet another aspect of Christy Mathewson was his courage to say what he thought was right. While every other person connected with the sport at the time denied that the White Sox were throwing the 1919 World Series, Mathewson, who was by then a Giants coach, was the only baseball man to bring it out to the public. In fact, two years before the Black Sox scandal, Mathewson tried to get Hal Chase, an outstanding first baseman of his time, banned from baseball for betting and gambling on baseball games.

Mathewson, whose 373 wins gives him the National League record in a tie with Grover Cleveland Alexander, was one of baseball's greatest pitchers.

WHO ACHIEVED THE WORST FIELDING PERCENTAGE IN THE MAJOR LEAGUES?

Charlie Hickman, New York Giants, 1900. A butter-fingered third baseman, Hickman muffed an average of almost one out of every five chances for an .836 fielding percentage. However, to Hickman's credit, he never committed nine errors in a game. That dubious claim to fame belongs to Andy Leonard of the Boston Braves. Then again, there was third baseman Mike Grady then of Philadelphia, who, in 1895, made four errors on a single ball.

For Grady, the problem started with a ground ball that he fumbled. As the runner crossed first safely, Grady pegged the ball over the first baseman's outstretched glove. The runner moved over to second, then dashed on to third. The toss to Grady at third was in time for the tag, but Mike dropped the ball for his third error. This time the runner sprinted home and, predictably, Grady hurled the ball over his catcher's head for the fourth and final miscue.

WHAT WAS THE WORST COMPLETE GAME BY A PITCHER?

Harley "Doc" Parker, who played for both the Chicago Cubs and Cincinnati Reds between 1893 and 1901, plumbed the pitching depths in 1901. The unfortunate hurler was allowed to remain on the mound for nine full innings during which he allowed 26 hits and 21 runs. Not surprisingly, Parker lost the game and hastened the use of relief pitchers.

WHAT PITCHER USED TO CALL IN HIS OUTFIELDERS AND INFIELDERS IN THE NINTH INNING AND PROCEED TO STRIKE OUT THE SIDE?

George "Rube" Waddell, arguably baseball's most eccentric eccentric, performed this feat many a time, usually successfully. However, despite the myriad fans who insist that they saw this event happen, Rube never was permitted by his manager, the legendary Connie Mack, to do this in a regulation major-league game. Still, Rube pitched an enormous amount of exhibition games, as there was extensive barnstorming in the pre-Ruth, pre-Cobb days when he pitched. He was a powerful drawing card for these barnstorming appearances, and the thousands who flocked to see the legendary Rube were often treated to this unique spectacle, with Rube usually striking out the side on nine pitched balls. Mack related this story of one particular time Rube pulled this stunt:

"I remember one game in Memphis when for some reason Mike Powers caught Rube instead of Ossee Schreckengost, his regular catcher. Harry Davis was managing the club for me that day and we had a 6–0 lead in the ninth when Rube called in his infielders and outfielders. He fanned the first two batters and struck out the third, too, but Powers dropped the ball on the third strike and the batter reached first.

"The next two batters hit little pop flies behind Rube and his tongue was hanging out chasing them. He wanted the players to return, but Davis insisted that Waddell work it out the best he could. He finally struck out the last batter with the bases filled, and this time Powers held the ball. Rube was just about exhausted by then."

Waddell was one of the greatest lefties of all time, with accolades coming from, among others, Cy Young. Rube earned some extraordinary marks such as his strikeouts-to-walks ratio in 1902, when he struck out 210 and walked 67, and 1904, when he struck out 349 and walked 81.

Rube Waddell may have been one of baseball's greatest eccentrics as well as one of the game's greatest lefties. *(National Baseball Hall of Fame)*

BEFORE NOLAN RYAN FANNED 383 BATTERS FOR THE CALIFORNIA ANGELS IN 1973, WHO HELD THE AMERICAN LEAGUE RECORD FOR STRIKEOUTS?

Rube Waddell, elected to the Hall of Fame in 1946, struck out 349 batters in 1904 for the Philadelphia Athletics, a record that stood for 69 years. Rube led the league in strikeouts six consecutive years, from 1902–1907. But as noted before, there was an eccentric side to Rube. For example, if there was a parade in town, Rube might very well skip the game to watch the parade—even if it took place on a day he was scheduled to start. Fishing, playing marbles, and sandlot baseball were other reasons for Rube to miss games. He once left the club for a week during the season to go on a fishing trip, without notifying the team of his whereabouts!

Many wondered how good this boyish pitcher could have been if he had applied himself. As it was, his fastball and curve ball were good enough to earn him a plaque in Cooperstown.

WHAT WAS THE WORST FIELDED GAME?

Detroit Tigers vs. Chicago White Sox, May 6, 1903. The American League rivals managed to commit a total of 18 errors—the record for a nine-inning game—Chicago being credited with 12 errors and Detroit with six.

FRANK CHANCE, CUBS FIRST BASEMAN IN THE LEGENDARY "TINKER TO EVERS TO CHANCE" DOUBLE-PLAY CONTRIBUTION, DID NOT BEGIN HIS CAREER AS A FIRST BASEMAN. WHERE DID HE PLAY?

From 1898 to 1902 Chance was a second-string catcher. The Cubs shifted him to first permanently in 1903 to get his bat in the lineup.

Frank Chance, of the famous "Tinker-to-Evers-to-Chance" battery on the Cubs, later managed the club. *(from the collection of Barry Halper)*

HOW DID BASEBALL'S WORLD SERIES DEVELOP?

When the Boston Pilgrims won the American League pennant in 1903, the Sox challenged the National League champion Pittsburgh Pirates. It would, the Sox insisted, be a true championship series. At first the Pirates' management refused the challenge, but the public insisted that it be played and, as a result, a best-of-nine "World Series" took place. The Pilgrims (soon to be permanently dubbed "Red Sox") won the series, five games to three, in a tremendous upset. No World Series was played in 1904 because of a dispute between the leagues, but by 1905 the annual fall classic was here to stay.

WHO WAS THE FIRST BATTER IN THE FIRST WORLD SERIES?

Ginger Beaumont, center fielder for the Pittsburgh Pirates, was the first batter in the first World Series played in Boston on October 1, 1903. Facing the Pilgrims' Cy Young, Beaumont flied out to Boston center fielder Chick Stahl. Although their leadoff man failed to get on base, the Pirates went on to score four runs in the first inning and eventually won the game, 7–3.

ONE OF THE GREATEST PLAYERS EVER WAS INTENT ON MAKING BASEBALL HIS CAREER AS A YOUTH IN GEORGIA. AT 17, HE WROTE LETTERS TO ALL THE CLUBS OF THE SOUTH ATLANTIC (SALLY) LEAGUE, ADVERTISING HIS TALENTS AND ASKING FOR A TRYOUT. WHO WAS THIS FUTURE STAR WHO RECEIVED NOT A SINGLE REPLY?

Tyrus "Ty" Cobb. Cobb was determined to be a big-leaguer, but Dad Cobb wanted young Ty to attend college and be a doctor. After Cobb's anonymous letters to the Sally League clubs got no responses, Cobb persisted and asked a friend to help him. So Reverend John Yarborough, Cobb's manager on the local Royston (Georgia) Rompers, agreed to assist. When Yarborough gave Cobb a letter of introduction to the owner of the Augusta club, he warned Cobb, "You are too bullheaded, quarrelsome, and resentful over being given orders. You will be fined and fired before the season is over."

Sure enough, only two games after Cobb was signed by Augusta, he was fired. Cobb's hard-boiled manager, Con Strouthers, told his feisty ex-player, "I only want players who follow orders."

But Cobb hooked up with a team in Anniston, Alabama, soon after the dismissal. Cobb wrote about the good news to his still-disapproving dad and received a return wire that said, "NOTE NEW ADDRESS. DO NOT COME HOME A FAILURE."

Cobb hit .370 in 22 games with Anniston before earning another chance with Augusta in 1904. Augusta's new manager, Bill Leidy, worked many hours giving Cobb the benefit of his vast knowledge. It paid off: Cobb won a spot in the big leagues and played in 41 games for the Detroit Tigers in 1905. He hit .240 in his rookie year.

Years later, Cobb partially credited his father's wire for some of his success. "That wire," Ty said, "spurred me on. I carried it with me for years. And I never did go back to Royston a failure."

Ty Cobb (shown here long after his playing days, with Fred Clarke, former player-manager of the Pittsburgh Pirates, left; Charles Gehringer, second from left; Cobb and Rogers Hornsby, far right) produced 4,191 hits in his 24-year career. To put this in perspective, Rogers Hornsby, shown here to Cobb's left, had 1,261 fewer hits in a 23-year career. *(from the collection of Barry Halper)*

A YEAR BEFORE FINALLY MAKING THE BIG LEAGUES, TY COBB WAS PRAISED BY THE IMMORTAL SPORTS SCRIBE, GRANTLAND RICE. WHO GAVE RICE HIS SCOOP ABOUT THE THEN-UNKNOWN MINOR-LEAGUER?

Cobb batted .237 in the South Atlantic League in 1904, but he knew he was destined for the major leagues. Sure enough, after that season, the *Atlanta Journal*'s Grantland Rice began receiving notes saying how good a seventeen-year-old prospect named Ty Cobb was. Based on these letters, Rice mentioned Cobb several times in his articles, printing notes to the effect that Cobb was attracting attention and showing big-league promise.

"This Cobb has great talent and may be one of the coming stars of baseball," wrote Rice. "Cobb hits well and has speed on the bases."

It turned out that the letters about Cobb that Rice received were not penned by Cobb admirers—they were written by Ty Cobb himself!

WHAT PLAYER HAD THE MOST SEASONS IN MAJOR-LEAGUE BASEBALL WITH A MORE-THAN-300 BATTING AVERAGE?

Ty Cobb had twenty-three .300-plus seasons.

WHO IS BASEBALL'S BEST HITTER?

Ty Cobb, "The Georgia Peach," of the Detroit Tigers. In his 24-year career, Cobb produced 4,191 hits in 11,429 at bats and a lifetime batting average of .367. To put Cobb's achievement in proper perspective, consider that Rogers Hornsby, the remarkable St. Louis Cardinals slugger, enjoyed a lifetime average of .358 over 23 years, yet had 1,261 fewer hits, while Pete Rose, who eventually broke Cobb's record of 4,191 hits, did so in the same 24-year career span, but had 14,053 at bats and a career batting average of only .303.

WHAT BROTHER PITCHING PAIR WERE BOTH CALLED "JEFF"?

The Pfeffer brothers, National League pitchers from 1905 to 1924, were really named Francis Xavier and Edward Joseph Pfeffer, but for some unknown reason, they both went by the moniker of "Jeff." To distinguish between the two, Francis was called "Big Jeff," with Joseph sticking to plain "Jeff." Big Jeff had great stuff with little control and disappeared from the majors after pitching a no-hitter. However, plain Jeff had season wins of 23, 19, 25, 17, 16, and 19 games respectively during his major league career.

WHAT WAS THE BEST PITCHING PERFORMANCE IN A WORLD SERIES?

Christy Mathewson of the New York Giants shut out the A's three times in the 1905 World Series.

The Philadelphia Athletics went into the 1905 World Series after surviving a late-season slump that threatened to knock them out of the top spot in the American League, which they had occupied since August. In addition, the A's lost their starter, Rube Waddell (26–11, 287 strikeouts), in an off-the-field accident. As if this weren't bad enough, they faced a New York Giants team that cruised to the National League pennant with a 105–48 record, capturing the flag by nine games. In this fall classic, the A's would have to face the great Christy Mathewson, who was in the midst of a brilliant seventeen-year career in which he gained 373 victories, placing him third on the all-time wins list, to go along with a career earned run average of 2.13. For the 1905 season, Mathewson had a record of 31–8, with a 1.27 ERA, while the team's second pitcher, "Iron Man" Joe McGinnity, had a regular-season record of 21–15 with an ERA of 2.87. The A's had little reason for confidence as they entered the Series, but it's doubtful that any of Connie Mack's men suspected that they would make such an undistinguished trip into the record books.

Mathewson was named to start Game One, and he swiftly dispensed with the A's on four hits, shutting them out, 3–0. In the second game, Philadelphia, relieved temporarily of Mathewson's tantalizing fadeaways, tied the Series by shutting out the Giants and McGinnity, 3–0. But then bad luck struck the A's in the form of a rainstorm that pushed the Series back one day and allowed Mathewson to return for game three. The result was another four-hit shutout, 9–0. After watching McGinnity get revenge by blanking the A's in the fourth game, 1–0, Mathewson took the mound for the clincher. Despite 18 previous innings of experience, the A's still could not solve Matty, and the result was a 2–0 victory and a world championship for the Giants in five games, each a shutout.

Mathewson's three Series shutouts in themselves were an incredible achievement that has never been duplicated; in fact, Christy's four lifetime World-Series shutouts also is a record. But consider this: in 27 innings, he allowed just 14 hits, walked one, struck out 18. He was so overpowering that not one Athletic runner reached third. This was against a club that led the American League in hitting (.339) and runs scored (617), and was second in home runs (24).

The Philadelphia A's must have had many winter dreams of Christy Mathewson's fadeaway, but they probably weren't able to hit it then either.

WHICH NOTABLE DOUBLE-PLAY COMBINATION WAS IMMORTALIZED IN POETRY BY AUTHOR FRANKLIN PIERCE ADAMS?

The Chicago Cubs' combination of Joe Tinker, Johnny Evers, and Frank Chance. Usually, the double play began with a ground ball to shortstop Tinker, who relayed the ball to second baseman Evers, who then pegged the ball to first baseman Chance.

In his poem, "Baseball's Sad Lexicon," Adams penned the following:

These are the saddest of possible words,
Tinker to Evers to Chance.
Trio of bear cubs, and fleeter than birds,
Tinker to Evers to Chance.
Thoughtlessly pricking our gonfalon bubble,
Making a Giant hit into a double—
Words that are weighty with nothing but trouble:
Tinker to Evers to Chance.

THE MOST FAMOUS INFIELD IN BASEBALL WAS THE SUPERBLY SYNCHRONIZED "TINKER-TO-EVERS-TO-CHANCE" DOUBLE-PLAY COMBINATION OF THE CHICAGO CUBS IN THE EARLY 1900's. WHO WAS THE THIRD BASEMAN ON THIS TEAM?

Harry M. Steinfeldt played the hot corner for the Cubs, anchoring the championship clubs of 1906–1908 and 1910. Never an outstanding hitter, Steinfeldt nonetheless performed well in the clutch, as his .471 average for the 1907 Series attests.

WHAT HALL OF FAMER NEVER WORE A WATCH BECAUSE OF HIS INTENSE APPROACH TO THE GAME?

Johnny Evers, the second baseman of the legendary Tinkers-to-Evers-to-Chance double-play combination of the Cubs. He was nicknamed "The Crab" because of his intensity and its effect on other people. Like Billy Martin, his desire to win was so overpowering, it made him impossible to get along with. His intensity became mythical, to the extent that it was said that his body was full of actual electricity. No one truly believed this, but watches supposedly would not keep accurate time while worn by him. Evers was given several quality watches as symbolic recognition of his outstanding play, but he couldn't wear any and have them work. Evers was always asking his teammates for the time, even during games.

WHAT ARE THE BEST SILENT FILMS ABOUT BASEBALL?

How the Office Boy Saw the Ballgame (1906), followed the next year by the almost identical *How Jones Saw the Ballgame,* and *Bush Leaguer* (1917).

WHO MADE THE MOST UNUSUAL STEAL OF HOME?

Fred Clarke, Pittsburgh Pirates, 1906. Player-manager of the Pirates, Clarke stole a total of eighteen bases during the 1906 season. His zaniest performance occurred during a game with the Chicago

Cubs. Pittsburgh had the bases loaded with Clarke edging his way off third. The count on the batter was three and one. When the pitch arrived, to everyone's amazement, the umpire said nothing. Clarke assumed if it had been a strike, the umpire would have suitably bellowed, "Strike two!" With that in mind, Clarke concluded that no announcement meant it was ball four, thus forcing in a run. So Clarke trotted nonchalantly home while the batter dropped his bat and ambled toward first. Meanwhile, the Cubs' catcher simply returned the ball to his pitcher.

Just as Clarke crossed the plate unimpeded, the umpire shouted: "Strike two!" As incredulous players turned to home, the red-faced umpire explained: "I got a frog in my throat—I couldn't say a word." The batter returned to the plate, but Clarke's run was allowed to stand. Since there is no other way of scoring it, Clarke was credited with a stolen base.

WHICH WAS THE WORST-HITTING TEAM TO WIN A PENNANT?

Chicago White Sox, 1906. Affectionately known as the "Hitless Wonders," the first-place White Sox put together a modest .230 team average, the worst in the entire league. Their best hitter, who would have had trouble cracking other lineups, was second baseman Frank Isbell, who hit .279. Despite their power shortage, the White Sox finished three games ahead of the New York Highlanders (later to be known as the Yankees). By contrast, the Highlanders had a team average of .266, 36 points higher than the champions.

Pitching was the White Sox's forte. They proved the point in the World Series, defeating the Chicago Cubs four games to two. The Cubs, who had a team hitting average of .262 during the regular National League season, were limited by White Sox pitching to a .196 average at bat. However, the "Hitless Wonders," world champions in 1906, were true to form in the championship. Over six games, their batting average was a measly .198.

WHAT WAS THE MOST UNUSUAL VICTORY
FOR A PITCHER?

Without throwing a single pitch, Nick Altrock of the Chicago White Sox was credited with a victory. It happened in 1906 after he was summoned to the mound in relief in the top of the ninth during a game when the White Sox were trailing by two runs. The opposition had the bases loaded with two out. As Altrock leaned in for the sign, the runners led off. Suddenly, Altrock wheeled and fired the ball to first, picking off the runner and retiring the side. In the bottom of the ninth, the White Sox rallied to win the game. Since Altrock was the last pitcher for Chicago, he was credited with the win under baseball's scoring rules. The victory was but one of twenty Altrock would produce for the pennant-bound "Hitless Wonders."

WHICH TEAM BEST EPITOMIZED MAJOR-LEAGUE
BASEBALL IN THE TWENTIETH CENTURY?

Chicago Cubs, 1906. Hollywood, the Bronx Chamber of Commerce, and Joe DiMaggio would have you believe it was any one of a dozen New York Yankees teams, especially the 1927 edition of "Murderers' Row." But the 1906 Cubs, with an unchallengeable record of 116 wins, only 36 losses, tops the Bronx Bombers anytime. In winning the National League pennant, the Cubs finished 20 games ahead of the second-place New York Giants, a club with a respectable 96 victories.

No doubt the 1906 Cubs lacked a good press agent. The Chicago team had innumerable stars, including Joe Tinker, Johnny Evers, and Frank Chance, who could execute double plays in their sleep. Leading an impressive corps of Cubs pitchers was Mordecai "Three-Finger" Brown, who produced a league-leading 1.04 ERA. The collective earned run average of the Chicago pitching staff was an arrestingly low 1.76. The Cubs also led the league in hitting with a .262 team average. They scored 704 runs, tops in that department. The only smudge on their otherwise unblemished 1906 record was an upset defeat at the hands of the Chicago White Sox in the World Series.

WHAT FIRST BASEMAN HOLDS THE RECORD FOR MOST CHANCES ACCEPTED IN A SEASON?

John Donahue of the Chicago White Sox had 1,986 chances in 1907.

WHO WAS THE FEATURED FEMALE IN THE TUNE "TAKE ME OUT TO THE BALL GAME"?

Nelly Kelly. Written in 1908 by Jack Norworth (lyrics) and Albert Von Tilzer (music), the tune has remained a standard ever since. However, most fans are familiar only with the chorus, which never mentions Ms. Kelly. She did, however, receive much attention in the two introductions. To wit:

> *Nelly Kelly loved Base Ball games,*
> *Knew the players, knew all their names,*
> *You could see her there ev-'ry day,*
> *Shout "Hurray"—when they'd play—*
> *Said to Coney Isle, dear, let's go,*
> *Then Nelly started to fret and pout,*
> *And to him I heard her shout.*
> CHORUS: *Take me out to the ball game . . .*

> *Nelly Kelly was sure some fan,*
> *She would root just like any man,*
> *Told the Umpire he was wrong,*
> *All along—good and strong—*
> *When the score was just two to two,*
> *Nelly Kelly knew what to do,*
> *Just to cheer up the boys she knew,*
> *She made the gang sing this song.*
> CHORUS: *Take me out to the ball game . . .*

WHO MADE UP THE "$100,000 INFIELD" OF CONNIE MACK'S PHILADELPHIA ATHLETICS AND WHY WERE THEY CALLED THAT?

Their nicknames were "Stuffy" McInnis, "Cocky" Collins, "Black Jack" Barry, and "Home Run" Baker. Connie Mack once said he would not take $100,000 for them.

Connie Mack once had such a superb infield on his Philadelphia Athletics team that he turned down a fortune for the trio. *(from the collection of Barry Halper)*

WHAT WERE THE CIRCUMSTANCES SURROUNDING THE INFAMOUS "MERKLE BONER"?

In 1908, there was a three-way battle for the National League pennant, with the Giants, Cubs, and Pirates waging the war. On September 4, the Cubs were playing in Pittsburgh, with a double shutout being pitched through the bottom of the ninth. There were men on first and third with two down in the inning when the winning hit came through. The man on first, the Pirates' Warren Gill, left the field as the hit was made and the game decided. The Cubs second baseman, Hall-of-Famer Johnny Evers, called for the ball and claimed a force at second for the final out of the crucial game. Since no run can score if the third out of the inning, made on the play, is a force, it seemed to Evers to be a legitimate appeal; however, it was denied by Hank O'Day, the umpire of the game. Frank Chance, the Cubs' Hall-of-Fame manager first baseman, urged Cubs owner Charles Webb Murphy to lodge a protest with National League president Harry Pulliam. Pulliam declined to rule an out on the play, being as it had never been done before, but conceded that it was a legitimate claim.

Nineteen days later, with the race still as tight as a coiled spring, the Cubs were in the Polo Grounds, facing living legend Christy Mathewson. It turned into a great pitchers' duel, with the score 1–1 going into the bottom of the ninth. That day, nineteen-year-old Fred Merkle played his first full game for the Giants at first base. With two out in the bottom of the ninth, the Giants had runners on first and third with Al Bridwell coming to bat. Merkle was the runner on first. Hank O'Day was again umpiring the game. Bridwell lined a pitch into center, and the runner on third, pinch-hitter Moose McCormick, galloped home with the winning run. Unfortunately, Merkle hadn't read about the Pittsburgh incident, and decided to jog into the clubhouse without touching second. Evers, always on top of things, again called for the ball. This time, however, the throw in was off the mark, and got by both Evers and Joe Tinker, the Cubs' shortstop. Floyd Kroh, a reliever sitting on the Cub bench, tried to retrieve the ball but was held back by Giants third base coach Joe McGinnity. Joe managed to hold Kroh off long enough to grab the ball himself and throw it into the stands. Mysteriously, Evers somehow obtained another ball in the meantime, and stood on second, again claiming a force-out. This time, umpire O'Day concurred, and called Merkle out.

However, by the time Evers finished his covert action, Giants fans had swarmed onto the field, making continuation of the game impossible. Quickly, Giants manager John McGraw called his players into the clubhouse, instructing them not to discuss the play with anyone. He sent Merkle off to a hotel in Brighton Beach, hoping he would be safe there from anyone with questions about the play, especially reporters.

Some even say that he told Merkle to go out to the Polo Grounds in the middle of the night and touch second so that he wouldn't be lying in any possible investigations.

Some newspapers, not aware of what had happened, reported the final score as Giants 2, Cubs 1, in the morning editions. In the meantime, McGraw protested to National League president Pulliam, basing his complaint on the grounds that O'Day was making a decision that had never been enforced previously in the game's history.

Chance, in a battle of protests, petitioned Pulliam to declare a game a 9–0 Cubs win by forfeit, as the Giants, the home team, couldn't clear the field so that the game could be continued. Pulliam ignored both protests, ruling in favor of his umpire, and decreed the game would be replayed the day after the end of the season if it had any impact on the standings.

It did, as the Cubs finished the season a half game ahead of Pittsburgh, tied with the Giants. The Giants lost the replayed game, with Christy Mathewson taking the crucial loss, 4 to 2. The "Merkle Boner"—although it was more O'Day's decision to make the call than Merkle's fault for making the mistake—cost the Giants the pennant.

WHAT WAS THE QUIETEST BASEBALL GAME
EVER PLAYED?

On April 18, 1909, a Sunday, the New York Highlanders played the Jersey City team in the Eastern League in an exhibition game. As was common at the time, there had been legal entanglements over playing baseball on Sunday, and the Jerseyites were worried about a run-in with the law. In order to prevent trouble, they distributed cards to all fans at the game asking them not to cheer for an event in the game, so as to keep the noise level down. The fans, surprisingly, followed the instructions, and the Highlanders won 6 to 3 in the quietest baseball game ever played.

WHAT ROOKIE PITCHER STARTED THE 1909 SEASON
WITH AN INCREDIBLE 10–0 STREAK?

The Philadelphia Athletics' Harry Krause had one of the most remarkable streaks in baseball during the 1909 season. By 1909, pitching rotation had matured out of the one-man-gang stage but was still not up to the regular five-man rotation employed throughout much of recent baseball history. The A's had a Hall-of-Fame rotation, featuring Eddie Plank, Chief Bender, and Jack Coombs, giving Krause a hard time finding work. Added to the oddities of 1909 schedule making, when a team could play five games in April and 40 in September, Krause had his first start of the year on May 8 in Philadelphia, and pitched a three-hitter for a 1–0 victory. He had to sit around for nine days before his next opportunity arose. This time he dueled into the 12th inning, winning a 1–0 decision, allowing five hits over the 12. Krause had to wait still another 12 days before his next chance, when he had 10 K's, giving up four hits in a 6–2 victory over Boston. He got another opportunity three days later for a change, and proved that the amount of rest he got didn't make that much of a difference, pitching another 1–0 shutout with eight strikeouts. He didn't start again until June 18, with the exception of a brief relief appearance squeezed in after 15 days' rest, and won 3–1. Finally, he started to get regular work, and reeled off still five more wins, giving up only one earned run in the next five complete game victories. Finally, Krause lost a start, and the special streak was ended, although he pitched well for the rest of the season, finishing up with a league-leading 1.39 ERA, going 18–8. Over the 10–0 streak, Krause had an 0.38 ERA, with 51 hits in 93 innings (all ten were complete games, including the 12-inning affair). It was a truly remarkable streak.

WHO WAS THE ONLY MAJOR-LEAGUE PLAYER IN THE TWENTIETH CENTURY TO HIT .400 IN HIS ROOKIE SEASON?

"Shoeless Joe" Jackson, later of Black Sox scandal fame, hit .408 in his rookie season, which was 1911.

WHY WAS THERE SO LITTLE INTEREST IN NO-HITTERS BEFORE 1911?

From the beginning of organized baseball, with pitchers pitching every day, there was relatively little interest in their accomplishment on a single day. In 1880, Lee Richmond and John Montgomery Ward pitched perfect games a few days apart, but the press, the fans, and the players themselves took virtually no notice of the occasion. This went on for years, and the normal mention of a no-hitter would be that of a "shutout without a hit." This blatant lack of recognition was still going on as late as the end of the twentieth century's first decade.

Exactly when this changed, no one seems to know for sure. There were rumors that a no-hitter was pitched sometime in 1910 or 1911, which captivated the public imagination, but since it doesn't show in the records, that is nothing more than hearsay. More likely, there was a quiet focus on no-hitters by the media, and the fans and players picked it up. In the *Reach Guide,* an early (maybe the first) baseball annual, a special section on the season's most memorable games was started about 1910, and this included a separate feature on no-hitters. The change in thinking came full circle by 1915, when a pitcher named Miles Main in the Federal League threw a no-hitter, and the newspapers began promoting Main as a future Hall of Famer, with the no-hitter his entrance requirement.

WHO WAS THE ONLY PLAYER IN BASEBALL HISTORY TO STEAL FIRST BASE?

Herman A. "Germany" Schaefer. A player who came into his own at the turn of the century, Schaefer variously was employed by the Chicago Cubs, Detroit Tigers, Washington Senators, New York Yankees, Cleveland Indians, and Newark of the Federal League. He was creative enough to be considered flaky by his more conservative teammates and opponents.

When Schaefer was playing for Washington against the Chicago White Sox in 1911, the game was tied with the Senators batting in the ninth inning. Schaefer was on first while a speedy base runner named Clyde Milan occupied third for Washington. On the first pitch to the next hitter, Schaefer sprinted for second base. His theory was that the catcher would attempt to throw him out at second and, in so doing, Milan would dash home safely from third. However, the White Sox catcher didn't fall for the bait. When Schaefer realized that his ruse wasn't working, he wheeled in his tracks and headed back to first. Surely, he thought, the catcher would try to nail

Herman A. "Germany" Schaefer. *(National Baseball Hall of Fame)*

him at first. But, alas, still no throw! Meanwhile, the umpires puzzled over what to do about a player who stole first base. After careful consideration the umpires decided that since no one ever had done it before—and there was nothing in the rule book to cover it—Schaefer was safe.

Once the dispute was settled, the White Sox pitcher cranked his arm for another pitch and Schaefer took off for second again. This time the catcher made the peg, but Germany evaded the tag and the runner scored from third.

Schaefer's antics were not always as productive. Another time he attempted to score from second on a short outfield fly. Upon his slide into home plate, Germany was signaled out by the umpire. "I beat the throw," shouted Schaefer, "and knocked the ball out of the catcher's mitt."

The umpire stared back at Schaefer, replying, "The hell you did." Then, he pointed to the ball, snug in the mitt.

"But," pleaded Schaefer, "he missed the tag. He never touched me."

"He got you, all right," the umpire insisted.

Finally, Schaefer turned to the grandstand. "Ladies and gentlemen," he begged, "does anyone have any more excuses? I'm plumb out of them myself!"

WHAT WAS THE BEST SEASON START FOR A PITCHER?

Rube Marquard, New York Giants, 1912. With an opening win over Brooklyn (18–3), Marquard became the most feared pitcher in baseball. By July 4, 1912, he had totaled a 19–0 record, the longest winning streak in a single season.

One reason for Marquard's success was the awesome hitting displayed by his teammates. During the 19-game streak, the Giants outscored their opponents, 129–49, averaging almost seven runs per game. Marquard's streak included only one shutout and it wasn't until his thirteenth win that he had to struggle, his team ahead only by one run.

His most dramatic victory was the nineteenth, a 2–1 triumph over Brooklyn. His pitching opponent was Napoleon Rucker, who allowed four Giants hits. One of New York's runs came as a result of a dropped pop-up by Bert Tooley, Brooklyn's shortstop. Brooklyn threatened in the ninth inning with the winning runners on base and one out, but Marquard struck out heavy-hitting Zack Wheat and ended the game with a fly-ball out. Rube's luck ran out on July 9 at Wrigley Field in Chicago. The Chicago Cubs routed Marquard and the Giants, 7–2. From then on Rube faltered and ran up a dismal 7–11 won-lost mark for the rest of the season.

Rube Marquard compiled an astounding 19-0 record in his first 19 outings with the New York Giants in 1912, until his streak was ended by the Cubs on July 9. This is Marquard, with Brooklyn, in 1916. *(from the collection of Barry Halper)*

WHY DID BILL LEINHAUSER AND SEVEN FELLOW STUDENTS FROM ST. JOSEPH'S COLLEGE OF PHILADELPHIA PLAY FOR THE DETROIT TIGERS FOR ONE DAY . . . AND ONE DAY ONLY?

On May 18, 1912, the Tigers were scheduled to play the Athletics in Philadelphia. At the time, Detroit's roster was minus Hall of Famer Ty Cobb who was under suspension for climbing into the stands in New York three days earlier to chase a heckler. In support of Cobb, his teammates decided to demonstrate for the Georgia Peach. "If Ty doesn't play, neither do we," they proclaimed. "We'll strike!" When the Athletics' manager, Connie Mack, heard about the strike, he suggested to Tigers' manager Hugh Jennings that he consider using collegians instead of the pros. Jennings agreed and immediately signed eight students from St. Joseph's College of Philadelphia and one sandlotter to regular contracts.

The nine new "Tigers" were hardly a match for the Athletics that day and went down to a humiliating 24–2 defeat. Aloysius Travers, who ultimately became a Catholic priest, pitched and set an all-time single game record, allowing all twenty-four runs. It's a record that still stands today.

The Tigers got four hits, two of which were triples hammered out by the sandlotter, Ed Irvin, who could boast a lifetime major-league batting average of .667. Of those who played, only Billy Maharg, who later became a professional boxer, continued in organized ball. He appeared in the 1916 outfield of the Philadelphia Phillies—for one game! And what about Bill Leinhauser? Well, he eventually joined the Philadelphia police force. He always recalled with fondness that on May 18, 1912, he was the proudest of the "neophyte nine" because he got to wear Ty Cobb's uniform!

WHEN DID THE RED SOX BEGIN TO PLAY AT FENWAY PARK?

Boston first began to play on the property of the Fenway Realty Co. —the red brick, single-decked Fenway Park—in 1912. The intimate midtown park occupies an entire city block. Jersey Street runs behind third base and Van Ness Street borders first base. Ipswich parallels Fenway, on the side known to most Bean Towers as the Green Monster in left, and Lansdowne is behind home.

Fenway's capacity of 33,536, the smallest in the big leagues, is distributed this way—7,418 bleacher seats, 12,274 grand stand seats, 13,250 field boxes, and 592 roof boxes. "The greatest ballpark in America," says New York sportswriter Phil Pepe, who has visited every major-league park. "It's one of those few parks that is a throwback to the old days."

"When we brought a Yankee ball club here," said Ralph Houk, "that Green Monster always haunted me. It's always an exciting game here because of that fence. You never have a game won until the last out. You can have a four- or five-run lead going into the ninth and still lose a game."

Pigeons are a familiar fixture at Fenway. Fat from popcorn and Cracker Jacks, these birds have even figured on the action in the field. In 1974, Willie Horton mortally wounded a pigeon with a foul ball. Another pigeon once got in the way of a Hal Peck throw. In 1945, Skeeter Nelson doubled off the rear of a pigeon. Luckily, the pigeon only lost a few tail feathers in the confrontation.

Fenway was refurbished in 1934. All of the commercial messages were removed in 1934, except for one. And the right-field corner still publicizes the house charity of the Red Sox—the Jimmy Fund. Though a few more signs have been added since, Fenway Park still looks basically as it has since 1912.

WHAT WAS THE WORST MISTAKE BY AN UMPIRE?

Bill Klem, a member of baseball's Hall of Fame, liked to boast that he never blew a call. However, one afternoon in 1913 he committed an egregious error during a game between the Pittsburgh Pirates and New York Giants. The hotly contested match produced a series of flareups that jangled Klem's nerves.

When the Pirates began needling him, Klem strode to the Pittsburgh bench and snapped: "If I hear anything else out of you guys I'll clear this bench! Not one more word!" For the moment, at least, the Pirates clammed up. Manager Fred Clarke then sent a young pinch hitter to the plate. Klem, who had never seen the kid before, asked the lad his name. The kid's reply was inaudible, so the umpire shouted: "C'mon, out with it!"

With a straight face, the rookie turned to the esteemed umpire and said: "Boo!"

Livid with rage, Klem ripped off his mask and ordered the young player out of the ball game. Fortunately, manager Clarke, sensing something was amiss, dashed out of the dugout to learn what was the matter. Klem promptly advised Clarke that nobody, especially a smart-guy rookie, was going to say "boo" to him.

"Sorry, Bill," Clarke replied, "but you'll have to make an exception in this case."

The rookie's name was Everitt Booe. He was, in the end, Klem's worst boo-boo.

WHAT PLAYER HIT THE MOST UNUSUAL HOME RUN?

George "Cullie" Cutshaw, Brooklyn Dodgers, 1913, at Ebbets Field. The Phillies and Dodgers were tied in an extra-inning game when Cutshaw came up to bat for Brooklyn in the last of the eleventh. Feared for his home-run-hitting ability, Cutshaw stroked the second pitch down the first-base line. It appeared that, with a little luck, he could stretch a single into a double. Meanwhile, Philadelphia's right fielder desperately pursued the ball, which was heading for the right field wall. At the very least, he would play the rebound off the wall and relay the ball back to the infield.

However, the ball was cooperating only with the Dodgers. It struck the embankment that abutted the fence but never ricocheted back to the right fielder. Instead, it climbed the wall and actually flew over the right-field fence and into Bedford Avenue on the other side. In those days, any ball that went over the fence—in any manner between the foul lines—was considered a home run. As a result, Cutshaw gained fame as the only ground-ball-hitting home-run swinger in baseball history.

WHAT FACTORS CONTRIBUTED TO BASEBALL'S ZANIEST HOME RUN?

Perhaps because it happened in the ill-fated Federal League, an outlaw circuit that functioned in 1914 and 1915 in competition with the American and National Leagues, the feat has been overlooked by sports historians. This is what transpired:

Umpire Barry McCormick failed to show up for the opening game of a series in Chicago between the Brooklyn Feds and Chicago Whales. McCormick's partner, Bill Brennan, worked the game alone from behind the pitcher's mound. Brennan survived without incident until the fifth inning. At that point a Brooklyn batter fouled off pitch after pitch, totaling twenty. Brennan trotted back and forth for more balls, and stuffed them in his shirt. It was a warm afternoon and soon Brennan had worked up a good sweat. In disgust, he dumped a pile of balls on the ground in back of the pitcher's mound, stacking them into a neat pyramid, and mopped his brow in relief as the batter was finally retired.

Up came Grover Land, the Brooklyn catcher who had jumped to the Feds from Cleveland, where he had been a battery mate of the celebrated Addie Joss. On the first pitch, Land rifled a line drive straight into the pyramid of balls, touching off a volcanic eruption of horsehides. In the resulting scramble, each Chicago infielder came up with a ball and was waiting for the hitter as he tore around the bases.

"I was tagged five times," recalled Land, "but Brennan ruled there was no put-out since it was impossible to figure out which was the fairly batted ball." Brennan decided to award Land a home run.

The Northside ballpark—now the site of Wrigley Field—resounded with the anguished screams of Joe Tinker, player-manager of the Whales, who later protested the decision to James A. Gilmore, the league president. After suitable deliberation, Gilmore ruled that he would not throw out the game unless the subsequent result had a deciding effect on the pennant race. It didn't, so Grover Land could always claim the world's record for freak home runs—with an assist, of course, from umpire Brennan.

WHICH TEAM WAS RESPONSIBLE FOR BASEBALL'S LONGEST WINNING STREAK, YET FINISHED FOURTH?

New York Giants, 1916. Managed by steel-tongued John McGraw, the Giants had come off a last-place finish in 1915 and were determined to make amends to their rooters in the new season. McGraw, the Captain Bligh of baseball, drove his team unmercifully to 17 consecutive road victories—an all-time record, but that still did not appease the bench boss. At mid-season he decided that many of his veterans had to be traded, and he dealt away such notables as pitcher Christy Mathewson and outfielder Eddie Roush.

On September 7, 1916, the Giants defeated Brooklyn and suddenly became a team possessed. A day later they met Philadelphia in a doubleheader. Pol Perritt, who won the first game for the Giants on the mound, pleaded with McGraw to let him pitch the second game after having been viciously needled by the Phillies. Demanding of his manager, "Let me beat those bums again," Perritt started the second game and came through with a four-hit shutout. Now the streak was for real.

By September 30, 1916, the Giants' undefeated streak had reached 25 games. Their next opponent, in another doubleheader, was the Boston Braves. McGraw's men won the opening game, lengthening their streak to 26, but they lost the second match and ended their remarkable streak that had lasted from September 7 through September 30.

Despite McGraw's ranting and raving, the Giants finished the season with 86 wins, 66 losses, nowhere near the top of the National League; however, they did enter the record books and for that they will long be remembered.

WHICH PITCHER HURLED THE MOST INNINGS IN A SINGLE WORLD SERIES GAME?

Babe Ruth, tossing for Boston's Red Sox in the 1916 World Series against the Brooklyn Dodgers, set a record by pitching fourteen innings. Ruth was on the mound in the second game of the Series in what turned out to be the longest World Series game ever played. After a first-inning homer by the Dodgers' Hy Myers, Ruth blanked the Brooks for the rest of the game. In the Red Sox third, the "Bambino" batted in the tying run. The score remained knotted until the bottom of the fourteenth inning when pinch runner Mike McNally scored from first on a pinch double by Del Gainor to give the Red Sox their victory. Boston ultimately won the Series in five games.

WHAT WAS THE BEST PERFORMANCE BY A RELIEF PITCHER?

Ernie Shore, Red Sox, June 23, 1917. Thanks to teammate Babe Ruth, Shore was able to make a name—albeit small—for himself in baseball history. Ruth had been named starting pitcher for Boston against the Washington Senators, but lasted for only one batter. The Babe, then known for his hurling more than his batting, walked the first batter and then uttered more than a few impudent remarks in the umpire's direction. Before Ruth could wind up for the second batter, the umpire ejected Babe for the game, whereupon Ernie Shore was called in from the bull pen as the unexpected reliever for Ruth.

As Shore tossed his first pitch to catcher Sam Agnew, the runner on first bolted for second. Agnew's peg was fast and accurate and the runner was called out. From there Shore was unbeatable. He pitched to the next twenty-six men, got all of them out, and achieved what remains to this day as the best relief performance in baseball history—all because of Babe Ruth's big mouth.

WHAT WAS THE MOST UNUSUAL NO-HITTER?

Chicago Cubs vs. Cincinnati Reds, 1917. Although the teams in question were less than spectacular, the Cubs and Reds boasted a pair of superb pitchers: Jim Vaughn for Chicago and Fred Toney for Cincinnati. Vaughn in fact produced three consecutive twenty-game seasons, while Toney, in 1917, was to score 24 victories. When the pair faced each other at Wrigley Field in Chicago, they attained the ultimate pitching accomplishment: after nine innings of regulation play, neither pitcher had surrendered a single hit—the only double no-hitter in baseball history. The overpowering Vaughn struck out ten, limiting his opponents to first base. Toney, by contrast, struck out three but permitted only one Chicago batter to reach second. The deadlock finally was broken in the top of the tenth inning when Cincinnati shortstop Larry Kopf delivered a clean single. Kopf reached third on a dropped fly ball and scored on Jim Thorpe's infield hit. The final score was Reds 1, Cubs 0.

THE BLACK SOX SCANDAL
(1919)

Baseball, like just about any other public part of life in the twentieth century, has had its share of scandals, but the most famous of all has to be the shame of the team that came to be known as "The Black Sox." Like most causers of so-called scandals, the Chicago White Stockings of 1919, perpetrators of this most famous of fixes, were merely the tip of an iceberg that had existed almost routinely in the sport, virtually since the days when it was played by white-flanneled blue bloods.

For instance, the infamous Tammany Hall boss, William Marcy Tweed, was also president of the New York Mutuals baseball team from 1860 to 1871, during which time Tweed's entire squad also happened to be on the city payroll! Every single team member was either a sweeper or clerk or some sort of civil servant—all to the tune of more than $30,000 a year for Gotham taxpayers.

Remember an old word for arena—hippodrome? Well, "hippo-droming" was popular long before the Black Sox scandal. Hippo-droming was when baseball players colluded with gamblers to fix scores or games. Fixing was so rampant that gamblers stood right out in the open in some parks, offering odds and taking bets. Rumor once suggested that the New York Haymakers club was actually owned and run by gamblers.

In California they had a popular, albeit boisterous, form of "fixing" games. When a fielder from the visiting team was right under a fly ball, strategically placed fans would whip out their six-guns and BANG! Off would go the revolvers. Throughout baseball, as well as other sports, there was "revolving," which was *not* the gunplay tactic just mentioned. Revolving was when a player would agree to sign with one club, accept "goodies" for signing, and then "revolve" to another club with the previous team's goodies in hand!

Despite the various common forms of "fixing" games, the twentieth century began with high hopes for baseball with the new, "cleaner" American League. For most of the first decade the high hopes were realized. But then the entire baseball world took a turn for the worse.

For several years previous to the Black Sox ignominy, the baseball scene threatened to collapse altogether, largely due to sagging gate receipts throughout the league, with one notable exception. Charles A. Comiskey's Chicago White Sox drew the largest crowds in baseball, while his players—even his stars—were among the lowest paid in either league. The poor Chicago White Stockings players were, in one sense, victims—victims of Comiskey's greed.

The Great War had just ended and a new order was coming in. It was an order that brought Prohibition and an attempt to legislate against gambling, gaming, and drink. The Black Sox probably weren't any more crooked than a world of athletes at that time, but they were bitter, disillusioned and, well, simply stupid—stupid for not realizing that "fixing" was no longer fashionable, or even tacitly acceptable.

WHAT SIGN WAS GIVEN BY THE CHICAGO WHITE SOX TO SIGNAL THAT THE FIX WAS ON, AND WHO GAVE IT?

Eddie Cicotte's second pitch in the opener plunked Cincinnati's second baseman, Maurice Rath, between the shoulders. By that act Cicotte passed the word to those on the inside that a conspiracy by the Sox to dump the Series was on.

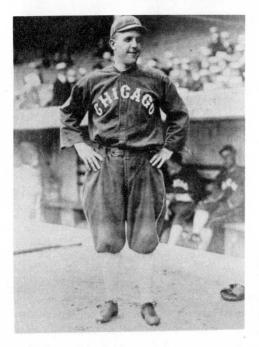

Eddie Cicotte, star pitcher for the about-to-become Chicago "Black Sox," supplied the key to whether the "fix" was on or not. *(National Baseball Hall of Fame)*

WHAT WAS SO UNUSUAL ABOUT THE LENGTH OF THE 1919 SERIES?

1919 was the first in a three-year trial of a best-of-nine-games World Series.

HOW MUCH WERE SCALPERS GETTING FOR TICKETS TO THE 1919 WORLD SERIES?

Tickets were being sold for $50 a pair, a huge sum in 1919.

WHO WAS THE FIRST PLAYER TO BECOME PART OF THE FIX?

Arnold "Chick" Gandil was the first White Sox player to agree to commit the fix and was responsible for recruiting the other players involved.

WHAT WAS "SHOELESS JOE" JACKSON'S SALARY AT THE TIME OF THE FIX?

Although Jackson was regarded as one of the greatest sluggers of his time, he never made more than $6,000 a season. This can be compared to Cincinnati's leading hitter, Edd Roush, who batted some 40 or 50 percentage points below Jackson, but made $10,000.

WHAT FAMOUS SONG-AND-DANCE MAN KNEW ABOUT THE SERIES FIX?

George M. Cohan was advised by former boxer Abe Attell that the Series was fixed after Cohan had already placed $30,000 on Chicago. Cohan couldn't call off the bet, but instead he made a call to his partner, Sam Harris, and had him hedge the bet and put a little extra on Cincinnati.

WHERE DID THE PHRASE "SAY IT AIN'T SO, JOE" COME FROM?

During the official investigation of the fix a year later, the September 30, 1920 *Chicago Herald and Examiner* provided this account: "As Jackson departed from the Grand Jury room, a small boy clutched at his sleeve and tagged along after him.

" 'Say it ain't so, Joe,' he pleaded. 'Say it ain't so.'

" 'Yes, kid, I'm afraid it is,' Jackson replied.

" 'Well, I never would've thought it,' the boy said."

Shoeless Joe Jackson was the central figure in the now-immortal phrase, "Say it ain't so, Joe . . ." *(National Baseball Hall of Fame)*

IT WAS REPORTED THAT AN OPPOSITE FIX WAS ON. WHAT WAS IT?

Cincinnati pitcher "Dutch" Ruether, scheduled to pitch the opening game, was seen drinking heavily the night before. It was rumored that a few Chicago gamblers were trying to get the whole Reds' pitching staff drunk in order to fix the Series for *Cincinnati* to lose.

WHO WAS THE FIRST PERSON TO TESTIFY AT THE GRAND JURY INVESTIGATION AND AT THE TRIAL?

Charles A. Comiskey, owner of the Chicago White Sox.

WHAT WAS THE FIRST NEWSPAPER TO BREAK THE NEWS OF THE FIX AND WHO REPORTED IT?

Chicago White Sox beat writer Hugh Fullerton of the *Chicago Inter-Ocean* was the one who wrote articles about the fix after the Series was finished. He took the material to his editor in Chicago and to his dismay, he was told it was too hot to publish. Few newspapers were prepared to tackle a story like this, out of fear of libel laws. Undaunted, Fullerton took his articles to New York where the *New York World* agreed to print them, providing he watered them down. Fullerton fought them, eventually arriving at a compromise. The articles were hot enough even without his direct accusations and the omission of a number of names.

On December 15, 1919, the *New York World* exploded Fullerton's bomb: "IS BIG LEAGUE BASEBALL BEING RUN FOR GAMBLERS, WITH BALLPLAYERS IN THE DEAL?" The World Series, he suggested, was tampered with to enrich gambling cliques in many American cities. Actually, he did not state explicitly that the series had been fixed. To avoid libel, his articles merely challenged the evasiveness of the National Baseball Commission in the face of some glaring suspicions.

WHO WERE THE PLAYERS INVOLVED WITH THE 1919 WORLD SERIES FIX AND HOW MUCH DID THEY RECEIVE FOR THEIR INVOLVEMENT?

Eddie Cicotte ($10,000), Charles Risberg ($15,000), Claude Williams ($5,000), Joe Jackson ($5,000), Oscar Felsch ($5,000), Fred McMullin ($5,000), and Arnold Gandil ($35,000). Buck Weaver, who was penalized for being part of the setup, never received any cash and maintained his innocence until his death in 1956.

WHAT WAS EDDIE CICOTTE'S 1919 REGULAR-SEASON RECORD?

Cicotte had completed all but 5 of 35 starts. He recorded 29 wins, 7 losses, and one save and had a 1.82 ERA.

HOW DID "SHOELESS JOE" JACKSON GET HIS NICKNAME?

While playing ball in Greenville, South Carolina, one day, Jackson developed blisters from a new pair of spikes that he had just bought. He wanted to sit out the next day's game, but his club turned up short an outfielder and he had to play. He put on his old shoes, but the blisters made the old shoes impossible to wear. In desperation, Jackson went out to play in his stocking feet. Nobody noticed until the seventh inning, when he blasted a long drive to right center and had to leg it hard. As he pulled into third, a leather-lunged voice from the opponents' bleachers blasted at him: "You shoeless bastard, you!"

The crowd laughed and picked it up. Fans and players around the league started calling him "Shoeless Joe" and it stuck.

WHAT WAS THE CALL ON THE FIRST PITCH IN THE 1919 WORLD SERIES?

Ball one!

WHO CALLED IT?
John Rigler was the umpire.

WHO WAS AT BAT AND WHO WAS PITCHING?
John "Shano" Collins was at bat for the White Sox and Dutch Ruether was pitching for the Reds.

WHO WAS THE FIRST COMMISSIONER OF BASEBALL AND WHY WAS THE POSITION CREATED?
In 1920, when it became known that the Chicago White Sox had conspired with gamblers deliberately to lose the 1919 World Series, baseball appointed the respected Judge Kenesaw Mountain Landis as its first commissioner in an attempt to restore public confidence in the game. Landis served from 1921 until his death in 1944.

HOW DID LANDIS GET HIS NAME?
Born in Millville, Ohio, on November 20, 1866, Kenesaw Mountain Landis was the son of a surgeon, Abraham Landis, who had been in the Union Army. Injured during the Battle of Kennesaw Mountain in 1864, Dr. Landis swore to God that if he recovered from his injury (they were about to amputate his leg) he would name his firstborn son after the Georgia battle site. No one knows why the future baseball commissioner's first name lacked an "n"!

A respected judge, Kenesaw Mountain Landis was appointed baseball's first commissioner in an effort to restore public confidence in the game after the "Black Sox" scandal of 1919. *(line drawing by Shirley Fischler)*

WHO WAS THE ONLY MEMBER OF THE 1919 CHICAGO WHITE SOX TO BE BANNED FROM BASEBALL EVEN THOUGH HE DIDN'T TAKE PART IN THE CONSPIRACY?

There were eight Chicago players banned from baseball, but one of them didn't throw any games. He was Buck Weaver, who wanted nothing to do with the plot but was thrown out of the game because he didn't reveal the conspiracy.

ALTHOUGH HE WAS BEING PAID OFF TO THROW THE SERIES, WHAT WAS "SHOELESS JOE" JACKSON'S BATTING AVERAGE AND WHAT DISTINCTION DOES HE HOLD?

Joe Jackson had a .375 batting average for the Series, the highest on the White Sox, and he hit the only home run of the Series.

WHAT HAPPENED WHEN KENESAW MOUNTAIN LANDIS PLACED A TWENTY-FIVE-CENT BET ON A GOLF MATCH?

Kenesaw Mountain Landis was a determined competitor besides being a tight-fisted baseball commissioner. Once, in a golf foursome in Clearwater, Florida, Landis and part-owner of the Cincinnati Reds, John Orr, lost a quarter apiece to George Daley, the sports editor of *The New York Tribune,* and famous journalist, Fred Lieb. But Landis insisted on a chance to win back his lost 25 cents. So a rematch in St. Petersburg's old Jungle Club was scheduled on a future date. When that day came, stormy conditions threatened, but Landis was determined to play.

"The sky looked threatening when we arrived at the first tee," recalled Lieb. "But Landis would tolerate no delay, let alone chickening out. It began raining when we were on the fourth hole. By the time we reached the sixth tee, it was pouring. Furthermore, it was downright chilly. We held a conference: Landis and Daley voted to continue, Orr and I to quit. So we flipped a coin, Orr and I won, and we started back for the clubhouse. We hadn't gone twenty yards when we met two stockily built Amazons wearing foul-weather gear and carrying their own bags over their shoulders. Landis couldn't stand it. 'Are you two sissies going to let these ladies enjoy this golf course by themselves?' he remarked disdainfully.

"Orr and I returned meekly to the sixth tee. In the most miserable of conditions we slogged our way for the full eighteen holes. Judge Landis was just as wet as any of us, but he was wearing a smile of beatific satisfaction. He had gotten in his daily round despite the elements. And he had won back his quarter."

WHO WAS THE BIG-TIME GAMBLER INVOLVED IN THE BLACK SOX SCANDAL AND WHO WAS HIS PRIZEFIGHTER SIDEKICK?

The gambler was Arnold Rothstein. Newspapers called him a "sportsman." His father called him a hoodlum. Whatever his moniker, Rothstein put together a fortune at two gambling dens in Manhattan. He mixed with such luminaries as oil magnates Joshua Cosden and Harry Sinclair, not to mention Charles Stoneham, owner of the New York Giants.

Rothstein's entourage included Abe Attell, who for twelve years had been the world featherweight champion. He fought 365 fights, lost only six, and was never knocked out. Attell was the contact when Billy Maharg and his partner, Bill Burns, met in 1919 at Jamaica Racetrack to outline the proposition that would rock the sports world.

WHAT FORMER PLAYER WAS UNDER SUSPICION FOR THROWING GAMES FOR TEN YEARS, YET CONVINCED PEOPLE NOT TO DO ANYTHING ABOUT IT?

Hal Chase, possibly one of baseball's all-time undesirables. His pockmarked, leering visage came to define the game and the way it was played at the time of his career. Chase started with the New York Highlanders in 1905, and anyone who saw him play was left gasping for superlatives. He was said to be the biggest drawing card in baseball, and many feel, even now, that he was the greatest defensive first baseman ever to play the game.

However, it didn't take long for Chase to establish a reputation for being a lazy bum who played the game strictly for the money.

He was accused of not trying to win the games, and briefly left the Highlanders in 1908 to join an outlaw league in California. He was suspended for a short while but later returned to New York during the 1909 season.

While commonly felt to be a bad influence on the game, Chase carried with him a charisma greater than any player's of his time. The New York press wouldn't write articles about the Highlanders' success or failure, but only about Chase. Chase managed to manipulate the firing of Highlander manager George Stallings, and installed himself as player-manager. But realizing his failure in this capacity, he resigned after one year. The team's next manager, ex-Cubs first baseman Frank Chance, accused Chase of "lying down" on the job, and traded him to the White Sox. He left the White Sox for the Federal League, and a year later joined the Cincinnati Reds.

Chase had his best years in Cincinnati, but before long, he was again accused of not trying to win, and Reds manager Christy Mathewson suspended Chase for the rest of the season and brought him up before the baseball commission on charges of ". . . attempting to cause any game of ball to result otherwise than on its merits under the playing rules."

Hal Chase was an enormously talented first baseman who also happened to be so corrupt that he was suspended by several teams and ultimately ousted from the game in 1919. Many claimed that it was Chase's shady dealings and questionable actions on the field that paved the way for the White Sox "dump." *(from the collection of Barry Halper)*

Chase was eventually acquitted, as it was suddenly "inconvenient" for many of his fellow players to testify against him. He was traded to the Giants, and spent the rest of his days in New York, a.k.a. Gambler's Heaven, until he was thrown out of the league in 1919 by the New York Giants' John McGraw.

Many contest that Chase made corruption fashionable, and that he started baseball down the long, dangerous road toward the Black Sox scandal. While a very good baseball talent, Hal Chase was a very bad—albeit colorful—baseball character.

WHAT TWO BASEBALL IMMORTALS WERE ALSO ACCUSED OF ATTEMPTING TO FIX THE LAST GAME OF THE 1919 SEASON?

In 1926, Ty Cobb was accused by Detroit pitcher Dutch Leonard of having conspired with Tris Speaker to fix the last game of the 1919 season. Cobb admitted he had written what appeared to be an incriminating letter to Cleveland's Joe Wood, but claimed innocence of any wrongdoing. Both Speaker and Cobb were acquitted by Judge Landis, although there were mutterings that the two had gained acquittal by making a secret agreement that the two could stay in the game but would never manage again. However, there has never been any concrete evidence of the secret agreement.

Tris Speaker was accused, along with Ty Cobb, of fixing the last game of the 1919 season. Both Speaker and Cobb were acquitted, although mutterings about the two persisted for some time. *(from the collection of Barry Halper)*

THE BABE RUTH ERA
(1920-1929)

The twentieth century was starting its third decade, baseball was finishing off its second half-century, and Prohibition was under way.

This was the "Roaring Twenties"—that infamous era of the speakeasy, the dance craze known as "The Charleston," bobbed hair, beaded dresses, and sporty roadsters with rumble seats.

This was the infancy of radio, talking movies, Ernest Hemingway and other expatriate American artists and writers in Paris. It was a boom time when the United States was in the full bloom of becoming a world powerbroker.

To a lot of people it looked as though the good times would never end, and everything seemed slightly larger than life: people flew across oceans, swam channels, and sat on flagpoles. It was a glorious age, a ridiculous age, an extravagant age.

The same applied in baseball, where one man who could outplay, outdrink, outeat, and just about out-anything anybody else became a symbol of the age. It wasn't just the Roaring Twenties. It was also the Babe Ruth Era . . .

One of my regrets is that I saw Babe Ruth only in the twilight of his career. Nevertheless, I have no compunctions about stating that Babe Ruth was the best player who ever walked onto the baseball diamond.

Why would I pick Ruth over, say, Ty Cobb or Hank Aaron, to name two great ones? Very simple. The Babe could do more things better than anybody. You can talk all you want about Cobb, but Ruth could hit equally well—and, of course, he outhit Cobb in the home-run department. But Ruth also was a superb pitcher, and even that may be an understatement.

What many present-day baseball fans may not realize is that Ruth, before he was traded from the Boston Red Sox to the Yankees, had been one of the best pitchers in the game. As a pitcher, The Babe was in a class with the Dodgers' great Sandy Koufax. Had Ruth continued on the mound, he surely would have made it to the Hall of Fame as a pitcher, because in the years 1915–1920, he was considered the best left-hander in the majors.

You take the fact of Ruth's pitching and combine it with the additional fact that he was the greatest home-run hitter who ever lived *and* could do many other things well on the field, and you have enough of a case to call Babe the all-time best. I'm convinced that if Ruth had played the years that Aaron did, he would have hit more than 900 home runs.

WHAT PRE-MODERN CATCHER WAS REGARDED BY MANY OLD-TIME SCOUTS AS THE BEST PLAYER IN BASEBALL HISTORY?

William "Buck" Ewing.

In 1919, the baseball *Reach Guide* had an article discussing the best players in the game. According to Francis Ritcher, the *Guide*'s editor, the three greatest players in the game at the time were Ty Cobb, Honus Wagner, and Buck Ewing, who played in the major leagues for 18 years (1880–1897). Richter went on to say: "It is a difficult, not to say ungrateful, task to select any one player as superior to all the rest, though we have always been inclined to name Buck Ewing as the greatest player of the game."

When the first nominations for the future Hall of Fame were being considered in 1930, the editor of the

Hall of Famer "Buck" Ewing has been called the greatest player in baseball history. *(National Baseball Hall of Fame)*

Spalding Guide, John Foster, selected Ewing as the greatest player he had ever seen, better than Cobb, Wagner, Ruth, Gehrig, etc. Ewing, who played for Troy (1880–1882), New York (1883–1892), Cleveland (1893–1894), and Cincinnati (1895–1897), was cited as having no weakness in his game, offensively or defensively, on the field or off. His career stats are good, with a lifetime batting average of .303. However, it was his defensive skills that made him a legend. Foster wrote that Ewing "handed the ball to the second baseman from the batter's box," and "as a thrower to the bases Ewing never had a superior." While the young fan may never have heard of him, the legend of Buck Ewing still lives on, in trivia questions like this.

THE NEW YORK YANKEES USED TO BE ON THE BOTTOM OF THE OLD EIGHT-TEAM AMERICAN LEAGUE WHEN JACOB RUPPERT AND TILLINGHAST L'HOMMEDIEU HUSTON PURCHASED THE TEAM FOR $460,000 IN 1915. LESS THAN FIVE YEARS LATER, THE EVENTS OF ONE DAY WOULD MARK THE VERY BEGINNING OF THE RISE OF THE YANKEES. WHAT HAPPENED?

Ruppert and Huston obtained the services of George Herman Ruth on December 26, 1919, from a financially strapped Boston Red Sox owner named Harry Frazee.

Known as the best left-handed pitcher in the American League and the best lefty hitter anywhere, the twenty-five-year-old Ruth became Yankee property in exchange for $125,000 cash and a $300,000 loan against the Fenway Park mortgage, which left the Yankees not only owning Babe Ruth, but, for a time, Fenway Park!

Ruppert and Huston's investment returned immediate dividends. In Ruth's first season as a Yankee in 1920, the New Yorkers finished only three games out of first place. The next year the Yankees won the American League pennant and attendance figures quickly doubled. Ruth smashed a phenomenal 54 homers in 1920 and 59 in 1921. The previous home-run high had been 29 by Ruth in 1919 when he was with the Red Sox (he pitched in only 14 games).

The mediocre divisional finishes of the pre-Ruth era were gone and a Yankees legend was born.

IN BIG-LEAGUE HISTORY ONLY ONE PLAYER HAS BEEN KILLED BY A PITCHED BALL. WHO WAS HE?

Ray Chapman, a right-hand-hitting Cleveland Indians shortstop, was struck by a fastball delivered by Yankee pitcher Carl Mays at the Polo Grounds. The pitch was intended to prevent Chapman from laying down a drag bunt in the top of the fifth inning of a game Cleveland led 3–0.

A twenty-game winner five times in his fifteen-year major-league career, Mays's deadly pitch rose as it neared the plate. Chapman, who seemed to freeze and make no attempt to dodge the pitch, was struck on his left temple and collapsed to the ground. Seconds later Chapman got up and with a ballplayer's instinct took two steps toward first base. But he then collapsed again, never to regain consciousness.

His teammates carried him to the center-field clubhouse, from where Chapman was rushed to a nearby hospital. He died at 3:30 A.M. the next morning, on August 17, 1920.

Ray Chapman is the only player in major-league history to be killed by a pitched ball. *(National Baseball Hall of Fame)*

WHAT SINGULAR PITCH WAS ONE OF THE MAJOR FACTORS BEHIND THE ADVENT OF THE "LIVELY BALL" ERA?

One of the most important changes in the history of baseball was the growing predominance of batting during the 1920's. There are many theories as to why this came about, but the most obvious was the limited ban of the spitball that was ordained in the winter of 1919–1920. This was done not out of disgust for the pitch felt by the beleaguered ballplayers, but because of its danger. This was never more apparent than on that August afternoon when Yankee submariner Carl Mays nailed Indians star shortstop, Ray Chapman. It was probably not a spitball that killed Chapman but a dirty gray ball that he couldn't see. From that moment on, a conscious effort was made to keep a clean, fresh, dry, and thus livelier ball in play.

Burleigh Grimes (shown here with Babe Ruth when Ruth was briefly a pitching coach for the Dodgers and Grimes was finishing out his career) was the last pitcher in the major leagues to be allowed to use the spitball. *(from the collection of Barry Halper)*

WHAT WAS CLEVELAND'S MOST UNUSUAL GAME OF THE ERA?

Cleveland Indians vs. Brooklyn Robins, World Series, 1920. In the fifth game of the World Series at Cleveland, which the Indians won, 8–1, a pair of extraordinary events took place. In the first inning, history was made when Cleveland right fielder Elmer Smith hit a bases-loaded home run over the right-field fence; it was the first grand slam ever in a World-Series game. The second unique episode occurred during a Brooklyn rally in the fifth inning. With runners on first and second and Clarence Mitchell coming up to bat, Robins' manager Wilbert Robinson signaled for a hit-and-run play; as soon as Mitchell swung, the runners were to take off. Mitchell did as instructed, belting a searing line drive toward second base. Indians second baseman Bill Wambsganss was so far from the base that he appeared unable to make a play on the ball.

"But," wrote Harry Cross in *The New York Times,* "Wambsganss leaped over toward the cushion and with a mighty jump speared the ball with one hand." Pete Kilduff, the runner on second, was well on his way to third and Otto Miller, the runner from first, was almost within reach of second.

The quick-thinking Wambsganss touched second base, retiring Kilduff. Miller, who was trapped between first and second, appeared mummified by the proceedings and remained rooted in his tracks. Wambsganss trotted over and tagged Miller for the third out. Thus, the first unassisted triple play was accomplished in the World Series. "The crowd," reported Cross, "forgot it was hoarse of voice and close to nervous exhaustion and gave Wamby just as great a reception as it had given Elmer Smith."

If that wasn't unusual enough, there was the added spectacle of Brooklyn pitcher Burleigh Grimes's humiliation. "No pitcher," wrote Cross, "has ever been kept in the box so long after he had started to slip. Uncle Robbie kept him on the mound for three and two-thirds innings and in that time he was badly plastered for nine hits, including two home runs and a triple. With a half a dozen able-bodied pitchers basking in the warm sun, Grimes was kept in the game until he was so badly battered that the game became a joke." When the score was 7–0, Grimes finally was removed.

In an ironic contrast, Cleveland pitcher Jim Bagby was hailed as a hero even though no other pitcher had ever been pounded for thirteen hits in a World Series and been able to emerge a hero. "He pitched," wrote Cross, "what was really a bad game of ball, but when it was over he was proud of it."

WHAT PLAYER DIED TWENTY-FIVE YEARS TO THE DAY AFTER HE WAS TRADED TO THE NEW YORK YANKEES?

Pitcher Herb Pennock was traded to the Yankees on January 30, 1923, from the Boston Red Sox for outfielder Camp Skinner, infielder Norm McMillan, pitcher George Murray, and cash. Pennock played on the famous "Murderers' Row" teams of the late 1920's. Twenty-five years later, on January 30, 1948, Pennock died of a stroke.

WHO TERMED YANKEE STADIUM "THE HOUSE THAT RUTH BUILT"?

Fred Lieb, a longtime baseball journalist, in 1923. Lieb also served as president of the Baseball Writers Association of America.

WHO IS BASEBALL'S BEST CLUTCH HITTER?

Babe Ruth. The heavyweight among the Bronx Bombers, Ruth drove in a run every 3.79 times at bat. His colleague on the New York Yankees, Lou Gehrig, is second with a 4.02 success ratio.

Babe Ruth (shown here shaking hands with Cards pitcher Dizzy Dean in 1935, as he played his poignant last games with the Boston Braves) will always be remembered as the best clutch hitter and slugger in the history of major-league baseball, even though Henry Aaron later eclipsed his epic home-run record. *(from the collection of Barry Halper)*

WHO IS THE BEST SLUGGER?

Babe Ruth. The slugging percentage is regarded by baseball statisticians to reflect the true value of a hitter's power. It is obtained by dividing possible total bases into actual total bases. Ruth's lifetime slugging percentage was .690. Ted Williams was second with .634, followed by Lou Gehrig at .632.

WHO HAS BASEBALL'S BEST HOME-RUN EFFICIENCY?

Babe Ruth. El Bambino hit a home run every 11.76 times at bat. Hank Aaron, owner of the all-time home-run record, only averaged a round-tripper every 16.23 times at bat. Ralph Kiner is second to Ruth with a homer every 14.11 times at the plate.

WHO WAS THE BEST PITCHER AGAINST BABE RUTH?

Hubert Shelby "Hub" Pruett, St. Louis Browns. Judging by Ruth's impotence at bat against Pruett, the Babe could have been mistaken for a fourth-string pinch hitter instead of "The Sultan of Swat." Pruett's efforts against Ruth would seem to qualify him for the Hall of Fame if not for his otherwise mediocre career won-lost record of 29–48 and 4.63 earned run average.

But against Ruth, Pruett looked like Grover Cleveland Alexander. The first time Hub—as a Browns' rookie—pitched against The Babe, he struck him out. Any suggestions that the feat was a fluke were soon dispelled. Ruth struck out nineteen out of the next twenty-three times he batted against Pruett.

HOW MANY GRAND SLAMS DID BABE RUTH SWAT IN HIS TWENTY-TWO-YEAR MAJOR-LEAGUE CAREER?

Of Ruth's 714 lifetime home runs, only two were grand slams.

"THE ONLY REAL GAME IN THE WORLD, I THINK, IS BASEBALL. YOU'VE GOT TO START FROM WAY DOWN, AT THE BOTTOM, WHEN YOU'RE SIX OR SEVEN YEARS OLD. YOU CAN'T WAIT UNTIL YOU'RE 15 OR 16. YOU'VE GOT TO LET IT GROW UP WITH YOU, AND IF YOU'RE SUCCESSFUL AND TRY HARD ENOUGH, YOU'RE BOUND TO COME OUT ON TOP, JUST LIKE THESE BOYS HAVE COME TO THE TOP NOW." NAME THE LEGEND WHO SPOKE THESE WORDS OF WISDOM.

Babe Ruth.

ONCE WHEN TRAVELING ON A TRAIN TO NEW ORLEANS WITH THE NEW YORK YANKEES, BABE RUTH ENCOUNTERED A NEAR-FATAL DISASTER. WHAT HAPPENED?

A renowned ladies' man, Ruth apparently went too far with a dark-eyed, dark-haired wife of a Louisiana legislator during a train stop at Baton Rouge. According to eyewitnesses, the enraged woman pulled a knife from her purse and pursued the panting Ruth, actually getting within five feet of him. But that's as close as she would get. Babe jumped off one of the Pullman cars and darted up the platform toward the front of the train. The woman could not keep up with Ruth, who was never a slouch on the base paths either.

Then, just as the engineer started up the train to New Orleans, Ruth hopped into the front car and the woman was left in Baton Rouge.

ACCORDING TO LEGEND, WHO IS THE BEST "TRENCHERMAN" AMONG PRO BASEBALL PLAYERS?

Babe Ruth. On an off-day "The Sultan of Swat" could also have been mistaken for "The Sultan of Suet." Eyewitnesses reported that Ruth could down three thousand calories as quickly as he could swing his forty-one-ounce bat against a fat pitch.

One such Ruth-watcher, former *Sporting News* publisher J. G. Taylor Spink, recalled a Ruthian culinary round-tripper. "In St.

Louis," said Spink, "Babe usually was to be found at Busch's Grove, an eating place in St. Louis County. He frequently would go there for breakfast. It was not unusual for Ruth to eat two fried chickens and wash them down with goblets of beer.

"For dinner The Babe would order a porterhouse steak, a double order of lettuce and Roquefort dressing, a double order of cottage-fried potatoes, a double order of pie à la mode, and a large pot of coffee. When Ruth finally called the waiter and asked for the check, there was not enough left on his plates to feed a sparrow!"

Paul Derringer, who pitched for the Cardinals, Reds, and Cubs, described his first meeting with Ruth in the dining car of their Pullman:

"I was eating breakfast at a single table and the seat opposite me was the only vacant one in the car. In came Ruth, alone. Seeing the empty chair, he sat at my table. The Babe called over a waiter and ordered a pitcher of ice, a pint of ginger ale, a porterhouse steak garnished with four fried eggs, fried potatoes, and a pot of coffee. He told the waiter to be sure to bring him the pitcher of ice and ginger ale right away.

"A few minutes later the waiter set the pitcher of ice and pint of ginger ale in front of Ruth. The Babe pulled a pint of bourbon out of his hip pocket, poured it over the ice, poured in the ginger ale, shook up the mixture—and that was Ruth's breakfast juice.

"Sometime later I happened to meet The Babe's roommate and related to him what had happened in the diner that morning. He told me that it was nothing more than a daily habit. Ruth generally drank a quart mixture of bourbon whiskey and ginger ale at breakfast, before attacking a steak, garnished with four or six fried eggs and potatoes on the side."

NAME THE POPULAR POLITICIAN WHO WAS "HIRED" TO REFORM BABE RUTH.

Jimmy Walker. Walker was a state senator and an avid baseball fan at the time when Babe Ruth was hitting towering home runs for the New York Yankees. However, "The Bambino," as the sportswriters had come to call the home-run king, liked to stay up late, drink whatever he pleased, and eat enough to feed a dozen men his size.

As a result, Yankees manager Miller Huggins threatened stiff punishment for Ruth.

At this point a group of baseball writers asked the persuasive Walker to attend a dinner that was being given for Ruth at the Elks' Club and plead with the guest of honor to reform. Ruth, who had no idea about the behind-the-scenes machinations, applauded when Senator Walker rose to speak, but the Yankee slugger was quickly stunned to the core by Walker's message.

"Babe Ruth," said Walker, "not only is a great athlete, but also a great fool. His employer, Colonel Jacob Ruppert, makes millions of gallons of beer and Ruth is of the opinion that he can drink it faster than the Colonel and his large corps of brewmasters can make it." Then Walker turned to Ruth and declared, "Well, you can't! Nobody can!"

Walker then pointed a finger at The Babe. "You are making a bigger salary than anyone ever received as a ballplayer. But the bigger the salary, the bigger the fool you have become."

Walker, who would later gain national prominence as New York's most flamboyant mayor, continued on this theme until the mighty Ruth was reduced to tears. Finally, "Gentleman Jim" placed a kindly hand on Ruth's shoulders and said: "If we did not love you, Babe, and if I myself did not love you sincerely, I would not tell you these things. Will you not, for the kids of America, solemnly promise to mend your ways? Will you not give back to those kids their great idol?"

According to biographer Gene Fowler, Ruth bawled louder than ever and finally kept his promise to Jim, set a new home-run record, and at the close of the 1923 season was voted the most valuable player of the year.

The Ruth-Walker link remained tight, especially when the senator decided to run for mayor against the incumbent, John Hylan. A tough politician, the aging and ailing Hylan attacked Walker for what he claimed would be the horrible things that would befall New York City if "Gentleman Jim" was elected to the mayor's office.

"Instead of replying to Hylan in the orthodox manner," wrote Fowler, "Jim met these onslaughts with full good humor." One day Walker was posing for a photograph with Ruth at Yankee Stadium when reporters informed him that Hylan had made a statement that Walker was a bosom friend of the underworld's.

Walker glanced at Ruth. "Please don't steal any bases today, Babe," he said, "unless you wish to embarrass both of us!"

WHO HOLDS THE RECORD FOR MOST YEARS LEADING A LEAGUE IN ERRORS?

Ivy B. Wingo, a career .260 hitter in a big league career that ran from 1911–1929 with Cincinnati and St. Louis of the National League, holds the dubious distinction. Wingo led the National League in errors in seven separate years.

WHAT YANKEE BAT BOY WAS FIRED FOR ALMOST KILLING BABE RUTH?

William Bendix, who, ironically, would later play The Babe in the movies.

When Ruth was at the apex of his career, the robust young bat boy worshipped "The Sultan of Swat" and The Babe, in turn, encouraged the young man to pursue a baseball career. Babe's every wish was Bendix's command. The kid would shine The Babe's shoes, run his errands, and provide Ruth with all the food the heavy-eating Babe required.

One day before a game, Ruth dispatched Bendix to obtain some soda pop and hot dogs. Dutifully, the kid returned with a dozen frankfurters and several quarts of soda. As usual, Ruth devoured everything that Bendix had delivered to the locker room.

But this time the feast took its toll. Later in the afternoon, Ruth collapsed with severe stomach pains and was rushed to the hospital. Headlines across the country proclaimed that Ruth was dying. When the Yankees' front office discovered that William Bendix had delivered the food to Ruth, the young bat boy was summarily dismissed.

The Babe recovered and continued hitting home runs and drawing fans to every ballpark in the American League. Meanwhile, the brokenhearted Bendix abandoned his pursuit of a baseball career and, instead, turned to the theater.

Bendix played hundreds of roles, many of them involving

sports figures. One of his most popular roles was that of "The Bambino" himself, in *The Babe Ruth Story.*

LOU GEHRIG FIRST BROKE INTO THE NEWSPAPER SPORTS PAGES WITH A FEAT HE DID WHILE IN HIGH SCHOOL. WHAT DID HE DO?

Gehrig hit a ball out of Wrigley Field in an intercity scholastic baseball game against Lane High Tech of Chicago. It wouldn't take him long to break into the majors.

Two years after earning a scholarship for football at Columbia University, Gehrig decided to turn pro in baseball with the New York Yankees as a twenty-year-old in 1923. Just before signing for a sizable bonus, he said: "No matter what I do now, ultimately I am

Lou Gehrig (shown here, right, with teammate Ruth, second from left, and Tigers Hank Greenberg, left, and Charles Gehringer, second from right) was a rare major-league ball player for his time when he came up to the big league in 1923. He had actually gone to college for several years. It would be decades before the major leagues would start drawing regularly from the college ranks for their baseball talent. *(from the collection of Barry Halper)*

going to be a ballplayer. I've now had two years of college, thanks to the scholarship and the sacrifices of my parents. But we are a poor family; we need money, and now it's my turn to earn money, real money, and make everything easier all around."

Hartford of the Eastern League, then Class AA, was where Yankee brass sent Gehrig for his first pro season. He hit .369 with 24 home runs in 59 league games there before the Yankees called him up for a chance to play in New York.

Gehrig did not waste his opportunity. He hit .423 in his first 13 games as a pinch hitter and a first baseman.

WHAT PLAYER RECORDED THE BEST MODERN SINGLE-SEASON BATTING AVERAGE IN MAJOR-LEAGUE HISTORY?

Rogers Hornsby hit an unprecedented .424 in his 10th season for the St. Louis Cardinals in 1924. Hornsby's career batting average of .358 is second on the all-time hitting list only to Ty Cobb's .367.

Rogers Hornsby (shown here, left) had a career batting average of .358 that is second only to Ty Cobb's .367. *(from the collection of Barry Halper)*

WHO HOLDS THE RECORD FOR MOST RUNS BATTED IN IN ONE GAME?

Jim Bottomley of the St. Louis Cardinals went six for six with 12 runs batted in on September 16, 1924, at Ebbets Field in Brooklyn. Bottomley had a bases-loaded single for two runs in the first. In the second, he doubled in another run. In the fourth, Brooklyn Dodger manager Wilbert Robinson walked the heavy-hitting Rogers Hornsby to load the bases for Bottomley, but Bottomley crushed a grand slam, bringing his RBI total to seven.

In the sixth, Bottomley cranked another shot over the fence with a man on. In the seventh, he singled home two more to tie the existing record of eleven RBI's, but he promptly broke it in the ninth by singling home Hornsby. The Cardinals won, 17–3.

LOU GEHRIG REPLACED WALLY PIPP AT FIRST BASE TO BEGIN HIS FAMOUS 2,130 CONSECUTIVE-GAME-PLAYING STREAK. WHY DIDN'T PIPP PLAY THAT DAY, JUNE 2, 1925?

Wally Pipp was an eleven-year veteran when Gehrig joined the Yankees in 1925. Pipp had hit .295 and driven in 113 runs the year before.

On June 2, 1925, Pipp complained of a nagging headache. Manager Miller Huggins told him to take the day off. Pipp would never start a game at first base for the Yankees again. Gehrig was not to be absent from the lineup again until May 2, 1939, a span of 14 seasons. Pipp moved on to Cincinnati in 1926.

In 1925 Gehrig played in 126 games and batted .295, which tied with his 1938 average as the lowest in his career.

WHO SERVED AS A MINOR-LEAGUE PLAYER, MANAGER, AND TEAM PRESIDENT ALL AT THE SAME TIME?

Casey Stengel was installed as a "one-man triumvirate" for the Boston Braves' Eastern League farm team at Worcester, Massachusetts, in 1925. At age 35, Stengel handled the responsibilities of club president, team manager, and player. He played in 100 of 125 games as the club finished in third place.

But by the end of the season, Stengel had had enough. He escaped by executing an unforgettable front-office triple play. Joseph Durso wrote: "As manager, he released Stengel the player. As president, he fired Stengel the manager. And as Stengel, he resigned as president."

WHICH WORLD SERIES PRODUCED BOTH AN UNDISTINGUISHED RECORD AND A MYSTERY CATCH?

The 1925 World Series between the Pittsburgh Pirates and Washington Senators proved an embarrassment to Roger Peckinpaugh, the Senators' shortstop and that season's Most Valuable Player. The usually redoubtable Roger committed a record eight errors, several of which played a role in the Pirates' taking the Series, four games to three (the Pirates became the first team to win a World Series after trailing three games to one). Roger's ignominious record stands today. "People always keep bringing up those errors," Peckinpaugh once said in an interview. "It used to bother me, but not anymore."

The 1925 World Series also produced a controversial catch by the Senators' right fielder, Sam Rice, following a belt off the bat of Earl Smith. In Game Three, Rice pursued Smith's drive and finally tumbled into the low bleacher seats among friendly Washington fans. Regaining his feet, Rice clambered out of the stands and triumphantly displayed the ball. Umpire Cy Rigler called Smith out. At that, the petulant Pirates stormed the field, contending that a fan had carefully placed the ball in Rice's glove as Sam lay behind the wall and out of sight. However, umpire Rigler refused to reverse his decision. In months and years to come Rice refused to discuss the catch, but he left a letter describing the incident with the Hall of Fame at Cooperstown, to be opened after his death. Immediately following Rice's death on October 13, 1974, the letter was opened before several witnesses.

The letter, dated July 26, 1965, read as follows:

It was a cold and windy day and the right-field bleachers were crowded with people in overcoats and wrapped in blankets. The ball was a line drive . . . and I turned slowly to my right and had the ball in view all the way, going at top speed.

About fifteen feet from the bleachers, I jumped as high as I could and backhanded the ball. I hit the ground about five feet from a barrier about four feet high in front of the bleachers with all the brakes on, but couldn't stop. So I tried to jump it to land in the crowd, but my feet hit the barrier about a foot from the top and I toppled over on my stomach into the first row of the bleachers.

I hit my Adam's apple on something which sort of knocked me out for a few seconds but McNeely (George, the center fielder) arrived about that time and grabbed me by my shirt and pulled me out. I remember trotting toward the infield still carrying the ball for about halfway and then tossed it toward the pitcher's mound. (How I wished many times I had kept it.) At no time did I lose possession of the ball.

WHAT TEAM MADE THE MOST EMBARRASSING MISTAKE EVER COMMITTED ON THE BASE PATHS?

Brooklyn Dodgers, 1926. The Dodgers, alias "Dem Brooklyn Bums," earned a reputation as baseball's "Daffiness Boys" because of an assortment of amusing blunders. The *faux pas* that symbolized the Dodgers' daffiness developed after they had loaded the bases with one out against the Boston Braves. Hank DeBerry was on third base, Dazzy Vance on second, and Chick Fewster on first. The batter was Babe Herman, a potent but occasionally laughable hitter.

Herman stroked the first pitch toward the right field fence. Without question, it would be an extra-base drive. As the ball bounced off the right-field wall, DeBerry easily trotted home from third while Vance and Fewster sprinted toward the plate and Herman raced for first. What seemed like a rudimentary run-scoring situation suddenly became a comedy of base-path errors when Vance, unaware that the ball was still bouncing around the outfield, became fearful that he would not reach home plate in time.

Ultracautious, Vance jammed on his brakes after rounding third and decided to return to the base rather than dash for home plate. Meanwhile, Fewster, normally an efficient base runner, believed that he could reach third base on the long hit. After rounding second, Fewster put his head down for an energetic dash to third, culminating with a vigorous slide.

Unlike Fewster, who took one brief look at the ball and ran like hell, Herman somehow had become mesmerized by his effort, and neglected to notice the traffic jam developing at third. What followed was a scene straight out of a Three Stooges' slapstick comedy. Three players from the same team slid headfirst to the same base.

Seconds later, the ball was pegged to third, where the Braves' third baseman, Eddie Taylor, tagged all three converging Dodgers. Then the four of them looked to the umpire for his decision. Vance, because he arrived there first, was awarded the base, but Herman and Fewster were called out. To further the Brooklyn tragicomedy, DeBerry's run did not count.

Among the more perplexed onlookers was a rookie on the Dodgers' bench who turned to manager Wilbert "Uncle Robbie" Robinson and inquired: "Mister Robinson, what kind of baseball is that?"

"Leave them alone," Uncle Robbie replied. "That's the first time they've been together all season!"

However, the perfect squelch was inadvertently provided by a taxi driver and his customer after the fare had left the ballpark a few days after the third-base incident had taken place.

As soon as the passenger closed the cab door, the taxi driver asked the fan how the game was going. "Pretty good," the fellow replied. "The Dodgers have three men on base."

"Oh, yeah?" replied the cabbie. "Which base?"

WHAT TEAM WAS THE BEST SLUGGING TEAM IN BASEBALL HISTORY?

New York Yankees, 1927. This was the club, managed by Miller Huggins, which added the name "Murderers' Row" to the baseball lexicon. The "murderers" in question included Babe Ruth, Lou Gehrig, Tony Lazzeri, and Bob Meusel, who pounded out a team slugging record of .489! Skeptics who believed that the record was a fluke were proven wrong just three years later when the Yankees' slugging average was .488. Six years later the Bronx Bombers slugged at a .483 clip.

Lou Gehrig may have been a member of the "Murderers' Row" Yankees of the late 1920's, but here he is with archrival, Giants pitcher Carl Hubbell, collaborating on a series of articles just before they faced each other in the World Series. *(from the collection of Barry Halper)*

HOW DESTRUCTIVE WAS THE ONE-TWO PUNCH OF BABE RUTH AND LOU GEHRIG ON THE MURDERERS' ROW YANKEES OF 1927?

The most lethal one-two punch in baseball history combined in 1927 for 107 homers, 339 runs batted in, 214 extra-base hits, and a combined average of .365 (Gehrig at .373, Ruth at .356). Those numbers would be very good combined for three players. Gehrig alone had 47 home runs and 175 runs batted in, a home run total that was second highest behind Ruth's 60 of the same year, and an RBI total that became a major-league record for the time.

WHICH MEMBER OF THE ST. LOUIS CARDINALS' GAS HOUSE GANG WAS ALSO A PROFESSIONAL STUNT MAN?

Ernie Orsatti, a Cardinal outfielder from 1927 to 1935, doubled as a stunt man in Hollywood during the baseball off-season. The Los Angeles-born Orsatti had a career batting average of .306 in nine seasons.

IN WHAT YEAR WERE UNASSISTED TRIPLE PLAYS TURNED ON SUCCESSIVE DAYS IN THE MAJOR LEAGUES, AND WHO TURNED THEM?

In 1927, Jimmy Cooney of the Chicago Cubs pulled off the feat. The next day, Johnny Neun of the Detroit Tigers also pulled one off.

WHO HOLDS THE MODERN RECORD FOR SINGLES IN A SEASON?

Lloyd Waner of the Pittsburgh Pirates, thanks greatly to his ability to beat out infield grounders, had 198 singles in 1927.

IN 1927 BABE RUTH HIT A THEN-RECORD 60 HOME RUNS. IN WHICH INNINGS DID RUTH HIT A MAJORITY OF THOSE ROUND-TRIPPERS AND HOW MANY WERE HIT AT YANKEE STADIUM?

Babe Ruth hit 16 of his 60 home runs in the first inning. The eighth inning accounted for nine of his shots and the fifth and sixth innings, seven apiece.

Of the 60 homers, Ruth hit 28 at his home ballpark, Yankee Stadium, and that included his first and last hit of the season. The first four-bagger was smashed on April 15 off the Philadelphia Athletics' right-hander, Howard Ehmke, and the final blast off Tom Zachary, the Washington Senators' lefty, on September 30. Zachary later admitted, "If I'd a known it was gonna be a famous record, I'd a stuck it in his ear."

WHICH FORMER RED SOX AND ATHLETICS FIRST BASEMAN WAS CALLED "A RIGHT-HANDED BABE RUTH"?

Jimmie Foxx broke in with the Philadelphia Athletics in 1925 and played sporadically with them until 1928 when he was in 118 games. He batted .328, hit 13 home runs, and had 79 runs batted in. Foxx continued to improve and hit 58 home runs—two short of Ruth's record 60—in 1932. He hit 48 home runs in 1933 and 50 in 1938 after being dealt to the Boston Red Sox.

"WHAT BASEBALL MEANT TO US THEN"

Babe Ruth, Frankie Frisch, and other notables from the 1920's-1930's era were revered in a manner that is different from the way contemporary fans view baseball stars. This is due in part to the manner in which the game is presented to the fans as well as the character and background of the fans themselves. Let's face it, the ballplayer of yesteryear was a different breed from his 1990's counterpart. Likewise, the fan of that era differed in many ways from today's spectator. One reason for that is the difference in background. Most of today's fans were born here, as were their parents and grandparents. When I was growing up in Brooklyn, many fans were first-generation Americans, including yours truly.

I was born about as far away from Ebbets Field and the Brooklyn Dodgers as one could possibly be; specifically, in a tiny Russian village called Soslov, in the Ukraine. Shortly after I was born, our family left under a certain amount of duress. My father shot a man during a pogrom and, because of that, left the country as quickly as he could. He had learned speed as that rarest of all things, a Jew in the Russian cavalry. He was, they tell me, quite a horseman, and as a young man had fought saber-to-saber against the Austrians. I was only a few weeks old at the time.

My father landed in Montreal ahead of the rest of the family, which included my grandfather (*zayde,* remember?), grandmother, my two uncles, my aunt, and, of course, my mother. We had to weave a perilous route through Poland before reaching the steamboat that would carry us across the Atlantic. I was four months old when we landed on Canadian soil.

But we weren't destined to become Canadians. Instead, after only a short while, we moved to the States because a cousin on my mother's side ran a kosher poultry market on Fort Hamilton Parkway and 36th Street, right off of the 36th Street stop on the Culver (BMT) line. He offered my father a job, and that was reason enough for the family to settle down in a town called Brooklyn.

I grew up during what was known as "The Great Depression," when unemployment was rife and businesses were closing left and right. It was a tough time across the nation, but as a kid, what did I know of problems? I had my punchball, my friends, a radio in the house, Ebbets Field nearby, and school. The Great Depression didn't depress me a bit.

What is it they say—"You can see the man in the crib"? Although I was born in Russia, my crib was Brooklyn. This was another way of saying Park Slope, Williamsburgh, Flatbush, Bay Ridge, Canarsie, Greenpoint (otherwise known as "Greenpernt"), Crown Heights, and Brownsville, among other lovely neighborhoods.

I'll always remember a sign that once greeted motorists coming off the Manhattan Bridge: "WELCOME TO BROOKLYN, POPULATION 2,000,000, SECOND LARGEST CITY IN THE COUNTRY." There was always something special about our universe on the other side of the East River and it wasn't only the Brooklyn Dodgers who gave us that identity, or our special language known to elocution teachers as "Brooklynese." Part of it had to do with the lay of the land and another part with what was on the land. Trolley cars, for instance. Brooklyn had more trolley cars than anywhere on earth, and that's a fact. For a nickel you could get on the Lorimer Street trolley in Greenpoint, and clang-clang your way from Box Street in the north, through Williamsburgh, and on to Bedford-Stuyvesant along Nostrand Avenue. After an hour, the wooden doors banged open and the motorman yelled out, "Last stop: Empire Boulevard, Ebbets Field!"

We had so many trolleys crisscrossing Brooklyn that residents spent a good amount of their waking hours dodging them. Which brings us to a favorite trivia question: How did the Los Angeles baseball team get its nickname?

As most of the civilized world knows, they once were the Brooklyn Dodgers before owner Walter O'Malley moved them west from Bedford Avenue and Sullivan Place. And the Dodgers part? Because of the overwhelming numbers of streetcars and the need to stay alive by avoiding—or dodging—them, Brooklynites became known as "Trolley Dodgers." Thus it was only natural that the National League baseball team representing the borough be named the Brooklyn Trolley Dodgers, a label that soon was shortened to Brooklyn Dodgers, which it remained until the day of that fateful, dreadful decision made by Walter O'Malley in 1957.

One of the best things about Brooklyn was the neighborhoods—distinct communities that could have passed for individual small towns, had they been located in Nebraska or Iowa. Each neighborhood was as different as the next and its inhabitants naturally figured their "turf" was the best in Brooklyn. Flatbush in those days was tree-lined and quite similar to what we call suburbia today. Williamsburgh, sitting right on the East River and including the huge Brooklyn Navy Yard, was lined with tenements and brownstones, while Crown Heights boasted that wonderful boulevard known as Eastern

Parkway, the poor man's Champs Élysées. Eastern Parkway touches vast Prospect Park on the north, while my neighborhood—a bit of a *cul-de-sac* between Borough Park and Greenpoint—was at the other end. Like most Brooklyn communities in those days, the residents were by today's standards somewhere between poor and middle class. But for me life seemed rich at the time: we had a home, the family had work, and there was good food on the table.

My family settled on Minna Street across from a sprawling burial ground known as Greenwood Cemetery. If Minna Street sounds strange, I should point out that the original owner of the land in our area had named the streets after his daughters, one of them being—you guessed it!—Minna.

Our neighborhood was predominantly Italian, although there was a sprinkling of Jewish families like the Mazers. If we differed in backgrounds, we immigrant children united behind the banner of sports. Sports was discussed in school, on the sidewalk, and in the candy store. Every Brooklyn neighborhood had several candy stores that carried such essentials as candy (of course!), cigarettes, cigars, ice cream, newspapers, magazines, and nearly always sported a soda fountain. In most communities the candy store passed for the equivalent of the country store, town hall, betting parlor, or even senior citizens' visitation center. More than anyone, the kids were the ones who called the candy store home. It was there that we bought our bubblegum picture cards of baseball stars, analyzed the Brooklyn Dodgers' problems, and indulged in our favorite candy-store pastime, arguing about the various merits of our baseball heroes.

Since our neighborhood was mostly Italian, many of my friends were partial to the best Italian baseball player of the time, Joe DiMaggio. It followed that since Joltin' Joe played for the New York Yankees, a large number of them rooted for the Bronx Bombers.

Nothing against Joe D., but since I wasn't Italian, I made a point of rooting for anyone who wasn't Italian, just to be different. One was Joe "Ducky Wucky" Medwick, a Polish-American outfielder who starred for the Gas House Gang St. Louis Cardinals and then the Dodgers. Ducky Wucky was an awfully good hitter and a terrific fielder. His specialty in left field was dashing pell-mell for a low line drive and sliding into the ball while snaring it at grass-top level in his mitt. When Medwick won the Triple Crown in 1937, I considered it a major event because Joltin' Joe, great as he was, had been shoved temporarily into the background.

Another favorite of mine was Oscar "Ox" Eckhardt, an outfielder who played in the bigs for the Boston Braves and then the Dodgers. The wonderful thing about Oscar was that he played with DiMaggio in the Pacific Coast League in 1935 at the age of 34, while Joe D. was just a kid. DiMaggio hit .3992 and Eckhardt hit .3997. Eckhardt turned out to be one of the greatest Pacific-Coast-League stars of all time—but a bust in Brooklyn! Still, I loved him and loved to kid my Italian friends about that record.

Years later, when I met Joe D. in person, I mentioned my idol Eckhardt and that season in the Pacific Coast League. Joe laughed and explained that on the final day of the season, Eckhardt had gotten three hits in the first game of a doubleheader, then had sat out the last game. DiMaggio had played in both of the games. Had Joltin' Joe quit after the first game, he'd have beaten out Eckhardt. But Joe had refused to quit.

Another time we got together Joe and I talked about Medwick, and DiMaggio actually defended himself about the 1937 season: "Of course, I was in the American League, but I had as good a year as Medwick did," he said. Then he started to reel off his batting average, his home runs, and his RBI's. I was astonished that one of the greatest ballplayers who ever lived remembered every one of his stats.

When I brought my baseball talk back home, my father invariably reacted as if I were discussing the manufacture of plutonium. He could not have cared less, considered sports a total waste of time, and shared this inability to understand the love of sports with most of the other immigrant parents in the neighborhood. Here the dads were trying to make an honest buck in a new country, but in 1934 their kids were constantly talking about Dodgers second baseman Lonny Frey, Dodgers right-hander Johnny Babich, and Dodgers first baseman Sam Leslie. Pop would say, "You know more about the least important things in life than anyone I've ever known!"

But in a way it was those ballplayers who turned us kids into Americans. If we couldn't stand on the corner or in the candy store arguing the relative merits of Joltin' Joe (whom I had the good fortune to see from the start of his major-league career in 1936, to the end in 1951) and Ducky Wucky Medwick, what would we have had to say to each other?

My mother, on the other hand, didn't share my father's antipathy to baseball. In those days there was a "philan-thropic" group called the "Knothole Gang," which allowed kids to get into Ebbets Field for nothing. Mom would take me and a group of my friends to games as often as she could. Sometimes she would even give us the supreme thrill of cross-ing the East River into Manhattan (which in those days was like a major border crossing), for the trek uptown to the Polo Grounds, home of the New York Giants.

When I say trek I mean *trek*. The Polo Grounds was located on East 155th Street near the East River, on an out-cropping of rock called Coogan's Bluff. Unlike Ebbets Field, which was a neat little bandbox of a ballpark, the Polo Grounds was, well, more suited for polo. It was built in the shape of a horseshoe with the uncovered center-field bleachers at the open end of the shoe, some 500 feet from home plate.

On the other hand, a good pull hitter could drop home runs into the left- or right-field grandstands, about 270 feet away. In fact, the first baseball game I ever saw was at the Polo Grounds, on July 2, 1933, when I had the pleasure of seeing the "Jints" play the St. Louis Cardinals of Gas-House-Gang fame. Carl Hubbell, one of the top fireball pitchers of any era, was on the mound for New York, while James "Tex" Carleton faced him for the Cards. The score was 0–0 after nine innings, then ten, then eleven, all the way to the sixteenth. Then the Cards finally yanked Carleton and replaced him with Jesse Haines. Hubbell stayed in there and won the game with a shutout in the eighteenth inning.

But that was only half the fun. The Giants and Cards were playing a doubleheader that day and I was allowed to stay for the second game. In the second Roy Parmelee of the Giants went up against the great Dizzy Dean. Parmelee won, 1–0, which meant that I had seen 27 shutout innings for the price of admission to one game. Not only that, I saw such Cardinals heroes as Joe Medwick, Rogers Hornsby, Frankie "The Fordham Flash" Frisch, and Leo "The Lip" Durocher. The trip back to Brooklyn, normally a long one, blew by faster than ever before, because my mind was filled with memories of what amounted to three full games at the Polo Grounds. I couldn't have asked for anything more had I been Ali Khan.

Only two days later I saw the inimitable Babe Ruth play. It was a July Fourth doubleheader at Yankee Stadium, which for me meant an even longer trip, because we had to go from Brooklyn to Manhattan and then cross the Harlem River into the Bronx. But to see the one and only Ruth, I'd have traveled around the world.

El Bambino's career was on the decline. He was thirty-eight years old when I saw him that first time, and getting pretty hefty around the waistline. A year earlier he had hit 41 home runs and batted .341, but in 1933 his average dropped to .301, and the number of roundtrippers sank by seven—but still pretty respectable numbers when you think about it. He was a piece of work that day against the Washington Senators and a presence unlike any athlete I had ever seen, before or since. It was a combination of his pigeon-toed walk, his majestic stance at the bat, and the mighty swing that gave me goose pimples, even when he missed the ball. The Yanks split the doubleheader that day, but I really didn't care as much about the score as I did about seeing Babe Ruth.

It was about that time that I began unconsciously storing up the knowledge that would amaze radio and television audiences decades later. In 1933, my observations on major-league baseball action didn't go over the airwaves but were immediately transferred to the streets of the neighborhood when I returned home—or, more specifically, got back to "the block." Like most Brooklyn kids, I had a special reverence for my block. As Brooklyn historian Elliott Willensky once said, "The whole world radiated from that piece of turf, the block. The rest was characterized by such expressions as 'around the corner' or 'over by the lots' or 'in the schoolyard.'" It was there, but mostly in the street or gutter, that we played what amounted to "The Official Sport of Brooklyn," punchball.

Precisely why punchball became such a popular pastime is a good question, particularly since there still was ample room in the neighborhood for baseball or softball. But punchball was ideally suited for Brooklyn in the 1930's. First of all, it was played in the streets, which, then, were smoothly paved and almost empty of cars, moving or parked. Secondly, punchball didn't demand much financial outlay for equipment —an absolute requirement in the Depression years. Last of all, we probably played punchball (as opposed to stickball) because there was less chance of breaking windows or slamming the ball out of sight when it was punched rather than swung at with a stick.

The punchball "court" consisted of home plate and three

bases. Home plate was an iron sewer cover sitting in the middle of the street. First base would be off to the right, chalked into the pavement alongside the curb about 20 yards or so from home. Second base would either be another sewer top or, if they were too far apart, another chalked base. Third was chalked alongside the left curb opposite first.

The ball we used was sometimes a beat-up tennis ball, with so little facial hair it was almost a rubber ball. Other times we'd use a "pimple ball," which was softer than a tennis ball, with tiny upraised bumps on its rubber surface. The ball used most often, though, was a plain, high-bouncing, smooth and usually pinkish rubber ball produced by the Spalding Company. In Brooklyn we called it a "spaldeen."

The basic difference between punchball and baseball—apart from the softness of the ball—was the pitcher and the catcher, or, rather, the lack of them. The batter would get up to home plate, bounce the ball once or twice in his hand to test the feel, then bounce it once off the ground, take one step forward, throw the ball upward, as in a tennis serve, and at about normal batting height, punch it as hard as he could. Once the ball was hit, the game was just like baseball: the batter ran to first, second, third and, if he was a great puncher, home. The same outs, double plays, and other basic rules applied—minus pitcher and catcher.

Brooklyn featured two versions of punchball. In the Williamsburgh game, a chalked line was drawn across the street from first to third. Any ball that fell in front of the line was considered an out, just as any ball that landed on the sidewalk was ruled out. The Crown Heights version eliminated the "out line" and allowed for the batter to hit grounders. Either way, punchball was a terrific game.

What also made the game so good was the fact that all you needed for a good game of punchball was four guys: two on each side. Invariably more kids would soon appear on the scene and you could change the team size at will.

Punchball also had various terms that were very special. "Hitting a sewer," for example, was the highest praise you could achieve on the block. Hitting a sewer meant that you were able to stroke the ball all the way past second base and on to the next sewer cover and to hell and gone down the street.

Since the distance between sewer covers wasn't uniform throughout Brooklyn, there were legends about punchball players who were able to hit *two* sewers! That was roughly equivalent to hitting the ball out of Yankee Stadium. I was definitely not a two-sewer man, but I did have my moments and loved the game.

Looking back at myself as an Orthodox Jewish kid growing up in an Italian-Catholic neighborhood, I imagine it was probably baseball that saved us all from succumbing to bigotry, that and the fact that I could play punchball. And I was smart. My father's presence probably helped, too. He was an imposing, physically strong man, built along the generous lines of a Gil Hodges.

My best friend of all was a kid named Pompeo Morazzo. Pompeo was an orphan who lived with his older sister, Yolanda, who took care of their house. Pompeo and Yolanda were always bugging me to eat at their house, which, of course, I couldn't do, because there was no way the Morazzo residence was observing Jewish dietary laws. Pompeo would complain, "But, Bill, I always eat at your house."

I'd explain, "You eat at my place because what you're eating there is kosher. You don't mind that, but I can't eat your food because it's against my religious principles—okay?" It was years later that Pompeo confessed to me that one of his lifetime unfulfilled ambitions had been to fill one of my kosher pastrami sandwiches with ham when I wasn't looking, just to see my reaction.

Once when I was about eleven, the big guys on the block had a major problem, which they came to me to solve. They had a baseball team that played its games in Prospect Park, about a mile from our neighborhood. These fellows, who were all four and five years older than I was (a really big deal at that age), wanted to dump their manager and bring *me* in as his replacement. Their spokesman, Pompeo's older brother Tony, said, "Bill, we want you to manage our club because you know more about baseball than we do."

In a sense Tony was right. I couldn't play the game as well as they could, but I *knew* the game. So there I was, eleven-year-old Bill Mazer, managing his first team in the Prospect Park League. Casey Stengel would have been proud!

No matter how crazy I might have been about sports, my dad saw to it that I maintained not only my regular schoolwork but Jewish studies as well. At first my dad had a twenty-year-old yeshiva student named Julius Funk give me private Hebrew lessons. Julius was as wild about baseball as I was and when he wanted to motivate me, he would say, "Bill, if you really do your Hebrew well—if you *really* work at this—I'm gonna take you to see the Giants play the Cardinals." Who could resist that kind of inducement? I studied my *aleph-bets* like crazy and Julius would take me to the Polo Grounds.

Once I graduated from junior high school, I decided—to my parents' surprise—that I wanted to go to yeshiva. I had thoughts about becoming a rabbi. The religious part I didn't mind, but the geography part nearly killed me. You have to remember that we lived in the middle of Brooklyn and the yeshiva was way up north on 186th Street and Amsterdam Avenue in Manhattan. This meant I had to get up at 6:45 A.M., say my prayers, eat breakfast, and walk over to MacDonald Avenue to catch the elevated train for Manhattan. Hebrew classes started at 8:45 and lasted until 2:45. At 3:30 we started English, which lasted until 7:30 at night. It may seem like an awful grind, but I considered it an obligation to fulfill, and did so every day of the week except Saturday. I started at the age of twelve and graduated before I was sixteen.

Once I had committed myself to the study of Judaism, it was hard to be around the gang as much as I had been. I couldn't even play ball or manage the Prospect Park team on my day off from yeshiva, because Saturday was the Sabbath and no ball playing was allowed for an Orthodox Jew. Surprisingly, the guys on the block understood. There was never once an anti-Semitic remark made and the ease between myself and the Italian kids was remarkable, particularly when you see what's happening in Queens and Brooklyn today between racial and ethnic groups.

It was around this time that my knack for recalling baseball history began to develop. A lot of my schooling relied on memory, and I seemed to have a particularly good one. Whereas other kids needed three hours to take a final, I could usually knock it off in less than half that time. And as for baseball facts, unlike today, there were no statistical bureaus, nor the volume of books and articles on the subject.

Memory has a lot to do with interest. You're either interested in something, or you're not, and my interest in sports in general and baseball in particular was nothing if not passionate. That, coupled with actually experiencing a lot of the history of the game, is what lodged those details in my cranium permanently.

For example, I had seen Dizzy Dean pitch at the Polo Grounds, so it was natural for me to follow up my interest in him in various ways. There would be the bubblegum picture card at the candy store that would list: Born—Jay Hanna Dean, January 16, 1911, in Lucas, Arkansas. I would commit that to memory. Taking that a step further, it wasn't hard for me to remember that Dizzy won 30 games in 1934 and that during the 1934 World Series he was bopped in the head with the ball while trying to bust up a double play. How could anyone possibly forget that Dean was taken to the hospital and then came home with this delicious and unforgettable quote: "They x-rayed my head and didn't find anything!"

These are events that I would always remember because they were part of the fabric of my life. Each day I would add more events and figures to my memory bank, and by the mid-1930's it was collecting interest.

But the interest really began to double and treble only when I was able to become a regular at the local ballparks and that would happen during The Great Depression, when men were selling apples on street corners and a little corporal in Germany was making big noises about conquering the world.

PART TWO

BASEBALL FROM THE GREAT DEPRESSION TO TODAY

THE GREAT DEPRESSION

(1929-1940)

A couple of weeks after Connie Mack's Athletics trounced the Chicago Cubs in the 1929 World Series, the bottom fell out of the world. The catastrophe took place on a street in Manhattan that was, more or less, midway between Ebbets Field and the Polo Grounds, a tiny, narrow thoroughfare known as Wall Street. With the stock market crash of 1929, the entire globe sank into an economic depression that would last until the cataclysm known as World War II brought an end to unemployment.

Baseball's immediate reaction to the Great Depression was to have a season of inflation—not in gate receipts or salaries, but in batting averages. Known as "the year of the hitter," 1930 would see the National League have a collective batting average of .303 and the American a less-dramatic .288, but still the highest collective average ever for the junior circuit. Bill Terry, at .401, was the last National Leaguer in the twentieth century to hit over .400. The St. Louis Cardinals had 11 batters who hit over .300 (including three backup players), and even the Phillies, National League basement dwellers, hit collectively for .315!

In the National League alone 12 players garnered over 200 hits and the Cards set a league high with 1,004 runs. League records were set for slugging percentage and, for the eight-team league, hits, doubles, total bases, runs batted in, and runs scored.

There was another inflated statistic that season, which stood to reason in light of the hitting numbers: earned run averages. The poor pitchers were practically wiped out of the game, with only four hurlers in the National League managing ERA's below 4.00. Dazzy Vance of the lowly Dodgers was the only National League pitcher having an ERA below 3.00, with 2.6. In fact, the reason the Phillies were so abysmal was because their pitching staff finished the season with a collective ERA of 6.71, another all-time high. The debacle was similar in the American League, with only the remarkable Lefty Grove of the Athletics managing an ERA below 3.00 (2.54).

What happened? The question has been asked for more than five decades. Did baseball owners introduce a "lively ball"? Was it the sacrifice-fly rule that was instituted in 1926, exempting a batter from a time at bat if he advanced a base runner with a fly ball? (The sacrifice-fly rule was cancelled in 1931, only to be reintroduced 20 years later.) Was it the banning of the spitball, or was it because strategy was out and the home run was in?

Probably it was all of the above, with a few other trends thrown in for good measure. It had been ten years since the introduction of the "lively ball" after Ray Chapman's death, and several years since the outlawing of the spitball. It was also three years after Babe Ruth set the home-run record with 60 in 1927 and the league became inundated with hitters who had learned how to make that uppercut on the pitch that produced homers. Whatever the case, it never happened again.

If "the year of the hitter" didn't really personify Depression baseball, what did?

For one thing, personalities rather than strategies would typify the Depression era in baseball. The old Ty Cobb kind of baseball was on its way out: earning runs hit by hit, with lots of bases stolen. Everybody was trying to blast the ball out of the park, and a lot did. Even though batting averages dropped after 1930, the number of homers hit each season stayed right up there.

As for personalities, it was a decade-plus of stellar characters who would disappear: Babe Ruth, Lou Gehrig, John McGraw, Rogers Hornsby—a veritable who's who of future Hall of Famers—retired or got fired. But as they faded from the scene a new host of stars appeared: Joe DiMaggio, Joe Medwick, Hank Greenberg, Ted Williams, Bob Feller.

There was so little actual change in the game of baseball during this period that the only real "first" was probably the introduction of night baseball. Another innovation occurred—the evening of August 26, 1939, when NBC televised a doubleheader between the Dodgers and the Reds from Ebbets Field. Few people were aware of it at the time since nobody had television sets. There were, however, several "institutions" surrounding baseball that began during the Depression, most notably the introduction of the Most Valuable Player award in 1931, the All-Star game in 1933, and the opening of the Hall of Fame in 1936.

One number that fell dramatically during the Depression was the attendance rate. In 1930, baseball attendance was 10,132,272—the greatest gate between the years 1901 and 1945. But it was all downhill after that. Most attribute the drop in attendance to the Depression, but some, like diamond chronicler Bill James, attribute the gate slump to the drop in hitting that occurred after 1930: "Every time there's a slump in hitting, there's a slump in attendance," said James, with the numbers to prove it.

The truth is, baseball wasn't keeping up with the times at all. There wasn't a major-league team west of St. Louis or south of Washington, D.C., but the population had already begun its exodus from the eastern corridor. The South was producing ballplayers faster than the majors could handle them, and even the West—notably the old Pacific Coast League—was producing a number of gifted players: both DiMaggio and Ted Williams were products of California baseball. But it would take years before major-league baseball responded to the pressure of growing numbers in the rest of the country.

IN 1929, THE YANKEES BECAME THE FIRST TEAM TO PUT NUMBERS ON THEIR UNIFORMS. HOW WERE THEY DISTRIBUTED?

The regulars were assigned numbers according to their spot in the batting order. Babe Ruth, the third hitter, received number 3, Lou Gehrig received number 4, and so on. All substitutes and pitchers were given numbers according to seniority.

NAME THE INNOVATIVE BASEBALL EXECUTIVE WHO ORIGINATED LADIES' DAY.

Margaret Donahue, an employee of the Chicago Cubs for thirty-nine years and the first woman to become a corporate executive of a major-league franchise, launched Ladies' Day in 1929. Although the idea has since become part of American life, Donahue's first day set aside for the ladies ended in disaster. She recalled the events leading up to the problem:

"There were 51,556 people in the park and more than 30,000 were women," she said. "People broke down the gates trying to get in. Box-seat holders were shut out and we finally had to summon the mounted police to break up the jam. Pregame practice was called off because we feared a stampede."

She solved the dilemma by asking women to write in for tickets, which were held to a maximum of 20,000 for each future Ladies' Day game.

Ladies' Day is not the only innovation credited to Donahue. In 1926, the cheerful lady was responsible for instituting the sale of season tickets to baseball games.

WHO HOLDS THE RECORD FOR THE MOST CONSECUTIVE SEASONS OF 30 OR MORE HOME RUNS?

Jimmie Foxx had 12 consecutive thirty-plus homer seasons from 1929 to 1940.

Jimmie Foxx (shown here, left, with Robert L. Johnson) still holds the record for most consecutive seasons of 30 or more home runs. *(from the collection of Barry Halper)*

WHAT WAS THE BEST PUT-DOWN OF AN AMERICAN PRESIDENT BY A BASEBALL STAR?

In 1930, the first year of the Great Depression, Babe Ruth signed a contract for $80,000. The Yankees had rewarded him with the then astronomical salary because of his popularity as a slugger and value to the team at the box office. Still, $80,000 seemed an outrageous amount of money. At least that was the opinion of one sportswriter, who asked Ruth how it felt to earn more money than Herbert Hoover, the President of the United States.

The Great Bambino mulled over the question for a moment and then shot back: "Well, I had a better year than he did!"

WHICH TEAM WAS THE BEST HITTING TEAM TO FINISH IN THE CELLAR?

Philadelphia Phillies, 1930. Although the third-place New York Giants set a record by hitting for an average of .319, the Philadelphia Phillies did almost as well, hitting .315, and belting 1,783 hits, 14 more than the Giants. The big difference was in the teams' pitching statistics, which is why the Phillies finished last in the National League.

WHICH TEAM HAD THE WORST PITCHING STAFF?

Philadelphia Phillies, 1930. At a time when big-league teams considered it horrendous to have a collective earned run average of more than 4.00, the 1930 edition of the Phillies finished the season with an earned run average of 6.71. During the entire season, the Philadelphia pitchers were able to put together only three shutouts.

NAME THE MAJOR-LEAGUE PITCHER WHO ONCE WAS KIDNAPPED?

Flint Rhem was one of the most dependable pitchers on the St. Louis Cardinals' staff during their winning years from the mid-twenties through the early thirties. Off the field, however, Rhem was as unpredictable as he could be—one of the most eccentric characters in the game.

In September 1930, the Dodgers, Cardinals, and Cubs were fighting for the pennant. The Cardinals, trailing the Dodgers by a single game, arrived at Ebbets Field for a three-game series and the pitching rotation had Rhem, who had enjoyed fair success against the Bums, scheduled to hurl the second game. Rhem was coming off six straight triumphs and, in general, had shown model conduct. But, unexpectedly, on the eve of the opener, he disappeared. Manager Gabby Street was at his wit's end for an explanation. His ace left-hander, "Wild Bill" Hallahan, who was supposed to pitch the first game, had injured his hand when a cabdriver, who was rumored to be a Dodger fan, slammed the door on him. Street wanted to switch to Rhem, but, alas, Rhem was nowhere to be found. When the players turned in the night before the first game, the pitcher still was missing. But, because it was Rhem, nobody worried very much. Flint was AWOL again, that was all. At least that was the prevailing thought.

The morning of the game arrived—and so did Flint Rhem, equipped with an explanation that soon would go down in baseball history. It seemed that Rhem had been standing in front of the team's hotel, getting some fresh air, when he was hailed by two men in a taxi. Rhem went over to speak to them and before he knew it, they grabbed him and shoved him into the cab. He was driven to a house somewhere in New Jersey (he thought). There, at gunpoint, he was forced to drink whiskey far into the night. That's what the man said!

WHO WAS THE LAST .400 HITTER IN THE NATIONAL LEAGUE?

Bill Terry hit .401 in 1930 as a thirty-three-year-old New York Giants first baseman. Terry played from 1923–1936 and managed the Giants from 1932–1941.

Bill Terry of the Giants was the last .400 hitter in the National League, hitting .401 in 1930. *(from the collection of Barry Halper)*

WHAT WAS THE BEST-HITTING TEAM IN BASEBALL?

The New York Giants, 1930. Playing at the horseshoe-shaped Polo Grounds in Harlem, the club managed by John McGraw hit for a collective average of .319. Those who made this mark possible included first baseman Bill Terry, whose .401 average led the Giants, third baseman Fred Lindstrom, second (with .379), on "The Pride of Manhattan," and right fielder Mel Ott, who not only batted .349 but hit 25 home runs.

Both Terry and Ott later became lionized, to a degree, as Giants managers. Terry did as much as any Giant to fan the flames of the then perennial Giants-Dodgers feud with his deathless line in 1934: "Brooklyn . . . are they still in the National League?"

Beloved for his soft nature and a unique right-leg kick before swinging, Ott could never be accused of antagonizing the Brooklyn foe with his rhetoric.

The Giants' pitching in 1930 was less awesome than the hitting. McGraw's pitchers finished with a collective earned run average of 4.59, third best in the National League.

(Note: The best hitting team of the nineteenth century was the 1887 Detroit National League club, which finished first and hit for a collective average of .347.)

JOHNNY LEONARD "PEPPER" MARTIN WAS A TWENTY-SEVEN-YEAR-OLD ROOKIE CENTER FIELDER WITH THE ST. LOUIS CARDINALS IN 1931. THE CARDS' TRAINER, HARRISON J. WEAVER, COINED ANOTHER NICKNAME FOR PEPPER DURING THE '31 WORLD SERIES. WHAT WAS PEPPER'S OTHER *NOM DE BASEBALL?*

Weaver called him "The Wild Hoss of the Osage" because of his penchant for running like the wind. Martin's reputation for fleet feet and his "country boy" image were so strong that a former minor-league teammate of Martin's once said, "Old Pepper goes out on the prairie and scares up a bunch of rabbits. He reaches down and feels the sides of these rabbits. If the rabbit is a bit thin, he lets him go. If the rabbit is nice and fat, old Pepper picks him up and puts him in his bag."

Pepper Martin (shown here post playing years, with Joe Medwick) was probably one of the fleetest of foot in the major leagues during his career and maintained his "country boy" demeanor throughout. *(from the collection of Barry Halper)*

WHO HOLDS THE AMERICAN LEAGUE RECORD FOR MOST RUNS BATTED IN DURING A SEASON?

Lou Gehrig had 184 RBI's in 1931.

WHICH TRAVELING VAUDEVILLIAN DURING THE WINTER OF 1931–32 HAD JUST SET A WORLD SERIES BATTING RECORD?

Pepper Martin made 12 hits in 18 at bats, a World Series record. In the second game against the Philadelphia Athletics in 1931, Martin had two hits and two stolen bases, scoring both Cards runs in the 2–0 win over the A's. In game five Pepper had three hits, including a homer in the sixth inning, and a long fly, to bat in four runs, as St. Louis took Philadelphia, 5–1. St. Louis won the Series four games to three.

After the fifth game, Commissioner Landis approached Martin and said, "Young man, how I'd like to be in your place tonight!"

Pepper thought the proposal over for a moment, then answered: "Well, Judge, $4,500 a year versus $65,000—I'll swap you!"

Martin didn't trade places with the baseball commissioner, but he did make up some of that salary differential by joining a traveling show in the off-season, for $1,500 a week.

WHAT WAS THE WORST GREETING RECEIVED BY A PRESIDENT AT A BASEBALL GAME?

Herbert Hoover, Philadelphia, October 6, 1931. One of baseball's most venerable traditions has been the appearance of the President of the United States at opening day of the season, and, frequently, at a World Series game. During the 1931 World Series between the Philadelphia Athletics and St. Louis Cardinals, President Herbert Hoover showed up for the third game. Hoover, a Republican, had been elected President in 1929, and was therefore generally held responsible for the Great Depression that had blanketed the nation. Nevertheless, it was traditional for fans to greet the presidential party with reverence and applause at such sporting events as the World Series.

When Hoover arrived at Philadelphia's Shibe Park that afternoon, there was a perfunctory pattering of palms behind the dugouts, whereupon Hoover waved his hat and smiled. But as the President approached his official box, someone booed. Then came another hoot and then another. Joe Williams, who covered the World Series for *The New York World-Telegram,* recalled how quickly the decibel count multiplied. "Soon," said Williams, "it seemed that almost everyone in the park was booing."

Prohibition was still in effect, and the crowd, *en masse,* seemed to realize that Hoover had lined up on the side of the drys, supporting the Prohibition law. Suddenly, the boos changed to a deafening chant: "We want beer! We want beer!"

As soon as the first inning was underway, the crowd's attention was distracted from Hoover to the Cardinals and Athletics. However, at the end of the eighth inning a voice boomed over the ballpark loudspeaker. "Silence. Silence, please." Hoover and his party were ready to leave the game. The public address announcer pleaded for courtesy and asked everyone at the stadium to remain seated.

The plea was ignored. Herbert Hoover, holding his wife by the arm, walked past the Athletics' dugout amid a cacophony of boos, followed by an equally deafening chant: "We want beer. We want beer!"

Hoover later explained that he walked out before the game's end because he had received two telegrams; one told of the death of a personal friend and the other revealed that the United States had gone off the gold standard. "Under the circumstances," said Hoover, "I decided I had no business watching a ball game." Despite the hostile reaction at the World Series game, Hoover continued to attend baseball games at various stadia in later years.

BILL TERRY, GIANTS FIRST BASEMAN IN THE 1920's, AND MANAGER JOHN McGRAW WOULD NOT SPEAK TO EACH OTHER AFTER TERRY ANSWERED BACK SHARPLY TO ONE OF McGRAW'S NOTORIOUS TIRADES. HOW WAS THIS SILENCE FINALLY BROKEN?
On June 3, 1932, McGraw broke the silence. Club owner Charles Stoneham decided to remove McGraw as manager because he had become increasingly irascible. Stoneham allowed McGraw to choose his own successor. McGraw called Terry into his office and offered him the job, which Terry immediately accepted.

WHAT PLAYER ACCUMULATED THE MOST HITS IN THE FIRST SIX YEARS OF HIS CAREER?
Joe "Ducky" Medwick amassed 1,064 hits in his first five years in the majors, 1932–37, with the St. Louis Cardinals. Kirby Puckett of the Minnesota Twins is a very close second with 1,062 in his first six years in the bigs.

Joe "Ducky" Medwick (shown here in later years, as a Brooklyn Dodger) accumulated more than a thousand hits in his first five seasons in the majors, with the St. Louis Cardinals. *(from the collection of Barry Halper)*

123

WHICH TWO IMMORTAL AMERICAN MUSICIANS SPONSORED BASEBALL CLUBS DURING THE DEPRESSION?

Although segregation would rule in major-league baseball for more than a decade, black baseball leagues were thriving in the depression era.

Gravel-voiced jazz trumpeter Louis "Satchmo" Armstrong sponsored the "Secret Nine" out of New Orleans, while a Cab Calloway team flourished at the same time.

WHICH BALLPLAYER CAUGHT THE OPENING GAME OF A DOUBLEHEADER AND PITCHED THE SECOND GAME?

Ted Radcliffe, one of the greatest black baseball players, was the catcher for Satchel Paige in a Negro-League doubleheader at Yankee Stadium in 1932 for the famed Pittsburgh Crawfords. The Crawfords won 5–0. Then Radcliffe took the mound and pitched a 4–0 shutout. As a result, Radcliffe earned the nickname "Double Duty," thanks to journalist Damon Runyon.

After seeing Radcliffe perform, Runyon wrote: "It was worth the admission price of two to see Double Duty out there in action."

Those who played with and against Radcliffe toasted his versatility. "He never got the recognition he should have," said shortstop Jake Stephens. "In my book he was one of the greatest."

Added catcher Royal "Skink" Browning: "Radcliffe could catch the first game, pitch the second—and was a terror at both of them."

WHAT WAS THE WORST PERFORMANCE BY A WINNING RELIEF PITCHER?

Ed Rommel, Philadelphia Athletics, July 10, 1932. A first-class pitcher for the A's from 1920 through 1932, Rommel appeared in 251 games as a reliever. In his final season with Philadelphia, Rommel appeared in a game that ran through eighteen innings. Rommel's opponents, the Cleveland Indians, were able to connect against him almost every inning, but the A's always rallied to save

Rommel for still another inning. In the eighteenth inning, Rommel finally stopped the Indians without a run, enabling Philadelphia to win the match, 18–17. During his career, Rommel won a total of 171 games, all for the Athletics, and later became a major league umpire.

WHO WAS THE PITCHER OFF WHOM BABE RUTH HIT HIS "CALLED SHOT" HOME RUN?

Charlie Root. The 1932 World Series between the New York Yankees and Chicago Cubs was one of the most bitterly played between National and American League teams. The Yankees won the first two games, 12–6 and 5–2, at Yankee Stadium, but the third and fourth games were scheduled for hostile Wrigley Field in Chicago.

Cubs fans not only resented the pompous Yankees, led by the thirty-seven-year-old Ruth and his home-run-hitting sidekick, Lou Gehrig, but they were angry that their team had dropped two games in a row. Prior to the game Ruth and Gehrig further enraged the crowd by smacking 18 "balls" into the bleachers during batting practice.

Ruth opened the hostilities by hitting a home run in his first at bat against pitcher Charlie Root in the first inning. But the Cubs rallied and when Ruth came to bat in the fifth inning the score was tied, 3–3. As Ruth glanced at the mound, fans taunted him with chants of "big belly" and "baboon." Root followed with a called strike, whereupon Ruth raised a finger on each hand. He did likewise until the count reached two and two.

At this juncture, Ruth lifted his arm and pointed to center field, clearly indicating to most onlookers that he was planning to plant the next pitch over the fence for another home run. The already-angry crowd became even surlier until Root delivered the pitch and Ruth drove the ball precisely where he had predicted it would go.

Instead of bombarding The Babe with more insults, the stunned crowd suddenly began applauding the man they had come to hate. Perhaps they realized that Ruth was in the twilight of his great career and that they never would see such a feat again. Whatever the case, New York swept the Series in four straight games, for Ruth's last appearance in a World Series. He retired two years later, claiming that his "called shot" was his "dumbest" move. "If I'd missed," Ruth explained, "I'd have looked like an awful fool."

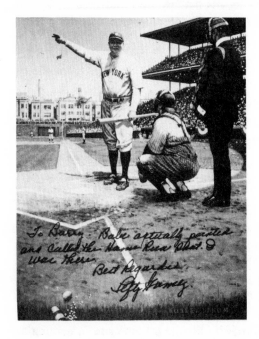

An artist's rendering of Babe Ruth's famed "called shot" of the 1932 World Series. *(from the collection of Barry Halper)*

WHEN WAS THE FIRST ALL-STAR GAME PLAYED AND WHO WON?

The American League won 4–2 over the Nationals in the first midsummer classic played in Chicago's Comiskey Park on July 6, 1933. Babe Ruth's two-run homer in the third inning proved to be the winning margin.

WHO WAS THE FASTEST BASEBALL PLAYER *NEVER* TO HAVE PLAYED IN THE MAJOR LEAGUES?

James Thomas "Cool Papa" Bell. At his peak in the thirties, Bell showed his speed in the Negro National League, the Mexican League, and the Cuban League, among others. Those who played with and against Bell claimed he was the original Kid Lightning on the base paths. "That man," said pitcher Satchel Paige, a Hall of Famer, "was so fast he could turn out the light and jump in bed before the room got dark." Observers insist that Bell was faster than Ty Cobb, Lou Brock, Jackie Robinson, and even Jesse Owens, one of America's greatest Olympic track stars. It was not unusual for Bell to score from first base *on a sacrifice*. In a 1934 East-West all-star game, he scored from second on a ground ball to win the game, 1–0. "They once timed me," said Bell, "circling the bases in 12 seconds flat." Pepper Martin, star base runner of the "Gas House Gang" St. Louis Cardinals, credited Bell with teaching him how to improve his base stealing.

HOW DID THE GIANTS' MANAGER, BILL TERRY, BLOW THE PENNANT FOR HIS TEAM IN 1934?

One early January day in 1934, Giants manager Bill Terry showed up at the Giants' offices to face a battery of writers. "We should win again this year," he said. "If we don't, we won't finish any lower than third. I think the Cubs, Pirates, and Cardinals will give us more trouble."

Roscoe McGowen of *The New York Times* asked, "What about Brooklyn, Bill?"

Terry replied in apparent innocence, "Brooklyn? Gee, I haven't heard a peep out of there. Are they still in the National League?"

Terry's question set off a storm of controversy and served to intensify the interborough rivalry. Letters, unsigned and with the Brooklyn postmark, came to Terry by the thousands. "Whaddya mean, yuh bum? Is Brooklyn still in the league? We'll show yuh. Wait'll yuh come to Brooklyn, yuh bum, yuh."

Just before the season started, Casey Stengel took over for the fired Max Carey as the Dodgers' manager. At his first press conference, Stengel quipped, "You can tell Terry the Dodgers are still in the league. I'll let our Mr. Van Mungo (Van Lingle Mungo) do a lot of arguing for me against the Giants this summer."

Through the summer, the Giants had first place for 27 games. However, the Cardinals came back and tied the Giants for the lead with two games to go for each. The Cardinals faced a pair with Cincinnati and the Giants squared off against the Dodgers who were intent on playing the spoiler.

Was Brooklyn still in the league? Thousands of fans from Ebbets Field showed up at the Polo Grounds holding up banners reading: YEP, WE'RE STILL IN THE LEAGUE. They screamed and whistled and yelled and rang cowbells, putting the Giants in the position of fighting for the pennant in their home park before a hostile crowd.

Stengel's Mr. Van Mungo pitched against "Tarzan" Parmelee on Saturday, and after four innings there was no score. In the fifth, Mungo singled, took second on a passed ball, and scored on a base hit by Buzz Boyle. In the sixth, Mungo drove in Len Koenecke with another hit. The Dodgers scored one in the seventh and twice in the ninth to back Mungo's five-hitter as the Dodgers won, 5–1. Meanwhile, Paul Dean and the Cards breezed over the Reds, 6–1.

On the final day, the Giants still had a shot at the pennant. They scored four times in the first, but then squandered the lead and Brooklyn put the Giants out of the race with an 8–5, ten-inning win.

The Dodgers proved they were still in the league. Stengel later said to Terry, "I would have come in to console you, but I thought better of it."

WHO RAN THE LARGEST AND MOST PRODUCTIVE FARM SYSTEM IN ORGANIZED BASEBALL?

Branch Rickey built up the St. Louis Cardinal organization to include, at one point in the 1930's, 50 farm teams and over 800 players. In fact it was Rickey who created the farm system of developing young players when he joined the Cards in 1916!

When Rickey joined the team, the Cardinals were so poor they couldn't afford to go south for spring training and worked out instead at Washington University in St. Louis. Since the team also couldn't afford to buy players, Rickey reasoned that if the Cardinals helped minor-league teams staff their clubs during their season, then the Cardinals could have "first dibs" on players after the minor-league season ended. This agreement became the basis for all farm-system-major-league relationships.

But in order to get the players he needed to "farm out" to the minors, Rickey instituted free-agent tryout camps, with some remarkable results. The first tryout camp produced Ray Blades, who would bat .311 over 11 years with the Cards. He later managed the team two seasons. Later camps produced stars like Red Schoendienst and even the great Dizzy Dean.

Branch Rickey (shown here between Hall of Famers "Pie" Traynor, left, and "Kid" Nichols, right) was the father of baseball's farm systems. *(from the collection of Barry Halper)*

WHAT WORLD CHAMPION BASEBALL TEAM FORMED A HILLBILLY BAND CALLED THE MISSISSIPPI MUDCATS?

It was the World Champion Cardinals of 1934, otherwise known as the Gas House Gang.

WHO WERE DIZZY AND DAFFY?

These were nicknames of the famous Dean brothers, of the 1930's: Jay Hanna "Dizzy" Dean and Paul Dee "Daffy" Dean came out of Arkansas with little education and soon captivated the public with their pranks on and off the field. Dizzy, the older, who was the more successful and zanier of the two, later became a successful broadcaster. The mother of a young boy once scolded Dizzy for the horrible grammar he used on the air, which, she claimed, was setting a bad example for her son. "You don't even know the king's English," the woman said.

"Old Diz knows the king's English," Dean protested. "And not only that—I also know the queen is English."

Pitcher Dizzy Dean (shown here, left, with Lon Warneke) was known for fracturing his English as well as putting a lot of English on his pitches! *(from the collection of Barry Halper)*

WHO SAID, "ME 'N' PAUL IS GONNA WIN FORTY-FIVE GAMES THIS YEAR"?

Dizzy Dean, boasting on behalf of himself and his brother during spring training in 1934. Dizzy also predicted that the St. Louis Cardinals would win the National League pennant.

So, what happened? Dizzy and Paul made good on both promises. The brothers racked up forty-nine victories that year—a record for brother tandems—thirty by Dizzy (30–7, the last National League pitcher to win 30) and nineteen by Paul. Next, in the World Series against the favored Detroit Tigers, Diz declared: "Me 'n' Paul can beat 'em all by us-selves." And they did, with each brother winning two games!

Another time, when Dizzy pitched a three-hit shutout in the first game of a doubleheader against the Dodgers, Paul came back with a no-hitter in the nightcap. "Shucks," said Diz after the game, "if I'd knowed Paul was gonna pitch a no-hitter, why I'd pitched a no-hitter too."

Dizzy Dean died in 1974 and Paul in 1981. Before he died, Paul, a grandfather of fourteen, lived in Springdale, Arkansas, and still dabbled in baseball, doing a little promotional work for the Cardinals' Triple-A team in Springfield, Illinois. How did he feel about the modern big-leaguers?

"I'll tell ya, podner," he drawled. "Them pitchers just can't hold the runners on base these days. I figure I could steal thirty bases today—and I weigh close to 300 pounds."

WHICH BLACK BASEBALL PLAYER STARRED AT EVERY POSITION?

Martin DiHigo. According to many observers who saw him play in the twenties and thirties for the Cuban Stars and Homestead Grays, DiHigo was one of the best ballplayers of all time. In a 1935 East-West all-star game, DiHigo started in center field and batted third for the East and, in the late innings, was called upon to pitch in relief. Buck Leonard, himself a star with the Grays, and others who played with DiHigo support the observers who labeled DiHigo one of the game's finest. He was used at every position by the Cubans and the Grays, and in 1929 he batted .386 in the American Negro League. When the Negro National League folded and blacks began to enter the major leagues in the late forties, DiHigo was too old to make it to the bigs. He played out his career during the fifties in Mexico.

WHO RECEIVED THE MOST UNUSUAL TREATMENT FOR A SORE ARM?

Guy Bush, Chicago Cubs. A major-league pitcher in the twenties and early thirties, Bush suffered a sore arm one afternoon before an important game. The Cubs' trainer, Andy Lotshaw, fancied himself an amateur psychiatrist and concluded that Bush's ailment was more psychosomatic than real. However, to placate the "injured" pitcher, Lotshaw produced a bottle that, he insisted, contained a secret potion guaranteed to cure the sore arm. The trainer then rubbed it vigorously from Bush's shoulder blade to his hand and then sent him out to pitch. Remarkably, Bush won the game and Lotshaw was immediately lionized by the pitcher.

When Bush received his next pitching assignment, he demanded more of the "secret" potion rubdown. Lotshaw obliged and, rejuvenated, Bush went on pitching for the Cubs until 1934 when he was traded. However, it wasn't until Bush ultimately retired that Lotshaw revealed the ingredients of his "cure." For the first treatment he reached into his bag for some liniment but discovered that none was left. Instead, he opened the first full bottle he could find and swabbed the dark brown, sparkly liquid on Bush's arm. The miracle cure was Coca-Cola.

WHO REPLACED BABE RUTH IN THE NEW YORK YANKEES' OUTFIELD?

George "Twinkletoes" Selkirk. In 1934, Selkirk, the son of a Huntsville, Ontario, funeral director, graduated from the International League to the American League Yankees. Unlike Ruth, Selkirk was extraordinarily fast and thus earned the nickname "Twinkletoes." Although Selkirk was hardly in Ruth's class as a slugger, he was a competent fielder and steady hitter. He was twice (1936 and 1939) selected for American League All-Star teams and batted above .300 five seasons.

Selkirk's most commendable moment occurred at his first at bat in the 1936 World Series when he hit a home run off the Giants' superb pitcher, Carl Hubbell. When Twinkletoes' playing days were over, he became a minor-league manager and, later, general manager of the Washington Senators in the mid-sixties. From time to time knowledgeable baseball fans would encounter Selkirk and introduce him as "the man who replaced Babe Ruth." Once a friend so introduced Selkirk to his grandsons. The kids looked at their grandfather and replied: "Who's Babe Ruth?"

WHICH NON-MAJOR-LEAGUER IS SAID TO HAVE HIT THE ONLY FAIR BALL EVER TO BE WHACKED OUT OF YANKEE STADIUM?

Josh Gibson, Pittsburgh Crawfords, 1934. The legendary black catcher—some consider him the most proficient of all time and a better slugger than Babe Ruth—hit the home run in a Negro National League game against the Philadelphia Stars. One witness was Jack Marshall of the Chicago American Giants, who recalled: "Josh hit the ball over the triple deck next to the bull pen in left field. Over and out! I never will forget that, because we were getting ready to leave to play a night game and we were standing in the aisle when that boy hit this ball!"

Baseball's bible, *The Sporting News,* credits Gibson with hitting a longer home run than Ruth ever hit *inside* Yankee Stadium, a drive that landed just two feet from the top of the Stadium wall circling the bleachers in center field, about 580 feet from home plate. It was estimated that had the blast been two feet higher it would have cleared the wall and traveled about 700 feet.

Catcher Josh Gibson is reputedly the only non-major-leaguer ever to hit a fair ball out of Yankee Stadium. *(from the collection of Barry Halper)*

Walter Johnson, one of the best pitchers of all time, watched Gibson in action and observed: "There is a catcher that any big-league club would like to buy for $200,000. His name is Gibson. He can do everything. He hits the ball a mile. And he catches so easy, he might as well be in a rocking chair. Throws like a rifle. Too bad this Gibson is a colored fellow."

One legend has it that Gibson was playing at Forbes Field in Pittsburgh one day and hit such a towering drive that nobody saw it coming down. After long deliberation, the umpire ruled it a home run. A day later Gibson's team was playing in Philadelphia when a ball suddenly dropped out of the sky and was caught by an alert center fielder on the opposition. Pointing to Gibson, the umpire ruled: "You're out—yesterday in Pittsburgh!"

WHO WAS THE LAST OF THE LEGAL SPITBALL PITCHERS?

Burleigh Grimes. Although the spitball—doctoring the baseball with saliva, tobacco juice, or sandpaper—was outlawed in 1919, eighteen spitball practitioners were permitted to continue throwing "wet ones" until the end of their careers. The mean, outspoken and fearless Grimes lasted the longest, racking up 270 victories in 19 seasons, with the Brooklyn Dodgers, Pittsburgh Pirates, and four other teams, before retiring in 1934.

Grimes was called "Ol' Stubblebeard" and he was revered as one of the most colorful characters of baseball. A hot-tempered Wisconsin farm boy, he became a big winner after mastering the art of the spitball. After his retirement as an active major-leaguer, Grimes turned to managing and always insisted that baseball never should have outlawed the spitball. In fact, he campaigned for its legalization as "a perfectly safe pitch, easier to control than the knuckle ball."

Grimes was voted into the Hall of Fame in 1964, and when he surpassed his eightieth birthday, Grimes told an interviewer that he was as fearless as ever. "I just got married again!" he laughed.

WHERE WAS MAJOR-LEAGUE BASEBALL'S FIRST NIGHT GAME PLAYED?

The first arc-light tilt was played before 20,422 fans in Cincinnati's Crosley Field on May 24, 1935, with the hometown Reds besting the Philadelphia Phillies, 2–1. After the game, the players were rather noncommittal about the event, but National League President Ford Frick said, "Night ball has merit, but I don't think there will be a steady diet of it."

Well, night ball did catch on—slowly at first—but it soon became more and more popular. By 1946, all National League parks with the exception of Chicago's Wrigley Field (which finally succumbed in 1988) boasted lights. Attendance figures that year were 8,902,000 paid admissions, compared to the 3,200,000 who had passed through the turnstiles in 1934.

In the American League as well, attendance experienced a steady upswing as lights were added. The Chicago White Sox and Philadelphia Athletics blazed the way with night ball in 1939. By

1948, the entire league was "lit up." Attendance in the American League in 1938 was 4,445,000; by 1948 it had climbed to 11,500,000.

WHO WAS THE "BEST DISGUISED" BASEBALL COLUMNIST?

"The Old Scout," *New York Sun.* For more than a decade, starting in 1935, a brilliantly written column appeared in the *Sun* with no byline other than "The Old Scout." The author was Herb Goren, a Brooklynite, who covered baseball and hockey for the paper. Goren inherited the column from Sam Murphy, the original "Old Scout," who did have his byline on the six-day-a-week opus. When sports editor Wilbur Wood decided to make a change, he gave the column to Goren. "Unfortunately," Goren recalled, "he couldn't let me put my byline on a column called 'The Old Scout' for a very good reason—I was only nineteen years old!"

WHAT BOXING PROMOTER COINED A DEATHLESS PHRASE FOR BASEBALL ("I SHOULD OF STOOD IN BED"), AND FOR BOXING ("WE WUZ ROBBED")?

Joe Jacobs. In October 1935, an ailing Jacobs was home in bed when he decided to attend the World Series in Detroit between the Tigers and the Chicago Cubs. Jacobs bet on Chicago, but Detroit won the Series. When Jacobs returned home to New York and resumed convalescence, he told reporters: "I should of stood in bed."

Jacobs's other remarkable remark had been delivered earlier when he was heavyweight Max Schmeling's manager. Schmeling was fighting Jack Sharkey on June 21, 1932, when Sharkey was awarded a controversial decision that thoroughly enraged Jacobs. It was then that he rushed to a nearby radio microphone and shouted, "We wuz robbed!"

THROUGHOUT MAJOR-LEAGUE HISTORY, SHORTSTOPS HAVE NOT BEEN AMONG THE GAME'S LEADING HITTERS. WHILE THERE HAVE BEEN SOME SHORTSTOPS KNOWN FOR THEIR OFFENSIVE STATISTICS, SUCH AS LOU BOUDREAU, ERNIE BANKS, AND HONUS WAGNER, THEY NUMBER FEW. WHO HOLDS THE MAJOR-LEAGUE RECORD FOR THE HIGHEST SINGLE-SEASON BATTING AVERAGE BY A SHORTSTOP?

In 1936, the Chicago White Sox's shortstop, Lucius "Luke" Appling, hit .388, the highest batting average for a shortstop in major-league history. Luke, who played from 1930 until 1950, teamed with Luis Aparicio to give the White Sox two of baseball's greatest shortstops ever, between 1930 and 1970. Although Appling was a lifetime .310 hitter, the .388 mark was a fluke for Luke. Playing regularly, he had never hit over .350 before.

Appling was said to know his hitting as well as almost anyone in baseball history. One story tells how he made many public appearances throughout his playing days, during which he would give away baseballs. This was great for the White Sox's public relations. But once, when Appling asked the Chicago management for more balls to distribute, the ungrateful front office said no. The next day at batting practice, Appling positioned a friend in a certain section of the seats in Comiskey Park. Appling then proceeded to hit eleven straight balls to this precise spot. He had his baseballs.

Appling occasionally used the foul ball for strategic purposes. Once, when he was facing Yankees pitcher Red Ruffing, Appling took two quick strikes and appeared headed for a quick exit from home plate. Luke was disturbed since the White Sox had two men on base and there were two out.

It was time to slow down Ruffing, so Appling fouled off the next four pitches until Ruffing threw one so wide that Luke didn't bother reaching for it. He then fouled off six consecutive pitches until Ruffing hurled two more egregiously bad pitches that Luke ignored. The count now was three and two as Ruffing bore down once more; but so did the king of the fouls. For his *chef-d'oeuvre,* Appling fouled the next fourteen pitches in a row before Ruffing, frazzled and furious, finally walked Appling to fill the bases.

Impatient, Ruffing grooved a magnificent strike down the middle, which the next batter, Mike Kreevich, lined for a bases-clearing double. That catapulted Yankees manager Joe McCarthy out of the dugout to remove his ace. On his way to the showers, Ruffing paused for a few words with Appling at third base: "You did it! You did it with those ———— foul balls!"

Though he enjoyed a great career, Appling listed his greatest thrill ever as happening years after his retirement, when in a nationally televised old-timers' game, Luke, almost eighty, hit a home run! The crowd went wild, and Pee Wee Reese, in the field, was so happy for Luke that he ran around the bases with him.

Luke Appling had the highest batting average in major-league history for a shortstop, hitting .388 in 1936. *(from the collection of Barry Halper)*

BESIDES APPLING'S HIGHEST BATTING AVERAGE FOR A SHORTSTOP, 1936 WOULD SEE TWO OTHER TWENTIETH-CENTURY RECORDS SET THAT HAVE NEVER BEEN BROKEN. WHAT WERE THESE RECORDS?

The highest batting average for a catcher—.367, by Babe Phelps of the Dodgers. Astoundingly, the second highest batting average ever for a catcher was Bill Dickey's .362, which came that same season.

The third record was the highest number of at bats in the 154-game schedule: 696 ups for Woody Jensen of the Pirates.

WHICH ST. LOUIS BROWNS PITCHER OWNED THE CATCHIEST NAME—AND NICKNAME?

His first name was Emil—not very exciting. But his last name was Bildilli, which had a sort of ring to it. His nickname was "Hill Billy." So, when the nickname and last name came together you got "Hill Billy" Bildilli. Now that's quite a name. Other than his name, "Hill Billy" Bildilli offered little for his fans to cheer about, because when it came to his pitching, he was far from a dilly. In five major-league seasons with the Browns—1937–1941—Emil "Hill Billy" Bildilli won four games and lost eight.

WHICH BATTER WAS RESPONSIBLE FOR ENDING DIZZY DEAN'S PITCHING CAREER?

During the fifth All-Star Game, played in Washington, D.C., on July 7, 1937, Earl Averill of the Cleveland Indians rapped a Dizzy Dean pitch right back at the big guy from Lucas, Arkansas. The drive fractured Dean's big toe on his right foot. Instead of patiently recuperating, Dizzy rushed back into action much too soon after the injury. As a result, he favored the wounded toe and altered his pitching motion, thereby permanently injuring his pitching arm. Dizzy never regained his top form. At the time of his injury, in the prime of his career, Dean was just twenty-six years old. A Cardinal since 1930, he could boast of a spectacular 134–75 record. Following the 1937 season, Dean was traded to the Chicago Cubs and pitched for the National League entry from the Windy City until 1941. His won-lost record with the Cubs was 16–8. Dean made a brief return in 1947 when he pitched for the St. Louis Browns and was credited with no decisions. Dean could well have been the greatest right-handed pitcher ever had he not been in so much of a hurry to pitch again in 1937.

WHO WAS THE LAST NATIONAL LEAGUER TO WIN THE TRIPLE CROWN?

Joe Medwick in 1937. "Ducky" led the league in at bats (633), hits (237), doubles (56), home runs (31), and batting average (.374).

WHO WAS THE OLDEST ROOKIE TO WIN 20 GAMES?
Jim Turner of the Braves was thirty-four years old when he performed the feat in 1937.

WHAT WERE THE CIRCUMSTANCES SURROUNDING THE END OF LOU GEHRIG'S CONSECUTIVE-GAME PLAYING STREAK?
In 1938, Gehrig had slumped to a .295 average, the lowest of his career, causing people to think that he was slowing down at age thirty-five. It was plain to all that he now swung hard but hit the ball softly. He also seemed to get nowhere when he ran, causing one teammate to say he looked like "a man running through waist-high water."

When the 1939 season began, it became apparent Gehrig could no longer play. Through eight games he had an average of .143 with only one run batted in. Manager Joe McCarthy contemplated a move for the team's—and Gehrig's—well-being.

On the night of May 1, an off day, Gehrig and McCarthy met in a Detroit hotel. They agreed that the streak would have to stop. The next day Gehrig brought out the lineup card as team captain, and received a thunderous ovation as the PA system announced that his streak was terminating.

Gehrig went to the Mayo Clinic in Rochester, Minnesota. The disease, amyotrophic lateral sclerosis, later nicknamed "Lou Gehrig's Disease," was diagnosed, and Gehrig was told he had two-and-a-half years to live. Gehrig died on June 2, 1941, sixteen years to the day he had replaced Wally Pipp at first base.

WHO WAS THE FIRST BASEBALL PLAYER TO HAVE HIS UNIFORM NUMBER RETIRED?
Lou Gehrig, 1939.

WHAT PITCHER PITCHED TWO CONSECUTIVE NO-HITTERS IN 1938?

Johnny Vander Meer of the Cincinnati Reds recorded a pair of no-hitters within four days in 1938. He is still the only pitcher in major-league history to have done it.

Vander Meer's first no-hitter came on June 11 against the Boston Braves, with the Reds winning 3–0 at Braves' Field. In his very next start on June 15, at the first night game played at Ebbets Field, Vander Meer blanked the Dodgers of Brooklyn, 6–0.

WHAT WAS THE MOST UNUSUAL ALIBI GIVEN BY A BALLPLAYER CAUGHT AFTER CURFEW?

Boots Poffenberger, Brooklyn Dodgers. Notorious for his carousing, Poffenberger was with the Dodgers briefly in 1939, when Leo Durocher was manager. Durocher was well aware of Poffenberger's habits when he obtained him from Detroit for the Dodgers, but the manager believed a pep talk could do the trick. "You're starting out fresh with me," said Durocher, "so let's forget all the stories I've heard about you."

All was well with Poffenberger and Durocher until the Dodgers checked into Philadelphia for a series with the Phillies. Durocher herded his men into the Bellevue Stratford Hotel and soon discovered that Poffenberger had reverted to form.

"If you've ever been to the Bellevue Stratford Hotel," said Durocher, "you know that tney had a cluster of clocks above the cashier's desk, a big one with the local time and smaller ones giving the times in various cities around the world.

"The first night in Philadelphia, half an hour past midnight, Dodger president Larry MacPhail and I were sitting in the lobby and somebody almost stepped on my shoe. I looked up and saw my new man, Poffenberger.

"The next morning I tapped Mr. Poffenberger's shoulder and asked him what time he'd come in. 'Eleven o'clock,' he said.

" 'You're a goddam liar,' I said. 'I was sitting right there in the lobby and it was twelve-thirty by the clock on the wall.'

" 'Well,' he said, 'it depends on which clock you were looking at. One of them clocks there said eleven and that was the clock I was going by!' "

WHICH LARGE "FELINE" LED THE NATIONAL LEAGUE AT ONE TIME OR ANOTHER IN EVERY SIGNIFICANT OFFENSIVE CATEGORY?

Johnny "The Big Cat" Mize led the National League in batting average (1939—.349), home runs (1939—28, 1940—43, 1947—51, and 1948—40), doubles (1941—39), triples (1938—16), runs scored (1947—137), slugging percentage (1938—.614, 1939—.626, 1940—.636, and 1942—.521), and runs batted in (1940—137, 1942—110, and 1947—138).

WHEN WAS A BASEBALL GAME CALLED "ON ACCOUNT OF A HURRICANE?"

On September 21, 1938, a killer hurricane spread its fury over New England. The Boston Bees (prior to 1936 and after 1940, they were known as the Boston Braves) were entertaining the St. Louis Cardinals for a doubleheader. During the second game, winds began to blow across the field with terrifying velocity. Umpire Beans Reardon decided he had better call the game because of the impending hurricane. And just what prompted Reardon's historic move? The umpire decided that something should be done when fly balls that started out to center field were being caught in foul territory by Boston catcher Al Lopez!

WHO HAD THE MOST TWO-HOMER GAMES IN ONE SEASON?

Hank Greenberg, who in 1938 challenged Babe Ruth's then-record 60 home runs by crushing 58. Along the way he had eleven two-homer games, including four in September.

Hank Greenberg (shown here, right, with Bill Veeck, then president of the Cleveland Indians) had the most two-homer games in one season, and the year was 1938. *(from the collection of Barry Halper)*

THE PLAYERS FOR WHAT TEAM HAD THE MOST UNUSUAL BATTING AVERAGE CHANGE FOR A GAME?

Chicago White Sox, 1940. The entire nine-man roster of the White Sox started and finished a game with precisely the same average before and after a match with the Cleveland Indians. Pitching for the Indians was Bob "Rapid Robert" Feller, who hurled a no-hitter. Since the event took place on opening day, 1940, the White Sox opened the game with averages of .000 and finished with exactly the same mark. It was the only occasion in major-league baseball history in which a club succumbed to a no-hitter without suffering any loss in its batting averages.

WHO CAME UP WITH THE BEST WAY TO
FOIL A BUNT?

Bert Haas, a Montreal Royals third baseman, was facing the Jersey City (Little) Giants in 1940 during an International League game. With runners on first and second, a Jersey City batter laid a perfect bunt down the third-base line. At that moment both runners took off, certain that the bunt would remain in fair territory.

Hoping that the bunt would roll foul, Haas suddenly realized that the baseball would hug the foul line on the fair side—unless he did something about it. At that point Haas ran to the ball, leaned over the horsehide, and began huffing and puffing in a desperate attempt to blow the ball foul. Finally, the ball, propelled by Haas's oxygen, rolled into foul territory.

The ingenious third baseman then picked up the ball and the umpire immediately ruled it a foul, nullifying the run that had just crossed the plate. Of course, were Haas to try his hot air trick in today's game, the ump would rule interference.

WHAT WAS THE MOST UNUSUAL "ERROR" MADE
BY PEE WEE REESE?

In 1940, while a young Brooklyn Dodgers shortstop, Reese was asked to do a special favor by Mrs. Dearie Mulvey, one of the Dodgers' owners. Mrs. Mulvey had heard about a crippled teenager, Dot DeMars, who was an avid Dodgers fan. Mrs. Mulvey invited the girl to be her guest at Ebbets Field so that she could meet her favorite player, Reese. Although Reese was hospitalized with an ankle injury at the time, he made a special trip to Ebbets Field for the occasion. After autographing a baseball and inscribing one of Dot's casts "Speedy Recovery," Reese returned to the hospital. He was accompanied by a *New York Daily News* photographer, who was driving, and *News* reporter Mary O'Flaherty, who was sitting between the driver and Reese on the right in the "death seat." On the drive back to the hospital, Reese committed an "error" that nearly cost his career, if not his life. As the auto sped along Flatbush Avenue toward the crowded shopping center at Fulton Street, the car swerved. The door suddenly flew open and Reese—in his cast—appeared about to fall out.

"I grabbed hold of Pee Wee," said Mary O'Flaherty, "while he pulled the door shut. How different the story of baseball might have been had he fallen out into the busy Flatbush Avenue traffic."

DURING THE DEPRESSION YEARS ADVERTISING SPROUTED UP ON MANY MAJOR-LEAGUE BALLPARK FENCES, AND MOST OF THEM CHALLENGED BATTERS TO HIT THE SIGN AND WIN A PRIZE. WHAT PARK BOASTED THE MOST DIFFICULT SIGN TO HIT IN THE MAJOR LEAGUES?

Ebbets Field, Brooklyn. Home of the Dodgers, Ebbets Field had a massive scoreboard located in right-center field. At the base of the scoreboard, a long, thin billboard approximately four feet high by forty feet wide proclaimed the advantages of shopping at Abe Stark's clothing shop on Pitkin Avenue in the East New York section of Brooklyn. In one corner of the billboard an invitation to batters proclaimed: "HIT SIGN, WIN SUIT!" Stark specialized in suits and gladly would have awarded one to any batter who whacked a ball off the sign. The only problem was that the sign was situated so close to the ground that it was virtually impossible to hit with a line drive. It was equally difficult to hit with a fly ball, because fly balls were usually flagged down by either the right or center fielder. The sign was immortalized in *The New Yorker,* except in the magazine cartoon the sign was moved to left field and Stark was drawn sitting in the front row with a baseball glove in his hand, leaning over the railing, ready to catch any ball hit toward his sign.

"A FAN GROWS UP
IN BROOKLYN"

Witnessing—or, more accurately, experiencing—baseball has been a major contribution to the store of trivia that seems to amaze my listeners. It was at this point in the history of baseball—the mid to late 1930's—that I began witnessing and experiencing major-league-baseball history in the making.

You had to be there to see it, literally, because television was more than a decade away and in the early thirties local baseball games were not even broadcast on the radio. I could listen to broadcasts of games from Boston on our big Stromberg-Carlson radio, but I couldn't listen, yet, to a game from Ebbets Field or the Polo Grounds.

When I went to my first major-league game in 1933, I was about to enter the yeshiva with the full intention of becoming a rabbi, or at least a Talmudic scholar, in the footsteps of my Russian *zayde.* So much for good intentions. Already in this new culture, this America, my proposed calling had serious competition from the sports scene. I was paying more attention to Van Lingle Mungo than I was to Moses.

I had the good fortune to see the 1934 All-Star Game at the Polo Grounds—this was only the second All-Star Game ever—and King Carl Hubbell was the star of this game. But

Hubbell was not the reason I had so eagerly schlepped from Minna Street to Harlem for the game. *The* reason was Van Lingle Mungo, the Dodgers' right-hander from Pageland, South Carolina, who was big and strapping and could throw the ball tremendously hard. Mungo had become a Dodger in 1931 and caught the fancy of the fans, even though the Dodgers didn't win many ball games for him. Still, Mungo managed 16 wins in 1933 and 18 in 1934—good enough to be named to the All-Star team.

I knew how important Hubbell was, but in my infinite Dodger-fan wisdom, I didn't think he could hold a candle to Mungo. I figured if Van Mungo had been on the Giants, he'd have been the biggest winner in the majors.

But it was Carl Hubbell who stole the show. Talk about unforgettable experiences, this was it. The first two guys up for the American League, Charlie Gehringer and Heinie Manush, reached base. The third American League All-Star batter was Babe Ruth. Hubbell bore down and struck out El Bambino, but King Carl's troubles were far from over. Coming up next was one of the great power hitters of all time, Lou Gehrig. The crowd held its breath and then—Whiff! Whiff! Whiff!—Gehrig was strikeout victim number two. The packed Polo Grounds was going wild, because there were two outs and the batter was none other than Jimmie Foxx, who could hit the ball as hard as Ruth and Gehrig. Sure enough, Foxx was strikeout victim number three. I can still hear the ovation King Carl received as he strode off the mound. Even the Dodger fans were cheering for him!

Hubbell stayed in his strikeout groove into the top of the second inning. His first victim was Al Simmons of the Chicago White Sox, followed by Joe Cronin of the Washington Senators. The next batter, Bill Dickey of the Yankees, came through with a single, but King Carl next faced Lefty Gomez and struck him out. I had seen six American League All-Stars go down swinging in the first two innings. Hubbell would go on to pitch three innings, by which time the National League was winning, 4–0. To show you what a difference Hubbell made, his successors were clobbered royally and the American League ended up winning, 9–7!

Hubbell was fantastic, but I was just a kid who was a fanatic Dodger fan, and I was positive that when Mungo took the mound the world was going to see the best ever. I was sitting next to a perfect stranger watching Hubbell strike out all of those Hall of Famers and I remembered saying to this guy, "You haven't seen *anything* until Van Mungo comes in!" The fellow looked me up and down as if I were a total basket case. I waited impatiently for Mungo's entrance and finally he got the nod. I was shivering with anticipation, but my enthusiasm dampened rapidly as Van Lingle Mungo was speedily blasted off the mound, as the American Leaguers began hitting everything that came their way. It was one of the most disappointing moments of my life. I remember saying to myself, What the heck happened to Van Lingle Mungo? How could he do this to me?

By the way, that 1934 All-Star Game produced one of the best trivia questions of all time: Eighteen players started that game, nine for each side, but only one man didn't make the Hall of Fame from that group. Who was it? Answer: Outfielder Wally Berger of the Boston Braves.

After a while I got used to the fact that the Dodgers had a lousy team, but I didn't care. All I could think about through most of the Depression was the Dodgers' getting better. But the Brooks caused such heartache that I hardly noticed there was a depression taking place.

To me guys like Ernest Gordon "Babe" Phelps, Tony Cuccinello (he later played for the New York City Department of Sanitation team) and Stanley "Frenchy" Bordagaray were stars, even though their batting averages and the experts might disagree. When I sought my first autograph, I didn't try to get it from Babe Ruth who coached the Dodgers briefly. I went after Johnny Frederick, an outfielder who also could play first. If it seems as though I had a distorted set of values, it only serves to emphasize how off-the-wall we Brooklynites were about the Dodgers.

Writer Neil Offen summed it up this way: "The fans of the Brooklyn Dodgers were the most fanatical, frenzied, outlandish, loony, wonderful group to form under the banner of one team."

The nickname "Daffiness Boys" was totally appropriate for our favorites and by the end of the 1930's, the Brooklyn fans had established themselves as no less daffy than their heroes. One of them was Bill Boylan, a milkman, who when game time arrived used to tie his horse and wagon (that's how milk was delivered in the thirties) to the gate outside Ebbets Field and then go in. He walked directly onto the field and pitched batting practice to Babe Herman. Herman had been in a slump and was firmly convinced that Boylan's pitching batting practice to him was the only way to get out of the slump.

Another wonderful fan was the Reverend Benney J. Benson of the Brooklyn Dutch Reformed Church, who held a service to pray for a pennant for the Dodgers on the steps of the Brooklyn Borough Hall at Fulton and Court Streets.

One great character was Tony Grimeli, who owned a bar just a knuckle-ball throw from Ebbets Field. Tony worked out a unique package deal whereby for three bucks he would provide transportation to the ballpark, a reserved seat, return transit, and all the free beer the fan wanted before and after the game. When someone mentioned to Grimeli that he would never break even that way, Tony explained, "At the bar only the beer is free. I know these people. The Dodgers make them very excited and when they come back here after the game and start to argue, they forget about the beer and drink whiskey!"

Another Dodger fan was a fellow who would sit by third

base, at the very top of the upper deck, with his trumpet. Between innings—between every inning—he would play the instrument. He played popular music and he played it quite well. "I'm just practicing," he would tell people. Ebbets Field was his rehearsal hall.

Finally, there was "Fierce" Jack Pierce, who had a box seat behind the Dodgers' dugout. After Harry "Cookie" Lavagetto joined the team in 1937, Pierce would bring a cylinder of compressed helium to every game. Every time Cookie stepped up to the plate to hit, "Fierce" Jack Pierce would blow up a balloon and float it into the air. He did this for six straight years.

The Dodgers were so bad in my rooting days that in 1936 Jimmy Powers of the *Daily News* decided what the club needed was a new name. Readers responded eagerly with more than seven thousand selections. Powers submitted the best of these to the players, who decided that the winning entry should be "Aces." But more than two million Brooklynites disagreed, and the team remained the Dodgers.

As for the possible derivation of the Dodgers' off-the-record nickname, "Dem Bums," there have been references made to a man referred to by a newspaperman as "The Spirit of Brooklyn" in the late twenties. This man would always sit under the Ebbets Field press box and scream out, over and over again, "You bums, you! You bums, you!" That was when the team was only doing badly. When the team was doing *very* badly, it was, "Youse bums, youse!" Maybe the first version was second-person singular and the latter, second-person plural, but nobody knows for sure. Very possibly this was how the Dodgers became known as "Dem Bums." At least this fellow was probably the inspiration for a cartoonist named Willard Mullin.

A sports cartoonist for *The New York World-Telegram* newspaper, Mullin was taxiing home from Ebbets Field one afternoon following a doubleheader when the cabbie asked, "How did our bums do today?"

"They split," Mullin answered, "won the first and lost the second."

Having mulled over the news, the driver concluded, "Oh, our bums win one and then their bums win one, huh?"

Mullin had heard the term "bums" attached to his favorite team before, but he had never translated it to the drawing board. Something about the way the cabbie said "Our bums win one" inspired him. He rushed to his studio and began a sketch that featured a tattered, wide-eyed caricature of a baseball-carrying bum, complete with holed shoes and patched pants resembling, now that I think of it, a great number of the poor, out-of-work people drifting through Brooklyn at the time. This figure would become an emblem as well known to Brooklynites as the stars and stripes are to all Americans and remained the Dodgers trademark, no matter how elite they would become in the 1950's, until the team left for Los Angeles.

It was the Dodgers' opening game of the 1937 season at Ebbets Field against the Giants that directly led to the coining of a term that would become synonymous with Brooklyn baseball, and it began with the first pitch of the game by my hero, Van Lingle Mungo. Umpire Beans Reardon called it a strike, whereupon Dick Bartell, the Giants' lead-off man, threw down his bat, turned around to argue violently, and while doing so was struck in the chest by a tomato flung from the stands. Only two seconds were necessary for the first hassle of the season, otherwise known in Brooklyn as a "rhubarb."

Although broadcaster Red Barber is generally credited with coining the expression, it was journalist Garry Schumacher who deserves the credit for coining it at the time. Schumacher recalled that children on the streets of Brooklyn used the term to indicate a controversy, usually one attended by confusion (it's now in Webster's dictionary). Barber later capitalized on its popularity and used it on the air so often that he became associated with "rhubarb" more than anyone else.

The Dodgers would always tease us fans into thinking they were going to be good, at the start of each season. It was the old build-'em-up-to-a-letdown syndrome, and the Brooks did it better than anyone. In that 1937 opener, for example, the Dodgers got three quick runs but managed to blow the game in the ninth, 4–3.

The inimitable Casey Stengel had been fired before the start of that season and was replaced by Burleigh Grimes, the former Dodgers pitcher and last man allowed to throw the spitball legally. But Stengel decided to go to that opening game despite being fired, to see if the Daffiness Boys had changed at all.

"They fooled me for a while," said Casey after the game. "Those spiffy new white and green uniforms had me baffled. But I recognized the boys in the late innings."

One day Casey wouldn't have recognized them. It was Memorial Day, 1937, at the Polo Grounds. The Giants-Dodgers doubleheader drew a crowd of 60,747, largest ever to see a National League game in New York. What's more, King Carl Hubbell was starting the opener with a string of 24 straight wins—16 in 1936 and eight so far in 1937.

King Carl was temporarily reduced to the ranks of serfdom in that classic. The Dodgers jumped all over him and routed the Jints, 10–3. I couldn't have been happier. Hubbell was knocked out of the box in the fourth, while Freddy Frankhouse coasted to the win. (Don't feel sorry for King Carl; he went 22–8 that year.)

But, despite the new kelly green caps and stockings, the Dodgers were going nowhere fast under Burleigh Grimes and finished sixth. Baseball historian Lee Allen had a good description of our Bums: "The Dodgers didn't know from one day to another who would be in the lineup and wandered around the league like a band of gypsies." Our beloved Brooklyns!

When I wasn't at the ballpark or at school. I had my ear to our big Stromberg-Carlson radio, listening to any broadcast I could pick up. From time to time I'd drift over to my aunt Bella's house, because her radio could pick up the game from Boston better. Boston, Chicago, Detroit, Cleveland—they all had major-league radio broadcasts, but not New York. The Dodgers, Giants, and Yankees all had the mistaken notion that if they aired the games on radio, it would hurt attendance at the ballparks.

One way to get the local scores fast was to hustle down to the neighborhood poolroom, which had a Western Union ticker. Half-inning scores from Ebbets Field were transmitted over the ticker and crowds of guys who gambled on baseball games would hang out around the ticker. My luck, I showed up at the pool hall one day just as it was being held up. I tried to sneak back out, but one of the holdup men whacked me on the backside with his pistol as I scooted by.

To tell you the truth, I was less fearful of being harmed by the gunmen than by my father. In our family the pool hall was considered a den of iniquity and I had been told emphatically never to trespass into a place like that even if I only wanted to learn a baseball score. I became hopeful, after a day or two went by, that my dad would never learn of my escapade. But Brooklyn neighborhoods were like small towns then, and parents had excellent radar. A couple of days later my father sat down with me in the living room and said, "What were you doing in the pool hall?"

After I recovered from the initial shock, I replied, "How did you know I was in the poolroom?"

He didn't answer but just glared at me, which was quite

enough punishment. Then, after a pause, he simply said, "If I ever hear again that you were in that place . . ."

I got the message. It didn't matter that I had merely been there to check the ticker. Dad figured I had wanted to play pool, which couldn't have been further from my baseball-crazed mind.

Fortunately for my backside, there were other ways to get scores, sometimes in the late afternoons I would run to a main street, like 13th Avenue, where there were lots of candy stores with newsstands. In those days we had a slew of evening papers, like the *World-Telegram, Sun, Evening-Journal,* and the *Post.* Their 5:30 editions would have the box scores on the front page. The game usually wasn't over, but the boxes of innings completed were filled in with the scores.

Another favorite gathering place for scores, especially late on Sunday afternoons, was on Fulton Street near the Loew's Metropolitan Theater, where the *Brooklyn Citizen* newspaper offices were located. The *Citizen,* like the *Brooklyn Eagle,* was a daily paper. The *Citizen* hung a huge scoreboard overlooking Fulton Street and an employee would fill in the scores of all Sunday games in chalk as they came over the ticker.

I learned a couple of things that 1937 season: for one thing, I learned that even though the Giants and my Dodgers supposedly despised each other, they weren't above exchanging players.

Bill Terry, who had been doing a wonderful job of running the Giants, eased a towering lefty named Cliff Melton into his starting rotation that year. Melton came through with a 20–9 record, but, more importantly to me, he became the catalyst of a famous Brooklyn-New York trade. Because Melton was working out so well, Terry felt he had leeway to begin restructuring his pitching staff. He was eying a Dodgers righty, Tom Baker, who he figured had a terrific future with the Jints. In exchange, he sent Brooklyn a veteran righty,

Frederick Landis Fitzsimmons, who had been with the Giants since 1925. Better known to us as "Fat Freddie," Fitzsimmons looked to be over the hill, at the outside good for another year or two if the Dodgers got lucky.

Get this: Baker was a total bomb. He lasted one season and then disappeared forever from the majors. Fat Freddie, on the other hand, was something else. Instead of wilting, he improved with age. He was 11–8 in 1938, went 16–2 in 1940 and 6–1 in 1941, when we won the pennant. More than that, Fat Freddie was another super Brooklyn character. He had a neat waddle on and off the mound and an outgoing personality that made him a fan favorite until he retired in 1944. Freddie didn't disappear, though. He opened the huge Freddie Fitzsimmons's Bowling Alley on Empire Boulevard right in the shadow of Ebbets Field and remained one of our heroes for a long, long time.

If Yankee Stadium was like a palace, then Ebbets Field was the hovel of baseball. For more than a decade the ballpark had been allowed to fall into a state of deterioration. The ushers, swearing a blue streak, used to fight for baseballs with the patrons. Yet there was always something homey and lovable about the place. And all of us, myself included, prayed for a winner.

Suddenly it appeared that my prayers were being answered in the persons of one Leland Stanford "Larry" Mac-Phail and Mr. Leo Ernest "The Lip" Durocher. Let me start with The Lip first. In the fall of 1937, Brooklyn sent Joe Tripp, Jimmy Bucher, and Roy Henshaw to the Cardinals for short-stop Durocher. One reporter said that Leo had "more brass than a Burmese junk shop; tailored to order for Brooklyn." Next MacPhail was imported from the Cincinnati Reds' front office to run the club on January 19, 1938. The minute he arrived, Larry called a press conference and announced that there'd be changes at Ebbets Field. And he wasn't kidding.

Just by reading the news stories, I could feel that an electrifying period was about to envelop the Dodgers. By this time I had not only graduated from yeshiva at the age of 16, but I was already in college at the University of Michigan. For the first time in my life I was following the follies of my Brooks in print rather than from the center-field bleachers of Ebbets Field.

Up until then I had felt that all of us Dodgers fans had lived in a baseball rooters' ghetto—we yearned to be in the upper class but doubted that we'd ever win that lottery. Like Aladdin's genie, MacPhail changed all that with a series of bang-bang moves that had everyone on Minna Street reeling.

First he got a loan of $50,000—*very* big money in those days—from the Brooklyn Trust Company and bought first baseman Dolf Camilli from the Philadelphia Phillies. Camilli, who had previously played for the Cubs, was a lefty power hitter who could make mincemeat out of the right-field wall only 297 feet from home plate.

Second, he dumped several of the old guard—Woody English, Heinie Manush, Johnny Cooney—and replaced them with several newcomers. My favorite was Goodwin George "Goody" Rosen, a Jewish right fielder from Toronto, Canada —how could I not like him?

And how could we not like MacPhail? In May 1938, he announced that he was installing *lights* at Ebbets Field and that the first night game would be played June 15 against Cincinnati. "With MacPhail," one of the baseball writers noted, "the fantastic was becoming commonplace."

Speaking of fantastic, how could I ever forget that first night game? Johnny Vander Meer, an apple-cheeked lefty, was the designated starter for the Reds. In his previous game, against the Braves, Vander Meer had pitched a no-hitter. Now, before a capacity house at our favorite ballpark, Vander Meer was mowing down Dodgers one after another. At first the fans booed him, but as they came to realize they were seeing history in the making, the hoots turned to roots. Vander Meer no-hit our Brooks, 6–0. It was awesome: the first Brooklyn game under lights and Vander Meer's second no-hitter in a row.

A witness to Vander Meer's magic was none other than El Bambino himself. A big crowd gathered around Ruth's box and this intrigued MacPhail, who missed absolutely no tricks when it came to promotions. Before the week was up, Larry hired The Babe as first base coach!

It helped at the gate but didn't do a heckuva lot on the field. By July 12 we had lost ten straight games to the Giants and were back in sixth place. Then came another game with the Jints at Ebbets Field and some interesting meat for the trivia collectors.

That afternoon the fans arriving at the main entrance noticed a huge message chalked on the pavement: "POSEDEL, PLEEZE BEAT THE GIANTS!" Bill Posedel was pitching that day. In the outfield was George Tuck Stainback, just acquired from the Phillies, and at third, Stanley "Packy" Rogers, promoted from the Dodgers' minor-league club in Elmira, New York.

For starters, Posedel beat the Giants 13–5, making July 12 an unofficial boroughwide holiday. Rogers, who would play only 23 games and hit a mere .189, was well on his way to miniature martyrdom as a Dodger that day. He clouted a triple, got two singles, a walk, and batted in three runs. Packy would hit only .097 against the rest of the league, but who cared? Against the Giants he hit .667! How effective, or should I say selective, was Packy? He rode the bench for 11 games after his debut, then got called upon to pinch-hit against the Giants and delivered a single!

"We didn't win many games," Cookie Lavagetto once said in marvelous understatement, "but there was always something to relieve the monotony."

One night after the Ebbets Field lights had been installed,

Gibby Brack misplayed a fly ball into a double, and the Dodgers' manager moaned, "Don't tell me the sun got in your eyes."

Brack looked up and replied, "You know, when I looked up, the moon did get in my eye."

MacPhail was known to erupt in best managerial fashion. Once after a terrible game, he went after Babe Phelps, Tom Winsett, Buddy Hassett, Cookie Lavagetto, and Gibby Brack. "You, Phelps," he began, citing his catcher as his first victim, whom he proceeded to lambaste. Then he went along the line: "And you, Winsett . . ." "And you, Hassett . . ." "And you, Lavagetto . . ." "And you, Brack . . ." "And you . . ." MacPhail paused and stopped, pointing a finger when he reached the next player. *Who are you?"* The trembling rookie responded, "I'm Pete Coscarart, your second baseman." The players couldn't contain their laughter and MacPhail conducted an orderly retreat out of the room.

But most of what MacPhail did was no laughing matter: the Dodgers were being transformed. He fired Burleigh Grimes and made Leo Durocher the Brooks' manager. To supplement our pitching hero, Van Mungo, he bought Whitlow Wyatt from Milwaukee and drafted two others: Hugh Casey from Memphis and Red Evans from New Orleans. Evans failed, but Wyatt and Casey were super. Whit became a 20-game winner and Casey became the most feared pitcher in the league. He also became a trivia subject: which Dodgers manager had a chauffeur who later became a Brooklyn hero? Answer: Uncle Wilbert Robinson had Casey as a driver when Hugh was still a high school boy in Atlanta.

MacPhail next went on to shore up the Brooks' outfield, which had been notoriously weak. He purchased Fred "Dixie" Walker from the Detroit Tigers, which many fans thought was a stupid move since Walker had already bounced from the Yankees to the White Sox and then to the Tigers. We thought he was washed up. But Dixie, at 29, emerged as the quintessential Flatbush hero, alias "The Peepul's Cherce." Dixie quickly endeared himself to fans because he batted .435 against the Giants in his first year—and .285 against the other seven clubs!

Dixie Walker is also the subject for a good trivia question: Why did Walker almost inspire a boycott of Dodgers fans? Answer: In the spring of 1941 MacPhail and Durocher thought the veteran Paul Waner, signed as a free agent after his release by Pittsburgh, should be the regular right fielder. After Waner was used daily in the exhibition games, a telegram signed by 5,000 Dodgers fans arrived at Ebbets Field and threatened a mass boycott unless Walker was put back in the lineup immediately, and kept there. As it happened, the threat was unnecessary; Waner hadn't measured up and Dixie gracefully moved back into position.

Incredibly Dem Bums began to climb: third in 1939, second in 1940, and—miracle of miracles—first place in 1941. The difference was the addition of Harold "Pee Wee" Reese at shortstop and Pistol Pete Reiser in center field. The climb to first meant a World Series coming to Brooklyn. It was a period of celebration (which I had to miss since I was back in Ann Arbor for my last year at Michigan)—and then tragedy.

The tragic part was typically Brooklyn. After exchanging 3–2 wins in Games One and Two, the teams moved to Ebbets Field, where the Dodgers' troubles started. The teams were scoreless going into the top of the seventh, thanks to Fat Freddie Fitzsimmons's superb pitching. With two out, Yankees pitcher Marius Russo lined a drive off of Freddie's knee that broke his kneecap. That was it for Freddie and the Brooks, as the Yanks went on to win, 2–1.

Game Four was worse. Brooklyn was leading 4–3 with two out and nobody on in the top of the ninth. Casey was on the mound and got Tommy Henrich to strike out on what some claim was a spitball. Catcher Mickey Owen couldn't handle it and Henrich hustled to first. The Bombers rallied and eventually salted away the game, 7–4.

The blunder so thoroughly demoralized the Dodgers, not to mention the entire borough, that the Brooks were useless the next day. "I don't think we could have beaten a girls' team," Billy Herman of the Brooks said. They lost the fifth game, 3–1, and the Series was over.

Still, MacPhail had performed miracles, and the transformation wasn't simply on the field. The club's kelly green trim was changed to royal blue and white. Larry insisted that ushers be courteous to Ebbets Field patrons, and he made sure that every seat was painted one shade of blue or another, with exits a flaming orange.

He also made two other pivotal moves that would affect the hearing of Brooklyn fans as long as the club stayed in Flatbush. One was the hiring of Gladys Goodding, and the other, Red Barber. Goodding was a petite professional organist who was installed in a loft behind home plate overlooking the field. She entertained the spectators with an assortment of pop tunes, and when the Brooks took the field, she'd launch into a stirring chorus of "Follow The Dodgers," one of the better team tunes of all time. Goodding was an accomplished musician and a lovely lady who eventually would become the subject of a trivia question when she was also hired to entertain at Madison Square Garden sporting events. (Who played for the Dodgers, Rangers, and Knickerbockers? Answer: Gladys Goodding!) Gladys forever won the hearts of Dodgers fans when, in one of her first performances, she impishly played "Three Blind Mice" as the three umpires strode onto the diamond.

Red Barber never would have made it to Brooklyn had MacPhail chosen to honor an agreement that had been cosigned by Horace Stoneham of the Giants, the Yankees' Ed Barrow, and the Dodgers' Steve McKeever, that none of the three New York teams would broadcast their home games.

McKeever had died, however, and MacPhail decided that his Brooks had nothing to lose by having their games described on the radio. He sold the Brooklyn game rights to sponsors for two years and imported Walter "Red" Barber from Cincinnati to handle the play-by-play.

If ever there was an unBrooklynlike personality, Barber was it. He was born in Columbus, Mississippi, and raised in Florida. As one critic described his style, "He had the home-spun vocabulary of a Southern senator, half hominy and half homily. His liberal references to black-eyed peas, catbird seats, and other quaint baggage of the grits circuit at first baffled Flatbush completely, and he might as well have spoken in Bulgarian. But gradually the borough came to understand him, and then he was one of their own: 'the verce of Brook-lyn.' " When you listened to Red, you listened to the best. There was never a better architect in setting up a game. It had a beginning, a middle, and an end. Believe me, when Red Barber said, "There's a bouncer wide of third base . . . ," that's where it was.

Barber and his Yankees counterpart, Mel Allen—he was as good as Red—had a profound influence on my broadcasting style in later years, though at that time I was not seriously thinking about sports work as a career.

How could I? Barber and Allen were among an exalted, precious few in the nation. You could count the number of name sportscasters on one hand. For a young Mazer to even *think* about reaching such a lofty plateau at that time would have been roughly equivalent to my aspiring to become America's first Jewish president.

BASEBALL FIGHTS THE "GOOD WAR"

(1941–1945)

For almost two generations of Americans raised in an atmosphere that questions the validity of our participation in Korea and, even more so, in Vietnam, the impact of December 7, 1941, upon this country may be difficult to understand.

The bombing of Pearl Harbor by the Japanese and America's immediate entry into World War II touched the entire nation, involved the whole country, and baseball was no different. Not only did the war mean a severe depletion of manpower—on baseball teams as well as in the factories—but it also meant shortages in supplies and goods. Worst of all to the baseball owners, at any rate, it meant a severe downturn in gate receipts: people simply stopped coming to ball games.

By April 1944—less than three years after our entry into the fray and almost a year and a half before it would end—more than 340 major-league baseball players and over 3,000 minor-leaguers were in military service. Just about every one of the 16 big-league teams had seen its roster decimated by the draft or enlistments, and this caused some unusual incidents. In Brooklyn, Leo Durocher hustled himself into the lineup as a replacement for second baseman Billy Herman, who had entered the service. On Durocher's first fielding chance, rookie shortstop Gene Mauch, all of eighteen years old, made a bad toss to Leo "The Lip" and the ball broke Durocher's thumb in two places. He went back to managing!

Cincinnati Reds coach Hank Gowdy, the first player to enlist during World War I, signed up again at age 53 and was commissioned an Army captain. (Which reminds me of a trivia question: who was the first major-league player killed in World War I? Answer: New York Giants infielder Eddie Grant.) However, Gowdy was far from being the only baseball personality who enlisted. Forty-one-year-old Chicago White Sox pitcher Ted Lyons had had a good 14–6 season in 1942. Lyons surely knew that he was sacrificing the last years of an outstanding career, yet he *enlisted* in the Marines. Buddy Hassett and George "Twinkletoes" Selkirk, both of the Yankees and both over 30, enlisted in the Navy, as did Ted Williams, who became a Navy pilot.

Williams's enlistment focused attention on Joe DiMaggio, who had accepted a deferment and was widely criticized for not helping the war effort. Finally, in February 1943, Joe D. joined the Army and never even told the Yankees, who had sent him a new contract. DiMaggio even refused the furlough that soldiers were allowed before donning the Khaki.

Not to be overlooked was then-Brooklyn hero, Larry MacPhail. He gave up a $70,000 salary in late 1942 for a commission as an Army lieutenant colonel. Many people had forgotten that MacPhail had been a hero in World War I and was involved in an incredible escapade shortly after that war. Along with seven other soldiers, MacPhail decided to kidnap Kaiser Wilhelm, Germany's wartime leader, who was living in a castle near Amerongen, Holland. MacPhail and company disarmed a guard and got as far as the Kaiser's drawing room before they were confronted by a squad of German soldiers. While conducting a strategic retreat, MacPhail managed to snatch one of the Kaiser's ashtrays, a souvenir he proudly displayed for years after.

One of America's leading airmen was Detroit Tigers catcher Birdie Tebbetts, who organized an Air Corps athletic program at Waco, Texas. At Tebbetts's urging, a number of major- and minor-league players joined the Air Corps at Waco, including pitcher Sid Hudson and outfielder Bruce Campbell of Washington.

One of the weirder uniformed-ballplayer stories involved Frank Mancuso, kid brother of big-league catching ace Gus Mancuso. Frank was with the St. Louis Browns when he joined up in 1942. He was commissioned a lieutenant and volunteered for the paratroops. After four successful jumps, Mancuso was almost ready for combat duty. But on his fifth jump there was a screwup and he mistakenly fell headfirst from the plane. Frank's legs caught in the parachute lines, and when he landed he broke a leg and wrenched his back. Bill Mead, who chronicled the Brownies' saga, wrote: "The back injury was so bad that Mancuso could neither stay in the Army nor, as the Browns soon discovered, look straight up for a pop fly."

Another unusual ballplayers-at-war story involved Buddy Lewis, who had been a star with the Washington Senators. Lewis served as a transport pilot in the Army Air Corps. Before going overseas, Lewis was stationed with other transport pilots at Lawson Field in Georgia. As part of their training, they were allowed to assemble a crew and fly to a city of their choice on weekends. Lewis landed a planeload at Washington's Andrews Air Base, took a cab to Griffith Stadium, home of the Senators, and went into the clubhouse. He told his ex-teammates he wanted to show them his plane. Then Lewis returned to Andrews Air Base and, as he put it, "broke every rule in the book." A few hours later when the game was in progress, he flew to Griffith Stadium and made a low dive over the ballpark. "I was low enough," Lewis said, "that I could almost read the letters on the uniforms."

Lewis's teammate George Case was the batter at that moment, and as the plane rose and turned to head back to Lawson Field, Case threw his bat in the air at his pal. Later Lewis said: "I was surprised that the people in the Pentagon didn't read about it in the paper and get in touch with my commanding officer."

Some players who had taken deferments still contributed their time to the war effort by making postseason tours. Bucky Walters and Johnny Vander Meer of the Reds, Bob Elliott of the Pirates, Stan Musial of the Cardinals, and Bill Dickey and Charlie Keller of the Yankees were among those who entertained troops in the South Pacific.

Even the Japanese got into the act on the South Pacific island of New Britain. As they charged a Marine emplacement, the Japanese soldiers were heard to shout: "To hell with Babe Ruth!" *The Sporting News* followed up the story with this comment: "Thirty Japanese struck out for good." Meanwhile three Germans posing as U.S. soldiers were exposed by their ignorance of the game and were shot (this later led to a rash of postwar movies in which the password was always some U.S. baseball term and some German trying to pass as a G.I. would blow the response and get killed).

Back home, Baseball Commissioner Landis decreed in January 1943 that spring training would take place north of the Mason-Dixon line, which supposedly reduced travel by five million "man miles." Pregame meals now consisted of fish instead of steak and even the baseball itself changed temporarily.

Baseball covers had been made traditionally from horsehide imported from Belgium or France, but the supply stopped as soon as those countries entered World War II. Horsehide from Bolivia was imported until 1943 when domestic horsehide was substituted. But the core of the ball had become a big problem. The War Production Board declared a shortage in cork and rubber, the ingredients for baseball cores, and major-league baseball turned to the use of "balata," the tough material used to cover golf balls. The result was a disaster. The ball Landis ordered the Spalding Company to produce was so dead that in a four-game series between the Cardinals and Reds opening the 1943 season, the two teams scored only six runs between them. Not a single home run was hit in the first 11 games of the season, and 11 of the first 29 games played were shutouts! In desperation, balls left over from 1942 were used until a new ball could be rushed into production. Finally, in 1944, the War Production Board took pity on baseball and made cork and synthetic rubber available.

Somehow, major-league baseball, like all of life on the "home front," continued despite fewer night games, dwindling rosters, and diminishing crowds.

WHAT KEY PLAYER FROM THE DETROIT TIGERS LEFT TO JOIN THE MILITARY BEFORE PEARL HARBOR?

Hank Greenberg was the key player from Detroit who was drafted in 1940. The loss of Greenberg hurt the Tigers, as they fell from first place in 1940 to fourth place in 1941. Greenberg actually finished his stint two days before Pearl Harbor, then immediately enlisted the day after Pearl.

Hank Greenberg (shown here, left, in auto, during Armistice Day parade in Detroit, immediately after World War II) was one of the major league's first players to enlist in the services. *(from the collection of Barry Halper)*

BESIDES LEFT FIELDER HANK GREENBERG OF THE DETROIT TIGERS AND RIGHT-HANDED PITCHER HUGH MULCAHY OF THE PHILADELPHIA PHILLIES, WHO WERE THE ONLY OTHER PLAYERS TO FACE INDUCTION IN THE SPRING OF 1941?

Cecil Travis and Buddy Lewis, both of the Washington Senators, were drafted in the spring of 1941. In 1940, Travis had hit .322, while Lewis had batted .317.

NOVELIST ERNEST HEMINGWAY, KNOWN FOR HIS MACHO PURSUITS, WAS KNOCKED OUT IN A BOXING MATCH BY A BIG-LEAGUE PITCHER. WHO WAS THE HURLER AND HOW DID HE DO IT?

Brooklyn Dodgers superb relief pitcher Hugh Casey did the drumroll on Ernest Hemingway's head in 1941. The episode came about when Dodgers boss Larry MacPhail decided to take his

Brooklyns to Havana, Cuba, for spring training. Hemingway, who was living in Cuba at the time, was a devout sports fan who also fancied himself a boxer and occasionally would invite his guests to go a round or two with him.

On this occasion, Dodgers broadcaster Red Barber had accompanied Casey to Hemingway's house. According to Barber, Hemingway looked Casey over and figured he had a pigeon on his hands. "Casey looked so innocent," Barber remembered. "He was a big man with a large stomach. He had rosy apple cheeks and spoke softly in his Georgia accent."

Shortly after Casey and Barber entered the author's house, Hemingway pulled out a set of boxing gloves. Casey later told friends what followed:

"Hemingway insisted I put on the gloves and spar with him. I didn't want to box with him. After all, when I was a little younger I'd done some fighting. But Hemingway wouldn't let me alone. Finally, I put on the gloves, and he said we'd just fool around. Before I knew it he was belting me as hard as he could. I told him to cut it out. He hit me harder than ever."

Hemingway, who thought he had calculated adroitly when first observing Casey, committed two *faux pas:* he didn't realize that Casey had been a fair-to-middling fighter and he underestimated the pitcher's burning pride. Too late Hemingway made this discovery. After the author had tagged the pitcher one time too many, Casey struck back at his host.

"I just knocked him down," Casey concluded, "and that ended the boxing for the night."

WHICH TWO PITCHERS STOPPED JOE DIMAGGIO'S CONSECUTIVE-GAME HITTING STREAK AT 56 GAMES?

Al Smith and Jim Bagby. The Cleveland Indians faced the Yankees in a night game on July 17, 1941, before 67,468 fans at Cleveland. A day earlier, DiMaggio, alias "The Yankee Clipper," had produced three hits to extend his streak to 56 games. To thwart Joe, the Indians came up with left-handed Smith, one of the better pitchers in the American League.

It looked like DiMaggio would come through on his first at bat when he whacked a hot ground ball along the third-base line, but the Indians' Ken Keltner stabbed the ball and pegged out DiMaggio. The second time up, Joe D. was walked. For his third trip, DiMaggio duplicated his first blow and, again, Keltner was the culprit, nabbing the ball and tossing Joe out at first.

But DiMaggio would get one more opportunity. In the eighth inning, with a runner on first. Cleveland's player-manager, Lou Boudreau, who played shortstop, brought in Jim Bagby, a right-handed knuckleballer, as relief pitcher, and DiMaggio responded with an erratically bouncing grounder to deep short. Boudreau got to the ball and converted it into a double play.

Joe DiMaggio logged a record 56-consecutive-game hitting streak the summer of 1941, just months before Pearl Harbor would pull the U.S. into World War II. *(drawing by Andrew Knipe)*

IN 1941, THE BROOKLYN DODGERS CAPTURED THEIR FIRST PENNANT IN TWO DECADES. THEIR WORLD SERIES FOE WAS NONE OTHER THAN THE CROSSTOWN RIVAL NEW YORK YANKEES. LEADING 4–3 IN THE NINTH INNING IN GAME FOUR, BROOKLYN WAS ONLY ONE STRIKE AWAY FROM EVENING UP THE SERIES AT TWO GAMES APIECE. HOWEVER, THE BOYS OF SUMMER WOULD FALL VICTIM TO A SINGLE MISTAKE THAT GAVE THE YANKS A CHANCE TO SPARK ONE OF THE MOST THRILLING COMEBACKS EVER. WHAT HAPPENED?

With two strikes on Yankee batter Tommy Henrich, Brooklyn bullpen ace Hugh Casey served up a fast-breaking pitch that Phil Rizzuto later said had to be a spitball:

"Sure, that's what he threw. When Henrich swung and missed, Owen didn't get near the ball. It exploded by him." Catcher Mickey Owen had let the third strike skip by wildly.

But the umpire at first only saw Henrich's missed swing and signaled him out on strikes. Police and jubilant fans spilled onto the field in reaction to the ump's call. However, Owen chased the ball and Henrich instinctively darted for first base. Owen turned to find his way to first blocked by a wall of fans, and Henrich was safe.

Casey now was forced to face Joe DiMaggio who began a slugging rally that was maintained by Charlie "King Kong" Keller, Bill Dickey, and Joe Gordon. By the time the Yankees were through with Casey, they had won the game, 7–4, taking a commanding three-games-to-one lead in the series. Not surprisingly, New York clinched the world championship the next day with a 3–1 win over the snake-bitten Dodgers.

HOW DID MAJOR-LEAGUE BASEBALL SUPPORT THE WAR EFFORT IN 1941?

Ford Frick, president of the National League, sent President Roosevelt a telegram that read: "Individually and collectively, we are yours to command." Philip K. Wrigley announced that he had planned to install a lighting system at Wrigley Field in Chicago in 1942, but instead would turn the electrical equipment in for defense use. Ed Barrow, president of the New York Yankees, offered civil defense authorities the use of Yankee Stadium as a bomb shelter, saying that citizens would be safe under the stands.

The first issue of *The Sporting News* printed after Pearl Harbor stated that baseball was ready to close down if asked to do so by President Roosevelt. An editorial in the paper said: "Born in America, propagated in America and recognized as the National Game, baseball and all those engaged in the sport are Americans first, last and always . . . In all the history of baseball there never was a conscientious objector, or a slacker in its ranks." (There was, however, a reported case of a minor-league pitcher, Tom Ananicz of Kansas City, who applied for combat exemption because he was a pacifist "by religion.")

Through the lobbying power of Washington Senators owner Clark Griffith, President Roosevelt wrote a letter to Commissioner Landis on January 15, 1942, which read: "I honestly feel that it would be best for the country to keep baseball going. There will be fewer people unemployed and everybody will work longer hours and harder than ever before. And that means that they ought to have a chance for recreation and for taking their minds off their work even more than before.

"Baseball provides a recreation which does not last over two hours or two hours and a half, and which can be got for very little cost. And incidentally, I hope that night games can be extended because it gives an opportunity to the day shift to see a game occasionally."

Baseball got the green light to continue operations.

Baseball Commissioner Ford Frick sent a telegram to President Franklin D. Roosevelt after Pearl Harbor, stating that baseball was FDR's "to command." *(from the collection of Barry Halper)*

WHICH MAJOR-LEAGUE BASEBALL PLAYER'S ENLISTMENT INTO THE NAVY WAS BROADCAST LIVE NATIONWIDE?

Bob Feller's. Feller was driving to Chicago for the major-league meetings on December 7, 1941. At about noon, while crossing the Mississippi River at Moline, Illinois, he heard about the Pearl Harbor attack on the car radio. He drove into Chicago, and on Monday morning at eight called Gene Tunney of boxing fame, who he knew was running the Navy's physical-fitness program.

Tunney met Feller at the courthouse the next morning and Feller signed up with the Navy while newsreel cameras and microphones recorded the event live and nationwide. Feller later explained his decision and the manner in which he had done it: "At that time anybody who was going to war from public life, it was a big thing. But we needed heroes. That's right—at that point we were losing the war."

IN 1941, TED WILLIAMS HIT .406 AND IN 1942, HE HIT FOR A TRIPLE CROWN. YET TWO OTHERS WON MVP HONORS IN BOTH THOSE SEASONS. WHO WERE THEY?

Joe DiMaggio achieved his 56-game hitting streak in 1941, eclipsing Williams for the MVP award. In 1942, Joe Gordon posted his best season as a Yankee, again overshadowing Williams's accomplishments, at least in the eyes of baseball writers who have voted the MVP award each season.

HOW DID THE UNITED STATES WIN A LESS-PUBLICIZED BATTLE AT THE BEGINNING OF WORLD WAR II?

J. G. Taylor Spink, editor and publisher of *The Sporting News,* wrote an editorial with a 1942 New Year's resolution asking that the major leagues "withdraw from Japan the gift of baseball which we made to that misguided and ill-begotten country."

Although there was nothing major-league baseball could do to take the game away from its enemy, the Japanese did it for them!

The Japanese government abolished baseball by decree as an "American influence" and ordered that Japanese translations replace those American baseball expressions that had come into use in the Japanese vernacular.

FOR THE 1942 SEASON THE NEW YORK YANKEES LOST A REGULAR TO MILITARY SERVICE UNDER UNIQUE CIRCUMSTANCES. WHO WAS HE?

The player was Johnny Sturm, a first baseman who hit .239 in 1941. Sturm was the first *married* major-leaguer ever to be drafted into the military service.

IN 1942, HARRY ADRIAN McCLURE, COMMANDER OF THE NORFOLK NAVAL OPERATING BASE, FORMED A TEAM THAT PLAYED EXHIBITION GAMES AGAINST MINOR-LEAGUE TEAMS AND WON 92 GAMES. WHICH MAJOR-LEAGUERS WERE ON THIS TEAM?

Pitcher Fred Hutchinson (Detroit Tigers), who finished the season with a 23–1 record; Bob Feller (Cleveland Indians) who was 19–3; catcher Vinnie Smith (Pittsburgh Pirates); and outfielder Sam Chapman (Philadelphia Athletics). The rest of the team was comprised of minor-leaguers who remained such.

WHICH WORLD-SERIES-WINNING TEAM BOASTED A CREEPY, A COAKER, AND TWO COOPERS?

The 1942 St. Louis Cardinals. One of the St. Louis infielders was Frank A. J. "Creepy" Crespi, who played alongside Jimmy Brown, Johnny Hopp, George Kurowski, Marty Marion and Ray Sanders. Coaker Triplett (along with Stan Musial, Enos Slaughter, Terry Moore, and Harry Walker) played in the St. Louis outfield. The Coopers comprised the Cardinals' famed pitcher-catcher brother act of Morton and Walker Cooper. Incidentally, the Cards defeated the New York Yankees in the 1942 Series four games to one.

AFTER THE 1942 CAMPAIGN, *THE SPORTING NEWS* SELECTED ITS MAJOR-LEAGUE ALL-STAR TEAM. THE NEXT YEAR FIVE OF THOSE ALL-STARS WERE IN THE MILITARY SERVICE. WHO WERE THE FIVE?

Johnny Mize, Johnny Pesky, Ted Williams, Joe DiMaggio, and Enos Slaughter were the five all-stars who had traded their baseball caps for kepis. The six who were not in military garb were: Joe Gordon, Stan Hack, Mickey Owen, Tex Hughson, Ernie Bonham, and Mort Cooper.

AFTER BEING CALLED UP FROM THE MINORS TO PLAY EIGHT GAMES WITH CLEVELAND DURING THE 1943 SEASON, GENE WOODLING, 21, ENTERED THE NAVY. WHAT HAPPENED TO WOODLING AFTER THE WAR?

Upon his return from the war, Woodling was traded to the New York Yankees where he played on the championship Yankee teams of the early 1950's, managed by Casey Stengel. After playing with the Bronx Bombers, Woodling stated that the Great Lakes squad of the World War II Navy may have been as good a team as the Yankees!

WHICH MEMBER OF BASEBALL'S HALL OF FAME WAS FIRED BECAUSE HE ADMITTED TO BETTING ON HORSES?

Rogers "The Rajah" Hornsby. In 1943, Hornsby was managing the St. Louis Browns in the American League when Donald Barnes, owner of the club, asked Hornsby about betting on horses. "The Rajah," wrote Dave Egan in Boston's *Daily Record,* "made the usual answer and appended the usual so-what-if-I-do. He was fired forthwith . . . fired out of the life he had known for a quarter of a century, because he had not been a hypocrite, and had not played it smart, had not told smooth lies. He did not drink and did not smoke and could not lie even if his career depended upon a success-ful lie." By February 1944, Hornsby, one of the finest hitters in baseball history, took a job as manager of the Vera Cruz team in the Mexican League.

WHO WAS THE YOUNGEST PITCHER EVER TO GO STRAIGHT FROM A HIGH-SCHOOL CLASSROOM TO A MAJOR-LEAGUE MOUND?

In June 1944, at the age of 15 years, 10 months, and 11 days, Joe Nuxhall was signed by the Cincinnati Reds and almost immediately was sent in to face National League opposition. Admittedly this was during World War II when many players were serving in the armed forces. Nevertheless, Nuxhall was exceptionally young. The poor youngster pitched one inning, gave up five runs, and was sent to the showers—for eight years! Nuxhall returned to the Reds in 1952 and became an ace of the Cincinnati mound corps, ultimately pitching 16 years and compiling a record of 135–117 with a 3.90 ERA.

Others have made a beeline directly from the classroom to the mound and remained in the majors. The most notable was Bob "Rapid Robert" Feller, who was only 17 when he turned pro with Cleveland in 1936. Feller pitched 62 innings, won five and lost three, struck out 76 and walked 47, while giving up 23 earned runs.

The majors have seen several 18-year-old whiz kids. One of the earliest was pitcher Waite "Schoolboy" Hoyt, who came up to the "bigs" at age 18 in 1918. Johnny Antonelli, would come directly from school to the Boston Braves in 1948, at the age of 18. In 1978, eighteen-year-old Mike Morgan would graduate from high school on a Monday and then sign the following Sunday with Charlie Finley's Oakland A's. Morgan promptly started against Baltimore, allowing 10 hits and two earned runs in a 3–0 loss.

WHICH BALLPARK HAD THE BEST SEATS FOR THE PRICE?

Ebbets Field, 1944. For fifty-five cents, a customer could obtain a seat in the Ebbets Field bleachers. If the patron arrived early enough, he or she could sit in the bleachers' boxes (still for 55 cents), a location unparalleled, considering the price in terms of proximity to the athletes. The first row of the upper bleachers over-hung center field, within easy conversational distance of the center fielder (useful during batting practice) and provided a panoramic, unobstructed view of the entire bandbox ballpark.

WHAT WAS THE LONGEST HIT FOR FEWEST BASES?

Josh Gibson, Homestead Grays. The legendary black catcher in the Negro National League, Gibson stroked his notorious elongated double-that-should-have-been-a-home-run at Dexter Park in Wood-haven, Queens, New York. Playing for the Grays against the Bushwicks, Gibson stroked a 500-foot drive to dead-center field. Dexter Park had no fence at center field, only a ten-foot hill on which *D-E-X-T-E-R P-A-R-K* was spelled out. The hill was topped by a flat plain onto which Gibson's ball rolled. A normal runner could have circled the bases twice, with ease. But Gibson, in his late forties, ran out of gas lumbering to second base. He stopped there, sat down on the bag, and watched as the Bushwicks' center fielder finally retrieved the ball and relayed it to the mound.

WHEN WAS THE MOST JARRING OUTFIELD COLLISION OF THE WARTIME ERA?

September 1944, between New York Giants outfielders Bruce Sloan and Steve Filipowicz. Sloan, the right fielder, was about five feet nine inches, but he weighed in at close to 200 pounds. A high fly went to right-center field and Bruce took off after it, looking like a roly-poly lightning streak.

Unfortunately for Sloan, center fielder Filipowicz—who later played for the football Giants, to give you an idea of his size and heft—was implacably parked right under the fly, looking much like the Colossus of Rhodes. Sloan and Filipowicz collided with such force that they literally disappeared in a dust cloud, and when the scene cleared, Sloan had to be carried off the field on a stretcher.

Filipowicz? He shrugged slightly at all the fuss!

WHAT FAMOUS SPORTSCASTER PUBLICLY APOLOGIZED ON THE AIR FOR DOWNGRADING A MAJOR-LEAGUE TEAM?

Bill Stern, for rapping the St. Louis Browns. During the 1944 baseball season, Stern was doing a daily sports program on the National Broadcasting Company network. On one show Stern opined that the Browns would not win the pennant unless they tried harder. A torrent of criticism poured into Stern's office, including objections from club owner Don Barnes and Jimmy Conzelman, a football coach who then was affiliated with the American League baseball team. "They told me in no uncertain terms," said Stern, "how wrong I'd been, how injudicious in my choice of words. I immediately aired a formal apology and appreciated the lesson."

The Browns confirmed their owner's opinion by winning the American League pennant that year.

NAME THE THREE PITCHERS WHO POWERED THE ST. LOUIS BROWNS TO THEIR 1944 AMERICAN LEAGUE PENNANT?

Denny Galehouse, Nelson Potter, and Bob Muncrief. The Browns, who would transfer to Baltimore ten years later, never won another pennant in St. Louis. But the 1944 team was a glorious edition backed by splendid pitching and the astute managing of James Luther Sewell. St. Louis finished atop the American League in 1944 with 89 wins and 65 losses. Galehouse (9–10), Potter (19–7), and Muncrief (13–8) were abetted by a few other solid hurlers including Sig Jakucki, Jack Kramer, and Sam Zoldak.

WHEN WAS THE ONLY ALL-ST. LOUIS WORLD SERIES?

1944, Browns vs. Cardinals, with all games played at Sportsman's Park. The Cinderella team of baseball, the Browns, provided the lordly Cardinals a large scare in the 1944 classic. The oft-mocked Browns opened the Series with a 2–1 win over the Cards, although the winners collected only two hits off ace pitcher Mort Cooper. In the second game, the Browns rallied to tie the game, 2–2, sending it into extra innings, but the Cards scraped together a run in the last of the tenth to tie the Series.

By now the entire country seemed to be pulling for Sewell's Browns, and they responded by taking the third game and a 2–1 Series lead with a convincing 6–2 win. But then the Cardinals' big guns began to produce. Stan Musial cracked a home run in the fourth game as the Cards triumphed, 5–1. Mort Cooper hurled a 2–0, seven-hit shutout in the fifth game, and Max Lanier got the win in the sixth and final contest, as the Cardinals prevailed, 3–1.

HOW DID BILL SKOWRON GET THE NICKNAME "MOOSE"?

"I got my nickname growing up in Chicago during World War II," explained Skowron. "My grandfather started calling me 'Mussolini' because he thought I looked like him.

"My friends changed it to 'Moose.' I didn't mind it—they called my brother 'Hitler'!"

THE WANING DAYS OF WORLD WAR II WOULD SEE THREE PHYSICALLY CHALLENGED BASEBALL PLAYERS MAKE BRIEF APPEARANCES IN THE MAJOR LEAGUES. WHO WERE THE THREE?

Pitcher Bert Shepard, who was missing a leg, appeared momentarily for Washington. Dick Sipek, who was deaf, played for Cincinnati, and outfielder Pete Gray, who had only one arm, appeared for the St. Louis Browns in 1945.

By far the best-known of the three, Gray (real name: Peter Wyshner), had been a star with semipro teams in the New York area. As a batter, Gray would take a normal swing holding the bat in his hand. In the outfield, Pete handled fly balls by catching them in a long, thin, unpadded glove. Then, in an intricate maneuver, he would slip the glove under his armpit, roll the ball across his chest to his throwing arm, and peg the ball to the infield. On grounders to the outfield, Gray would trap the ball with his glove, push the ball to his feet, slip off the mitt, then toss the ball back to the infield.

Despite the fact that he had replaced Mike Kreevich, who had been a .300-plus hitter the year before (and who quit baseball in disgust when he was replaced by Gray), Gray was not a gimmick. He hit .218 and was an adequate fielder. After the 1945 season, however, Gray returned to the minors, where he played for several more years.

BASEBALL HAS STAGED AN ALL-STAR GAME EVERY SEASON SINCE 1933 . . . EXCEPT FOR ONE. WHICH YEAR LACKED THE ALL-STAR EVENT, AND WHY WASN'T THE GAME PLAYED?

The midsummer classic of 1945 was never played. The country and "The Game" were so engulfed by the Second World War that the game was canceled. Instead, Baseball Commissioner Happy Chandler scheduled exhibition contests played by major-league teams against minor-league clubs, military clubs (often laced with major-league stars), and college teams. The proceeds were diverted to the war effort.

BASEBALL'S
LAST GOLDEN AGE

(1947–1957)

While I was going through my "minor-league" years as a broadcaster, major-league baseball would flower into an era of great players and record-breaking moments, much as it had during the "Ruth Era" after World War I.

It seems that whenever baseball goes into one of its "great" periods, the New York Yankees have powerhouse clubs, and the late forties through the tragic move of the Dodgers to Los Angeles in 1957 was no exception. The Yanks won the World Championship *seven* times in the decade from 1947–56. How could they not, with veteran stars like DiMaggio and Yogi Berra still on the club and budding luminaries like Mickey Mantle coming on strong?

But the real heartbreaker for me, the Brooklyn boy, was that five out of those seven Series wins were earned by beating my Brooklyn Dodgers! By 1947, Brooklyn had the majors' first black ballplayer, Jackie Robinson, at first base, Pee Wee Reese at short, Carl Furillo, and Gil Hodges. In fact, I've always felt that if the Yanks hadn't been sitting up there in the Bronx in that decade, with all of their heavy artillery, the Dodgers would have won more than the single World Series they managed to grab from the Bronx Bombers in 1955.

Interestingly, the Dodgers didn't win a pennant for the duration of the war, but as soon as hostilities ceased, they were back on top. In 1946, they finished in a dead heat for first place with the

Cardinals and lost the play-off, but a year later the Brooks made it to the top without mistake. One reason for their success was the addition of the talented Jackie Robinson. Once again the Yankees provided the opposition, but this time the Brooks made it tough for the Bombers.

With the Yanks leading the Series, two games to none, the Dodgers took over at Ebbets Field, winning the third game in a 9–8 squeaker. This was followed by two of the most memorable games ever played. In Game Four the Yankees started Floyd Bevens, a right-hander who had a 7–13 record for the year.

By the bottom of the ninth, Bevens had allowed no hits, but eight walks. The Yanks led 2–1 (Trivia question: How did the Dodgers get the run? Answer: Two walks, a sacrifice, and a ground out.) This was the first time a World Series pitcher had a no-hitter going into the ninth.

With one out, Carl Furillo walked, but Spider Jorgensen fouled out. Al Gionfriddo went in to run for Furillo while Pete Reiser batted for pitcher Hugh Casey. Gionfriddo stole second and Reiser was purposely walked. The winning run was on, but Bevens still had a no-hitter. Eddie Miksis ran for Reiser. The next batter was Harry "Cookie" Lavagetto, an all-time favorite, but now in the twilight of his career.

Cookie drove Bevens's second pitch high off the right-field wall, scoring Gionfriddo and Miksis. The Dodgers won, 3–2. What had been quiet streets of the borough suddenly erupted into bedlam as residents shouted out of the windows in a manner that rarely has been duplicated for a sporting event.

It almost didn't matter that the Yanks rebounded to win the next game, 2–1, and take a three-games-to-two Series lead—which brings us to the next "finest hour" in Brooklyn baseball history.

This one was at Yankee Stadium. Brooklyn was ahead, 8–5, in the bottom of the sixth with two men on base for the Yanks. It was then that Joe DiMaggio walloped a tremendous drive toward the left-field bleachers. It looked like a home run as left fielder Al Gionfriddo raced toward the bleachers. When he reached the gate to the bull pen, the hitherto unknown utility player reached up and made a one-handed grab in front of the 415-foot mark. Brooklyn won the game, 8–6.

The Dodgers' hopes for a first World Series win were snuffed out in Game Seven. The final score was 5–2, and once again the cry was heard throughout the borough: *"Wait 'til next year!"* But it would be two years before we would meet and lose to the Bombers again in 1949. And I don't have to tell you about Bobby Thomson's "shot heard 'round the world" off Ralph Branca in 1951. That merely added to the Dodgers' curse.

By now the Dodgers had assembled the team that became known as "The Boys of Summer." It was one of the best clubs of all time, but it had the misfortune of playing the Yankees in both the 1952 and 1953 series and—what else?—lost them both. There was a brief interlude in 1954 when the Giants swept the Indians before the Dodgers and Yankees collided once more. Those of us who remembered 1941 wondered whether there was such a thing as a law of averages. You certainly couldn't prove it by the Brooklyns.

What made 1955 different from the other years is a good question, as far as the Dodgers were concerned. Walter Alston's cool, firm, and astute managing certainly didn't hurt. Nor did the fact that the Brooks finished a fat thirteen and a half games ahead of Milwaukee, or that Don Newcombe enjoyed a twenty-win season on the mound. Yet, it was still the Yankees in the other dugout and anyone who had suffered the pangs of depression after so many other Dodgers-Yankees confrontations could hardly exult over another battle with the Bombers. After all, an 0–7 Series record suggests that a team is doomed to defeat. When the Yanks swept the first two games, we figured history was merely repeating itself.

Even when the Dodgers won the next two games at Ebbets Field, fans of Dem Bums refused to get overly optimistic. Then the Dodgers won again, 5–3, but still Brooklyn fans contained themselves. This proved to be a good move; the Yankees rebounded at home, 5–1, and once again the Series was down to the seventh game.

Alston decided to go with Johnny Podres, the young lefty who had won Game Three. Veteran Tommy Byrne was on the mound for the Yanks. The Brooks got a run in the fourth and a second run in the sixth. It was 2–0 Dodgers in the bottom of the sixth, when Sandy Amoros moved to center stage. Amoros hit only .247 that year, but he was inserted in left field by Alston, for defensive purposes. Talk about brilliant managing.

Podres walked Billy Martin to start the inning and then Gil McDougald beat out a bunt. The elements for another Dodgers tragedy were in place when Yogi Berra stepped to the plate. Because

Berra normally pulled the ball to right, Alston moved Amoros close to center field. This time Alston didn't look so good. Berra lifted a long, high fly down the left-field line. From the looks of things, it would either be an extra-base hit or, if the wind took it, a home run.

At the crack of the bat, Amoros knew he was in trouble. The ball sailed toward the left-field line as the Cuban dug his cleats into the turf. It seemed that Amoros ran almost endlessly and, at the last second, strained to get his glove on the ball. He got it all right, but that was only Part One of the miracle. Sandy then wheeled and pegged the ball to Pee Wee Reese, who relayed the ball to first, nailing McDougald for a double play. The score remained 2–0 and stayed that way right through until the end. It was over—all the years of frustration had ended for those who had suffered with the Brooklyn Dodgers.

But one Series win was not enough to eliminate the scars of 1941, 1947, and the incredibly bitter loss to the Giants in 1951. A year later the Yanks got even, beating Brooklyn in seven games again. The seventh game, at Ebbets Field, was symbolic. It was a bitter cold day—writers in the press box wore winter coats and still froze—and Newcombe was even colder. He was knocked out in a hurry and the Yankees walked away with a depressingly easy 9–0 decision.

Shortly thereafter, the unthinkable was being discussed. Was O'Malley really planning to move the Dodgers from Brooklyn to Los Angeles? At first nobody took the rumors seriously; after all, this was Brooklyn and the Dodgers—a team that did excellently at the gate, year in and year out. But O'Malley wasn't satisfied. Ebbets Field was too old and too small and he wanted more money. Ultimately the move was made. To make matters worse, the Giants followed the trek out West, taking with them one of the greatest young players the game would see, the "Say Hey Kid," Willie Mays.

It turned out to be a bonanza for O'Malley and a disaster for Brooklyn. In one fell swoop the borough lost its identity and its confidence. Thousands of fans across the country became cynics overnight and a new, less glorious era was upon the game of baseball. Some would call it the era of greed. When O'Malley switched his loyalty from Brooklyn to the buck, all bets were off in terms of traditional values.

Perhaps the last vestige of that quality we call loyalty was displayed by that game warrior, Jackie Robinson. In December 1956, O'Malley sold Robinson to the hated Giants for $35,000 and Dick Littlefield, a left-handed pitcher. Rather than play for the Giants, Robinson simply hung up his uniform for good.

Musical baseball teams was about to occur. New York City lost two clubs, and some sports soul, forever. "Go west, young man!" had infected baseball teams across the country.

A BROOKLYN DODGER LAUNCHED A POST-WORLD-WAR-II BASEBALL-PLAYER REVOLUTION. WHO WAS HE?

Luis Francisco Rodriguez Olmo was the player who jumped to the Mexican League from the Dodgers. It all happened immediately after World War II when big-leaguers wanted minimum yearly salaries of $5,000, shorter spring schedules, and a limit on salary cuts. Those who were discontented looked to the Mexican League, much as American pro football players now find an alternative in Canada. Defectors, such as Olmo, drew three-year suspensions. Soon after his return to Brooklyn, Olmo was shipped to the Boston Braves. Before leaving Brooklyn, Luis played with the Dodgers in the 1949 World Series and hit a home run.

NAME THE HURLER WHO POPULARIZED THE "EPHUS" PITCH?

Rip Sewell, a square-jawed hurler for the Pittsburgh Pirates who died in 1989, would lob the ball some twenty-five feet into the air, higher than a slow-pitch in softball. When the horsehide eventually floated down, it looked bigger than a beachball to the batter who would then proceed to miss hitting it by at least two feet. There never had been a pitch quite like it in the history of the game. Right from the start, when Sewell began serving up the pitch in 1943, batters cursed the "ephus" (pronounced "E-fuss" and sometimes referred to as a "blooper" pitch).

Probably the most famous "ephus" pitch was thrown in the 1946 All-Star game at Fenway Park, Boston. In this game, won handily by the American League, 12–0, Ted Williams expected and received a Sewell "ephus" pitch. Williams, whose reflexes were the best in baseball, waited, timed the "ephus" perfectly, and rapped the ball some twenty rows back in the right-field bleachers.

FOR WHOM WAS JACKIE ROBINSON PLAYING WHEN HE BROKE PROFESSIONAL BASEBALL'S COLOR LINE?

The Montreal Royals. Signed to a professional contract in December 1945 by Brooklyn Dodgers general manager Branch Rickey, Robinson was assigned to the Dodgers' top farm team, the Montreal Royals of the International League. Robinson, who had starred for the all-black Kansas City Monarchs, made his professional debut in the all-white league on April 27, 1946, when he took the field for the Royals against the Jersey City Giants at Roosevelt Stadium in Jersey City.

At first the twenty-seven-year-old rookie was nervous. He grounded out in his first turn at bat and erred on a ground ball on his first fielding attempt. But in the third inning, Jackie came to the plate with two men on base and whacked a home run into the left-field stands. His confidence returned, Robinson became a scourge on the base paths. He singled a few innings later, stole second, reached third on a daring sacrifice, and scored after he induced the enemy pitcher to balk. He completed the game with four hits in five times at bat, helping Montreal to a 14–2 victory. The Royals finished first and went on to win the Little World Series. A year later Robinson was a member of the Brooklyn Dodgers, the first black to make it to the major leagues.

Jackie Robinson in action, the man who broke the "color" barrier in major-league baseball with the Brooklyn Dodgers. *(from the collection by Barry Halper)*

WHEN JACKIE ROBINSON BROKE THE COLOR LINE WITH THE MONTREAL ROYALS IN APRIL 1946, THE ROYALS HAD A SECOND BLACK MAN ON THEIR ROSTER. WHO WAS HE?

John Wright, a twenty-seven-year-old right-handed pitcher. Prior to signing with the Brooklyn Dodgers' organization, Wright had starred with the Newark Eagles, Pittsburgh Crawfords, and Homestead Grays. While Robinson was an instant International League star, Wright made only two appearances in relief for the Royals before being optioned to Three Rivers, Quebec, in the Class-C Border League. He finished the season there, was unconditionally released by the Dodgers' organization that winter, and returned to the Homestead Grays.

Why did Robinson succeed and Wright fail? Robinson once explained: "John had all the ability in the world, as far as physical abilities were concerned. But John couldn't stand the pressure of going up into this new league and being one of the first. The things that went on up there were too much for him, and John was not able to perform up to his capabilities.

"In a number of cities, we had very little pressure. But there was always that little bit coming out. It wasn't so much based on race—I think most of the Negro players could have done it as far as race. But because John was the first Negro pitcher, every time he stepped out there he seemed to lose that fineness, and he tried a little bit harder than he was capable of playing. He tried to do more than he was able to do, and it caused him to be a lot less of a pitcher than he actually was. If he had come in two or three years later when the pressure was off, John could have made it in the major leagues."

When Wright was optioned out in May 1946, the Royals added another black pitcher, Roy Partlow, a thirty-year-old. But later in the season he too was optioned to Three Rivers. Thus, Robinson was the only black player to survive the entire season with the Royals. Meanwhile, the Dodgers signed Roy Campanella, who had starred for the Baltimore Elite Giants, and Don Newcombe, a pitcher with the Newark Eagles, and assigned both to Nashua in the Class-B New England League.

HOW DID LAWRENCE PETER BERRA GET THE NICKNAME "YOGI"?

One of Berra's teammates from an American Legion team in St. Louis began calling him Yogi. Nobody remembers exactly why, but old neighbor and teammate Joe Garagiola pointed out, *"What else could you call him?"*

Lawrence Peter "Yogi" Berra shows his catching form. *(from the collection of Barry Halper)*

WHICH TEAM ONCE OFFERED THE YANKEES THE THEN-ASTRONOMICAL SUM OF $50,000 FOR THE SERVICES OF YOGI BERRA?

The New York Giants.

WHO WAS YOGI BERRA'S CATCHING COACH IN 1949?

Yankee all-time great Bill Dickey was assigned to help Yogi who, in his early years, was a good hitter but a less-than-adequate catcher defensively. Yogi had a scatter arm, and he also had trouble with low pitches. A writer asked Yogi about his progress. He replied, "Bill is learning me all his experience."

HOW DID YOGI BERRA TURN AN UNASSISTED DOUBLE PLAY BY TAGGING OUT TWO RUNNERS?

During a game against the Browns in his rookie season, Berra got a chance to get back at the St. Louis bench for taunting him about his scatter arm. With a runner on third, a St. Louis Browns batter tried to lay down a squeeze bunt. Berra pounced on the ball, tagged the batter before he got out of the box, then dove for the plate and nailed the runner from third. Afterward, Yogi explained the play: "I just tagged everybody in sight, including the umpire."

WHO WAS THE FIRST BALLPLAYER TO EARN A SIX-FIGURE SALARY?

In 1947, the prolific hitter Hank Greenberg was released by the Detroit Tigers. Greenberg decided to retire rather than play for the Pittsburgh Pirates, to whom he had been sold. The Pirates coaxed him to play by offering him $100,000 and he responded by hitting .249, with 25 home runs and 74 runs batted in. Possibly he made it an even better investment for the Pirates by becoming the role model and mentor for a young Pirate outfielder named Ralph Kiner, who went on to be a prolific home-run hitter himself.

JACK "LUCKY" LOHRKE MADE THE MAJOR LEAGUES IN 1947 AS A TWENTY-THREE-YEAR-OLD THIRD BASEMAN WITH THE NEW YORK GIANTS. BUT THE FACT THAT LOHRKE WAS EVEN ALIVE IN 1947 WAS A MIRACLE. WHAT TWO MIRACLES EARNED LOHRKE THE NAME "LUCKY"?

Lohrke was a man of uncanny luck. While in the minors, Lohrke missed a team bus. That bus never reached its destination. It was involved in a fatal crash that left no survivors.

During a stint in the service, Lohrke was the recipient of even more luck. He got bumped from the passenger list of an over-crowded plane that later crashed.

HOW MANY GRAND SLAMS DID GIL HODGES HIT AS A DODGER?

Hodges hammered 14 base-clearers in his years as a Dodger from 1947–1958 (Hodges also played one game for Brooklyn in 1943).

WHO WAS THE WORST "MOST VALUABLE PLAYER"?

Bob Elliott, Boston Braves, 1947. Never to be confused with Joe DiMaggio, Willie Mays, or Roberto Clemente, Elliott hit .317 for a third-place Braves team. Everything Elliott did that year, it seems, was the right move, in terms of his career before and after. He hit 22 home runs and drove in 113 runs, but never again in his twenty-nine-year career did he come close to matching his MVP effort of 1947.

WHO WAS THE FIRST PLAYER IN MAJOR-LEAGUE HISTORY TO PINCH-HIT A HOME RUN IN THE WORLD SERIES?

In the third game of the 1947 World Series between the New York Yankees and the Brooklyn Dodgers, Yogi Berra pinch-hit a dinger.

WHO WAS THE FIRST BLACK PLAYER IN THE AMERICAN LEAGUE?

Larry Doby of the Cleveland Indians, 1947.

WHO WAS THE MOST UNUSUAL CANADIAN PLAYER?

Mike Goliat, Toronto Maple Leafs. Although he was a rugged son of the Pennsylvania coal-mining country, Goliat was adopted by Canadians when he came to play for the Toronto Maple Leafs of the International League in 1947. (He played for the Philadelphia Phillies in 1951, but returned to the Leafs in 1953.) "Mike," said *Toronto Star* writer George Gamester, "was one of Toronto's most colorful athletes."

Goliat once hit a ball into a distant corner of Maple Leaf Stadium in Toronto but was thrown out at third base because he nonchalantly stopped to pick up his cap when it flew off his head on the base path. Once, in a game against the Havana Sugar Kings, Goliat faced pitcher Emelio Cueche. Because Goliat was more than a fair hitter, Cueche decided to throw Mike an intentional base on balls. Mike disapproved, reached across the plate, and smacked one of Cueche's wide pitches over the right-field wall for a home run.

ONE PITCHER ABOVE ALL OTHERS WAS LOVED BY HIS TEAMMATES BUT HATED BY THE CONCESSIONAIRES? WHO WAS HE?

John T. (Jack) Salveson, who hurled for four major-league teams, but spent most of his twenty-one-year career in the Pacific Coast League, could empty a park faster than a towering inferno. This was because Salveson was one of the fastest pitchers the game has known. As a result, Jack was not a favorite among the fellows who dispensed hot dogs and beer. Once he finished his business in an hour and twenty minutes. How did Salveson do it? While a well-pitched game today might require 100 to 120 pitches, the right-handed Salveson usually tossed under 90. "The great conservationist," Lefty O'Doul said of Jack. When he pitched and won a 20-inning affair for Portland in 1947, Salveson threw 54 pitches in one nine-inning stretch, precisely six a frame. "I don't monkey around with fancy pitches," he said. "I think those screwballs, knucklers, and sliders are freak pitches." Salveson liked the fastball. He also played the role of a pitcher in the Lou Gehrig movie, *Pride of the Yankees*. One of his jobs was to hit Gary Cooper, playing Gehrig, on the head with the ball. Since the ball was made of cotton with stitches to make it look like a real baseball, the usually accurate Salveson required seven tosses to hit the target. "It just wouldn't go straight," he moaned.

HOW DID THE PITCHER LEROY PAIGE GET THE NICKNAME "SATCHEL"?

The greatest of all black pitchers before blacks were freely allowed to pitch in the majors, Paige was not nicknamed "Satchel" because of a penchant for carrying shoulder bags. He did, however, receive the nickname because of the size of his feet, which looked as big as satchels.

Others who watched him pitch believe his nickname should have been "Whiz-bang." Joe DiMaggio declared Paige was the fastest pitcher he ever saw. In the thirties and forties, Satchel bested Dizzy Dean in six out of eight exhibition games and beat Bob Feller in his prime. Finally, in 1948, when he was said to have been forty-two years old (although others insist Paige was older), he signed with Bill Veeck's Cleveland Indians and pitched superbly. He later pitched for the St. Louis Browns until 1953, always dispensing cheery homilies. Eventually, he was admitted to the Baseball Hall of Fame, but he never really quit the game. In 1977, he served as pitching coach for New Orleans in the American Association and pitched batting practice. Asked his age, Paige replied: "Somewhere between 85 and 100!"

Leroy "Satchel" Paige may well have been the greatest pitcher ever, but he was forced to play his best years in the Negro Leagues, only arriving in the majors in 1948, well over 40 years old. *(from the collection of Barry Halper)*

WHICH BALL PARK HAD THE MOST UNUSUAL MUSICAL BAND?

Ebbets Field, which housed the Brooklyn Dodgers Sym-Phony from 1938–1957. Occupying Section 8, Row 1, Seats 1 through 6, the Dodgers' Sym-Phony was regarded as the zaniest musical combination ever to have a long run at a major-league park.

At their most serious, the Sym-Phony played such immortal tunes as "The Brooklyn Baseball Cantata" and warbled lines including:

> *Leave us go root for the Dodgers, Rodgers,*
> *They're the team for me.*
> *Leave us make noise with the boisterous boys*
> *On the BMT.*

Irving Rudd, who was the Dodgers' publicist during the halcyon days of the Sym-Phony, once described them thusly: "They had a dual purpose: to amuse the crowd at the ballpark and to harass opposing players. There was Jojo Delio on the snare drum, brother Lou Soriano belted the bass drum and was the Sym-Phony conductor. There was Patty George and Jerry Martin and Joe Zollo and his son Frank."

The Sym-Phony would toot and drum an opposing batsman—especially if he struck out—back to his dugout with a rhythmic cadence and waited until the player sat down, at which time they

The Brooklyn Dodgers' Sym-Phony in full dress serenade "Bums" Spider Jorgensen (left) and Bobby Bragan. *(from the collection of Barry Halper)*

blared forth with a big chord. If it took a long time for the player to sit down, the Sym-Phony waited patiently, but the big blare always came as soon as the flannel trousers touched the bench.

"Back in July 1951," said Rudd, "Local 802 of the American Federation of Musicians questioned the amateur standing of the Brooklyn Dodgers' Sym-Phony Band and threatened to throw a picket line around Ebbets Field. The Dodgers thereupon scheduled a 'Musical Unappreciation Night.' Admittance was free as long as you brought a musical instrument. And so they came, more than 30,000 strong, with harmonicas, drums, kazoos and every conceivable type of portable instrument including—yes!—even two pianos, which were brought into the rotunda at the main entrance.

"What a night for music! The weird noises unleashed by the capacity crowd of roof-raisers must have traumatized music lovers for miles around." So much for the threat from organized labor.

The Sym-Phony members wore frock coats and top hats and directed their musicianship not only toward needling the opposition but also toward the resident umpires, whom they denigrated with a snappy rendition of "Three Blind Mice." When the National League added a fourth umpire to each umpire team, it disturbed Soriano. "How the hell," he asked, "can you play 'Four Blind Mice'?"

Brother Lou claimed that the Sym-Phony's finest hour occurred in 1948 when the group was invited to stroll the aisles during the Republican Convention in Philadelphia. "Governor Tom Dewey said we were great," said Soriano after the affair, "and when he wins the election we're going to give a concert in the White House. Now that's beautiful, because it's a sure thing that Harry Truman can't win!"

WHAT WAS THE BIGGEST "STEAL" OF PLAYERS FROM ONE LEAGUE TO ANOTHER WITHOUT COMPENSATION TO THE "ROBBED" LEAGUE?

Stars of the Negro National League such as Monte Irvin, Larry Doby, and Don Newcombe made their way to the National and American Leagues (Irvin went to the New York Giants, Newcombe to the Brooklyn Dodgers, and Doby signed with the Cleveland Indians) after learning their baseball skills in the black professional leagues. Yet, the white-owned major-league teams refused to sufficiently compensate the leagues or teams in which stars such as Newcombe were trained.

One such black owner, Mrs. Effa Manley, tried in vain to obtain compensation from the Dodgers for Newcombe, who developed into one of major-league baseball's outstanding pitchers. "I wrote to Branch Rickey," said Mrs. Manley, "but he didn't even answer our letters, let alone give us anything. The thing was, he knew we were in no position to challenge him. We got nothing for Newcombe, $5,000 for Irvin, and $15,000 for Doby. Rickey even tried to take our parks, but he couldn't. But he did take our ballplayers. He outmaneuvered us completely."

WHAT WAS THE BEST JOKE BY A MANAGER?

It was told by Leo Durocher. Although Leo later changed the venue of this gag from Ebbets Field to the Polo Grounds, the story he told on himself originally had a Brooklyn locale. As Leo said it, the gag went as follows:

"A horse trotted up to me in the dugout and said he wanted to play for the Dodgers. 'Okay,' I said, and went out to the mound to pitch a couple in to him. The horse takes the bat in his teeth and hits two or three in the stands.

"So I says to him, 'Not bad, but can you field?'

"So he trots out to the outfield and I fungo a few, and this nag snares each one cleanly between his teeth.

" 'Pretty good,' I have to admit to him. 'But one more thing. Can you run?'

" 'Run?' the horse whinnies. 'If I could run, do you think I would be out here looking for a job?' "

Over the years the punch line was altered to fit the occasion, i.e., "If I could run, I'd be at Belmont!"

Still another version had the horse actually belting an inside-the-park blast 500 feet to the foot of the Polo Grounds' clubhouse but being pegged out at home plate. In this gag, Durocher demands, "Why the hell didn't you run faster?" To which the nag snaps: "If I could run, I'd win the Derby!"

WHO IS THE ONLY BALLPLAYER EVER TO PLAY 1,000 GAMES EACH IN THE INFIELD (FIRST BASE) AND THE OUTFIELD (ALL THREE POSITIONS)?

Stan "The Man" Musial, "Mister St. Louis Cardinal," performed the feat over a twenty-two-year major-league career. Of all the positions, Musial named right field as his favorite spot to play. It was while Musial played that position in 1948 that he put on a show long to be remembered. He missed by just one homer becoming the only hitter ever to lead in all of the following departments in one season: batting, base hits, doubles, triples, home runs, runs batted in, and slugging percentage. The wiry, left-handed batter who made the number six famous with his crouched, coiled stance, batted .376 —43 points higher than runner-up Richie Ashburn, and had 230 hits, the most in the National League since Joe Medwick's 237 in 1937. Stan's total bases, 429, were the most since Rogers Hornsby's league record set in 1922. With 46 doubles, 18 triples and 39 home runs (one behind Ralph Kiner and Johnny Mize who blasted 40 each), he had 103 extra-base hits, four shy of Chuck Klein's league high in 1930. Musial's slugging percentage (.702) was the highest since Hack Wilson's .723 in 1930 (the year Wilson set the league record with 56 homers and the major-league standard of 190 RBI's). Scoring 135 runs and driving in 131, Musial had what amounted to a piece of the best production of several great hitters. It was hardly surprising that in 1948 Musial was named the National League's Most Valuable Player. But he was not cited as "Player of the Year," a distinction earned by the Cleveland Indians' Lou Boudreau, who led his team—as manager and star shortstop—to the American League pennant.

Stan "The Man" Musial is the only ballplayer ever to play 1,000 games each in the infield and the outfield. *(from the collection of Barry Halper)*

WHICH BASEBALL TEAM PLAYED BASKETBALL ON A STAGE?

The Brooklyn Dodgers. During the off-season the popular Dodgers frequently would seek employment in and around New York City, and once, to the delight of Brooklynites, they put together their own basketball team and played "home" games on the stage of the vast Paramount Theater in downtown Brooklyn. Diagonally across the street a tavern was appropriately renamed The Dodgers Cafe.

LIKE MANY BALLPLAYERS, MICKEY MANTLE WAS DISCOVERED WITH THE HELP OF A LITTLE LUCK. WHAT HAPPENED?

Mantle played baseball at his high school in Oklahoma and for a local semipro team called the Baxter Springs Whiz Kids. One summer night in 1948, a scout named Tom Greenwade was on his way through Baxter Springs to watch another prospect play in another town. But Greenwade saw the Baxter Springs field beside the roadway and decided to pull over and watch the game.

Greenwade, a New York Yankee scout, watched a sixteen-year-old Mantle stroke three home runs—one left-handed and two right-handed. One blast even splashed into the river beyond the outfield. Greenwade approached Mantle after the game, but when he learned Mantle still had one year of school left, he realized he could not make any offers. So Greenwade promised to return in a year.

He came back the next year indeed, and saw Mantle hit two more homers. Greenwade offered Mickey a $1,500 signing bonus plus $140 for the rest of the summer and Mantle became a Yankee prospect in 1949. In 1951, Mantle became a New York Yankee rookie and hit .267 with 13 homers and 65 RBI's in 96 games.

WHICH BASEBALL SLUGGER CAMPED AT AN EDITOR'S DOORSTEP TO REGISTER A BEEF?

Jeff Heath, Cleveland Indians. A sensitive soul, Heath, who was a member of the Boston Braves' 1948 pennant-winning team, was offended by a story written about him in *The Sporting News*. The story so bothered Heath (often called "Lord Jeff") that he decided to stop off at the conclusion of the season to see *The Sporting News'* publisher, J. G. Taylor Spink, as he drove home to Washington State. "I just wanted Taylor to know my side of the story," said Heath.

Unfortunately, Heath's timing was poor. He crossed the Mississippi River to downtown St. Louis at six in the morning. "I decided," said Heath, "that the only thing I could do was to drive to *The Sporting News* building and sleep in the car until Mister Spink came to work. I assumed that that would be around nine or ten in the morning. I drove to his office, parked, and tried to sleep, but I was uneasy, afraid some guy might come down the street and steal my expensive shoes. So, a few minutes after seven, I locked the car and went to see if I could get into the building to doze off. Maybe there'd be a night watchman or janitor. The door was unlocked. I climbed the stairs and whom did I meet but Spink himself!'"

WHO WAS THE CANADIAN-BORN PITCHER WHO PINCH-HIT A BASE HIT IN HIS FIRST MAJOR-LEAGUE AT BAT?

Oscar Judd. A farm boy from Rebecca, Ontario, Judd could hit as well as he could pitch and proved it by being named to the 1943 American League All-Star Team. After seven outstanding minor-league seasons, he had been promoted to the Boston Red Sox in 1941, and it was early in his rookie stint that Boston manager Joe Cronin sent Judd up against the great Bob Feller, whereupon Oscar came through.

Once his pitching arm came up lame, Judd, a slow-talking, fast-running Canadian, made a comeback in the National League before drifting down to the Toronto Maple Leafs of the International League. Despite his lingering arm trouble, Judd took the mound on May 4, 1949, for Toronto before 22,206 fans at Maple Leaf Stadium, Toronto's biggest opening-day baseball crowd, prior, of course, to the Blue Jays' debut. He held the strong Newark Bears to three hits in eight innings as the Leafs won, 4–3. The following year he retired.

WILLIE MAYS WAS SITTING IN A MOVIE THEATER IN 1951, WATCHING A DOUBLE FEATURE WHEN THE HOUSELIGHTS WENT ON AND A MAN WALKED OUT ON STAGE AND SAID, "IF WILLIE MAYS IS HERE, HIS MANAGER WANTS HIM AT THE HOTEL." WHAT WAS THE NEWS MANAGER TOMMY HEATH HAD FOR WILLIE?

When Mays, who was enjoying the day off with the New York Giants' Minneapolis farm club of the American Association, got back to the hotel, Heath was grinning and holding out his hand. "Congratulations," he said.

"For what?" Willie asked.

"You're going to the big leagues."

Willie Mays, the "Say Hey" kid. *(from the collection of Barry Halper)*

WHO WAS THE FIRST NATIONAL LEAGUER IN THE TWENTIETH CENTURY TO HIT FOUR HOMERS IN A NINE-INNING GAME?

Gil Hodges accomplished that feat on August 31, 1950.

WHO WERE THE TRIO OF YANKEES WHO COMPRISED "THE THREE MUSKETEERS"?

Mickey Mantle, Whitey Ford, and Billy Martin.

Billy Martin (shown here in a three-part sequence, being tagged out by Roy Campanella) was a member of the Yankees' Three Musketeers: Mickey Mantle, Whitey Ford, and Martin. *(from the collection of Barry Halper)*

WHO WAS FORMER CLEVELAND INDIANS GENERAL MANAGER FRANK LANE DESCRIBING WHEN HE SAID, "HE'S A FEISTY LITTLE SON OF A BITCH. HE'S THE KIND OF GUY YOU'D LIKE TO KILL IF HE'S PLAYING FOR THE OTHER TEAM, BUT YOU'D LIKE TEN OF HIM ON YOUR OWN SIDE, THE LITTLE BASTARD"?
Billy Martin.

IN HIS FIRST SEASON WITH THE NEW YORK YANKEES, BILLY MARTIN QUICKLY EARNED HIS FEISTY REPUTATION WITH TWO MEMORABLE FIGHTS IN A TWO-WEEK SPAN. WHO WERE MARTIN'S FOES?
Jimmy Piersall and Clint Courtney. Before the first game of a June 1950 Yankee-Red Sox series at Fenway Park, Piersall was needling Martin about the size of his nose and ears. Never one to swallow an insult, Martin shot back. So did Piersall. Finally, the insults became increasingly personal until Billy challenged Piersall to meet him under the Fenway stands. Piersall accepted the invitation and before anyone could interrupt the battle, Billy flattened Piersall. Not lacking any courage, Piersall regained his feet only to absorb another two licks that dropped him to his knees and bloodied his mouth. That was it, for Piersall.

Afterward, Yankee manager Casey Stengel, a noted brawler during his own playing days, was particularly pleased by Martin's spirit. "This should wake my other tigers up," Stengel said. "It's

Billy Martin was once paid to get hit with a pitched ball. Meanwhile here he is being hit with a caught ball! *(from the collection of Barry Halper)*

about time they realize they got to fight harder this year. I just hope Martin's fighting spirit spreads to the others."

Martin soon got involved in another altercation, this time with Clint Courtney. Courtney was a rugged ballplayer and was already intensely disliked by Martin. He recalled, "Down in Phoenix I missed one game and a kid by the name of Eddie Lenne was playing second base and Courtney jumps into him and spikes his leg open. That kid Eddie was a neighbor of mine in Berkeley and we played ball together. He later got killed in Korea. I couldn't get Courtney that day because I was in the stands. But from that day on, every time I got the chance, I took a punch at him. Every time."

Martin's first chance came in 1952 at Yankee Stadium. Courtney had been traded by the Yankees to the St. Louis Browns and was making his first appearance against his former team. Before meeting Courtney and the Browns, the Yankees discussed the roughhouser's tactics in the locker room. "Someone has to take care of him," Mickey Mantle suggested.

"I'll take care of him!" Billy said.

Martin needed no urging. He got his chance in the St. Louis half of the eighth inning. Courtney was on first base with two outs. He tried to steal second base. Yogi Berra threw a strike to Billy, covering the bag. Courtney barreled into second base with his typical flagrant recklessness, but Martin was ready, slamming the ball into Courtney's mouth.

Billy, with his fists ready for battle, waited for Courtney to get up and retaliate. But Courtney was still stunned by the taste of Martin's rawhide sandwich and Billy turned away. Suddenly, Courtney regained his feet and started in a fury toward Martin. "Watch out!" shouted pitcher Allie Reynolds from the mound.

In one motion Martin turned and landed a blow to Courtney's jaw. Courtney fell and got up, only to run into some more blows from Billy. The bout ended when the umpires separated the combatants.

"A fellow has to take care of himself," Martin explained. "He also has to take care of his friends."

NO PITCHER GAVE UP MORE HOME RUNS TO WILLIE MAYS THAN THIS HALL-OF-FAME LEFT-HANDER. WHO IS HE?

Warren Spahn yielded 17 of Mays's 660 career four-baggers. No pitcher gave up more to Mays.

Spahn yielded Mays's first major-league hit, a home run on May 28, 1951. Spahn also gave up Mays's 200th career home run. A total of 433 home runs were hit off of Spahn during his career.

WHAT WAS THE BEST CONTRACTUAL SQUELCH?

When Hank Greenberg was general manager of the Cleveland Indians he once received an unsigned contract from one of his players. Greenberg immediately dispatched a telegram to the player: IN YOUR HASTE TO ACCEPT TERMS YOU FORGOT TO SIGN CONTRACT.

A few days later, Greenberg received an answering wire: IN YOUR HASTE TO GIVE ME A RAISE YOU PUT IN THE WRONG FIGURE.

WHO WAS BASEBALL'S FIRST $100,000 BONUS PLAYER?

Paul Pettit, a pitcher for the Pittsburgh Pirates from 1951–1953.

BOBBY THOMSON'S "SHOT HEARD 'ROUND THE WORLD" IS STILL ONE OF THE MOST FAMOUS SINGLE MOMENTS IN BASEBALL HISTORY. WHAT WERE THE CIRCUMSTANCES PRECEDING THOMSON'S DRAMATIC BLAST?

On August 12, 1951, Thomson and the New York Giants trailed the first-place Brooklyn Dodgers by a thick thirteen and a half games. Fueled by manager Leo Durocher's goading and cajoling, the Giants reeled off 16 straight wins. Also, by winning 39 of their last 47 games, the Giants hustled their way into a first-place deadlock with the stunned Dodgers. The two clubs headed into the last day of the season tied, and after each club won its last regular-season game, they remained tied, so the National League pennant would be decided by a best-of-three play-off.

The Giants won the first game at Ebbets Field, and the Dodgers earned a big win the next day at the Polo Grounds behind a shutout by rookie Clem Labine.

Both clubs had their aces on the hill for the deciding game. Don Newcombe pitched for Brooklyn and Sal Maglie went for New York. Newcombe took a seemingly safe 4–1 lead into the bottom of the ninth, but the Giants generated a rally that echoed their final six weeks of the regular season.

Alvin Dark singled to right. Don Mueller also rolled a single to right. Whitey Lockman doubled in a run one out later. With Giant runners on first and third, right-hander Ralph Branca was brought in to save the pennant for the Dodgers.

Bobby Thomson hit the second offering from Branca on a line to left, the ball sailing over the wall. Bedlam erupted at the Polo Grounds. Giants fans went crazy, and Dodgers fans sat in frozen astonishment. All had just witnessed one of the most dramatic moments in sports history.

WHEN BOBBY THOMSON HIT THE "SHOT HEARD 'ROUND THE WORLD" ON OCTOBER 3, 1951, WHO WAS ON DECK?

While Thomson was busy making history, there was a rookie center fielder on deck. His name was Willie Mays.

WHAT BASEBALL PLAYERS APPEARED IN THE DIAMOND SEQUENCES OF *THE WINNING TEAM* (1952), STARRING RONALD REAGAN AS GROVER CLEVELAND ALEXANDER?

Bob Lemon (Cleveland Indians), "Peanuts" Lowrey (St. Louis Cardinals), George "Catfish" Metkovich (Pittsburgh Pirates), Irv Noren (Washington Senators), Gerry Priddy (Detroit Tigers), Hank Sauer (Chicago Cubs), and Al Zarilla (Chicago White Sox).

WHAT WAS THE BEST ANSWER BY A BASEBALL PLAYER TO A REPORTER'S QUESTION?

A product of the New York City sandlots, Billy Loes of the Brooklyn Dodgers made his way to the majors amid much fuss and fanfare, especially in the Manhattan dailies. The lean, lanky Loes was admired for his droll and occasionally bizarre humor. His most widely reported retort was delivered during the 1952 World Series when he mistook the velocity of a ground ball hit to the mound and erred on the play. Questioned about the error, Loes replied with a straight face: "I lost it in the sun!"

A lesser, but philosophically better, line was delivered later in Loes's career. Many observers wondered why a pitcher with so much natural talent could continually fail to win more than fourteen games a season, even though he was backed by a strong club. When a reporter questioned Loes about his perennial failure to reach the twenty-win plateau, Billy mulled over the query for a moment and then candidly commented that such a Promethean effort would be damaging to his psyche: "If you win twenty," said Loes, "they want you to do it every year."

WHICH TEMPESTUOUS CATCHER OWNED THE NICKNAME "SCRAP IRON"?

Clint Courtney, a major-leaguer for ten years, was dubbed "Scrap Iron" by his teammates while playing for the St. Louis Browns in 1952. It was during spring training that Courtney bet New York sportswriter Milt Richman $100 on a footrace between the two.

The challenge took place at a railroad station in Colton, California, using the roadbed as the track. The race was won by Richman in a convincing manner, but Courtney claimed the newsman bumped him and requested and got a rematch. The results of the second race were the same except that at the finish line Courtney tripped and dived headfirst onto the cinder-strewn racecourse. His clothes were torn to shreds and his body cut all over. It took the trainer well over an hour to treat Courtney's wounds. At breakfast the next morning, Browns manager Rogers Hornsby, who had not witnessed the race, looked up at Courtney and asked, "What the hell happened to you?"

"I was in a race," replied Courtney, who closely resembled a mutilated mummy.

"How did you do?" asked Hornsby.

"I lost," answered Courtney, grimacing with every syllable.

"Okay," said Hornsby. "It will either be a $250 fine or you can catch today's game against the Indians."

On the assumption that any physical torture would be preferable to another fiscal setback, Courtney said, "I'll catch!"

That afternoon Courtney collected three singles off Early Wynn, the Indians' future Hall of Famer, and earned the undying admiration of his teammates. Considering his reputation as a battler, it was ironic that Clint Courtney should die after suffering a heart attack while playing, of all things, Ping-Pong.

THE VERY LAST ST. LOUIS BROWNS PLAYER WHO WAS ACTIVE IN THE MAJOR LEAGUES WAS A NOTABLE PITCHER. WHO WAS HE?

Don Larsen, the only pitcher (as a New York Yankee) ever to hurl a perfect game in the World Series. The big fellow broke into the majors with the Browns in 1953, their last year in St. Louis before becoming the Baltimore Orioles. As a Brown, Larsen posted a 7–12 record and a 4.16 earned run average. He concluded his major-league career in 1967 with the Chicago Cubs where he had no decisions and a hefty 9.00 ERA. In between, Larsen pitched for the Yankees, Kansas City Athletics, Chicago White Sox, San Francisco Giants, and Houston Astros. Another member of the final Browns team in 1953 was Billy Hunter, who later became manager of the

Texas Rangers. Hunter, a shortstop, hit .219 that year and in the true tradition of the Browns, finished last among American League players who qualified for the batting championship.

WHO WAS THE ONLY MAJOR-LEAGUE PITCHER TO HURL A NO-HITTER IN HIS FIRST STARTING ASSIGNMENT, WHEN HE SHOULD HAVE BEEN IN THE MINORS?

On May 16, 1953, Alva L. "Bobo" Holloman of the St. Louis Browns tossed a no-hitter at the Philadelphia Athletics in his very first start.

Ironically, Holloman was supposed to be en route to the minors when the Browns decided to give him a "token" start. The right-hander defeated the A's, 6–0. Even more amazing is the fact that the no-hitter was the only complete game Holloman ever pitched in the majors. He remained with the team for the 1953 season posting a singularly unimpressive 3–7 record. It would be Holloman's only season in the majors.

Ted Breitenstein also pitched a no-hitter in his first start for St. Louis of the Old American Association. Breitenstein's 8–0 no-hitter occurred on October 4, 1891.

Charlie "Bumpus" Jones tossed a no-hitter in his first game for Cincinnati of the National League. Jones's no-hitter on October 15, 1892, resulted in a 7–1 win over Pittsburgh.

ON APRIL 17, 1953, MICKEY MANTLE SWATTED THE FAMOUS 565-FOOT HOME RUN IN WASHINGTON. WHAT DID HE DO TWO YEARS EARLIER, TO THE DAY?

He appeared in his first regular-season game, going one-for-four and driving in a run during a 5–0 Yankee win over the Red Sox at Yankee Stadium.

Mickey Mantle swatted his famous 565-foot homer on April 17, 1953. *(from the collection of Barry Halper)*

WHAT IS THE BEST ALLUSION TO BASEBALL IN A NON-BASEBALL MOVIE?

Mogambo (Metro-Goldwyn-Mayer), 1953. Grace Kelly, responding to Clark Gable's identification of a group of scurrying animals as "Thomson's gazelles," asks: "Who is this man Thomson that gazelles should be called after him?"

Ava Gardner, in jealous pursuit of Gable's charms, and definitely another kind of lady, answers sardonically: "He's a third baseman for the Giants who hit a home run against the Dodgers once."

According to experts on film, this could be the closest adherence to baseball fact ever achieved in a Hollywood production. "Baseball movies," wrote film critic Paul Ringe, "traditionally have been viewed with suspicion by baseball fans. But *Mogambo* did justice to both Bobby Thomson and gazelles."

WHAT DO BASEBALL'S HANK AARON AND HORSE RACING'S LOUIS WOLFSON HAVE IN COMMON?

There would seem to be little to connect Hank Aaron, the home-run king, with Louis Wolfson, owner of Triple-Crown winner Affirmed. Yet were it not for Wolfson, Aaron's career might have taken a turn for the worse.

When Aaron was climbing up through the minors in 1953, he

was signed by the Jacksonville, Florida, club owned by Sam Wolfson, brother of Louis. A nasty bloc of white militants in Jacksonville took exception to the signing of a black ballplayer. They threatened that if Aaron played, the ballpark would be set afire. Sam Wolfson went to his brother, Louis, for advice.

"What should I do, Lou?" he asked.

"You play Aaron and see what happens," Louis Wolfson counseled.

Aaron played, there was no fire at the ballpark, the racial barrier at Jacksonville was broken, and Hank Aaron went on to become a superstar.

WHO WAS THE ONLY KNOWN PROFESSIONAL BASEBALL PLAYER TO APOLOGIZE PERSONALLY TO A PITCHER OFF WHOM HE HAD HIT A SINGLE?

Archie Wilson, Toronto Maple Leafs. A balding, clutch-hitting left fielder with the International League Leafs, Wilson wore number three on his uniform and liked to say it was "me and The Babe," as in Ruth. During a game against Buffalo in 1954, Wilson came to the plate in the ninth inning with two outs against the Maple Leafs and nobody on base. The pitcher was Frank Lary, who was one out away from pitching a perfect game, having retired the first 26 men he faced. But Wilson stroked a single to ruin Lary's bid. When the game was over, Wilson, ever the sportsman, walked to the Buffalo dressing room and formally apologized to Lary.

IN 1954, THE CLEVELAND INDIANS WON 111 GAMES AND LOST ONLY 43, FINISHING EIGHT GAMES AHEAD OF THE SECOND-PLACE YANKEES. ALTHOUGH THE INDIANS SHOWCASED SUPERSTARS SUCH AS LARRY DOBY, BOB FELLER, AL ROSEN, BOB LEMON, AND EARLY WYNN, THE AMERICAN LEAGUE MVP DID NOT COME FROM CLEVELAND. TO WHOM DID THE BASEBALL WRITERS GIVE THIS PRESTIGIOUS AWARD?

From 1951–1955, Lawrence Peter Berra, known to most as Yogi, won three American League Most Valuable Player Awards, in

1951, 1954, and 1955. In 1954, his .307 batting average, 22 home runs, and 125 runs batted in led the Yankees to a 103-win season. Ironically, this was the best win total the Bombers would produce from 1949–1958, but marked the only season during this time period that they failed to win a pennant.

Berra would also set a record for the most World Series played in, 14, as well as belting 358 home runs throughout his career, establishing an American League mark for catchers. However, as great as he was, Berra was as well known for his malapropisms and one-liners as he was for his playing abilities.

After going four-for-four in one game, Yogi noticed that the box score in the following day's newspaper said he went only three-for-four. After complaining to the official scorer, he was told that it was a typographical error.

"Baloney," said Yogi, "it was a clean hit up the middle."

Then there was the time Yogi was doing a radio show with a renowned sportscaster. Receiving a check for his services that said "Pay to Bearer," Yogi was insulted. "You've known me all these years and you still can't spell my name?" Yogi lamented.

WHAT POETESS WROTE OF THE DODGERS' GLORY AFTER THEIR SERIES VICTORY IN 1955?

Dodger fan and world-renowned poet Marianne Moore, of Fort Greene, Brooklyn, penned a poem to the Dodgers, entitled "Hometown Piece for Messrs. Alston and Reese." It ended thus:

> *You've got plenty: Jackie Robinson*
> *and Campy and big Newk, and Dodgerdom again*
> *watching everything you do. You won last year. Come on.*

Alas, they did not "come on" the next year.

WHO HAD THE BEST BIRTHDAY FOR A PLAYER?

Pee Wee Reese, Brooklyn Dodgers. For Reese's birthday, on July 23, 1955, the Dodgers' captain was hailed with a "night" in his honor. He was overwhelmed with gifts, including an automobile (in which his mother, to Pee Wee's surprise, was sitting), but the *pièce de résistance* came when the houselights dimmed and 33,000 fans lit matches and sang "Happy Birthday" to Reese. The effect of the matches against the black backdrop of the stands was awesome.

WHO WAS THE WORST HOME-RUN HITTER?

Floyd Baker, a journeyman who alternately played for the St. Louis Browns, Chicago White Sox, Washington Senators, Boston Red Sox, and Philadelphia Phillies. Never to be confused with "Home Run" Baker, Floyd came to bat for a total of 2,280 times in his major-league career during which he hit exactly one home run. Baker retired in 1955 with a lifetime .251 batting average.

NEW YORK YANKEE ROOMMATES WHITEY FORD AND MICKEY MANTLE HAD A REMARKABLE ABILITY TO PRODUCE WHEN MONEY WAS ON THE LINE. HOW DID FORD'S AND MANTLE'S ALL-STAR-GAME PERFORMANCES COMPARE WITH THEIR CAREER WORLD-SERIES STATISTICS?

Mantle and Ford played unspectacular baseball in the mid-season classics. But when a World Championship was at stake, the duo put up phenomenal numbers.

In All-Star games, Ford pitched six times and went 1–2. He gave up eleven earned runs in twelve innings for an earned run average of 8.25. Mantle batted 43 times and hit eight singles and two homers while also striking out 16 times.

But the duo's World Series appearances and performances were another story altogether. From 1950–1964, Ford pitched in 22 games and allowed 44 runs in 146 innings, for an ERA of 2.71. Of those 22 games, Ford won ten (still a World Series record) and lost eight.

In his 230 World Series at bats Mantle set records for runs batted in (40), total bases (123), home runs (18) and runs (42).

Ford and Mantle saved their best for when it mattered the most.

Whitey Ford's pitching rose to clutch occasions. *(from the collection of Barry Halper)*

WHO ARE THE ONLY TWO PLAYERS SINCE 1901 TO HAVE FIVE EXTRA-BASE HITS IN A GAME?

Joe Adcock of the Milwaukee Braves hit four home runs and one double on July 31, 1954 and Lou Boudreau had four doubles and one home run on July 14, 1946.

WHO PITCHED THE ONLY WORLD-SERIES PERFECT GAME?

Don Larsen's 2–0 perfect game against the Brooklyn Dodgers in Game Five of the 1956 World Series lifted the New York Yankees to a three-games-to-two lead. (The Yankees won Game Seven, 9–0.) It was only the sixth complete game Larsen pitched in 1956.

Yogi Berra, the catcher for Larsen's gem, said: "I can still remember that last pitch to pinch hitter Dale Mitchell that Larsen threw. I called for a fastball. He didn't shake me off during the whole game. It was high, the pitch, and I dunno whether it was a strike or not. I just ran out there to the mound. I jumped on Larsen and I said something like, 'Great game, Don!'

"In the dugout you sometimes talk about a no-hitter when a guy has one going, and we might have if the score had been 8–0 or something like that. But a walk and a home run could have tied the game in the ninth and we could've lost it, so nobody said anything. People have asked me what I did in that game. I had to look it up because I couldn't remember. I just remember Larsen."

"THE 'FAN'
BECOMES A PRO"

In many ways, the post-World War II era produced some of the most engrossing baseball I ever had the pleasure to witness. Not only did we enjoy the return from the armed forces of such notables as Joe DiMaggio and Pee Wee Reese, but there was the thoroughly gripping saga of Jackie Robinson, who led the Black revolution in the game. And along with that came the rise of the Brooklyn Dodgers—alias The Boys of Summer—as a major power.

It was quite a treat being a sports journalist in those days, and I have to laugh when I think that I could very well have been a physician then rather than a professional broadcaster. After all, I had originally planned to be a doctor, which is why I enrolled at the University of Michigan before the outbreak of World War II.

I could have stayed in the New York area and gone to any number of colleges for premed, but I decided it was time to go out of town. As it turned out, it was a brilliant move—not so much for a budding medical career, but rather for sports.

Any regrets I had about removing myself from Ebbets Field and the Dodgers was mitigated by the Ann Arbor sporting scene. Michigan had great Big Ten football. Tom Harmon, one of the top football players of all time, was there. Tom was so good he made the cover of *Time* magazine. Michigan also fielded a super baseball team, a marvelous swimming team, and one of the nation's top wrestling squads. I had gone to the Great Midwest to take the oath of Hippocrates and instead found myself immersed in sports—sports I'd only read about. I even tried out for, and made, the freshman basketball team.

Playing basketball for a college as important as Michigan was something special, and I was pretty good at it, too. But I ended up paying a price for the time involved in sports. I finished the season well in "hoops," but I wound up getting a *B* in one course. When my father heard about it, he was furious. He said, "Did I send you to Michigan to become a basketball player or a doctor?"

You have to keep in mind that in the late thirties the business of getting into medical school was no easy feat for a Jew. Jews were openly discriminated against and quota systems—ten percent maximum for Jews—were the norm. It also meant that higher grades were expected from Jews, so even one *B* was practically a catastrophe in my father's eyes. Pop laid it right on the line: "Which is it—do you want to be a doctor or do you want to become a basketball player?"

Put in those terms, my choice was pretty clear. I knew my limitations. I was a decent basketball player. A great one? Never. Even if I made the varsity team, so what? There was no NBA in those days; pro basketball was a fly-by-night operation that paid peanuts. So it was back to the books.

But as I progressed through my sophomore and junior years, I became more pessimistic about medicine as a career. It was becoming obvious that my chances of getting into a reputable medical school—because of my religion, not my grades—were slim to none. Ultimately I said, "Screw 'em! What does it matter?"

I began branching out, and sports became an integral part

of the changes in my life. I covered basketball for the *Michigan Daily* newspaper and took English courses up to my nose. In my senior year I began thinking seriously about becoming a sportswriter. I also took a speech course and took to sitting in at the campus broadcasting studio, where I began to get the notion that it would be fun to be a radio announcer, although the thought of becoming a sportscaster never occurred to me. One day when I got behind the mike for kicks, somebody remarked, "Hey, you have a good voice." It came as a complete surprise to me, and had I known then what I know now, I'd have taken voice lessons, singing lessons—the whole bit. But I never got that close to sportscasting at Michigan, although I stayed close to sports. How could it be otherwise with all our terrific teams and Detroit nearby?

Going to Detroit to see the Tigers play at Briggs Stadium was a major event in my life, because the home club had one of the greatest Jewish athletes of all time in Hank Greenberg. In my freshman year at Michigan, Greenberg had his finest year at the plate and on the final day of that 1938 season had 58 home runs, just two short of Babe Ruth's record.

I remember his final run at Babe Ruth's record so clearly, although I didn't attend the doubleheader at Briggs Stadium on the last day of the season. It was the Tigers against the Indians and I was praying that Greenberg would hit two homers. Unfortunately, in the opener he faced Rapid Robert Feller, one of the best fastball pitchers of all time.

Feller won the battle of the titans, striking out 18 batters to set a new one-game strikeout record. Greenberg went one-for-four and the "one" wasn't a home run. The best he could do was blast a double. I was crushed after the second game; Hank had three hits, but they were all feeble singles.

Still, my favorite remained Greenberg, of whom Paul Richards once said, "No power hitter ever looked better standing up at the plate. He stood almost straight up, with that bat cocked high behind his right ear, and he was a picture of confidence. I used to think of two things when I saw Hank standing there: he knows he can hit, and he enjoys it."

Another player who was a pleasure to watch at the plate was Dick Wakefield. He played for the University of Michigan and eventually became baseball's first "bonus baby." Wakefield played seven games for the Tigers in 1941, then became a regular two years later. He played a total of nine years in the majors—one with the Yankees and one with the Giants—but he never came close to fulfilling his early notices.

Wakefield was a friend of mine, and we'd hang out at the campus poolroom together. This wouldn't have bothered my father because the Michigan poolroom was lovely. I even played on one of the Michigan pool teams that won a national championship in pocket (straight) pool. Wakefield loved to play pool, and I beat him a lot of times, although we never gambled. In fact, I have never bet on a game—of any sort—in my entire life.

While Wakefield was heading for the major leagues, Mazer was heading for the armed forces. Even before the Japanese dropped their bombs on Pearl Harbor, a Selective Service System had been implemented by the government and a draft of all able-bodied men began. After Pearl Harbor, just about every young American figured he'd get the call. For me it came in the fall of 1942.

But in the months between graduation and my being drafted, I began what would become my career. Right after getting my degree, I heard about an announcer's job in Grand Rapids, Michigan, and applied for the job. Lo and behold, I was hired, and I began working as a staff announcer for radio station WOOD-WASH. (It was a weird station—it was WASH in the morning and WOOD at night!) The whole episode at WOOD-WASH was truly strange, for among my duties was reading the Bible on the air. That's right . . . organ music in the background . . . Dum, dah, dah . . . Bill Mazer reads the Bible: "And in the beginning . . ." I even read poetry!

It was shortly after getting this bizarre job that the war intruded on my budding career. I had heard that because of guys being drafted right and left there were some openings at NBC. NBC Radio had two sections in those days: the Blue Network, which was WJZ in New York, and the Red Network, which was WEAF in New York. I got an audition to announce for a show on the Blue Network called "The Chamber Music Society of Lower Basin Street," which at one time featured that wonderful comic, Zero Mostel. From what I gather, the audition was well received, but before I was hired I got my induction notice.

Despite the fact that this would interrupt my nascent career, I was as gung-ho to do my bit as everyone else in the early forties. There was an *esprit de corps* in the country the likes of which is probably unthinkable today, but it was a part of our lives then. There was no question in our minds that we *had* to defeat the Axis powers, and considering the atrocities Hitler was perpetrating against our people, there was an even more compelling feeling for a Jew like me. That I could personally participate in the destruction of the bad guys became an enthralling possibility.

I was drafted into the Army Air Force, but since my eyes weren't so hot, there was no way I was going to be a pilot. Instead, I was trained to be a radio operator-gunner for the B-17 bomber, the famed "Flying Fortress."

After finishing basic training, I expected to be sent overseas, either to the European theater or the Pacific. But just before I got my marching—or flying—papers, word came that the Air Force had decided to send me to communications school. I was sent to Sioux Falls, South Dakota, for radio-operator school, where I did so well they decided to send me for officers' training in Abilene, Texas.

At Abilene, fate stepped in and probably saved my life. Fate took the form of a young southern officer who took an instant dislike to me almost from the moment I arrived, when he thought I had been rudely staring at him, and took offense. In fact I had been gaping blindly because I'd broken my glasses in transit and was just trying to find my way around the base. I explained to him what had happened but made the mistake of making a joke about it and for some reason the S.O.B. hated me from that moment. Thank God, because the unit he would have assigned me to went to Normandy and was wiped out, almost to a man.

Instead, I was transferred to North Carolina and eventually New Haven, where I was to meet "Dutch," the proverbial girl of my dreams and the woman I've been happily married to for more than 40 years. She has suffered the nickname all those years, since it was shorter than "The Duchess of Arthur Street," as I originally called her. Her real name is Dora, and I met her while I was in rehearsals for an Army Air Corps Band show I was going to emcee. It was only three dates later that I proposed, but since I could have been shipped overseas at any moment, her parents put the kibosh on any marriage plans.

Sure enough, I was soon shipped out to the Pacific in the Transport Command. While we were flying to the Philippines delivering supplies to the GI's, the Japanese took a shot at us and, believe you me, that was enough to scare the white corpuscles out of my bloodstream. Our C-47's were completely unarmed. I quickly found out what it was like to be the proverbial duck in a shooting gallery.

On one supply mission, I happened to be sitting in the cockpit with the pilot when I took to admiring the skyscape up ahead. "Geez," I said to the pilot, "those sure are puffy little clouds." His chin dropped. "Puffy little clouds? My God, that's *antiaircraft . . . flak!*" As he yelled those words, he was already executing a steep dive. We got the heck out of there—one of several close calls.

Another time at the base, I was watching a Humphrey Bogart movie when the air-raid sirens suddenly began blaring. My buddy, Irving Rich, and I dove for the nearest shelter and then realized we were in the latrine. Jumping to his feet, Irving turned to me and barked, "If we're going to die, we're not going to do it lying in the crapper."

I can't say my Army Air Corps service was particularly notable, nor was it Congressional Medal of Honor stuff, but I was glad to serve, because this was "the good war." Ultimately it would have a major influence on my career, partly because when I had filled out my induction papers, I had put down "radio announcer" as the job I'd had in civilian life. Soon my colonel requisitioned me to emcee dances and shows, then I announced an Air Corps baseball game and ended up an announcer on the "Aviation Cadet Hour."

Anyway, despite Japanese ack-ack and assorted other threats to my person, I made it to V.J. Day and finished my tour of duty on a remote Pacific atoll called Kwajalein, which would later make the history books, along with another remote atoll named Bikini, as the site of postwar atomic bomb tests. It was there that I had a chance encounter that would help shape my broadcasting career.

I had become commander of the air base radio group by this time—mind you, I wasn't even twenty-four yet—but the war was now over, and we were all awaiting orders to ship home. There was a lot of time to kill, which I did mostly at the local officers' club, and one day I saw a familiar face. No, it wasn't Ted Williams or Joe DiMaggio, but someone I had remembered playing football and running track for James Madison High School in Brooklyn.

Marty Glickman had been one of my early sports heroes, but now he was a professional sportscaster on loan to the Marines. Glickman worked for WHN (ancestor of New York's current all-sports station, WFAN) handling a variety of sports broadcasting assignments. We got to talking and I mentioned that I had been doing a bit of announcing and was interested in doing it professionally when I got back home.

"Give me a call when you get back to New York," Glickman said with a chuckle. "I'll have your name in lights and your ass in tights!"

Easy to say when you're standing in a military lounge on a remote Pacific atoll, thousands of miles from Broadway. But Marty would be true to his word.

The first order of business as soon as I got back to the States was to make sure that Dutch—who, unbelievably, had waited for me—became Mrs. Bill Mazer. Then, and only then, did I begin the hunt for a job.

Just like the ballplayers who returned from the war, I found myself competing with a lot of returning vets as well as youngsters totally wet behind their microphones. But I remembered what Marty Glickman had said, and I had the temerity to call him when we got back to Manhattan, even though he was definitely in the big time at WHN, New York.

As promised, Marty got me an audition, which went well. All indications were that I'd be doing sports for WHN, when WHN family business intervened. The sports director at WHN was Bertram Lebhar, otherwise known as Bert Lee. He was a chap I had listened to doing New York Rangers play-by-play before the war. Bert Lee liked me, but unfortunately he liked Bert Lee, Jr. better. It mattered not that Bert junior was a teenager with absolutely no broadcasting experience. He *was* the sports director's son, and he got the job.

Undaunted, I made the rounds, including checking back with NBC, where I had almost been hired at the start of the war. No luck—all the announcers who had been off to war had returned and there were no openings. My poor "duchess" was currently the breadwinner for the Mazer family, while I marched up and down Manhattan waiting for my break.

One break did come in a new medium that was just starting up business—they called it television. CBS was getting enthused about TV and they were looking for a guy to do sports for them. Next thing you know, I was doing basketball for the CBS Television Network in New York and Washington. If this sounds like a big deal, keep in mind that in those postwar years, TV people like me used to pray that somebody in radio would hear us and give us a good job. TV was nothing at that time and would remain small potatoes for some years. To give you an idea of how "nothing" television was, my *zayde* would often say to me, "What are you, a bum? Why don't you go out and get a real job?"

It would be Marty Glickman who would give me my break in radio. The most important aspect of this tale is that Marty remembered. In this business a lot of promises are thrown around, but Marty didn't have to promise. He just remembered at the right time. And the right time was when a New York broadcaster, Guy Lebow, was hired to take over as sportscaster at WKBW in Buffalo and never showed up to take the job. When the station discovered they didn't have the New York announcer they had hired, somebody telephoned Glickman and asked him to "quick, find somebody!" Marty remembered his buddy from the officers' club on Kwajalein and recommended me for the job.

I wasn't certain that I wanted to leave New York, particularly since I was getting comfortable in this new thing called TV. But the television work wasn't really making me a living, and besides, Marty said, "If you're any good, you'll be back in New York in a year." He would prove to be only sixteen years off!

In 1948, I began my long stint in the "minors" of broadcasting: Buffalo, New York. How good I was is a matter for debate, but I sure as heck worked: baseball, football, boxing, basketball, hockey—you name it, Mazer did it. I worked a Sugar Ray Robinson boxing bout almost as soon as I got there, and as far as baseball was concerned, I handled play-by-play for the Buffalo Bisons in the International League.

Before major-league baseball expanded west, the International League was as powerful as any league short of the majors, featuring good kids on the way up and big-league veterans no longer good enough for the bigs but with some savvy and talent left. One of my immediate favorites was Coaker Triplett, an outfielder from Boone, North Carolina. Triplett had a southern accent you could cut with a knife and was overflowing with homegrown homilies like, "You can't make chicken salad out of chicken shit—just remember that, Boy!" Triplett had been with the Cubs, the Cards, and then the Phillies, but would never see the majors again.

Another of our ex-big-leaguers was Chet Laabs, who had earned a niche in baseball annals for two different reasons. First and foremost, he helped Bob Feller set a record on October 2, 1938, when Rapid Robert struck out 18 batters. Laabs was with the Tigers at the time, and Feller said this about him: "I struck out Laabs five times, including the last out of the game that gave me the record. The last pitch was a fastball, a called third strike. Laabs had a lot of power for a little guy, but he couldn't hit a fastball. He had a blind spot two feet high."

Laabs's other claim to fame was his playing on the only St. Louis Browns team ever to win a pennant—the famed 1944 edition that had the effrontery to beat out the Yankees on the final weekend of the season, when Laabs contributed two homers.

The Bisons' manager was Paul Richards, a dour type who knew baseball inside out and later would be a big-league manager. He was the first guy I ever saw bring a pitcher in from the bull pen to relieve a pitcher and not take the starter out of the game! Instead, Richards put him at first base. He then let the relief hurler pitch to one man, took him out of the game, and brought his starting pitcher back to the mound from first base. He was an inventive man who won an International-League pennant in 1949 for Buffalo but never won the Little World Series between the International League and American Association.

The beauty of broadcasting minor-league baseball was in watching the unfinished product being molded. It was like seeing a painter begin a canvas rather than seeing the completed work of art. One such developing product in Buffalo was Johnny Groth, an enormously talented outfielder who looked as though he could end up in the Hall of Fame. Duke Snider was starting to make it big in the Dodgers' outfield at the time, and Groth had all of Snider's trappings. Unfortunately, he got beaned in the majors and although he played in the bigs for 15 years, he never fulfilled his promise.

When I wasn't doing baseball, I was behind the mike for Buffalo Bisons hockey games in the American Hockey League, or for Little Three college basketball—Canisius College, Saint Bonaventure, and Niagara. Red Barber once said a person could only be an expert at one sport, but I disagree with that. Each sport has a kernel, an essence, to it that a sportscaster can, and should, find.

Finding the essence of a sport in order to broadcast it wasn't the only thing I was discovering in Buffalo. Just as many minor-league baseball players found themselves beholden to do a lot more than just play ball (there's a trivia question you'll find about a ballplayer who was kept on the roster because he cleaned out the locker room) I often had to do a lot more than simply broadcast.

One season, when we were less than two weeks away from

baseball opening day, the station owner walked in and tersely announced, "We don't have a sponsor for the games." If we didn't have a sponsor, we weren't doing the games—it was that simple.

There was only one thing to do: get a sponsor, and *pronto.* One of the station salesmen and I hopped in a car and drove to Syracuse, where Sylvania Electric Company had its headquarters. We managed to sell Sylvania on the idea of backing the broadcasts and, poof, we were back in business.

My next challenge was to get people out to the ball games, and my basic spiel was, "Come on out to the ballpark —it's a home away from home. Bring the family. Enjoy the comfort, the excitement." To me that was really what baseball was all about, and it was surprising how many people came, bringing their portable radios with them so they could watch the game and hear Mazer do it.

When I wasn't at the local stadium with the fans, I was doing the games from the studio. When the Bisons had an away game, we did what Red Barber and the Dodgers once had done in the early days of Brooklyn baseball on radio: do a ticker-tape account of the game.

What with TV, instant replays, and all the modern video conveniences, contemporary ball fans might find it difficult to conceive of doing ticker-tape baseball. But back in the postwar years, owners felt it was too expensive to send a broadcast team on the road. Instead, we sat in the studio behind a mike reading the ticker as fast as we could and attempting to re-create the action, with canned fan noise in the background. There were tricks to be learned, as I rapidly found out.

It happened during a game between the Bisons and Toronto, and I had a guy hitting a home run with the bases loaded. At least that's what the ticker said, and I had already reenacted the bases-clearing clout for my listeners. Suddenly, tick, tick, tick . . . "Cancel that call," came the message and then, ". . . the ball was caught." That moment taught me in one fell swoop that I had to stay a couple of pitches behind the tape.

Another embarrassing moment happened the night Bisons pitcher Dick Marlowe pitched a perfect game. By this time I was faithfully staying a couple of pitches behind the tape—until I received the Teletype message telling me that he had pitched the perfect game. Instead of retaining my composure and continuing the play-by-play, I acted like a complete jerk and shouted, *"I don't want to keep you in suspense! Marlowe pitched a perfect game!"* I did it because I wanted to be an honest reporter and didn't want to keep my audience in suspense any longer. But it was a stupid thing to do. After all, I had carefully built up that suspense and then blew it all!

It was at about this time that I began to get into the trivia shtick. It all started with a kid at the station who fancied himself a sports maven. He said he had read something that day about the longest win streak in the history of sports and challenged me to come up with the answer.

"Well," I said, not realizing what I was getting myself into, "at least give me a clue—tell me what sport it is."

"No," he insisted, "then you'd know it right off the bat."

The challenge was too great to resist: "How about the Passaic, New Jersey, Wonder Five in basketball?"

The kid was flabbergasted. "You're absolutely right!" he said. Then he demanded, "How did you know that?"

Ah, the perennial question. I think I answered, "I must have seen it in 'Ripley's Believe It Or Not.'"

Who can keep track? My mind, and yours, is like a computer, but, unlike a computer, I can't trace where all the information comes from. Furthermore, back then I had nothing like the Elias Sports Bureau to keep statistics for me. I had to remember them myself. In any event, my answering that question must have impressed some people because word soon got around Buffalo sporting circles that Mazer could recall an amazing number of sports facts and had the stories to go with them. Never did I dream that I would someday turn trivia into a personal trademark. All I was dreaming about then was getting back to New York.

Once, I thought I had my wish fulfilled. Red Barber left the Brooklyn Dodgers' broadcasting team, leaving Connie Desmond (one of the best voices of all time) and Vin Scully to handle the chores. They wanted another sportscaster on the team, and I was one of the people invited to Manhattan for the interview. I can't begin to tell you how excited I was about the opportunity.

I got the chance because the ad agency handling the Dodgers' broadcasts was Batten, Barton, Durstine, and Osborn (their accounts were Dodgers sponsors Lucky Strike cigarettes and Schaefer Beer). Alex Osborn of the agency was a Buffalonian and a big fan of mine. He recommended me to the Dodgers.

When I came to New York I met all of the ad guys, but then it was necessary to sit down with the Dodgers' boss, the one and only Walter O'Malley, otherwise known as "The O," or "The Big Ooom." One might describe him as a quiet George Steinbrenner. O'Malley, like Steinbrenner, wanted to run New York baseball, but he did his thing with considerably less bluster.

At last I met with The Big Ooom and almost immediately after being introduced, he asked me what "Mazer" meant. For a second I didn't know what to make of his question. "Are you asking me what my people's nationality is—or their religion?"

He took a puff on his big, black cigar and said, "Well, both."

"They came from Russia," I responded, "and they're Jewish."

He blew some smoke, then said, "You know, Jewish people are very critical of their own."

Now, what the hell did *that* mean? I thought of about

three smart-ass cracks to make but bit my tongue and finished the brief interview, shook hands, and left.

Was O'Malley being anti-Semitic? Who knows? To this day I regret not asking him why he asked the question, but I didn't and that was that. All I could do was wait and see if I got the job.

It didn't take me long to learn that the job went to a fellow named Andre Baruch. What a blow! Baruch had been an emcee on the *Lucky Strike Hit Parade,* but as far as I knew, he had never broadcast a baseball game in his life. I was crest-fallen, to say the least—can you imagine the possibilities of Mazer and Vin Scully working together?

So I shuffled on back to Buffalo, where I stayed until after my beloved Brooklyns had left for Los Angeles. In fact, it would be the 1960's before I began the broadcasting road back to New York City, and it meant a tour in Milwaukee first!

I had become a big fish in the proverbial small pond by this time and I had developed my own style. I inserted my personality into the broadcasts because I have always firmly believed that broadcasting was no different from sitting and talking across a dinner table. I always have a picture of "you" sitting there, and I simply talk directly to "you," whether it's over the airwaves or into the television camera. And it was television that began the break from Buffalo. In 1964 I got a call: "Would you be interested in doing games on Milwaukee television?"

Would I? It was only weekend work, but it was the major leagues, and that was all the difference in the world. Don't let any ballplayer kid you; the minors may have all kinds of satis-fying elements, but the major leagues is why you're in the game in the first place. I went to my boss at the Buffalo station and told him I wanted to take the Milwaukee gig. He could have nixed the deal, but he understood. "Go ahead," he said. "We'll cover for you on weekends."

Well, you know the old saw, "It never rains but it pours"? I had just started weekending in Milwaukee when I got a call from New York: NBC wanted me to do a radio talk show. I went to my boss again: "How about it?"

"You've waited all your life for this . . ." He never finished what he wanted to say. He just started to cry. I did, too. The man was a big fan of mine and I was very fond of him.

It would be difficult to recapture the feeling of ecstasy I experienced when I learned that I was, in fact, hired by NBC in New York City to do a sports telephone talk show, the first of its kind in America. My break came because of a guy named Mike Joseph, who programmed NBC as a talk station. Joseph's idea was for me to do general sports talk at what then was the unheard of "afternoon drive" hour. The show was geared in part to the thousands of motorists driving home from work.

A lot of people in the business thought it wasn't going to succeed, simply because it had never been done before. But it did. I was the right guy at the right place at the right time. It worked because I came across as a "family-style" kind of guy, and a family show is what it was. I just picked up the phone and talked to listeners.

This was also the time when the trivia angle was becoming important for me. Three times a day we had what was called a "Challenge Round," when listeners would call in and try to stump Mazer on the air. Those who foiled me would win prizes, but we didn't give many of them away, because my recall was never better than it was then.

The New York City to which I returned had been transformed, at least in the baseball sense. Gone were Ebbets Field and the Polo Grounds. My beloved Dodgers were basking in the California sunshine, along with my hated enemy, the "Jints." Television ruled the sportscasting business.

As for The Game itself, it was, as they say, a different ball game—and a less enjoyable one at that. A lot of people are to blame, but none more than the infamous owner of the Dodgers, Walter O'Malley. Whenever I think about baseball's entry into the age of cynicism, I am reminded of a story about a luncheon conversation between New York journalists Jack Newfield and Pete Hamill. They were discussing the state of the world when Newfield suggested that each write on a napkin his opinion of the three worst personalities of the century. When they showed each other their picks, each had the following: 1) Adolf Hitler; 2) Joseph Stalin; and 3) Walter O'Malley.

When O'Malley greedily and unnecessarily removed the Dodgers from Brooklyn, he effectively stripped the borough of two million people of its spirit, while concomitantly turning millions of fans into abject cynics. For that, he will never be forgiven.

THE AGE OF CYNICISM
(1958–1969)

By the time Dutch and I got back to New York City—and we had three kids by this time: two girls and a boy, Arnie, who would one day play "Swede" Risberg in the Broadway show of the Black Sox scandal, *Eight Men Out*—there was no more Ebbets Field, no more Polo Grounds.

But, there was a new team in New York, and they had been in town for a couple of seasons when the Mazer family returned. They, too, would eventually become known as "The Amazin's," although until they performed the miracle of 1969, they would be known more for their bathos and pathos than their winning. Still, fans seemed to love the Mets, in their new Shea Stadium in Flushing Meadow, Long Island. It wasn't Brooklyn, and it wasn't the Dodgers, but by golly, there were days when I could almost hear the cry: "Youse Bums, youse!"

The irony was that during the post-Golden Years of 1957 through 1969, Brooklyn's previous nemesis, the New York Yankees, would win three more World Series, but *so would the Dodgers.* That's right, the California sun seemed to agree with the transplanted Bums, and they have been a periodic contender ever since.

It wasn't simply that clubs moved. For the first time in more than 50 years the game actually expanded from its sixteen-team limits. (Of course one reason why they did finally expand was because the venerable Branch Rickey threatened to come out with a new league, the Continental.) The American League would add teams in Washington and Los Angeles in 1961; the National League would follow suit for 1962 with teams in Houston and the aforementioned New York Mets.

As with any era, talent would age and disappear, as new stars came into ascendancy. Ted Williams, "The Splendid Splinter," retired after the 1960 season. But new names and faces were at their peak. Chicago fans could watch two future Hall of Famers: Ernie Banks on the Cubs and Luis Aparicio on the White Sox. The great Hank Aaron and Eddie Mathews were practically the entire offense for the Milwaukee Braves, who had moved west from Boston in 1953. There were superb ballplayers, no doubt: Willie Mays, Maury Wills, Gil Hodges, Sandy Koufax.

But while the game itself was the same, other changes were occurring and it wasn't merely the faces of the new players. Television, of which I would soon become a part, had taken over baseball. The broadcast overkill of television and radio from the new major-league cities would ultimately destroy much of the minor-league and baseball farm systems that existed in the country. Television was also making movie stars of ballplayers, and superstars and super stats and super salaries were not a long way off. Baseball players now owned restaurants and discos, and began to look at their careers in terms of how many TV ads and endorsements it would mean. It wasn't just the Babe Ruths who overate and overpartied and overindulged in general; it seemed to become endemic to the game—to all major-league sports, for that matter.

Walter O'Malley had proven he was in the game for the money, by moving Dem Bums to Tinseltown; now a raft of young players would prove the same thing. The Age of Cynicism in baseball had arrived.

WHAT WAS THE FIRST MAJOR-LEAGUE FRANCHISE SHIFT IN HALF A CENTURY?

Boston Braves to Milwaukee, National League. Once a baseball institution, the Braves vacated Boston for Milwaukee in time for the 1953 season. Although few baseball barons would admit it at the time, the switch served as a catalyst for many more franchise moves. In 1954, the St. Louis Browns moved to Baltimore and became the Orioles, and in 1955 the Philadelphia Athletics packed for Kansas City. Following the 1957 season, the Brooklyn Dodgers and New York Giants moved from New York City to become the Los Angeles Dodgers and San Francisco Giants, respectively.

The Braves turned out to be the prime carpetbaggers. After a relatively short stay in Milwaukee, the erstwhile Boston nine moved to Atlanta after the 1965 season.

The spate of transfers eventually inspired lawsuits. For instance, in 1969 the City of Seattle filed a $11,000,000 suit against the American League and its twelve clubs after the league decided to move the expansion Seattle Pilots to Milwaukee and change the club's name to the Brewers. The city of Seattle eventually dropped its legal action when the American League promised to deliver a new franchise, eventually known as the Seattle Mariners.

WHAT HAPPENED TO EBBETS FIELD AFTER THE DODGERS LEFT FOR THE WEST COAST IN 1957?

The memory-filled, thirty-two-thousand-seat stadium where the Brooklyn Dodgers participated in nine World Series was boarded up and eventually destroyed by wrecking ball. The site of the historic field was converted into what is still a housing development.

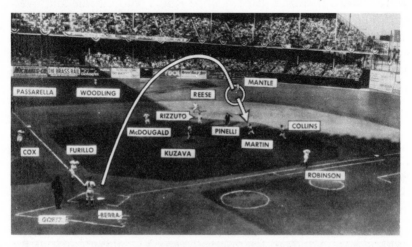

Jackie Robinson pops one out to the Yankees at Ebbets Field shortly before the Bums pulled up stakes and moved west, leaving the historic ballpark to the wrecker's ball. *(from the collection of Barry Halper)*

WHAT'S THE LONGEST RECORDED THROW OF A REGULATION BASEBALL?

Canadian Glen Gorbous threw a baseball 445 feet 10 inches on August 1, 1957, while playing for the Philadelphia Phillies.

WHICH FORMER NEW YORK YANKEES SECOND BASEMAN WAS KILLED IN A FREAK COMMUTER-TRAIN ACCIDENT?

George H. "Snuffy" Stirnweiss. On September 15, 1958, the popular Stirnweiss, who played for the Yankees from 1943 to 1950, was riding in the second car of a five-car commuter train pulled by two diesel locomotives. The Jersey Central Railroad's Train No. 3314 was rolling toward the Bayonne, New Jersey lift bridge, from Bay Head Junction on the Atlantic coast. It was a normal run that carried businessmen to Jersey City, from where they took the Hudson Tubes to Manhattan.

But this time a mysterious event took place. The big lift bridge had been raised to allow the dredge ship *Sand Captain* to pass through. Normally, several precautionary devices would be brought into play to prevent the train from plunging into the river. Three signal lights were spaced along each railroad approach to the bridge. Nevertheless, the engineer apparently ignored the lights and, despite the shrieking warning signals from the *Sand Captain,* the locomotives and two forward coaches sank in a giant geyser of water.

All passengers in the second coach, including Stirnweiss, died in 35 feet of water.

George H. "Snuffy" Stirnweiss (shown here scoring one for the Yanks in 1947) died in a freak commuter-train accident in 1958. *(from the collection of Barry Halper)*

WHO WAS THE OLDEST PLAYER IN THE HISTORY OF THE MAJORS TO WIN A BATTING CROWN?

Ted Williams was 39 when he hit a league-leading .388 in 1957. One year later, Williams won his sixth and final batting crown by hitting .328 at the age of 40.

Ted Williams was the oldest player in the history of the majors to win a batting crown—at age 40 in 1958. *(from the collection of Barry Halper)*

THE LOS ANGELES DODGERS' FIRST GAME IN L.A. WAS PLAYED ON APRIL 18, 1958. WAS THE WEST-COAST DODGER DEBUT A SUCCESSFUL ONE?

Yes. The Dodgers even set a National League single-game attendance record at the time, as 78,672 fans packed into the Los Angeles Coliseum. The Dodgers did not fail to satisfy the huge crowd: L.A. edged the San Francisco Giants, 6–5.

WHO HOLDS THE MAJOR-LEAGUE RECORD FOR MOST CONSECUTIVE PINCH HITS?

Philadelphia's David Philley had nine successful pinch hits spread from September 9, 1958 to April 16, 1959.

WHO WAS FIRST BASEMAN BILL "MOOSE" SKOWRON'S DEFENSIVE REPLACEMENT WHEN SKOWRON PLAYED FOR THE NEW YORK YANKEES?

It was Marvin Eugene Throneberry, the "Marvelous Marv" of New York Mets "fame." Yankee manager Casey Stengel used Marv to replace Skowron in the late innings during the 1958 and 1959 seasons, because Skowron's glove was notoriously porous. Of course Marv, who established his fame as a Met, never challenged for a Golden Glove award either. But the fact remains that Throneberry started his major-league career as a defensive specialist.

A ROUSING TRIBUTE FOR A FORMER GREAT INCLUDED THE LARGEST CROWD IN BASEBALL HISTORY AT THAT TIME. WHOM DID 93,103 PEOPLE TURN OUT TO HONOR ON MAY 7, 1959?

Roy Campanella. The largest crowd in history turned out that night to honor the former Los Angeles Dodgers catcher at a special exhibition game in the Los Angeles Coliseum against the New York Yankees, world champions at the time. An estimated 15,000 fans had to be turned away at the gate. Campanella never played after 1957 as a result of the tragic automobile accident in New York that left him paralyzed from the chest down.

Satchel Paige joined thousands of others to pay tribute to Roy Campanella, 1959. Campy was paralyzed from the chest down after a tragic auto crash. *(from the collection of Barry Halper)*

231

The tribute to Campanella was heart-touching and unforgettable. With the Coliseum lights turned off, a spotlight suddenly showed Campanella being wheeled onto the field by former teammate Pee Wee Reese. For everyone in the crowd that night, it was a most dramatic and emotional event.

WHAT WAS THE WORST LOSS FOR A PITCHER?

Harvey Haddix, Pittsburgh Pirates, May 26, 1959, County Stadium, Milwaukee. Pitching against the Milwaukee Braves, Haddix pitched 12 innings of perfect ball and retired thirty-six consecutive Braves batters. Yet, after 12 innings, the Pirates and Braves were locked in a scoreless tie. In the bottom of the thirteenth inning, Felix Mantilla of the Braves, a .215 hitter, led off with a ground ball to Pirates third baseman Don Hoak, who threw the ball away for an error. Eddie Mathews sacrificed Mantilla to second and then Henry Aaron was purposely walked. He was followed by long-hitting Joe Adcock, who delivered a home run to right-center.

Curiously, Adcock passed Aaron on the base paths in the ensuing celebration and a dispute arose over the final score. It finally was declared a 1–0 game, the toughest loss of Harvey Haddix's career.

HOW DID WALTER ALSTON MANAGE TO WIN A PENNANT FOR THE DODGERS THE SAME SEASON HE WAS "FIRED" BY THEM?

The year was 1959. Alston was skipper of the transplanted Brooklyn Bums, now the Los Angeles Dodgers. His boss was Walter O'Malley's hatchet man, General Manager Emil "Buzzy" Bavasi.

The Dodgers, who had won a World Series under Alston's baton in Brooklyn, were alternating between mediocre and miserable early in the 1959 season, and Bavasi (not to mention O'Malley) was becoming restive, if not wretched.

Walter Alston helped the Dodgers win a pennant, while he was unofficially fired! (from the collection of Barry Halper)

Finally, Bavasi decided that Alston had to go; the new Dodgers manager would be the ever-popular shortstop, Harold "Pee Wee" Reese.

Apart from O'Malley and Bavasi, only a privileged few in the Dodgers' high command knew that Alston was about to get the gate.

Even Alston didn't know.

On a day that the Dodgers were scheduled to play a night game at home, Bavasi decided to tell Alston he was finished as the dugout boss.

There was only one hitch; he couldn't locate the "Skipper." Persistent calls to Alston's home went unanswered. In the meantime, a press release was drawn up announcing Reese's appointment.

It so happened that a former Dodgers employee, who had worked with the club in Brooklyn but had declined to go West with them, was visiting Los Angeles at the time and dropped into the office of Allan Roth, the club's statistician.

Roth told his visitor that Alston was finished and Reese was the new manager, except that it hadn't been announced yet and mum was the word until Alston was advised.

That night the visitor from Brooklyn went to the ballpark, fully expecting to see Reese running the club from the dugout.

"When I got to my seat," the former employee recalled, "I was astonished to see Alston's wife sitting next to me as if nothing had happened to her husband. I thought to myself how sporting it was for her to show up under such terrible circumstances."

But then, the former employee looked up into the Dodgers' dugout and there was Alston, himself, running the club.

"I couldn't believe my eyes," he recalled, "so I headed up to the press box and cornered Roth. He pulled me over to the side and quietly told me that Alston had been at the dentist's all day. 'We couldn't let him go with such short notice,' Bavasi said. 'I guess they'll tell the Skipper tomorrow.' "

Roth and his friend chuckled. "Wouldn't it be something," the Brooklyn visitor said, "if Los Angeles wins tonight and then rolls up ten more in a row and takes the pennant!"

The two laughed at the absurdity of it all and then sat down to watch Alston manage his "last" game for the Dodgers.

Almost.

Roth and his friend from Brooklyn watched in astonishment—and more than a touch of pleasure—as the Dodgers delivered an emphatic win that night.

"Bavasi decided to hold off for another day or two," the other remembered, "just to see what would happen."

What happened was that the Dodgers refused to lose in the next couple of weeks. In fact, they played so well that in no time at all they marched all the way to the pennant.

Alston's walking papers never were delivered and, thanks to a visit to the dentist, he remained the Dodgers' manager for many more years.

His kingdom for a cavity!

FROM WHOM DID THE YANKEES ACQUIRE ROGER MARIS?

Maris first donned Yankee pinstripes in 1960 after he was obtained from the Kansas City A's on December 17, 1959, along with infielder Joe DeMaestri and first baseman Kent Hadley, for outfielders Hank Bauer and Norm Siebern, pitcher Don Larsen, and first baseman Marv Throneberry.

NAME THE TWO MAJOR LEAGUE MANAGERS WHO WERE TRADED FOR ONE ANOTHER?

On August 10, 1960, an unprecedented swap took place when manager Joe Gordon of the Cleveland Indians and manager Jimmy Dykes of the Detroit Tigers switched jobs. At the time the Indians were in fourth place and the Tigers in sixth. Bill DeWitt, the Tigers' president, said he proposed the trade as a joke in a conversation with Frank Lane, Cleveland's general manager. "We were discussing player trades," DeWitt recalled. "I said, 'Frank, we're getting nowhere on this, so let's trade managers.' I meant it to be facetious."

Lane, one of the greatest wheeler-dealers, later said: "I considered Bill's remark in a jocular vein. We were only one game out of first place at the time. But then when we began to stumble, it became no joke to me." On the day the managerial switch was arranged, the Indians lost for the fourteenth time in eighteen games. The swap didn't help either club. Detroit never climbed out of sixth place and Gordon was fired at the end of the year. After finishing fourth with the Indians in 1960, Dykes lasted through the 1961 season, when he, too, was fired.

WHAT BALL CLUB WAS OUTHIT BY 31 HITS, OUTHOMERED BY SIX, AND OUTSCORED BY 28 RUNS IN THE SEVEN-GAME, 1960 WORLD SERIES, YET STILL SOMEHOW MANAGED TO CAPTURE THE CHAMPIONSHIP?

The Pittsburgh Pirates edged the New York Yankees in seven games despite being outhit 91–60, outhomered 10–4, and outscored 55–27 over the remarkable series. The Yankees deadlocked the deciding Game Seven with a pair of runs in the top half of the ninth inning. As the Pirates prepared for the bottom of the ninth, almost everyone knew that Pittsburgh had not won a world championship in 35 years. But now, only a single run away from winning the 1960 World Series, the Pirates refused to hesitate. Stocky Bill Mazeroski led off the Pirate ninth against Ralph Terry. He took ball one from the fifth Yankee pitcher of the long October 13 afternoon. The next offering, a fast, chest-high slider, never reached Johnny Blanchard's catching glove. Instead, the ball sailed over the left-field wall and the quiet crowd of 36,683 erupted into a jubilant celebration. Mazeroski flung his cap into the autumn air and waved his arms wildly as he rounded second base.

The Pittsburgh fans spilled onto the field to be near their heroes. As the celebration spread out onto the streets, the Yankees wondered in silent shock how they had lost the series they had so dominated.

WHITEY FORD CONCOCTED HIS OWN FORMULA TO IMPROVE HIS PITCHING GRIP ON THOSE COLD APRIL DAYS WHEN IT WAS HIS TURN TO PITCH. HOWEVER, FORD'S SECRET SUBSTANCE ONCE FOUND ITS WAY ONTO THE ARMPITS OF AN UNSUSPECTING YOGI BERRA ON OPENING DAY, 1961, IN DETROIT. WHAT HAPPENED?

Ford's mixture of turpentine, baby oil, and resin was helpful stuff. It was white and sticky: "Like Elmer's Glue," marveled Ford. On chilly days it worked wonders for Ford's ball grip.

Anyway, here's what happened to Berra, according to Ford:

"The thing was that Yogi was always borrowing everybody's stuff—their aftershave lotion or shaving cream or hair tonic. He'd be on his way to the shower room and he'd just reach into your locker and help himself to a dash of whatever he needed. Nobody minded too much, even though the guys would pretend to run him off.

"I even found a sophisticated way to keep my magic elixir stashed away. I bought a roll-on deodorant, took out the ball, emptied out the deodorant stuff, and poured my sticky stuff into the little can.

"Well, leave it to Mickey to put two and two together. Mickey Mantle always knew what I was up to; we didn't have any secrets. He knew that Yogi was always mooching stuff from guys' lockers, so after this game with the Tigers, he went and put my sticky stuff on the shelf in my locker—where Yogi would be sure to use it.

"Sure enough, Yogi came out of his own locker and saw the deodorant can on my shelf and helped himself. All the writers were still crowded around me because I'd just won the opener, but the next thing we heard was Yogi bellowing: 'Son of a b——! What the hell is this stuff?' He was off to the side there cursing and writhing around—no kidding, his arms were stuck to his sides.

"Mickey and I were the only guys on the club who knew what it was and with the writers hanging around trying to interview me we didn't want to give it away. So we got Yogi into the trainer's room and the trainer had to use alcohol to dissolve all that stuff, and finally he had to cut the hair under Yog's arms to release him. Boy, was he boiling. I can imagine how it must've hurt him to get all stuck together like that, but that was his tough luck. I was afraid that he might spill the beans on my sticky stuff, but he never did."

A GREAT OLD-TIME PITCHER ADMITTED THAT HE SOMETIMES USED A CUSTOM-MADE RING WITH A SHARP EDGE TO CUT BASEBALLS. WHO COMMITTED THIS TRICK?

Whitey Ford. Late in his career, Ford had a jeweler pal of his make up a special ring. Ford had the design of the ring all planned out: "A half-inch by quarter-inch piece of rasp, all nice and scratchy like a file." Then the hunk of rasp was welded to a stainless steel ring. The cost of the ring was $100.

A lefty, Ford wore the devious ring on his glove hand, like a wedding ring. "During games I'd just stand behind the mound like any other pitcher rubbing the new ball and I'd take my glove off and rub the ball. The rasp would do some job on it, too. Whenever I needed a ground ball, I'd cut it good. It was as though I had my own tool bench with me.

"To hide it, I even got a skin-colored Band-Aid and wrapped it around the ring to match my finger. Camouflage and all. I've got to admit it worked like a charm. Nobody got onto it, and I didn't go around talking about it in the dugout or anything like that—guys get traded to the other teams, and I didn't want *that* to get around."

Ford eventually abandoned the ring when Cleveland Indians manager Alvin Dark grew suspicious and saved some foul balls from a game. Then Dark showed his evidence to umpire Hank Soar. Soar approached Ford and while asking Whitey how he was cutting the ball, he spotted the ring.

Soar got right to the point, asking, "What's that?"

Ford answered, "My wedding ring."

Amazingly, all hell did not break loose. Soar apparently did not realize that the ring was slicing the ball. But Ford took no chances of getting caught with the evidence. He knew the officials were onto him. Ford got rid of the ring at the end of that inning.

WHAT FUTURE HALL-OF-FAME PITCHER STRUGGLED OVER THE FIRST SIX YEARS OF HIS CAREER TO A LOSING 36–40 MARK?

Sanford "Sandy" Koufax did not establish himself as a dominant pitcher until his seventh major-league season in 1961, at age 25. In that year the great lefty went 18–13. Koufax's best seasons were in

1963, 1965, and 1966. He won the Cy Young Award in each of those years with sparkling numbers: 25–5, 1.88 ERA in 1963; 26–8, 2.04, in 1965; 27–5, 1.73, in 1966. The Dodgers also won the World Series in '63 and '65.

In 1972, at age 36, Koufax became the youngest person ever elected to the Hall of Fame.

Future Hall of Famer Sandy Koufax struggled through his first six years in the majors. *(from the collection of Barry Halper)*

WHOM DID WARREN SPAHN FACE TO ACHIEVE HIS 300th VICTORY?

He beat the Chicago Cubs on August 11, 1961, by a score of 2–1.

AT THE END OF THE 1961 SEASON, BABE RUTH'S LONGSTANDING RECORD FOR MOST HOME RUNS IN A SEASON, 60, WAS IN JEOPARDY OF BEING ERASED. ON THE FINAL DAY OF THE SEASON, WHO WOULD REWRITE THE SINGLE-SEASON HOMER MARK?

Roger Maris. The Yankee outfielder was attempting to set the famous record in the New Yorkers' final three-game home set against the Boston Red Sox. Throughout the season Maris was repeatedly bugged with the same question: "Will you break Ruth's record?"

Of course, Maris grew a bit testy about being asked the same thing over and over. "Don't ask me about the d—— record anymore!" he would yell. "I don't give a d—— about the record. All I care about—all I'm interested in—is that we win the pennant." (New York would beat Cincinnati, four games to one, in the World Series.)

The three-game series with Boston included a controversy ignited by Commissioner Ford Frick. Frick ruled that if Maris hit number 61, it would be inscribed in the record book with an asterisk to indicate that Ruth had totaled 60 home runs in a 154-game season whereas Maris had played in a season of 162 games.

Roger Maris would rewrite the single-season home-run record in 1961. *(from the collection of Barry Halper)*

Frick's ruling irked the Yankee fans. To show their dismay, Yankee supporters brought banners to the games that announced: "Frick—up your asterisk." Maris wasn't quite as bothered as his fans. "Commissioner Frick makes the rules," he said. "If all I am entitled to is an asterisk, it will be all right with me."

The Red Sox pitchers were determined to blank Maris over the series and keep him from breaking Ruth's thirty-four-year-old record. They nearly did.

Maris was homerless against 6'6" Sox righty Don Schwall in the first game. And Maris was stopped in the second game by Bill Monbouquette.

It came down to the final day of the season. Maris's obstacle on October 1 was a twenty-four-year-old right-hander named Tracy Stallard. Stallard retired Maris in his first at bat. But in the fourth inning, Maris got good wood on the ball. By the time it landed, in the right-field deck about 360 feet away, the 23,154 fans—and Maris—knew there was a brand new home-run record in the books. After his home-run trot, the congratulatory Yankees formed a human wall and would not allow Maris in the dugout. Four times Maris tried to enter the dugout only to be gently pushed onto the field by his teammates. Finally, Maris raised his cap to the jubilant fans and to a moment that would go down in major league history.

Fittingly, Maris's sixty-first homer was the only run of the ball game as New York edged Boston, 1–0. "If I never hit another home run," Maris said later, "this is the one that they can never take away from me."

WHO WAS THE WORST ROOKIE OF THE YEAR?

Don Schwall, Boston Red Sox, 1961. A pitcher who compiled a 15–7 record and 3.22 earned run average, Schwall dropped to a 9–15 level a year later and a 4.94 earned run average. He soon was shipped to the Pittsburgh Pirates.

DID THE FABLED "M & M BOYS," MICKEY MANTLE AND ROGER MARIS, EVER APPEAR TOGETHER ON THE SILVER SCREEN?

Yes. The Yankee sluggers were paired in the 1962 film *Safe at Home,* about a Little Leaguer who runs away to the Yankee spring training camp to ask the outfield stars to appear at a Little League banquet.

HOW MANY MANAGERS DID CHARLES FINLEY EMPLOY BETWEEN THE YEARS 1961 AND 1978?

In eighteen major-league seasons (1961–78), Finley hired a total of thirteen different men as managers. "Charley O" purchased the Kansas City Athletics in December, 1960, and, beginning with Joe Gordon, there followed Hank Bauer, Eddie Lopat, Mel McGaha, Haywood Sullivan, Alvin Dark and Luke Appling. Moving to Oakland in 1968, Finley shortened the team nickname to the A's, but lengthened his list of managers. The first for the American League entry from the Bay Area was Bob Kennedy, then Hank Bauer for a second time, John McNamara, Dick Williams, Alvin Dark again, Chuck Tanner, Jack McKeon, Bobby Winkles, and, once again, Jack McKeon. In May, 1978, Winkles resigned, saying, "I don't want to give Finley the pleasure of firing me."

WHERE DID THE NEW YORK METS PLAY IN 1962 AND 1963 BEFORE SHEA STADIUM WAS OPENED IN 1964?

The old Polo Grounds, formerly inhabited by the New York Giants.

WHO WAS THE NEW YORK METS' FIRST OFFICIAL MASCOT?

Homer, the beagle. The idea of Homer came from Phillip Liebman of Rheingold Beer. Rheingold was a major sponsor of Mets telecasts in 1962.

Homer led a luxurious life. He lived in the Waldorf Towers, was trained by Rudd Weatherway of Lassie fame, and worked game days by occupying a stage set atop four box seats behind home plate at the Polo Grounds. His room and board, including the cost of the seats, was estimated to be $20,000 a year.

WHO WAS THE WINNING PITCHER IN THE FIRST NEW YORK METS WIN?

The Mets had started off their debut season by dropping their first nine contests. Jay Hook recorded the first ever Mets victory on April 23, 1962, a 9–1 nod over Pittsburgh.

WHAT THREE MEN COMPRISED THE NEW YORK METS' ORIGINAL BROADCASTING TEAM?

Bob Murphy, Lindsay Nelson, and Ralph Kiner. Prior to joining the Mets broadcasting team, Murphy gained experience in the booth at Boston and Baltimore. The cheerful Nelson was a college football broadcaster and also worked NBC's *Game of the Week* baseball telecasts. Kiner was the Pittsburgh Pirates' home-run king. They were together for 17 years, the longest of any baseball broadcasting trio.

Ralph Kiner (shown here as Pittsburgh Pirate) was a member of the original New York Mets broadcasting trio. *(from the collection of Barry Halper)*

241

WHO RAN THE BASES BACKWARD AFTER HITTING HIS 100TH CAREER HOME RUN?

Jimmy Piersall rounded the bases in proper order, but did so running backward. Piersall's 100th homer came as a New York Met against Philadelphia right-hander Dallas Green in July of 1963. Soon after, he was released by manager Casey Stengel, who said, "There is room for only one clown on this team."

WHICH NEW YORK METS PINCH HITTER COMPLETED PHILADELPHIA PHILLIES PITCHER JIM BUNNING'S PERFECT GAME?

John Stephenson. It happened on June 21, 1964, before a Father's Day throng at New York's Shea Stadium. Bunning, then a crafty thirty-two-year-old veteran who had previously hurled a no-hitter while pitching for the Detroit Tigers, completed his masterpiece by striking out the bewildered Stephenson on three pitches.

WHICH FORMER LOS ANGELES DODGER PITCHER APPEARED IN SUCH TELEVISION SHOWS AS *THE LAWMAN* AND *THE BRADY BUNCH?*

Don Drysdale.

ANOTHER DODGER ALSO APPEARED IN *THE BRADY BUNCH* TELEVISION SERIES. WHO WAS THE PLAYER?

Wes Parker, a Dodger first baseman and outfielder from 1964 through 1972.

WHICH NATIONAL LEAGUE CATCHER THREW A "BEAN BALL" IN 1965, THEREBY PRECIPITATING ONE OF BASEBALL'S BIGGEST AND MOST NOTORIOUS BRAWLS?

Catcher John Roseboro of the Los Angeles Dodgers. It happened in 1965 in a game against San Francisco in which Juan Marichal, a native of the Dominican Republic and ranked among the best pitchers in the majors, was throwing for the Giants. The two teams were archrivals in a bid for the pennant. In the fourth game of the series, Marichal hurled a viciously hard fastball at the head of Los Angeles star Maury Wills. Wills ducked in time, but the Dodgers vowed revenge. The first Dodger pitch to Marichal sailed wide. Catcher John Roseboro caught the ball and returned the horsehide to the mound. However, the ball met an obstacle enroute—Marichal's ear! The brawl was on. Armed with his bat, Marichal made for Roseboro. He hit the catcher at least three times and received an eight-day suspension and $1,750 fine. As for Roseboro, his "bean ball" was considerably less expensive, apart from the bruises he suffered.

Juan Marichal, native of the Dominican Republic, ranked among the best pitchers in the majors. *(from the collection of Barry Halper)*

WILLIE McCOVEY'S BIGGEST AT BAT OF HIS CAREER CAME IN THE SEVENTH GAME OF THE 1962 WORLD SERIES AGAINST THE YANKEES WITH TWO OUT IN THE BOTTOM OF THE NINTH AND TWO ON IN A 1–0 GAME. WHAT HAPPENED?

With the Giants down to their last out, and the winning run at second, McCovey made the loudest final out of any World Series by crushing a line drive that was stabbed by a leaping Yankee second baseman, Bobby Richardson. One foot either way and the Giants would have been champs.

WHO HIT THE FIRST HOME RUN EVER IN THE ASTRODOME?

In an exhibition game between the New York Yankees and the Houston Astros on April 9, 1965, Mickey Mantle cracked the first homer in the major league's first domed stadium in a 2-1 Yankee loss in 12 innings.

WHICH TWO MAJOR LEAGUERS HAVE THE UNIQUE DISTINCTION OF HAVING PLAYED EACH OF THE NINE FIELD POSITIONS IN A SINGLE BIG-LEAGUE GAME?

Bert Campaneris did it first on September 8, 1965, when his team, the Kansas City A's, announced that he would. Campaneris played one inning at each position, including the eighth inning as pitcher. And in his one-inning stint on the mound he permitted just one run.

Cesar Tovar equaled Campaneris's feat three years later, on September 22, 1968, as a Minnesota Twin. Tovar pitched a scoreless first inning and his first successful out was the lead-off batter, Bert Campaneris.

WHAT BIG-LEAGUE PITCHER FROM THE LATE 1960's TO 1980 WAS ACTUALLY SIGNED AS A $100,000 BONUS BABY INFIELDER?

Skip Lockwood was a third baseman in 1965 with Kansas City, but he was converted to a pitcher in 1967, and to a reliever in 1974.

HAS ANY TEAM EVER USED AN INFIELD WHERE ALL FOUR MEMBERS WERE SWITCH HITTERS?

Yes. During the 1965 World Series against the Minnesota Twins, the Los Angeles Dodgers used Wes Parker, Jim Lefebvre, Maury Wills, and Jim Gilliam, all switch hitters, in the same game.

WHAT DO RICK MONDAY, SAL BANDO, DUFFY DYER, LENNY RANDLE, CRAIG SWAN, KEN LANDREAUX, JIM PALMER, GARY GENTRY, BOB HORNER, ALAN BANNISTER, FLOYD BANNISTER, AND REGGIE JACKSON HAVE IN COMMON?

They all played baseball at Arizona State University.

WHAT WAS REGGIE JACKSON'S MAJOR AT ARIZONA STATE?

Mr. October majored in Biology.

REGGIE JACKSON ORIGINALLY WENT TO ARIZONA STATE UNIVERSITY IN 1964 ON A FOOTBALL SCHOLARSHIP WITH ASPIRATIONS OF BECOMING A PROFESSIONAL FOOTBALL PLAYER. WHAT EVENT INSPIRED REGGIE TO GIVE UP FOOTBALL AND CONCENTRATE ON A BASEBALL CAREER?

Football coach Frank Kush moved Jackson from tight end to the starting cornerback position early in fall practice of 1965.

"I liked football. I liked contact," Reggie said. "But I realized when I was switched, football wasn't for me. I wanted the offense, the glamour position. I was a glamour guy. I didn't want defense."

By the following Arizona State baseball season in 1966, Jackson was well prepared.

"Rick Monday had set all the home-run and strikeout records here in 1965," recalled Dick Mullins, the University's sports information director. "Reggie broke them all in 1966."

THE KANSAS CITY A's CHOSE REGGIE JACKSON SECOND OVERALL IN THE 1966 FREE-AGENT DRAFT. WHICH TEAM CHOSE AHEAD OF THE A's AND WHOM DID THEY SELECT?

The New York Mets picked an eighteen-year-old high school catcher named Steve Chilcott. Chilcott developed shoulder problems and never played in the major leagues. Then the A's picked, and club owner Charles O. Finley smiled as he walked to the microphone. "I take Reggie Jackson," he said.

THE NEW YORK METS RECEIVED THE RIGHTS TO TOM SEAVER BY HAVING THEIR NAME SELECTED OUT OF A HAT. WHAT HAPPENED?

Seaver was originally signed by the Atlanta Braves after the twenty-one-year-old's last season at the University of Southern California had ended. The Braves awarded the native Californian a $50,000 bonus. However, it was determined that the Braves' signing of Seaver was in violation of a college rule. Commissioner William Eckert nullified the contract and declared Seaver a free agent. Under the commissioner's ruling, any club was free to deal with the young pitcher, just as long as they agreed to match the Braves' guaranteed bonus. Only three teams showed interest and a method to settle the matter was needed. On April 3, 1966, Commissioner Eckert wrote the names of the three teams on slips of paper and dropped them into a hat. Eckert closed his eyes and picked one out. The slip read "Mets." The Mets signed Seaver the following day.

IN THE 1960's AND 1970's, WHO WAS THE MAJOR LEAGUES' BEST PITCHER WITH THE MAJOR LEAGUES' WEAKEST TEAM?

Tom Seaver, New York Mets. A mediocre pitcher can win a spate of games if his team scores enough runs for him. But a superior pitcher is one who wins despite inferior hitting and fielding behind him. Tom Seaver suffered such a fate through many seasons with the Mets. Yet, by the start of the 1977 season, Seaver had amassed 182 wins and 107 losses.

From 1967, when Seaver first broke in with the Mets and won the National League's Rookie-Of-The-Year award, to the beginning of 1977, the Mets had not quite won 50 percent of their games. However, in that span, Seaver won nearly 65 percent of his decisions.

Tom Seaver may well have been the best pitcher with the weakest team of its day in the history of major-league baseball. *(from the collection of Barry Halper)*

WHO DROVE IN 90 OR MORE RUNS IN 11 CONSECUTIVE SEASONS?

Cincinnati first baseman Tony Perez was one of the most consistent RBI men of all time, driving in at least 90 in 12 of his 23 seasons. He did that eleven straight years as well, from 1967 to 1977, playing with the Montreal Expos the last season of the eleven.

NAME THE NATIONAL AND AMERICAN LEAGUE PITCHERS WHO HAD THREE WORLD SERIES WINS IN THE 1967 AND 1968 CLASSICS RESPECTIVELY?

Bob Gibson of the St. Louis Cardinals overwhelmed Boston's Red Sox in the 1967 World Series. The fireballing right-hander earned three complete game victories while striking out 26 Boston batters to give St. Louis the championship in seven games. In 1968, the Detroit Tigers' Mickey Lolich turned the same trick—against the Cardinals. The crafty left-hander earned his third win of the Series and a championship for Detroit by beating none other than Bob Gibson in the seventh game, 4–1.

Bob Gibson earned three complete game victories in the 1967 World Series, helping his Cards defeat the BoSox in seven games. *(from the colllection of Barry Halper)*

WHO HOLDS THE RECORD FOR MOST WORLD SERIES GAMES PLAYED?

Yogi Berra played in 75 World Series games for the Yankees. In fourteen World Series, he hit .274 with 12 homers and 39 RBI's.

WHICH PITCHER STRUCK OUT (IN THE FOLLOWING ORDER): WILLIE MAYS, WILLIE McCOVEY, BROOKS ROBINSON, ROBERTO CLEMENTE, MAURY WILLS, AND HARMON KILLEBREW?

No, it wasn't Carl Hubbell or Tom Seaver. It was Eddie Feigner (pronounced "Fayner"). Feigner was the "King" of "The King & His Court," a four-man softball team that had been barnstorming the world since 1946—hardly ever losing a game or even allowing as much as a squibble single up the middle because of Feigner's strikeout proclivities.

Feigner mixed his large assortment of windups, speeds, and different pitches, for just the right combinations to strike out those famous major-leaguers.

WHO HOLDS THE RECORDS FOR CATCHERS IN RESPECT TO MOST CHANCES WITHOUT ERROR, MOST CONSECUTIVE GAMES WITHOUT ERROR, AND MOST PUT-OUTS?

Yogi Berra of the New York Yankees had 950 consecutive chances without an error, 148 consecutive games without an error, and 8,696 career put-outs as a catcher.

BILLY MARTIN'S FIRST MAJOR-LEAGUE MANAGERIAL JOB CAME IN 1969 WITH THE MINNESOTA TWINS. WHICH OFFER HAD MARTIN TURNED DOWN IN 1967?

Charles Finley's offer to manage the Kansas City Athletics.

DENNY McLAIN WAS THE LAST PITCHER IN THE MAJORS TO WIN 30 GAMES, WINNING 31 IN 1968 WITH DETROIT. WHO WAS THE MAJORS' LAST 30-GAME WINNER BEFORE McLAIN?

Dizzy Dean won 30 for the Cardinals in 1934.

Denny McLain was the last major-league pitcher to win 30 games in one season. *(from the collection of Barry Halper)*

WHO WAS THE WORST STRIKEOUT BATTER?

Bobby Bonds, 1970. Although Babe Ruth, Duke Snider, and Mickey Mantle struck out with a flourish, nobody could match the frequency of Bonds during the 1970 season when he batted .302 for the San Francisco Giants. Despite his 26 home runs and 78 runs batted in, Bonds struck out 189 times.

WHO PLAYED FOR EIGHT MAJOR-LEAGUE TEAMS IN A CAREER THAT BEGAN IN 1968?

Bobby Bonds played for eight teams in 14 years, from 1968–1981. Bonds started his career with the San Francisco Giants in 1968. He went to the New York Yankees on October 22, 1974, in exchange for Bobby Murcer. After hitting .270 for the Yankees in 1975, Bonds was traded to the California Angels on December 11, 1975, for Mickey Rivers and Ed Figueroa. Bonds played two seasons with the Angels and hit .265 and .264.

Again, Bonds found himself traded, on December 5, 1977. This time he was sent, along with Thad Bosley and Rich Dotson, to the Chicago White Sox, for Brian Downing, Chris Knapp, and Dave Frost. Bonds would only play 26 games with the White Sox in 1978. He was traded in mid-season on May 16, 1978, to the Texas Rangers for Claudell Washington and Rusty Torres. Would longevity finally be in store for the nomadic Bonds in Texas? No.

After the 1978 campaign, Bobby had yet another new city to adjust to. This time Bonds was sent to Cleveland with Len Barker in exchange for Jim Kern and Larvell Blanks. Bonds hit .275 with 25 HR's and 85 RBI's with the Indians in 1979. However the Indians traded Bonds in December of 1979 to St. Louis for John Denny and Jerry Mumphrey. Of course Bonds played one season in St. Louis before he was sent to the Chicago Cubs on June 4, 1981, for cash.

In total, Bonds was traded seven times, for a total of twelve players. From December, 1977, through June, 1981, Bonds was traded five times—that equals five trades in only three years and six months.

Bonds played in 1,849 games, posted a career batting average of .268, and slugged 332 home runs.

WHAT WAS THE WORST PERFORMANCE BY A BATTER WINNING THE BATTING CHAMPIONSHIP?

Carl Yastrzemski, Boston Red Sox, 1968. When the Red Sox won the American League pennant in 1967, Yastrzemski batted .326 and led the league in home runs with 44 and in RBI's with 121. A year after winning the "Triple Crown," Carl repeated as the American League's best hitter. However, in that "year of the pitcher," his league-leading batting average was only .301.

Carl "Yaz" Yastrzemski, hitting phenom for many years with the Boston Red Sox. *(from the collection of Barry Halper)*

WHAT PLAYER HOLDS THE MAJOR-LEAGUE RECORD FOR MOST CAREER SAVES?

Rollie Fingers collected 341 saves in his seventeen-year career, which spanned the years 1968 to 1985. Fingers played in Oakland, San Diego, and Milwaukee.

WHICH ST. LOUIS CARDINAL BOUNCED INTO A GAME-ENDING DOUBLE PLAY AND ENABLED THE 1969 METS TO CLINCH FIRST PLACE IN THE EASTERN DIVISION OF THE NATIONAL LEAGUE?

Ironically, it was a man who would later manage the Mets, Joe Torre. On September 24, 1969, Torre bounced into a double play that gave the Mets a 6–0 victory and their first-ever championship. The victory also meant overtime for the Shea Stadium ground crew when many of the 54,928 fans spilled onto the field shouting, "We're Number One!" They ultimately dug up home plate, ran off with the bases, and ripped up chunks of the outfield grass for souvenirs.

WHO HOLDS THE MAJOR-LEAGUE RECORD FOR INTENTIONAL WALKS IN A SEASON AND MOST SEASONS WITH 20 OR MORE INTENTIONAL WALKS?

In 1969 Willie McCovey received 45 intentional passes. He had five seasons of 20 or more intentional walks, leading the National League four times.

WHICH EXPANSION TEAM MOVED AFTER JUST ONE SEASON?

The Seattle Pilots, who played one season in the great Northwest, packed up in 1969 and moved to Milwaukee where they became known as the Brewers.

The failure of the Pilots could mostly be blamed on poor ownership and an old, run-down stadium. Dewey Sariano, a former ship pilot with the Coast Guard and their minority owner, was responsible for naming the Pilots. Majority owner William Daley spent the majority of the season attempting to sell the franchise and very little time on the team's performance on the field.

The Pilots played their home games in Sicks Stadium, a rickety structure holding only 28,000 spectators. That, combined with the American League's highest-priced tickets and a last place team, brought only 677,944 fans to see the Pilots.

After their disastrous first season, the American League gave the City of Seattle until November 9 to meet three conditions: one, expand Sicks Stadium by 25 percent; two, complete groundbreaking on the proposed multimillion-dollar domed stadium; and three, come up with enough local money to purchase the Pilots from Daley. None of these conditions was met and the team left for Milwaukee.

The City of Seattle had to wait eight years until it had its next taste of baseball, when the American League expanded once again in 1977. This time there was stable ownership and the domed stadium originally meant for the Pilots, the Kingdome.

WHAT WAS THE BEST STRIKEOUT PERFORMANCE IN A LOSING EFFORT?

Steve Carlton, St. Louis Cardinals vs. New York Mets, September, 1969, Busch Stadium. Carlton's problem was that he was facing "the Amazin' Mets" during the year when they surmounted a nine-and-one-half game deficit in late August to win the National League's East Division crown by eight games. "It was the best stuff I ever had," said Carlton of his effort that night, and the records substantiate his claim. He struck out 19 batters, a record, yet the Mets won the game, 4–3, on two home runs by Ron Swoboda. Carlton struck out the side in four out of nine innings and struck out the side in the ninth to set the record. However, Carlton himself allowed that his performance was flawed: "When I had nine strikeouts, I decided to go all the way. But it cost me the game because I started to challenge every batter." It was a two-strike pitch that Swoboda hit for his first home run in the fourth inning, and a 2–2 pitch that Swoboda pulled into the seats in the eighth, giving the Mets a 4–3 lead.

Steve Carlton once struck out 19 batters, a record, yet lost the game to the Amazin' Mets in 1969. *(from the collection of Barry Halper)*

WHICH OFF-BROADWAY PLAY WAS BASED ON THE ANTICS OF REAL-LIFE BASEBALL FANS?

"Bleacher Bums." The show portrayed a group of zealous Chicago rooters noted for their boisterous support of the beloved Cubs during the 1969 season.

The bleachers in Wrigley Field had been renowned as the private solarium for class cutters, meditating hippies, and elderly pensioners. But suddenly, in 1969, the Cubs began winning and these bleacher regulars soon were sitting side by side with a group of rough young men who were noted for their yellow construction helmets and their habit of hurling many different heavy objects at visiting players. The Cubs' management took no action to calm them down and the Chicago players encouraged them.

Dick Selma, a Cubs reliever, surfaced as a cheerleader and, in his free moments in the bull pen, would direct the Bums' cheering section. When the Cubs won a home game, Ron Santo, the third baseman, played to the fans by kicking his heels together as he cavorted toward the clubhouse in the left-field corner. The Bums were crazy about Santo's act and probably would have torn down the park had he ever failed to perform. By contrast, visiting teams were furious with the Bums. Pete Rose was vilified with uncomplimentary names; Lou Brock was showered with white mice; and "Mudcat" Grant's handsome face was the target of a flying transistor radio battery. One afternoon, Tommie Agee of the Mets was told by the Bums that his wife was working the streets. "Shows how stupid they are," teammate Ron Swoboda muttered. "Tommie isn't even married!"

The play was first staged by the Chicago-based Organic Theater, and was presented in nine "innings" rather than the usual two or three acts. "It's a play about people, not about a baseball game," said Stuart Gordon, founder and director of the theater company. "Our feeling was that the real stars of the Cubs were the fans. The players change, but the fans stay. Why do all these people come every year? What's it all about? What this is about is hope."

ASTROTURF AND ALL

(1970–1990)

Baseball, like other sports, arts, and entertainment, reflects what's happening in our country—in our culture, if you will. With the wild events of the late 1960's, it was inevitable that the hippy-yippy-activism would sooner or later seep into the sport. And it did.

One relatively harmless manifestation of the "counterculture" mentality that arrived was in style, and the Oakland A's personified this "new" look. The A's won three straight World Series, in 1972, 1973, and 1974, with a teamful of talent—and a team that also sported the longest sideburns and handlebar mustaches since the last century.

That was the irony of it. Here they were, the most "modern" team around in terms of performance, and yet their sideburns-mustache look became perfectly nineteenth century as soon as they donned their baseball uniforms. To complete the picture the A's had redesigned their uniforms into the style worn in baseball's infancy. It seemed silly, but people got a big kick out of it.

That may have been the least disturbing sign of baseball's moving into the difficult modern era. Baseball moved indoors in several places and because real grass could no longer bask in the filtered sunlight of these covered arenas, Astroturf—artificial turf—became the playing surface. But grass wasn't the only thing that became artificial in baseball.

The last twenty baseball seasons have seen the arrival of drug and alcohol problems (or at least the *admission* of these problems), gambling, sex, violence, overinflated salaries, free agency, designated hitters, player strikes, and other such thorny dilemmas. Some say baseball has become a circus; others lament that the game is being destroyed—sometimes simultaneously—by the owners, the players, free agency, the officials, television . . . you name it.

In fact, as the French say: "The more things change, the more things stay the same." Baseball has survived everything from the Black Sox scandal through the Pete Rose "scandal," and I have every expectation that it will be thriving on controversy and scandal a century from now. But it will also thrive on good pitching, fielding, and hitting. Whatever happens, it's still *The Game.*

WHY DID THE HOUSTON ASTROS INSTALL ARTIFICIAL TURF AT THE ASTRODOME?

It wasn't planned that way. Originally, grass grew under the Texas dome, bathed in brilliant sunlight. However, when outfielders began complaining about the glare, the dome was painted opaque. Unfortunately, the grass then stopped growing. The only alternative was the installation of artificial turf, which had just been developed by the Monsanto Corporation. Thus emerged "Astroturf," the "grass" that revolutionized baseball!

NAME THE PITCHER WHO SMACKED A GRAND SLAM IN THE 1970 WORLD SERIES?

Dave McNally's grand slam and complete game victory fueled the Baltimore Orioles to a 9–3 win over the Cincinnati Reds in Game Three of the 1970 World Series. The Orioles went on to win the Series, 4–1. The next grand slam in World Series action occurred in 1987. Dan Gladden, of the Minnesota Twins, slugged that one in a 10–1, Game-One victory over the St. Louis Cardinals. Minnesota won the 1987 World Series, 4–3.

WHAT WAS THE NAME CHARLES O. FINLEY TRIED TO GET VIDA BLUE TO LEGALLY CHANGE TO?

Finley wanted Vida to change his first name to "True." Finley said, "It will be more colorful (no pun intended), and you'll get famous faster."

Blue graciously declined, saying he appreciated Finley's suggestion but explaining, "I like my name. It was my father's before it was mine."

Vida Blue began his major-league career by resisting Oakland-owner Charles Finley's demand that he change his name. *(from the collection of Barry Halper)*

WHO SAID THIS: "EVER SINCE I WAS A KID I WANTED TO BE A SPORTS STAR, A FOOTBALL HERO, A BASEBALL HERO. THAT'S ALL I WANTED: THAT'S ALL I'D DREAMED OF. THEN IT HAPPENED. IT WASN'T LIKE I EXPECTED. THEY CHEW YOU UP AND SPIT YOU OUT. PEOPLE USE YOU FOR YOUR RECORDS, YOUR WINS, YOUR NUMBERS. YOU ARE NOTHING BUT A DAMN WON-LOST RECORD. THAT'S ALL YOU ARE"?

Vida Blue.

THE 1971 ALL-STAR GAME, PLAYED IN DETROIT, MARKED THE FIRST TIME THAT THERE WERE TWO BLACK STARTING PITCHERS IN THE MIDSUMMER CLASSIC. WHO WERE THE RECORD-SETTING PAIR?

The Oakland A's Vida Blue and Pittsburgh Pirate ace Dock Ellis started the game, with the American League winning, 6–4. The story of the game, however, was not the pitchers, but Reggie Jackson. Invited to the game by American League manager Earl Weaver as a replacement for injured Minnesota Twin star Tony Oliva, Jackson entered the game as a pinch hitter in the third inning. The American League was down 3–2 with Luis Aparicio on first and two out when Jackson walloped an Ellis fastball. The ball soared and soared until it finally crashed into an electronic transformer at the top of Tiger Stadium high above the right-center-field stands. The spot where the ball hit measured nearly 600 feet from the initial point of contact. Many believe Jackson's shot to be the longest ever hit in a big-league game.

WHICH BIG-LEAGUE PITCHER PLAYED FOR TEN DIFFERENT CLUBS AND FOURTEEN DIFFERENT PITCHING COACHES, THEN WENT ON TO BECOME A PITCHING COACH HIMSELF?

Bob Miller, who pitched in the major leagues for 17 years was, for a time, pitching coach of the Toronto Blue Jays and certainly had to be qualified to know quite a bit about the art of hurling.

In those 17 years, Miller pitched for ten ball clubs, two of them twice. The list reads like a travel agent's dream: the St. Louis Cardinals, the New York Mets (in 1962 and again in 1974), the Los Angeles Dodgers, the Minnesota Twins, the Cleveland Indians, Chicago's Cubs and White Sox (in the same season), the San Diego Padres (the other two-time stop), the Pittsburgh Pirates, and the Detroit Tigers. Miller even played with three teams each in three different seasons (the 1970, 1971, and 1973 seasons).

This meant that when Miller coached the young Toronto hurlers, he was giving them the combined experience and know-how of 15 pitching coaches: himself, Al Hollingsworth, Howie Pollet, Red Ruffing, Joe Becker, Lefty Phillips, Early Wynn, Art Fowler, Cot Deal, Les Moss, Roger Craig, Mel Wright, Johnny Podres, and Rube Walker—all of whom had tutored Miller!

WHO WERE BASEBALL'S FIRST TWO FREE AGENTS?
Pitchers Andy Messersmith and Dave McNally.

WHAT DO MAJOR-LEAGUER PETE LaCOCK AND ACTOR PETER MARSHALL HAVE IN COMMON?
Ralph Pierre "Pete" LaCock, a former first-baseman-outfielder for the Kansas City Royals, is the son of Peter Marshall, who hosted the popular TV game show, *Hollywood Squares.* Pete LaCock began his major-league career with the Chicago Cubs in 1972, was traded to the Royals after the 1976 season, and retired from baseball in 1980.

FOUR MEMBERS OF THE LOS ANGELES DODGERS HAD BIT PARTS IN THE CLASSIC MOVIE, *GODFATHER II.* WHO WERE THE MOVIE-STARS-FOR-A-MOMENT?
Tommy Lasorda, Tom Paciorek, Steve Yeager, and Bill Buckner all appeared with Al Pacino in *Godfather II.*

WHOM AND WHAT DO DICK ALLEN, REGGIE JACKSON, MIKE SCHMIDT, AND NELSON LIRIANO ALL HAVE IN COMMON?
Each one has broken up a Nolan Ryan no-hitter with one out in the ninth inning.

IN THE EARLY 1970's THE OAKLAND A's WERE CALLED "THE MUSTACHE GANG." WHY WAS THIS CURIOUS MONIKER APPLIED?
A's owner Charles O. Finley came up with an idea that would separate his club's image from the rest of baseball. Finley sponsored a "Mustache Day" promotion at Oakland. Cash prizes would be awarded to fans who grew the best mustaches and beards. Finley also told his players he would pay them $100 if they grew mustaches and beards. Until 1972, baseball players generally had to

remain clean-shaven. That all changed thanks to Finley. Almost the entire Oakland team—those who were able—grew mustaches and beards. Reggie Jackson grew a beard, while Rollie Fingers grew the finest handlebar mustache seen on a baseball diamond since the turn of the century. Even conservative manager Dick Williams grew one.

"The world had changed, and baseball had changed with it," Williams said afterward. "If I could identify with my players with a mustache, why not?"

Finley expected the players to shave after the promotion. Most of them did not, not even manager Williams.

WHAT PITCHER ONCE LED THE NATIONAL LEAGUE IN FIVE PITCHING CATEGORIES WHILE HURLING FOR A LAST-PLACE CLUB?

Steve Carlton led the league in wins (27), ERA (1.97), strikeouts (310), and innings pitched (346), even though the Philadelphia Phillies finished the 1972 campaign at 59–97, 37½ games behind the first-place Pittsburgh Pirates.

Lefty's best season earned him his first Cy Young Award at the age of 27. He would go on to win it three more times, in 1977, 1980, and 1982—the only pitcher to win the prestigious award four times in his career!

WHAT UNIFORM NUMBER DID WILLIE MAYS WEAR WHEN HE JOINED THE NEW YORK METS IN 1972?

His old 24. Thanks to the graciousness of Jim Beauchamp (who gave up the number), Willie wore the same number that he made famous during his 21 seasons with the New York and San Francisco Giants.

THE NEW YORK METS' DEBUT OF WILLIE MAYS SEEMED TO BE PERFECT FOR A SCRIPT OF A HAPPY ENDING HOLLYWOOD MOVIE. WHAT HAPPENED?

Mays's first series as a Met in 1972 was at Shea Stadium, New York, ironically against the San Francisco Giants. Many assumed there was an unwritten agreement that Willie would not see action against his former team, but the fans wanted to see Willie play, regardless. They chanted "We want Willie" throughout Friday night's opening game of the weekend series. Mets manager Yogi Berra said he wanted to use Mays against left-handed pitchers only, and when Berra opted to use young John Milner as a pinch hitter on Friday, the Shea fans booed the rookie for no reason except that he wasn't Willie Mays. Still, Milner walked and the Mets won, 2–1.

Mays again remained on the bench the following day as the Mets won again, 1–0, but on Sunday, San Francisco manager Charlie Fox gave the starting assignment to Sam McDowell, a lefthander. To the delight of many, Berra made Mays his lead-off batter for the game.

It was a chilly Mother's Day plagued by drizzling rain. In his first at bat, Willie drew a walk and scored on Rusty Staub's grand slam. Next, he struck out in the third. By his next turn up, in the fifth inning, the Giants had rallied back to tie the game at 4–4. It was then that Mays demonstrated with living proof that, at age 41, he had not lost his uncanny ability to create drama.

With a full count worked by righty reliever Don Carrithers, Mays ripped the ball over the left-field fence and into the visitors' bull pen. It was his first home run as a Met, and the 647th of his incredible career. The fans stood and cheered Willie for several minutes, as did his new teammates.

The home run was the difference as New York swept San Francisco, 5–4.

"It was super," Staub said afterward of Mays's heroics. "I was ecstatic over my own home run, but I can't tell you how I felt when Willie hit his."

"I had feelings for both sides," Willie said. "I wanted to help the Mets, but at the same time, I had certain feelings for the Giants. I didn't think I would do anything to win a ball game. I thought I would be so nervous I wouldn't hit the ball at all."

Eddie Yost, the Mets' third-base coach, summed it up the best: "You couldn't have written a better script."

WHO IS THE ONLY PLAYER TO HIT TWO HOME RUNS IN HIS FIRST TWO WORLD SERIES AT BATS?

Gene Tenace did it for the Oakland A's in 1972 in the second and fifth innings.

WHO HIT TWO HOME RUNS IN AN INNING TWICE?
Willie McCovey, on April 12, 1973, and June 27, 1977.

WHO WAS THE FIRST DESIGNATED HITTER IN MAJOR-LEAGUE HISTORY?
Ron Blomberg of the New York Yankees went 1-for-3 on April 6, 1973, in Fenway Park. He drove in a run and scored a run in the Yankees' 15–5 loss to the Boston Red Sox.

WHICH TEAM POSSESSED THE MOST DURABLE INFIELD IN BASEBALL HISTORY?
The Los Angeles Dodgers had four infielders who stayed together from 1973 to 1981: Steve Garvey at first, Davey Lopes at second, Bill Russell at short, and Ron Cey at third.

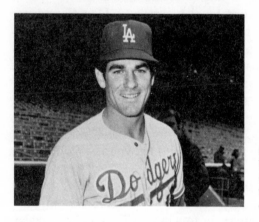

Steve Garvey was a member of baseball's most durable infield (the Los Angeles Dodgers) from 1973 to 1981. *(from the collection of Barry Halper)*

WHAT PLAYER MADE THE BEST INDIVIDUAL COMEBACK?
John Hiller, Detroit Tigers, 1973. A relief pitcher, Hiller won 10 games and saved 38 for the Tigers as the top reliever for the Detroit club. To accomplish this, Hiller first had to overcome the after-effects of a heart attack.

On the advice of physicians, Hiller missed the entire 1971 season following the attack. After recuperation, Hiller obtained his doctor's permission to work out during the Tigers' batting practice. The medical sabbatical had no apparent effect on Hiller's ability to throw a strike, so manager Billy Martin restored him to the active roster in 1972. The rejuvenated pitcher responded with a 2.05 earned run average, the best of his career to that point. A year later he pitched well enough to become the ace of the Tigers' bull-pen corps.

THE INFAMOUS PETE ROSE-BUD HARRELSON BATTLE IN THE THIRD GAME OF THE 1973 NATIONAL LEAGUE CHAMPIONSHIP SERIES SO ANGERED THE SHEA STADIUM CROWD THAT IT ALMOST CAUSED A FORFEIT FOR THE HOME TEAM. WHAT HAPPENED?

The Mets were on their way to taking a 2–1 lead in the best-of-five series with a 9–2 lead in the fifth inning of Game Three when mayhem erupted. Rose was running from first base when John Milner fielded Joe Morgan's ground ball and threw to Harrelson at second. Harrelson's quick throw to first was in time for the double play, which ended the inning, but Harrelson and Rose began to argue after Rose barreled into Harrelson, hard. Soon their words led to actions and in an instant, the 200-pound Rose was on top of the 150-pound Harrelson. Players charged from both benches and bull pens. Mets third baseman Wayne Garrett jumped Rose and some other players tried to settle the riot, but another one erupted when Reds reliever Pedro Borbon went out of control and began taking wild swings at anyone wearing a Mets uniform. Though order was eventually restored, it would be only temporary.

The hostility of the Mets fans against Rose, who had gotten much the better of Harrelson, had not dissipated. When Rose took his position in left field in the bottom of the fifth inning, he was bombarded with bottles and other debris and soon another debacle was under way. The bombardment from the left-field stands continued with such intensity that Cincinnati manager Sparky Anderson pulled his team off the field. The angry fans were warned over the public address system that the Mets might have to forfeit if the rooters continued their obscene behavior, but the appeal had little effect.

Finally, National League President Chub Feeney came up with a solution. He asked Yogi Berra, the Mets manager, and Willie Mays to go out to left field and plead with the fans to stop. They were joined by Tom Seaver, Cleon Jones, and Rusty Staub. The plan worked. The Reds were able to safely take the field and the two teams played out the Mets' 9–2 victory.

WHAT WAS THE WORST TEAM TO WIN A PENNANT?

New York Mets, 1973. When the National and American leagues each agreed to split into two divisions for the 1969 season, purists argued that a team with a .500 record could conceivably win a pennant, especially in view of the best-of-five series that would decide the divisional championships. In 1973 the Cincinnati Reds had little trouble winning the Western Division championship in the National League with a record of 99 wins and 63 losses. But the Eastern Division race was extraordinarily close. The New York Mets and St. Louis Cardinals matched each other's record through the final day of the regular season.

However, due to earlier rainouts, the Mets were required to play a doubleheader with the Chicago Cubs on the day following the end of the regular schedule because the two games had originally been postponed earlier in the schedule. If the Mets could win one of the two games, they would win the championship. If they lost both ends of the doubleheader, they would have to hold a playoff with St. Louis.

On a gloomy, drizzly day in Chicago, the Mets won the first game of the doubleheader—the second game became irrelevant and was cancelled—and entered the championship series with a conspicuously mediocre record of 82 wins and 79 losses. Militantly unimpressed with the favored Reds, the Mets conquered Cincinnati on the arms of pitchers Tom Seaver and Jon Matlack. Carrying their extraordinary luck to the World Series, the Mets took the Oakland Athletics to seven games before losing the final match. Never in baseball history has a team with so little gone so far.

WHAT PITCHER APPEARED IN A RECORD SEVEN GAMES IN THE 1973 WORLD SERIES?

Darold Knowles, Oakland Athletics.

WHAT MAJOR-LEAGUER DID NOT EVEN PLAY BASEBALL IN HIGH SCHOOL OR COLLEGE, BUT STILL SOMEHOW MANAGED TO WIN THE AMERICAN LEAGUE ROOKIE OF THE YEAR AWARD?

Mike Hargrove was a twenty-four-year-old rookie in the 1974 Texas Rangers training camp. Hargrove, with little previous baseball experience, impressed manager Billy Martin enough to win a spot on the roster. He then impressed the baseball world enough to win Rookie of the Year honors.

HOW DID SLUGGER REGGIE JACKSON DESCRIBE HITTING?

"Hitting is concentration. Free your mind of everything. Study the flight of the baseball. Do not think of fine summer nights or fine wine or beautiful women. Think of seeing that white baseball, that spinning sphere, those seams turning over and over again as it gets closer to you. See it from the pitcher's hand to the contact of the bat. See it, see it, see it."

Reggie Jackson (here as a California Angel) once said, "Hitting is concentration." *(from the collection of Barry Halper)*

265

WHAT PITCHER WAS ONCE ELECTRONICALLY CLOCKED AT A SPEED OF 100.9 MPH?

Nolan Ryan threw the ball at that speed in Anaheim Stadium as a member of the California Angels on August 20, 1974.

WHO WAS THE ONLY PLAYER IN BASEBALL HISTORY TO WIN THE ROOKIE OF THE YEAR AND MOST VALUABLE PLAYER AWARDS IN THE SAME SEASON?

Fred Lynn became the first player to win both awards with his phenomenal 1975 season. That year, Lynn batted .331, hit 21 home runs, and boasted 105 RBI's. Lynn also lead the league with 103 runs.

THE FINALE OF GAME SIX OF THE 1975 WORLD SERIES BETWEEN BOSTON AND CINCINNATI PROVIDED ONE OF THE GREATEST MOMENTS IN BOSTON'S BASEBALL HISTORY. TRAILING 6–3 WITH TWO OUTS IN THE EIGHTH INNING, AND JUST FOUR OUTS FROM ELIMINATION, THE RED SOX RALLIED. WHAT HAPPENED?

Pinch hitter Bernie Carbo stepped to the plate with two men on base and two outs. The streaky-hitting reserve outfielder took one strike and then swung late and missed wildly on the second strike—a fastball. The umpire had already called the pitch a ball, before Carbo swung at it.

However, one pitch later, Carbo more than redeemed himself. He rebounded with the most important home run of all the 96 he garnered in his twelve-year major-league career.

"I knew I hit the ball good," Carbo said. "I ran to first, looked up, and saw the center-fielder's back and knew the ball was gone. I was happy, so happy. I thought I might have missed first base, but I was just jumping around too much to worry about it."

Suddenly, miraculously, the score was 6–6 and Fenway Park was beyond ecstasy.

When Carbo came to bat again in the eleventh, Reds catcher

Johnny Bench mumbled to Carbo, "I don't believe it. I just don't believe it."

"I don't believe it either," Carbo said.

An inning later, the game would reach its thrilling climax. In the bottom of the twelfth, Carlton Fisk led off against Cincinnati pitcher Pat Darcy. The Boston catcher smashed a high, arcing shot down the left-field line, which threatened to sail foul. As he proceeded to first base, Fisk, waving both arms, exhorted his fly ball to stay fair. When the ball bounced off the foul pole, Fisk, his teammates, and 32,205 fans went crazy. The Red Sox won, 7–6, to force a seventh game.

Cincinnati won Game Seven the next day, 4–3, on Joe Morgan's bloop single with two outs in the ninth inning. The victory was Cincinnati's first World Championship in 35 years.

Massachusetts governor Michael Dukakis sent 20 pounds of codfish to Ohio governor James Rhodes after the Series was over.

"Imagine our problem if we had won," joked Dukakis. "I don't know anyone in Massachusetts who would want ten pounds of Lake Erie Perch and ten pounds of Ohio River Catfish."

NAME THE STARTING LINEUP FOR THE WORLD CHAMPION BIG RED MACHINE OF 1975 *AND* 1976.

1B Tony Perez
2B Joe Morgan
3B Pete Rose
SS Dave Concepcion
OF George Foster
OF Cesar Geronimo
OF Ken Griffey
 C Johnny Bench

WHEN WAS A GAME-WINNING GRAND-SLAM HOME RUN NULLIFIED AND FOR WHAT REASON?

On April 10, 1976, with the New York Yankees leading the Milwaukee Brewers 9–6 in the ninth inning, Don Money of the Brewers came to bat with no outs and the bases full. He slammed the ball over the left-field fence, only to find that the first-base ump, Jim McKean, had called time before the pitch. Why? Yankee manager Billy Martin had been shouting pitching instructions to Sparky Lyle, but the crowd noise was too intense for Lyle to hear Martin, so first baseman Chris Chambliss asked for time. Apparently, no one, including Sparky Lyle, heard McKean grant time out. After a lengthy debate, Money stepped back in. He struck out, and the Yankees won, 9–7.

WHO WAS THE FIRST MAN TO HOMER IN THE "NEW" (RENOVATED) YANKEE STADIUM?

The Minnesota Twins' Dan Ford connected on a monstrous drive over the center-field fence off Rudy May on April 15, 1976. The Yankees won the game, 11–4.

WHO BECAME THE FIRST PLAYER TO HOMER INTO THE THIRD DECK OF YANKEE STADIUM AFTER IT WAS REMODELED IN 1976?

Joe Charboneau, the 1980 American League Rookie of the Year, slugged a homer into the third deck on June 28, 1980.

WHAT IS THE RECORD FOR THE MOST CONSECUTIVE VICTORIES BY A PITCHER BEFORE THE FIRST LOSS OF HIS CAREER?

Twelve, a record achieved twice, once by a National League starter many years ago and once by a reliever, in baseball's modern era.

The starter, George "Hooks" Wiltse of the New York Giants, went from May 29 to September 15 of 1904 before enduring the first loss of his career. He finished the season with a 13–3 record.

The reliever, Butch Metzger, won the first twelve decisions of his career *over three seasons.* He won one game in 1974 for the San Francisco Giants, another in 1975 as a member of the San Diego Padres, and then won his first ten decisions with San Diego in 1976.

He completed that season with an 11–4 mark, good enough to share the National League Rookie of the Year Award with Pat Zachry of the Cincinnati Reds.

Wiltse won a total of 139 games over his career; however, Metzger won only six games after his record-tying streak.

The American League streak for both starters and relievers is nine. Whitey Ford did it for the Yankees in 1950, as he went 9–1 as a starter, and Joe Pate, a Philadelphia Athletics reliever, was 9–0 in 1926.

Ford won 236 games in his career and has a place in the Hall of Fame. Pate, like Metzger, enjoyed little success after his flash of brilliance. Pate never won again, finishing his career with a record of 9–3.

WHICH RED SOX PLAYER WAS INVOLVED IN TWO BRAWLS WITH THE NEW YORK YANKEES?

Carlton Fisk faced off against the Bronx Bombers in a "preliminary" bout in 1973, and helped ignite the "main event" in 1976.

Home plate at Fenway was transformed into a war zone in 1973, all because Gene Michael of the Yankees missed a suicide squeeze bunt. The runner from third, Thurman Munson, noticed Fisk, Boston's pride of home plate, catch the ball and brace himself for a collision between the two best young catchers in the American League. Munson was ready, too—with elbows way up. *Bang!* Fisk absorbed the full impact of Munson's 188 pounds, landed on his American Express card, and came up swinging. Both Munson and Michael then attacked Fisk, leaving him with a bruised eye and a scratched face.

"The Yankees and Red Sox have played this way since baseball was invented," says Fisk. "I must admit we get out there against them with a lot of intensity. Sometimes we get carried away."

In 1976, on a warm Thursday night in May, Boston's flaky left-handed pitcher, Bill Lee, almost had to be carried away himself, following a bench-clearing brawl with the hated New Yorkers in the newly refurbished Yankee Stadium. The defending American League champs trailed the first-place Yankees by six games as the two clubs met in the first game of a crucial four-game weekend series.

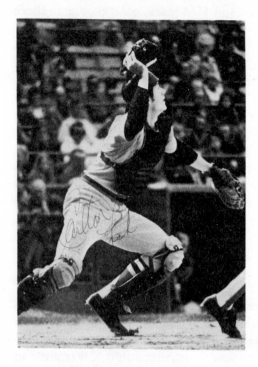

Carlton Fisk, Red Sox catcher and tilter with Yankees! *(from the collection of Barry Halper)*

In the bottom half of the sixth inning, New York was threatening to add to their precarious 1–0 lead with Lou Piniella on second base and Graig Nettles on first. The batter, Otto Velez, lined a Lee fastball into right field. The Sox's Dwight Evans, who earlier had thrown out Yankee Fred Stanley at home plate, again was challenged to retire a base runner.

As Piniella chugged around third base with the green light from coach Dick Howser, the charging Evans scooped up the ball, reared back, and fired an accurate one-hop throw to catcher Fisk.

The Sox's talented backstop received the skidding throw on the first-base side of the plate, turned on his knees to meet the sliding Yankee runner, and tagged him out. But it didn't end there.

Piniella thought the ball had been jarred loose by the collision and tried desperately to kick it away so that umpire Terry Cooney would see it. Instead of the ball, Piniella inadvertently kicked Fisk.

"I was down on my knees with the ball," Fisk said, "and the next thing I know, his knees are at my head. We went down and he's rolling and kicking all over the place. It was his kicking that started the whole thing. He was being malicious."

Having suffered several painful groin injuries on previous plays like this one, Fisk took exception to Piniella's actions. He tagged him with the ball a second time—only harder—in the jaw. Lou grabbed the catcher's chest protector and Fisk rapped him again on the chin, this time with the ball in his bare right hand. Then the donnybrook began.

At that moment, Boston first baseman Carl Yastrzemski and Yankee on-deck hitter Sandy Alomar raced to home plate to act as peacemakers. The rest of the players figured Yastrzemski and Alomar were going to fight, too, so they stormed to the diamond with fists cocked.

Bill Lee was the next player to join the fracas, followed by the Yankees' Velez and Nettles, who put both his arms around the Boston pitcher to try to drag him off the pileup of players.

"I heard him (Lee) yelling that his shoulder was hurt," Nettles recalled. "If I wanted to punch him right there I could have killed him, but I didn't. At that point I just wanted to break it up."

Meanwhile, New York outfielder Mickey Rivers, who also charged out of the dugout to lend physical support, jumped Lee from behind, dragged him to the ground with a hammerlock, and uncorked a number of vicious hammering punches in a windmill-like manner.

With Boston's ace left-hander now lying on the ground in pain, Nettles tried to explain to a few of Lee's teammates that he only wanted to pull the Boston pitcher off the pile. Suddenly, Lee got up, walked over to Nettles, and delivered a barrage of invectives that made the Yankees' third baseman sorry he even attempted to make peace. At one point, Lee told Nettles, "If you ever hurt my shoulder again, I'll kill you." That was all the usually mild-mannered Nettles had to hear.

"He started screaming at me like he was crazy," Graig said. "There were tears in his eyes. He told me he was going to get me, and that's when he started coming after me. I wasn't going to back off anymore."

Nettles then connected with a right cross to the eye, which decked Lee. They finished their private war on the ground. By now the pain in Lee's shoulder was excruciating. Red Sox trainer Charley Moss rushed to the aid of the fallen pitcher and escorted him to the dressing room. It turned out to be Lee's last appearance in uniform for six weeks.

The rest of the casualty list read like a weekly National Football League injury report. Carl Yastrzemski suffered a bruised thigh, Mickey Rivers injured his foot, Lou Piniella hurt his hand, but, miraculously, the injury-prone Carlton Fisk escaped unscathed.

"It was the worst fight I've ever seen," Yankee first-base coach Elston Howard commented after the fist swinging subsided.

A FORMER NATIONAL LEAGUE PITCHING ACE WON 13 CONSECUTIVE GAMES OVER THE LOS ANGELES DODGERS FROM 1976 THROUGH 1980. WHICH PITCHER MANAGED THIS MASTERY OVER THE DODGERS?

Six-feet-eight-inch, two-hundred-twenty-two-pound James Rodney "J.R." Richard of the Houston Astros.

THREE GREAT BASEBALL BOOKS CAME OUT OF THE '70s . . . WHAT WERE THEY?

BALL FOUR, a frank and funny expose by former pitcher-turned broadcaster Jim Bouton; *The Boys of Summer*, Roger Kahn's love-hate affair with the Brooklyn Dodgers and *Nice Guys Finish Last*, Leo Durocher's story of fifty riotous years in baseball.

WHAT AMERICAN LEAGUE ROOKIE WAS THE TOAST OF BASEBALL IN 1976 WITH HIS PHENOMENAL FIRST-YEAR SUCCESS?

Mark Fidrych went 19–9, including 24 complete games and a league-leading ERA of 2.34 as a twenty-one-year-old Detroit Tiger right-hander.

Mark "The Bird" Fidrych (left) was a rookie phenom and the toast of baseball in 1976, while Randy Jones (right) won the Cy Young Award that same season. *(from the collection of Barry Halper)*

A BIG-LEAGUE PITCHER PROUDLY DISPLAYS HIS CY YOUNG AWARD IN A CAR WASH! WHO IS HE?

The 1976 National League winner of the Cy Young Award was Randy Jones of the San Diego Padres, who now hangs the plaque in his Poway, California, car wash. The year Jones won the award, he fashioned 22 victories, giving him a total of 42 wins over a two-year period, so the Padres were confidently looking to the future for better things from the twenty-six-year-old curly blond southpaw. But somewhere along the line Jones snapped the motor nerve in his left biceps and suddenly his career was in jeopardy. After the 1976 season, Jones underwent apparently unsuccessful arm surgery. He came up with a dismal 6–12 record for the 1977 campaign but didn't actually retire until 1982.

WHICH TWO NEW YORK YANKEE PLAYERS WERE ONCE FINED $100 EACH FOR SLEEPING THROUGH A GEORGE STEINBRENNER "PEP TALK"?

Sparky Lyle and Ed Figueroa.

PRIOR TO SIGNING REGGIE JACKSON IN 1977, NEW YORK YANKEES OWNER GEORGE STEINBRENNER INVITED THE POPULAR SLUGGER TO NEW YORK CITY FOR A TWO-DAY GET-TO-KNOW-EACH-OTHER MEETING. WHAT WAS THE ELABORATE GIFT STEINBRENNER GAVE JACKSON?

A Rolls-Royce. Steinbrenner handed Jackson the keys to a $63,000 automobile at the end of the two-day meeting the owner had initiated. "Reggie, the car is yours," Steinbrenner said. "No strings attached, whether you sign with the Yankees or not."

An impressed Jackson soon after signed a reported five-year contract worth $2.93 million. "George Steinbrenner took it on his own to hunt me down," Jackson said. "He's like me. He's a little crazy, and he's a hustler. It was like trying to hustle a girl in a bar. Some of the clubs offered several hundred thousand dollars more, but the reason I'm a Yankee is that Steinbrenner outhustled everybody else and there are certain things he said to me, and certain ideologies and philosophies that we talked about and reached an accord on. And another important thing. I didn't come to New York to become a star. I brought my star with me."

IN 1977, A NEW YORK YANKEE BECAME ONLY THE SECOND PLAYER TO HIT THREE HOME RUNS IN A WORLD SERIES GAME. WHO WAS THE YANKEE SLUGGER WHO EQUALED RUTH'S 1926 AND 1928 FEATS?

Reggie Jackson slugged three homers in Game Six of the 1977 World Series against the Los Angeles Dodgers. The Yankees led the Series three games to two and were attempting to clinch the World Championship at Yankee Stadium.

But the Yanks trailed the Dodgers 3–2 in the fourth inning when Jackson approached the plate to duel with Dodger starter Burt Hooton with one man on. Jackson won the duel. He smashed a Hooton fastball into the right-field seats and the Yankees led, 4–3.

One inning later, Jackson came up to bat again with a man on base. This time Jackson would face Tommy Lasorda's new reliever, Elias Sosa. But again Jackson slugged a homer into the right-field seats as New York took a commanding 7–3 lead.

Then in the eighth inning, Jackson strode to the plate again to the hometown crowd's loud chants of *"Reggie . . . Reggie."* Charlie Hough tried to pitch carefully to "Mr. October," but there was simply no stopping Jackson on this October 18 evening. Hough's low knuckle ball eventually landed in the center-field bleachers. Just a few minutes later, the Yankees were celebrating their first World Championship since 1962.

AFTER REGGIE JACKSON'S FIRST HOME RUN OF THE 1978 SEASON, THE YANKEE STADIUM CROWD PAID AN UNUSUAL TRIBUTE TO MR. OCTOBER. WHAT DID THE FANS DO?

They showered the field with Reggie Bars. In the off-season, following Jackson's unforgettable three-home-run game in the last game of the 1977 World Series, a candy company came up with the idea of creating a new candy bar called the Reggie Bar.

Yankee management then decided to use the Reggie Bars as a promotional giveaway in a game against the Chicago White Sox on April 13, 1978. Jackson's first homer of the season, against Chicago's Wilbur Wood, resulted in the unusual tribute.

WHEN BASEBALL PLAYERS REFER TO THE "MANAGER'S BAR," WHAT DO THEY MEAN?

In baseball, off-field traditions are as important as playing the game on the field by the "book." Many years ago, some manager decided that when his team was on the road, the hotel bar would be the province of the manager and no player could imbibe at that particular watering hole. The custom became a tradition maintained for the most part down through the years. But in 1978, that tradition was challenged by then-player representative Dock Ellis of the Texas Rangers, who suggested to team members that they test the rule on manager Billy Hunter. Ellis made his statement on the team bus and was promptly interrupted.

"Shut up, Dock," snapped Billy Hunter, "and sit yourself down. You're not going to change the rule."

So Ellis resigned his player rep position with this retort: "I feel that some of these rules are juvenile and not for grown men."

Not all managers agreed with Hunter. One of them was Billy Martin, occasional manager of the New York Yankees.

When Ellis was the Yankees' player rep in 1976 and the early part of the 1977 season, Ellis often discussed problems with Martin in the hotel bar.

"I used to meet Billy, get my four gin and tonics free, and leave," recalled Ellis with a laugh. "I went the whole year without paying."

WHICH MAJOR-LEAGUER PLAYED FOR FOUR TEAMS DURING THE 1977 SEASON?

Dave Kingman played for four teams in 1977—The New York Mets, San Diego Padres, California Angels, and then finally the New York Yankees—a major-league record. For that travel-filled season, the 6'6", 210-pound Kingman managed to hit .221 with 26 homers and 78 RBI's.

AN AMERICAN LEAGUE PITCHER ONCE STUNNED THE SPORTS WORLD BY ADMITTING THAT HIS MANAGER WAS RIGHT IN FINING HIM. WHO WAS THE HONEST MAN?

On May 7, 1978, Jim Palmer made a pair of hasty exits during a Baltimore Orioles loss to the Minnesota Twins.

The first departure, from the pitcher's mound, cost him his second defeat of the season. The second exit took a chunk of cash out of his wallet as he was fined by the club for not staying around until the game's conclusion. Manager Earl Weaver had a club rule insisting that all players be present in the clubhouse after every game. When the manager discovered Palmer's absence, he announced that his pitcher would be fined. "I hate to fine a player," said Weaver, "and I especially don't like fining someone like Palmer who doesn't cause problems. But I had to do something. Believe it or not, I even asked Jim what he thought I should do."

To which Palmer replied: "It was a misunderstanding on the field between me and Earl. There were extenuating circumstances, but you can't condone my actions. I knew the rule."

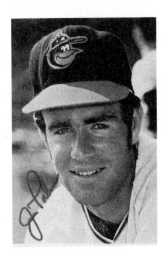

Jim Palmer, the Orioles' ace, was once fined by manager Earl Weaver for a pair of hasty exits. *(from the collection of Barry Halper)*

HOW DID A MAJOR-LEAGUE MANAGER OVERCOME HIS TEMPTATION TO USE A TIRED AND OVERWORKED RELIEF PITCHER IN YET ANOTHER BALL GAME?

During the 1978 season, Atlanta Braves manager Bobby Cox vowed that his relief specialist, Gene Garber, wouldn't pitch in a game—and Cox personally saw to it that he wouldn't succumb to the temptation.

Insisting that Garber needed a day off, manager Cox wrote Garber in on the starting lineup as "center fielder." But when the right-hander was scheduled to bat in the first inning, Rowland Office pinch-hit for Garber, thus denying Cox the option of using Gene as a relief pitcher. "I knew he needed a day off," said Cox, "and with him out of the game, I couldn't use Garber if I wanted to."

WHICH FORMER GIANTS SCOUT TOLD TEENAGER PETE ROSE HE WAS TOO SMALL EVER TO PLAY IN THE MAJORS?

Charlie Fox, who later became general manager of the Montreal Expos, made his biggest bonehead decision ever, when he was scouting for the Giants in Cincinnati. At the time, Pete Rose was a high school baseball star with dreams of making it in the major leagues. Fox took one look at Rose and shook his head. "I told him he was too small," Fox recalled, "and didn't have enough to make it. Of course, he only weighed about 140 pounds then and looked like a midget. He had no power. I know what he has done since, but when I saw him, he lacked too much. In fact, I told him, 'I can't put you in a Giants uniform; you'd look like a Giant midget.' "

Rose not only emerged as a Reds "giant." On the night of July 25, 1978, Pete shattered the first of the many records he would eventually break, as he safely hit in his thirty-eighth consecutive game, eclipsing Tommy Holmes's National League record. Ironically, Rose was born April 14, 1941—the same year that Joe DiMaggio, "The Yankee Clipper," batted safely in 56 straight games. Ah, if only Charlie Fox could have seen the future.

IN 1978, THE NEW YORK YANKEES MET ARCHRIVAL BOSTON AT FENWAY PARK IN A THRILLING ONE-GAME PLAY-OFF TO DETERMINE THE AMERICAN LEAGUE EAST'S REPRESENTATIVE IN THE AMERICAN LEAGUE CHAMPIONSHIP SERIES. WHO WON THE GAME?

The Yankees were victorious in the match-up, which seemed to be taken right from a Hollywood script. Boston was the hot team, winning ten of its last 12 games to reach first place on the final day of the season. But the Yankees had won nine of 16 against Boston that year and their ace, Ron Guidry (24–3), was set to take the mound at Fenway. However, at Fenway Park, Boston was always hard to beat: they were 59–23 (.720) in 82 home games. Boston's starter would be Mike Torrez, who just the year before had worn the Yankee pinstripes.

On that afternoon of October 2, almost 33,000 fans jammed into Fenway to cheer on their heroes. Millions more saw the game on national television or heard it on their local radio stations.

"That one game surpasses any other that I've been connected with," recalled Yankee broadcaster Frank Messer. "Those two teams . . . and the whole season boiling down to just one game at Fenway . . . It was quite a moment for everyone who was there or watched on TV."

Boston jumped to an early lead when Carl Yastrzemski came to the plate in the second inning. Yaz stroked a home run down the right-field line to give Boston a 1–0 lead.

"I thought that when 'the old man' hit the home run, that was going to do it," said former Boston announcer Ken "Hawk" Harrelson. "Mike was throwing the ball real well and he wanted that win."

In the third, fourth, and fifth innings, the Red Sox generated more offense, yet were unable to score any more runs. But they were gaining confidence against Guidry, who was pitching on only three days' rest. Finally, in the sixth inning, Boston produced another run. Rick Burleson doubled and was moved to third on Jerry Remy's bunt. Then Jim Rice singled home Burleson to make the score 2–0, much to the pleasure of all Boston.

And Torrez was rolling along, too. He only permitted two hits in six innings and Fenway was sensing victory. However, the events of the Yankee half of the seventh would prove to sour the sweet mood of all Red Sox fans.

Torrez's troubles began when Chris Chambliss and Roy White singled. Following pinch hitter Jim Spencer's fly out, Torrez would face the light-hitting shortstop, Bucky Dent. "Mickey Rivers was on deck," recalled Messer, "and he noticed a crack in Bucky's bat. He called it to Bucky's attention." Dent decided to use Rivers's bat in favor of his cracked one as he confronted Torrez.

Inside their dugout, the Yankees were shouting encouragement to Dent. In the stands, fans were rooting for Torrez to retire the Yankee batter. Dent would not oblige. He got good wood on Torrez's pitch, which soared over the Green Monster into the left-field netting. Chris Chambliss, Roy White, and the rest of the Yankees congratulated Bucky Dent with loud applause, but the stadium was suddenly silent. With one swing of the bat, Boston had lost control of the game and now trailed, 3–2.

Torrez also lost his pitching control and walked the next batter, Rivers. That was all for Torrez. Rivers soon scored on Thurman Munson's double, making it 4–2. Rich Gossage, the Yankees flamethrower, came on to shut down the Red Sox in the seventh. Then Reggie Jackson's center-field home run shot off a Bob Stanley fastball made it 5–2.

"When it wound up in the bleachers, I just thought it was an extra run," says Jackson.

Jackson soon learned that his home run was something just a little more than "an extra run."

Hope was still alive in the bottom of the eighth as the Fenway faithful tried to rally the homeboys. Jerry Remy's double off Gossage sent Fenway into a frenzy. Yastrzemski routinely singled in Remy and the score was 5–3. Carlton Fisk supplied another single and then Fred Lynn's clutch base hit brought in Yaz to make it a one-run game. But Gossage managed to regroup amid the pandemonium by striking out George Scott on a fastball to end the furious Boston rally.

After the Yankees were swiftly retired in the top of the ninth, the entire season for the two rivals came down to the Red Sox's last three outs. After Gossage got the first out, Burleson worked for a base on balls against the Goose. Up came Remy. Gossage pitched carefully to the contact hitter until Remy punched the ball to right field. Just as Lou Piniella reached the ball, it dropped in front of him. Eddie Yost was screaming from the coach's box at third base for Remy to come to third. But Remy, in his best Hamlet, hesitated and remained at second as Piniella's throw reached Graig Nettles.

Up next came Rice, attempting to slug his forty-seventh and most important home run of the season. Gossage served up a fastball, but Rice's swing was a bit late. Piniella made the catch in deep right as Remy tagged up and advanced to third base. The Red Sox were down to their last out.

The stage was set for a dramatic battle. Carl Yastrzemski was the batter. Yaz had had 17 homers and 81 RBI's in the 1978 season, even though he had been hampered by back and wrist injuries. And the longtime darling of Boston had tagged Gossage for an RBI single in his last at bat.

"I wasn't going to mess around with my breaking stuff," the Goose said after, "and get beat by anything but my best. Yastrzemski is the best player I've ever played against. I just wound up and threw as hard as I could. I couldn't tell you where."

Old Number Eight, the 1967 American League MVP, took the first pitch for a ball. Gossage's second pitch tailed away from Yaz, but the legend swung with all his might anyway. He didn't get all of it. The ball sailed harmlessly toward third base. Nettles followed it and made the easy catch near the coaching box as the Yankee dugout erupted. Yaz strode off in disgust.

The Yankees won, 5–4. They had just overcome Boston's one-time fourteen-game lead and edged the Red Sox for the American League East Championship.

AN ANTI-DISCO PROMOTION AT COMISKEY PARK RESULTED IN CHAOS. WHAT HAPPENED?

"Disco Demolition Night" was proposed to the Chicago White Sox by a local disco-hating, album-rock disc jockey in 1979. The deejay proposed that each fan who brought a disco record to Comiskey Park on July 12 would be admitted for 98¢. Each disco record brought to the park would then be blown up on the field between games of the doubleheader against the Detroit Tigers.

White Sox owner Bill Veeck okayed the promotion, which attracted a sellout crowd of more than 50,000. But the mayhem of the evening began early. Many fans began hurling firecrackers and records onto the field during the first game. Then the detonation of the thousands of records in a big container ignited pandemonium. An estimated 7,000 fans swarmed onto the field where several clashes between disco and anti-disco groups broke out.

In all, the melee triggered 37 arrests and after a 76-minute delay the umpires declared the field unplayable. The White Sox had to forfeit the second game.

WHO WERE THE ONLY TWO PLAYERS EVER TO TIE FOR THE MVP AWARD, AND WHEN DID THAT HAPPEN?

In 1979 Keith Hernandez of the St. Louis Cardinals and Willie Stargell of the Pittsburgh Pirates shared the award when they tied in the voting. Hernandez had led the National League with a .344 average while picking up a Gold Glove. Stargell led the Pirates to the world championship.

THE PITTSBURGH PIRATES DID NOT WIN ANY CHAMPIONSHIPS IN THE 1980's. THEIR LAST WORLD SERIES VICTORY CAME IN 1979, WHEN THE "PITTSBURGH LUMBER COMPANY" DEFEATED THE BALTIMORE ORIOLES IN SEVEN GAMES. MVP WILLIE STARGELL WAS ONE OF THEIR BEST POWER HITTERS, BUT WHAT WAS WILLIE'S *WEAKEST* POINT?

The Pirates were a team based primarily on offense, with hitters such as Bill Madlock and Dave Parker. The main man, however, was Willie "Pops" Stargell, who took MVP honors for the 1979 Fall Classic, not to mention the National League co-MVP award for the regular season.

Stargell, elected to the Hall of Fame in 1988, his first year of eligibility, hit 475 home runs throughout his illustrious career. "Pops" was known for his friendliness and was one of the most popular players in baseball history, with both fans and players alike.

Many power hitters are inept at base stealing. Stargell was no exception. In one of his more notable attempts at a stolen base, Stargell started his slide when he was nowhere near second base, and came to a stop about ten feet from the bag. Ivan DeJesus, the Chicago Cubs' shortstop, was about to make the tag on Stargell when the quick-witted base runner came up with an idea. Standing up, Stargell made a *T* sign with his hands, and yelled "Time Out!" to the umpire. After being called out, Stargell returned to his dugout, where his teammates were on the floor with laughter. And what statement did "Pops" give to defend himself? "I was told the bases were only seventy feet apart."

Willie Stargell, MVP of the 1979 Pittsburgh Pirates. *(from the collection of Barry Halper)*

WHAT WAS THE ONLY LEAGUE CHAMPIONSHIP SERIES TO HAVE FOUR OF ITS FIVE GAMES GO INTO EXTRA INNINGS?

The 1980 National League Championship Series between the Houston Astros and the Philadelphia Phillies went into extra innings four times in the best-of-five match-up. Steve Carlton beat the Astros in Game One by a score of 3–1. The next four went into extra innings. In Game Two, the Astros scored four times in the tenth inning and held on to win, 7–4. Larry Christenson of the Phillies and Joe Niekro of the Astros engaged in a scoreless duel in Game Three before Houston pulled it out, 1–0, in eleven innings. Game Four saw Houston tie the game in the bottom of the ninth, only to lose 5–3 in ten innings. In the fifth game, Astros pitcher Nolan Ryan could not hold onto a 5–2 lead in the eighth inning and the Phillies, with a run in the tenth, secured their first pennant since the 1950 Whiz Kids.

WHAT PLAYER MADE A RUN AT HITTING .400 IN 1980?

George Brett of the Kansas City Royals sported a .400-plus average throughout the summer and into the final stanza of play. However, he was overtaken by small injuries and the haunting pressure of the media to finish the season at .390, the highest major-league average since Ted Williams hit .406 for the Red Sox in 1941.

WHAT SAN DIEGO PADRES SLUGGER MADE HEADLINES AFTER THE 1980 SEASON?

Dave Winfield, who hit .276 with 20 home runs and 87 runs batted in for the last place Padres, entered the free-agent draft and got a then-record million and a half dollar per-season contract from the New York Yankees.

Dave Winfield bagged what was then a record preseason contract after the 1980 season. *(from the collection of Barry Halper)*

IN WHAT YEAR WAS THERE NO TWENTY-GAME WINNER, THE ONLY TIME IN THE HISTORY OF THE GAME?

This feat was accomplished in 1981, the year of the players' strike. The most wins by a pitcher in the majors that year was 14.

HOW MANY GAMES DURING THE 1981 SEASON WERE CANCELLED DUE TO THE PLAYERS' STRIKE?

During the 43-day strike by the Baseball Players' Association, 713 games were lost along with an estimated 98 million dollars in players' salaries, and ticket, broadcast, and concession revenues.

WHOM DID DAVE RIGHETTI STRIKE OUT TO COMPLETE HIS ONLY NO-HITTER?

Dave "Rags" Righetti stood on the mound at Yankee Stadium on July 4, 1983, and stared over at Wade Boggs, who was emerging as the American League's top hitter. Undaunted, Rags struck out Boggs to complete his no-hitter.

WHAT HAPPENED TO HOUSTON ASTROS PITCHING ACE J. R. RICHARD?

James Rodney Richard was set to take the mound for the Houston Astros in 1980 when he felt a sharp pain in his neck, followed by total numbness. Richard was carried off the field on a stretcher and taken to the hospital where it was discovered he had suffered a crippling blood clot in his neck. Up to that point, J. R. was 10–4 with a 1.89 earned run average and 119 strikeouts.

Richard later attempted a comeback but was unable to overcome the sickness. It was discovered afterward that he had experimented with illegal drugs.

WHAT SAN FRANCISCO GIANTS SHORTSTOP ATTEMPTED TO MAKE A DRAMATIC COMEBACK IN 1980?

Roger Metzger tried to return to the Giants in 1980 after losing four fingers in an off-season accident. Unfortunately, Roger failed in his comeback, with a .074 batting average in 28 games.

WHICH FORMER NATIONAL LEAGUE FIRST BASEMAN IN THE 1930's HAD A RACEHORSE NAMED AFTER HIM IN THE 1980's?

A pacing standard-bred horse, "Ripper Collins," raced on harness tracks for the better part of the 1980's. James Anthony "Ripper" Collins was born in 1904 in Altoona, Pa. He played nine seasons with St. Louis, Chicago, and Pittsburgh in 1931–38 and 1941. Collins's career average of .296 included four .300-plus seasons.

Collins was a member of the 1931 and 1934 world champion St. Louis Cardinals. He also played for the 1938 Chicago Cubs, who lost the Series four games to none to the New York Yankees.

ONLY THREE MAJOR-LEAGUE BASEBALL PARKS STILL USE HAND-OPERATED SCOREBOARDS. WHICH ARE THEY?

Boston's Fenway Park, Chicago's Wrigley Field, and the Oakland Coliseum each employ hand-operated scoreboards.

THE GREEN MONSTER IN FENWAY PARK HAS A MORSE CODE MARKING INSCRIBED ON IT. WHAT DOES THE MARKING READ?

Marked vertically on the scoreboard face are the Morse code initials of the deceased former Red Sox owner, Thomas A. Yawkey, and his loving wife, Jean R. Yawkey.

WHO HOLDS THE NATIONAL LEAGUE RECORD FOR THE MOST CAREER GRAND SLAMS?

Willie McCovey had 18 bases-loaded dingers in his career.

Willie McCovey holds the National League record for most career grand slammers. *(from the collection of Barry Halper)*

FROM 1977 TO 1983 ONLY TWO MEN IN BASEBALL BATTED .300 OR OVER FOR EACH OF THOSE SEVEN CONSECUTIVE SEASONS. WHO WERE THEY?

Rod Carew and Cecil Cooper.

WHO WAS THE WINNER OF NINE STRAIGHT GOLD GLOVE AWARDS FROM 1978 TO 1986?

Keith Hernandez, with the St. Louis Cardinals and New York Mets, won nine straight awards for his excellent play at first base.

WHO WERE THE FOUR LOS ANGELES DODGERS TO WIN THE NATIONAL LEAGUE ROOKIE OF THE YEAR AWARD FOUR CONSECUTIVE YEARS, FROM 1978–1982?

Pitcher Rick Sutcliffe won the award in 1979, pitcher Steve Howe won in 1980, pitcher Fernando Valenzuela in 1981, and second baseman Steve Sax in 1982.

WHICH PLAYER HOLDS THE RECORD FOR MOST HITS IN A WORLD SERIES GAME?

Paul Molitor, Milwaukee Brewers, had five hits on October 12, 1982, against the St. Louis Cardinals.

IN THE CRUCIAL FOURTH GAME OF THE 1981 WORLD SERIES BETWEEN THE LOS ANGELES DODGERS AND THE NEW YORK YANKEES, A JOURNEYMAN DODGER OUTFIELDER HIT A PINCH-HIT HOME RUN TO HELP BEAT THE YANKEES. WHO WAS THIS OUTFIELDER?

In a nineteen-year career spanning 1966 to 1984, Jay Johnstone played for eight different teams. Mostly a platoon player, he compiled a .267 career batting average. His greatest moment, however, did not occur until the 1981 World Series, when his two-run pinch-hit homer off Ron Davis helped the Dodgers win the game, 8–7, and tie up the Series at two games apiece.

If there was one thing that Johnstone was famous for, it was his sense of humor, not his pinch-hitting. For years he was known around clubhouses, especially the Dodger clubhouse, as a master of the practical joke.

For instance, in spring training one year, Johnstone was scheduled for a urine test. Instead of urine, he filled his vial with apple juice. After setting the vial in front of the nurse, who remarked how cloudy it was, Johnstone poured the contents of the vial into his mouth, explaining that he would run it through again. By this point the nurse had started screaming, and Johnstone went off to the bathroom, telling her that he would bring another sample back. The doctor later chided Johnstone for this prank, because the nurse was elderly and got very scared.

Ex-Dodger pitcher Dave Goltz won't forget the stunt Johnstone pulled on him. Johnstone stuck some red hot Capsolin goo (a medication for sore muscles that produces the sensation of heat) in Goltz's shorts. Then he covered it with white powder, so Goltz wouldn't see the red substance.

The ride home from that game was supposedly the quickest of Goltz's life. Arriving home, he leaped out of his car, and ran inside to the shower, leaving his wife and kid in the car.

KEITH HERNANDEZ WASN'T PLEASED WHEN HE WAS TRADED TO THE NEW YORK METS ON JUNE 15, 1983. WHAT DID HE SAY ABOUT HIS NEW TEAM?

Hernandez was being traded away from a world championship team to a perennial basement club. The Mets had finished sixth or next to last in the National League East in each of the last six years. That prompted Keith to comment that he was being sent to the "Siberia of baseball."

Keith Hernandez (here as a Cardinal) wasn't delighted when he was traded to the New York Mets. *(from the collection of Barry Halper)*

WHO IS THE ONLY AMERICAN LEAGUER TO GET 3,000 HITS AND 400 HOME RUNS?

Carl Yastrzemski finished his brilliant twenty-three-year career with the Boston Red Sox after the 1983 season. He had a career total of 3,419 hits along with 452 homers in 11,988 at bats. Yastrzemski's final average was .285.

HOW DID DON MATTINGLY WIN THE 1984 BATTING CROWN?

Mattingly and Dave Winfield, Yankee teammates, were in a tight race for the American League batting crown that went down to the last game of the season. Winfield was ahead, .340 to .339, entering that last game. Winfield went 1-for-4 and Mattingly went 4-for-5, giving the fans some drama in an otherwise meaningless game. Mattingly won the crown, .343 to .340.

WHO HOLDS THE NATIONAL LEAGUE RECORD FOR MOST CONSECUTIVE GAMES PLAYED?

Steve Garvey of the Los Angeles Dodgers played in 1,207 consecutive games.

WHO BECAME THE ONLY FIRST BASEMAN IN MAJOR-LEAGUE HISTORY TO GO THROUGH A FULL SEASON WITHOUT A SINGLE ERROR?

Steve Garvey of the San Diego Padres went through a full season in 1984—161 games—without a single error.

TEAM MASCOTS HAVE BEEN A PART OF BASEBALL FOR OVER ONE HUNDRED YEARS. TEAMS PAY PERFORMERS TO DRESS UP IN ANIMAL OUTFITS AND DANCE ON THE FIELD, TO TRY TO GET THE FANS MORE INVOLVED IN THE GAME. THE SAN DIEGO CHICKEN AND THE PHILLIE PHANATIC HAVE BEEN TWO OF THE MOST POPULAR MASCOTS EVER. STILL THERE HAVE BEEN TIMES WHEN A TEAM'S EFFORT TO EXCITE THE FANS WITH MASCOTS HAS NOT WORKED. WHO WAS THE MOST UNPOPULAR MASCOT IN BASEBALL HISTORY?

In the early 1980's, the mascot craze was at its highest level ever. It seemed as if almost every team had a mascot, except the San Francisco Giants. So the Giants decided to poll the fans on what sort of mascot they wanted. The majority of the fans voted to have no mascot at all. However, Giants management disregarded the fans' wishes, and, in 1984, the San Francisco Crab was born. Never has there been a more unpopular mascot in baseball history. During the middle of the fifth inning, when it would make its entrance, the fans would throw trash and beer, and boo the crab mercilessly. Little children, whom the crab was supposed to entertain, were frightened of it. The grounds crew sprayed their hoses on the crab if he got too close. Eventually, anti-crab T-shirts started to appear.

The San Francisco Crab was put out of its misery when the person inside the costume expressed concern about the possibility that a frustrated fan might carry a gun into the stadium.

How crabby of him!

WHO HOLDS THE MAJOR-LEAGUE RECORD FOR CONSECUTIVE GAMES WITHOUT AN ERROR?

Steve Garvey had an errorless streak of 193 games, in which he successfully handled 1,633 chances, a National League record.

WHOM DID PETE ROSE REPLACE AS MANAGER OF THE CINCINNATI REDS FOR THE 1985 SEASON?

Vern Rapp.

WHICH TEAM ONCE BEGAN A GAME WITH THREE HOME RUNS?

The San Diego Padres are the only big-league team to achieve the feat. The three homers were hit by Marvell Wynne, Tony Gwynn, and John Kruk, against San Francisco Giants pitcher Roger Mason. However, San Francisco still won the game, 13–6, on April 13, 1987.

WHO IS THE FIRST, LAST, AND ONLY PITCHER IN THE HISTORY OF THE MILWAUKEE BREWERS TO HURL A NO-HITTER?

Juan Nieves became the first Brewer to throw a no-hitter against the lowly Baltimore Orioles on April 15, 1987. Nieves struck out seven in the game and walked five, but he did not allow any base runners beyond first base.

WHO WAS THE FIRST MAJOR-LEAGUER TO HIT HOME RUNS FROM BOTH SIDES OF THE PLATE IN CONSECUTIVE GAMES?

Eddie Murray achieved this unique feat with the Baltimore Orioles in May, 1987.

WHOSE UNIFORM NUMBER IS THE ONLY ONE RETIRED IN THE HISTORY OF THE KANSAS CITY ROYALS?

The late former manager Dick Howser's number 10 was retired on July 3, 1987, after Howser succumbed to a brain tumor. It's the only retired uniform number in Kansas City's twenty-year history.

**IN APRIL, 1988, CINCINNATI REDS MANAGER PETE
ROSE WAS SUSPENDED THIRTY GAMES FOR SHOVING
AN UMPIRE, DAVE PALLONE, DURING AN ARGUMENT.
WHILE OTHER UMPIRES OBVIOUSLY ABHORRED
ROSE'S BEHAVIOR, MANY OF THE "MEN IN BLUE"
WERE ALSO QUICK TO CRITICIZE PALLONE FOR HIS
BEHAVIOR IN THE INCIDENT. PALLONE'S
COLLEAGUES ALSO SPOKE OF THEIR DISLIKE FOR
HIM PERSONALLY. CAN YOU RECALL WHAT MADE
THIS UMPIRE SO UNPOPULAR AMONG
OTHER ARBITERS?**

In 1979, when the regular umpires went on strike, four umpires got their jobs by crossing the picket lines. Dave Pallone was one of these. Almost ten years later, many signs of hatred toward Pallone remained among other umps, the most obvious being former umpire Ron Luciano's derogatory statements about Pallone on national television.

But players weren't immune from attacking Pallone verbally. In 1984, Reds shortstop Dave Concepcion got thrown out of a game after arguing with Pallone. A teammate of Concepcion's who had observed the incident could not understand why the ejection occurred, since it sounded to him like Concepcion was only calling the umpire a "cab." But that was just Concepcion's Venezuelan accent —he was really calling Pallone a "scab."

HOW DID PETER SEITZ ALTER THE COURSE OF BASEBALL HISTORY?

Baseball players love him; owners loathe him! Peter Seitz is the man responsible for eliminating the sport's controversial reserve clause that indefinitely bound players to their teams. Following the 1975 baseball season, pitchers Andy Messersmith and Dave McNally, both of whom had played without contracts that season, appealed to the Major-League Players' Association for assistance. The union took the position that the players were free agents.

At that time when players did not sign, management had the "right" to renew their contracts, contending this "right" existed indefinitely from year to year. The players maintained that a contract could be renewed for only one year, now known as the option year.

In order to settle the dispute, professional arbitrator Peter Seitz was called in for a decision. This was not the first time the league powers had agreed to outside arbitration, having agreed to it in 1973 to successfully avoid a players' strike. He ruled in favor of Messersmith and McNally, thus ending the baseball reserve clause. Seitz later became arbitrator for labor-management disputes in the National Basketball Association. Asked if he believed that arbitration was now a necessity in professional sports, he replied in the affirmative.

"It has become a part of all industry," said Seitz, "so it is necessary in sports. It's either an arbitrator or the courts. An arbitrator is faster and cheaper." He concluded, tongue in cheek: "Be it observed that I did not kill baseball, and for all I know, someday—I should live so long—revisionists will suggest that I should be immortalized in the pantheon in Cooperstown, New York."

PART THREE

TOUCHING
ALL THE BASES

TIMELESS TRIVIA

Sure, "the times they are a'changin' " in sports, but never as much as someone from the "good ol' days" (probably myself included) would have you think. Largely, only the names have been changed to protect innocent memories.

What has changed is the emphasis on value that is placed on various aspects of the game. For one era it'll be hitting and home runs will be the bottom line. For another it'll be the decade of the pitching duel, and the ERA will be the dominant stat.

Today seems to be the era of musical managers: if a team falls below a certain level of performance, the tendency is to fire the manager before messing with the basic makeup of the team itself. If a new manager doesn't work, then and only then do they start lowering the boom on the players. It's virtually impossible today for a baseball manager to achieve the records set by the game's winningest pilots, Joe McCarthy and Casey Stengel. Joe McCarthy managed three teams in his 24-year career (1926 through 1950) and won seven World Series between the years 1932 and 1943. Note that he managed for six seasons before he won a Series (all of his were won with the Yanks) *and* he managed for five and a half seasons with two clubs, the Yankees and Red Sox, *after* he won his last Series.

For Stengel, it was the same thing. "The Old Perfesser" managed four teams for a total of 25 years, over a span of *four* decades

—and all of his Series wins were with the Yanks, also. Davey Johnson, on the other hand, after six years at the helm of the Mets, had two divisional wins, one Series win, and with two years left on a reputed $675,000 contract, was rumored to be dead in the water (as the Mets certainly were) by the end of the 1989 season. Johnson, luckily, survived.

In other words, being a manager who ends up with the right team at the right moment counts for a lot in the baseball business.

Jimmy Dykes once called Joe McCarthy a push-button manager. In other words, McCarthy had all the best players and all he had to do was push the right buttons at crucial moments—yet at the same time he still has the reputation of being the greatest manager of his time. But take a look at the teams he managed: with the greatest hitters of all time and some of the finest pitching ever, you can't help but say, "Hey, I could win with that ball club, too."

If you take a look at the club Johnson managed, then you realize that the dynasty potential—and face it, dynasties are what make Hall of Fame managers—for the 1980's Mets was minimal. As good as their pitching was, it wasn't the greatest and they just couldn't pull it off again after 1986. It was the same with the Miracle Mets of 1969: they had three great pitchers in Seaver, Ryan, and Koosman, but couldn't pull it off again in 1970.

To win the crucial games—to win the Series more than once and become classified as a dynasty—a club needs at least one "franchise player." To me it's doubtful that Darryl Strawberry is that franchise player and I think it has been proven by now that he does not have the ability to carry a team like Babe Ruth did, or Joe DiMaggio or Mickey Mantle. That's when the manager has to step in and show himself as more than a button pusher.

But how can a manager motivate in today's game? I spoke to my old friend Jimmy Frey, general manager of the Cubs, just before the 1989 play-offs and we discussed the fact that he had been Darryl's hitting instructor when Strawberry was in the minors. Frey said that it looked to him as though Darryl had long ago stopped having fun in the game, and that when he was a kid, he had needed a lot of motivating. Without coming right out and saying so, Frey implied that Strawberry should have been pushed a lot harder with the Mets. But how can a manager motivate? One of the recurring themes with Strawberry and the Mets has always been that Straw had problems with the pressures he felt in New York, with the implied expectation for him to become "The Franchise." And Johnson, as much as any manager in the bigs, was under such public scrutiny himself that putting demands on Darryl invariably brought out stories of dissension on the team, of star pouts and managerial tyranny. Managing a major-league baseball team today would seem to be a no-win situation.

Tommy Lasorda may very well be the only exception, and he proves my rule that a manager has to be given time and lots of it in order to get results and achieve immortality. Lasorda, through the 1989 season, had been in charge of the Dodgers for 14 seasons (although he only managed for four games in 1976), during which time the Dodgers won six division championships (1977, '78, '81, '83, '85, and '88), four league championship series (1977, '78, '81, and '88) and two World Series (1981 and 1988). But, he had managed the club more than five seasons before they won their first Series (à la Joe McCarthy) and then it took the team another seven years to repeat.

I've known Tommy for 40 years—he was a pitcher for the Dodger Montreal farm club while I was covering Buffalo. If you had told me back then that such a clown emeritus would become the manager of "my Dodgers," I'd have bet you a million to one! This guy was the Rodney Dangerfield of the minor leagues.

"I'm the best left-hander in the league," he'd insist, "but I don't get no respect." He also took credit for Sandy Koufax's rise to stardom: "What is all this baloney? If it hadn't been for me, there'd've been no Koufax!" In a sense, he's right; Tommy was sent down to the minors to make room for Koufax.

For all his buffoonery as a player, Lasorda is unquestionably a first-rate manager. The way he managed the 1988 World Series, even from a purist's point of view, was incredible. Still, the only real criterion for Lasorda, or any big-league manager, would be matching McCarthy's and Stengel's record of seven World Series wins.

If this had been the case when someone like Leo Durocher was managing, he'd never have lasted as long as he did in New York. It's a strange thing about Leo Durocher: his record proves that he managed for 24 years, over parts of *five* decades, with four clubs. But he achieved only one World Series win, with the Giants in 1954, when he had a franchise player named Willie Mays. Leo set the mold for guys like Gene Mauch, managers who try to outthink everybody else. In retrospect, his record can only be compared to Casey Stengel's in terms of longevity, but he was definitely a thinking-man's manager.

Casey was simply the greatest. The only time I was ever with him for any length of time was at a sports dinner in Rochester, and he didn't act like the unpredictable Casey Stengel I had always heard about. No double-talk. No clowning around. He spoke like an educated man who had gone to dental school, which he had.

The one thing that exemplifies Stengel most in my mind comes from something I was told by Jerry Coleman, who played under Stengel from 1949 to 1957: "When the Yankees won a pennant or a World Series, Stengel made us feel as though we hadn't accomplished a thing. He was the greatest motivator I've ever been around."

He drove them further and further. Mickey Mantle has told me that in a way Casey hurt him, because Casey always wanted him to do more than Mickey thought he was physically capable of doing. Stengel kept telling Mick that he had the potential to be the greatest ballplayer of all time—better than Ty Cobb, better even than the Great Babe.

Mickey said, "Stengel never took into account that although I may have been physically faster than them and certainly as strong, I just wasn't as good. He really pushed me to the limit." Mantle resented that a little, but he respected Stengel and looked to him as a father figure.

I doubt if any of today's managers could measure up to the standards set by Stengel or McCarthy, but as I said, in today's world I seriously doubt whether any of them would be given the time to build a legacy, what with baseball's current high-pressure, big-business, bottom-line climate. If anything, it's the money aspect of baseball that has changed the game more than any "dead" ball, DH rule, Astroturf, or scandal.

George Steinbrenner epitomizes this evolution. I've known him for a long time, and it's strange how he can be so likable and so dislikable almost at the same moment. Here's a guy who sometimes presents himself poorly when there's no need for it. I don't like bullies, which George can be, but I also can see that it arises from his being such a terrific competitor—he just plain wants to win *all* the time. One year he'd go out and literally buy a team that could win the Series—1978, for instance—and declare that he was going to leave well enough alone. Then before you knew it he'd start fiddling with the mix the minute things didn't go just the way he wanted them to.

I think George would be better served if he went less on instinct and more on business acumen. He should have had more patience and confidence in his choices of good baseball people and allowed them to make important judgments. I'm sure he wasn't about to ask Billy Martin what he thought about shipbuilding. By the same token it made no more sense for him to consider himself a better judge than Billy Martin—or Dallas Green or any of a host of other Yankee managers—on baseball matters. Maybe it's time for George to face the fact that he simply isn't willing to go out and buy another Series-winning roster.

But high-profile owners are certainly nothing new. Bill Veeck was anything but a silent partner and he changed the game, much to the dismay of "The Lords of Baseball," as the late Dick Young used to call the establishment owners. Veeck was a maverick with all his promotional gimmicks, but he understood the game. He was a fan more than anything else. I think he was a visionary, years ahead of his time, but to the staunch conservatives running baseball, he was a threat to the spirit of the game.

It's the old story: if you're a purist, you're not going to like the designated hitter rule or an owner like Veeck, who once put a midget in his lineup. Truth is, though, the owners are running a business and they're going to do whatever they think will get people into the ballpark. But then, of course, they don't even have to get fans out to the parks anymore, not with fat TV deals.

Owners can't be making that many mistakes if a guy like George Steinbrenner can get a $500 million cable TV contract. Is a single major-league market worth that much for TV rights? That cable deal sounds as out-of-sight to me as any ballplayer's inflated contract. But then I think ballplayers are worth whatever they can get. Sure, a manager has the right to go over to a player who's had a bad year and say, "You stank up the joint, kid." But if that player has a $2 million salary, he still gets that $2 million. End of discussion.

But if television has brought money to the game, it has also brought changes. Not only has television eroded the strength and number of minor-league teams and farm teams, it has also turned the World Series into an almost completely Night Series. But more than all of this, it has turned platoons of players into movie stars. In the old days, there was only one "movie star," Babe Ruth. He was succeeded by Joltin' Joe. These were guys who had no private lives, whose every move was captured in the papers and in the newsreels. They were constantly in the hands of the public. Today most major-leaguers are "movie stars," and they act that way both on and off the field.

You never used to see members of the winning team run out of the dugout to shake hands with the players coming off the field after the game's last out. You'd think it was the end of the World Series, or maybe the first win they'd had all year. In the National Hockey League the handshaking takes place only after the final game of the Stanley Cup—with the opposing team. In baseball it's become an everyday occurrence. My old friend, Dr. Jim Nicholas, who has tended major-league bones in almost every sport, attributes this ritual to the omnipresent TV cameras.

Then again, playing to an audience shouldn't be automatically viewed as offensive. I had dinner in Chicago with Felipe Alou one night and at one point I called one of Milwaukee's players a "hot dog." Felipe, a Dominican, turned to me with a hurt look on his face.

"I'm disappointed in you," he told me. "You're the last guy I ever expected to hear that term 'hot dog' from." I asked him why.

"Why do you think that your culture is superior to Latin culture?" he asked me, and after protesting that I didn't, he said, "Have you ever been to a bullfight?"

"No," I said, "but I've seen films."

"When the toreador or the matador makes a great move, he struts in front of the audience," Felipe explained. "In America, that would be considered 'hotdogging.' In my country we not only expect it, we love it."

I objected. "But this isn't bullfighting, and you're not that way yourself."

"Only by personal choice," he responded. "But I don't think there's anything wrong with it. Why does everybody have to be like *you* want them to be?"

That conversation made a tremendous impression on me. Although I still consider some players to be hot dogs, now I think of the term as meaning that they're artists. When Willie Mays used to lose his cap, guys would say, "You never saw Joe DiMaggio lose his cap." Does that make Willie a bad person or a poor ballplayer? Certainly not. No one has ever been sued or arrested for showing off on the field.

But more than on the field, the rules are changing for athletes off the field (just as they have changed for politicians). The private lives of movie-star athletes no longer exist. The peccadillos of today's ballplayers were never documented in such graphic detail in the past. Wade Boggs didn't invent adultery. Babe Ruth's sexual prowess was probably on a par with his home-run hitting, but nobody ever talked about it publicly. The saddest part of the Boggs episode was what his ex-lover, Margo Adams, revealed to me when I interviewed her while she was doing a promotional tour for the book she had compiled on their clandestine relationship (what else!). She related that even as Wade stood at a press conference holding his wife and professing his undying love for her, he was cheating on her yet again, only this time the "other woman" wasn't Margo! (I always wondered whether it upset Margo that she wasn't the other woman that time.)

Ballplayers put themselves in a position of public scrutiny these days largely because they lend themselves to it. They do television commercials in which they appear as role models—and if you're going to play a role model in America, you've got to be squeaky-clean. No matter how sophisticated the American public allegedly has become, it still expects the ballplayer on the front of the Wheaties box to be like Caesar's wife: above reproach.

Still, it was ironic to see the great hue and cry that followed Rickey Henderson's accusations that his teammates drank too much between games. Come on, drinking is still part and parcel of our culture—and its most accepted vice. I just don't think drinking is frowned upon in our society as much as the size of that story implied. It certainly isn't frowned upon as much as the use of drugs.

As far as the drug problem is concerned, I have never "done drugs" in my life and so I sit and ask myself if I really want to be "holier-than-thou" on the subject. The late baseball scribe, Dick Young, was almost rabidly outspoken on the subject, urging that athletes with drug problems be thrown out of the human race—let alone the major leagues—after the first offense. I think the Bible offers a more understanding viewpoint: it's just too easy to cast stones. How many chances should somebody have? On an intellectual basis, I'd take a liberal point of view. But on a gut basis, if I were an owner, manager, or commissioner, I'd know I would have to be tough—for the player as well as for the game.

After all, there are three strikes in baseball and then that's it. After the third strike, you can't just say to the ump, "Hey, give me another chance." In terms of drug usage, I think three strikes and yer out—after that, psychiatric help is what a player needs rather than coddling.

It'll take time, but I have no doubt that baseball will come to terms with chemical abuse. Changes are already evident. Unfortunately, the winds of change are not even vaguely evident in another critically important area.

It's patently fishy that in a sport with as many black athletes as baseball, there is so minuscule a number of black managers. The only argument I've ever heard, and this was years ago, was that the owners were afraid to hire blacks to manage because they'd never be able to fire them—don't forget that the premier facet of being a manager today is expendability. That was the argument, and it's as specious today as it was then.

On the other hand, I'm saddened by the fact that several former star ballplayers—Hank Aaron and Joe Morgan, for instance—turned down managerial offers because the salaries were lower than their salaries as players or what they could make in the business world outside baseball. Hey, the job comes with a pay cut: Dallas Green maybe made $350,000 when he managed the Yanks, which was maybe a third of what Mattingly made as a player. If you want to manage, no matter what color your skin is, you'd better know you can't make what you did as a player, at least if you were a star.

Occasionally we do see a minority hiring, such as Frank Robinson with the Giants and Orioles, but if baseball has really changed as much as people like to complain that it has, then why did the hiring of a guy like Cito Gaston hit the headlines as big as it did?

Mind you, all of this hot controversy, gossip, and argument simply becomes fodder for the trivia mills of the future. With that in mind, it's time for trivia that exists outside of time, where the era in which it occurred is entirely irrelevant!

BROOKLYN DODGERS MANAGER WILBERT ROBINSON ONCE CLAIMED THAT HE COULD CATCH A BASEBALL DROPPED FROM AN AIRPLANE 525 FEET IN THE AIR AND THE FORMER CATCHER SOON HAD HIS CHANCE TO PROVE IT. WHAT HAPPENED IN WHAT TURNED OUT TO BE ONE OF BASEBALL'S ZANIEST GAGS?

Frank Kelly, the Dodgers' trainer, volunteered to go up in a plane and drop the baseball to Robinson waiting below. But Casey Stengel had other ideas. The master pranksman handed Kelly a large grapefruit instead of a ball.

As Robinson prepared himself for the catch, the airplane reached position at 525 feet directly above. Kelly dropped it and Robinson saw what looked like a ball coming down. As Robinson tried to grab the missile, it smashed him to the ground, leaving his face and body a juicy, drenched mess.

"Oh God, I'm killed! I'm blind! It's broke open my chest. I'm covered with blood! Somebody help me!"

When Robinson heard the roaring laughter, he got up quickly. A short while later he couldn't help but laugh himself at one of the zaniest stunts ever pulled in baseball.

WHICH PLAYER DID MANAGER CASEY STENGEL KEEP ON HIS BOSTON BEES TEAM BECAUSE HE SWEPT OUT THE CLUBHOUSE?

During the late thirties and forties, Casey Stengel kept a young, skinny utility player on the team because he always swept out the clubhouse and Casey liked keeping things clean. The player was Whitey Wietelmann, who later became a rather hefty coach of the San Diego Padres, where he continued to keep things in order. He fixed clocks, mended suitcases and trunks, patched furniture, and repainted chairs.

"Sometimes," said Whitey, "pitchers throw chairs. You can fix anything if you have the right tools."

Whitey became a part of baseball folklore by accompanying Stengel the night "The Perfesser" was supposed to have been hit by a taxi. The incident prompted Dave Egan, a Boston writer, to propose that the cab driver be given an award for having done the most for Boston baseball that year by striking Stengel. Wietelmann's version of the historic event is different. "I was sitting in a bar with Casey, having a couple of beers," said Whitey. "Afterward, Casey had to go across the street to the Miles Standish Hotel. He wore a big black coat and a black hat. He walked right into that cab—that's what happened."

Wietelmann also had a fling as a manager in the minors. In Yuma, he found his ballplayers by advertising in the newspapers and, besides managing, he was the groundskeeper and concessions manager. He was also ingenious. "When I got kicked out of a ball game, I'd go up in the stands and sell beer. I had an arrangement with one of my pitchers: if I had two bottles in my hand it meant bunt. If I was drinking from the bottle, it meant something else. Those were my signs."

CORRECTLY IDENTIFY THE ACCOMPLISHMENTS OF THE TWO SPORTS FIGURES NAMED TEX RICKARD.

The "original" Tex Rickard was a Texas-born promoter who came to New York to become one of the city's most renowned sportsmen. He was most prominently associated with boxing but also helped organize a group of financiers who built Madison Square Garden on 50th Street, the predecessor to the contemporary Garden. Originally the Garden, which opened in 1925, was to feature boxing, but it later became the home of hockey and basketball teams. The New York Rangers were so named because of Rickard and his Texas background—hence Tex's Rangers.

A few decades later another Tex Rickard appeared on the New York sports scene. The latter-day Rickard was the public address announcer at Brooklyn Dodgers games at Ebbets Field and a character who became legend for his misuse and abuse of the language and attendant malapropisms. Once, a visiting team complained to the umpires about coats and jackets that were draped over the railing in center field.

Dutifully, the umpire walked over to Rickard, who manned the public-address microphone, and asked him to make a plea over the p.-a. system about the disturbing coats and jackets.

Rickard obligingly took microphone in hand and intoned: "WILL THE LADIES AND GENTLEMEN IN THE CENTER-FIELD BLEACHERS PLEASE REMOVE THEIR CLOTHING!"

WHO ARE THE ONLY TWO NATIONAL LEAGUERS TO HIT OVER .400 IN THIS CENTURY?

Rogers Hornsby and Bill Terry. Hornsby did it three times—1922 (.401), 1924 (.424), and 1925 (.403) with the St. Louis Cardinals. Terry, whose playing career began in 1923, hit .401 in 1930 with the Giants and had a lifetime average of .341. Hornsby, who started playing in 1915, finished his career with a lifetime average of .358.

WHAT WAS THE MOST UNUSUAL MANAGERIAL BIRTHDAY CELEBRATION OF MODERN TIME?

When "Jolly" Charlie Grimm managed the Milwaukee Brewers of the American Association, he was approached by his boss, Bill Veeck, who realized that Grimm's birthday would arrive soon. Veeck asked what his manager would like for this birthday.

"A good left-handed pitcher," replied a smiling Grimm, expecting nothing more than a short beer in return.

But Milwaukee had a long tradition of honoring its baseball managers' or coaches' birthdays with lavish on-the-diamond fetes prior to the game and Grimm was toasted with such a celebration at the pitcher's mound.

A huge cake was wheeled onto the field, whereupon manager Grimm was presented with a $1,000 savings bond, compliments of the Brewers. When Charlie took the giant knife in hand to cut the cake, he discovered that his wish had been granted. Hidden inside the cake was one José Acosta, a left-handed pitcher whom Veeck had secretly purchased from Norfolk for his manager's birthday.

"I called the Norfolk owner," said Veeck, "and said I'd give him $7,500 for Acosta and another $5,000, providing nobody knew he had been bought. Wild horses couldn't have torn the secret out of him."

Grimm was suitably astonished and delighted with Veeck's thoughtfulness. "Well, Charlie," said Veeck, "it is the birthday present you wanted—a left-handed pitcher."

The grateful manager started his new acquisition in the second game of that afternoon's doubleheader. Although he lost the game in thirteen innings, Acosta struck out seventeen batters and later proved to be a major factor in the Brewers' American Association pennant drive.

WHO WAS THE MOST UNUSUAL PUBLISHER
IN BASEBALL?

J. G. Taylor Spink. One of the most unpredictable men in baseball, Spink was publisher of *The Sporting News* and reigned as king of baseball journalism through most of the first half of the century. Spink was both amusing and terrifying. He had a habit of waking his correspondents—working newspapermen in the big cities—at all hours of the night. The reporters loathed him for that, but there were others who loved him. President Franklin Delano Roosevelt wrote Spink a fan letter during World War II. The Commander in Chief of the armed forces saluted Spink for getting 400,000 copies of *The Sporting News* to servicemen every week during the war. At a testimonial dinner for Spink in 1960, the Athletic Goods Manufacturers' Association honored Spink with a silver Revere bowl as "America's Foremost Sports Publisher."

Colleagues remember Spink for his eccentricities. He was obsessive about punctuality and hard work. Once a member of the staff was two hours late at the office, whereupon Spink demanded an explanation. "I was kept awake all night by a toothache," said the writer, holding his jaw. To which Spink snapped: "If you couldn't sleep, there was no reason for you to be late this morning."

According to Gerald Holland of *Sports Illustrated,* Spink probably fired most of the correspondents who worked for him at one time or another. In most cases, however, the staff members returned. "When Spink's temper cooled," said Holland, "Spink usually told them a humorous story, by way of indirect apology, and frequently gave them a raise or a gift to assure them that all was forgiven."

When Spink died in 1962, one of the first to arrive at the publisher's funeral was Dan Daniel, longtime baseball columnist for *The New York World-Telegram* and the New York correspondent for *The Sporting News.* When someone asked Daniel why he had arrived so early, the reporter replied: "If I hadn't, Spink would have fired me for the forty-first time."

Before the invention of radar, Spink had a knack for locating his distant correspondents and cartoonists (such as award-winning Willard Mullin of *The New York World-Telegram*) wherever they might be hiding. "Spink," said Mullin, "could get you on the pipe from any place, to any place, at any time."

Once Mullin was invited by a friend to play golf on a course that he had never seen before. "All was well," Mullin recalled, "until we were putting on the sixth green. Suddenly a messenger came galloping from the clubhouse, tongue hanging out, with the 'message from Garcia' (Spink). I don't know how the hell he found me, but he did!"

On another occasion, Spink pulled the telephone off his office wall after seeking inside information on negotiations to move the Braves from Boston to Milwaukee. The publisher had been calling Lou Perini, one of the principals in the deal, night and day in an attempt to get the scoop. After several dozen calls, he phoned Perini one morning and said, "Hello, Lou. This is Taylor."

Then there was a pregnant pause.

"Whaddya mean, Taylor who? *Taylor Spink.*"

Then came another pause to consider the question from the other end. "*Spink—S-P-I-N-K,* you son of a bitch."

At which point the phone was ripped off the wall. Spink eventually got the scoop, at the expense of his phone and the wall.

Carl Benkert, former executive for the baseball-bat company Hillerich and Bradsby, once attended the Kentucky Derby with Spink. "Throughout the preliminary races," said Benkert, "Spink checked the racing form and yelled at people countless times, asking opinions about which horse would win the Derby. He even went to the window to buy his own tickets."

Finally, the Derby began and several companions wondered which horse the publisher eventually selected. When Middleground crossed the finish line first, Spink leaped for joy. "I had him! I had him! I had $100 on his nose!"

The publisher's companions were suitably impressed until Spink's wife, Blanche, turned to her husband and then her friends. "I have news for you. He also had $100 on each of the other thirteen horses in the race!"

During a trip to New York in the forties, Spink was heading for Ebbets Field in Brooklyn when he noticed that the taxi driver's license read Thomas Holmes. Spink was curious. "Are you Tommy Holmes, the baseball writer? The one who works for *The Brooklyn Eagle?*"

The cabbie's voice turned surly. "I am not," he replied to Spink. "But some crazy son of a bitch out in St. Louis thinks I am and keeps telephoning at three o'clock in the morning!"

Red Barber, the beloved radio announcer, found a soft spot in the publisher's heart when he visited Spink's office and noticed an out-of-print book on the shelf. Spink gave it to Barber and the broadcaster immediately offered to pay for the prize antique. Spink refused. "What could I do for you?" asked Barber.

A smile crossed Spink's face. "Be my friend," he said.

WHICH MAJOR-LEAGUE TEAM IS NOTED FOR STAGING THE MOST UNORTHODOX APPROACH TO THROWING OUT THE FIRST BALL ON OPENING DAY?

Bill Giles, executive vice president of the Philadelphia Phillies (son of Warren Giles, former National League president), instituted a "dropping"-the-first-ball ritual in place of the popular "throwing out" the first ball and it appeared the Veterans Stadium faithful appreciated the change. Among Giles's best "droppings" were: a "Parachute Man" who dropped the ball to a waiting Phillie seconds before landing; a "Helicopter Man" who did the same thing; the Flying Wallendas; and probably his most spectacular act, Joseph Guzman traversing a high wire on a motorcycle, and Monique hanging from a trapeze beneath. This duo performed a series of stunts some 100 feet above home plate and culminated their performance by dropping the first ball, which was caught by Phillies catcher, Bob Boone.

HOW MANY PITCHERS HAVE REGISTERED 100 OR MORE WINS IN BOTH THE AMERICAN AND NATIONAL LEAGUES?

Three. Cy Young won 289 games in the National League, pitching for Cleveland (which was in the National League in the late 1800's), St. Louis, and Boston. His 222 wins in the American League came with Boston and Cleveland, after the franchise joined the American League.

Jim Bunning, who had a total of 224 career wins, picked up 118 American League victories while with the Detroit Tigers from 1955 to 1963. Traded to Philadelphia after that season, Bunning went on to amass 106 wins in the National League, with the Phillies, the Pittsburgh Pirates, and the Los Angeles Dodgers.

Cy Young (shown in uniform, many years after his playing career ended, with Connie Mack, left) is one of three pitchers to log 100 or more wins in both the American and National Leagues. *(from the collection of Barry Halper)*

Gaylord Perry, with 314 wins over a 22-season career, was credited with 175 National League wins while pitching for the San Francisco Giants, San Diego Padres, and Atlanta. With the Cleveland Indians, Texas Rangers, and, very briefly, the New York Yankees, Seattle Mariners, and Kansas City Royals, Perry ran up a total of 139 victories in the American League.

One other fellow should be mentioned because he came within a single victory of joining the select group: Milt Pappas, who managed to pitch 110 victories for the American League Baltimore Orioles between 1958 and 1965. When he switched to the National League and played for the Cincinnati Reds, Atlanta Braves, and Chicago Cubs, Pappas posted 99 wins, just missing that elusive 100th victory by one game!

WHICH BALLPARK HAD THE BEST BILLBOARD IN BASEBALL HISTORY?

Dexter Park, Woodhaven, Queens, New York. An optician bought billboard space at the home park of the semipro baseball team, the Bushwicks.

"DON'T KILL THE UMPIRE, MAYBE IT'S YOUR EYES"
was the message that then suggested that irate fans visit the Queens
optician for an eye exam.

WHICH FAMOUS BASEBALL EXECUTIVE HAD AN EVEN MORE FAMOUS FATHER—A POPULAR MOVIE COMEDIAN WHO STARRED IN TWO BASEBALL MOVIES?

The late comedian, Joe E. Brown, who starred in *Elmer the Great*
and *Alibi Ike,* was the father of Harry Joe Brown, former Pittsburgh Pirates general manager.

THE LOS ANGELES DODGERS HAVE ONLY HAD TWO MANAGERS. WHO ARE THEY?

Since the Dodgers made the move from Brooklyn to Los Angeles on
that fateful day in 1958, they have had only *two* managers: Walter
Alston and Tom Lasorda.

WHO HOLDS THE RECORD FOR THE MOST INNINGS PITCHED AND MOST STRIKEOUTS IN ALL-STAR GAME HISTORY?

Don Drysdale, with 19 strikeouts in 19 innings pitched.

WHO WERE THE ONLY PLAYERS TO MAKE AN UNASSISTED TRIPLE PLAY?

There are eight who can stake this claim: the first was Neal Ball in
1908; then came Bill Wambsganss in 1920; George Burns, 1923;
Ernie Padgett, also 1923; Glenn Wright in 1925; Jimmy Cooney,
1927 and Johnny Neun in the same year; and Ron Hansen more
than 40 years later, in 1968.

CASEY STENGEL WAS WELL-KNOWN FOR HIS ZANY ANTICS AND REPUTED MALAPROPISMS. LAUGHING AND TALKING TO FANS WAS TYPICAL STENGEL WHEN HE WAS STILL PLAYING AS AN OUTFIELDER. WHAT WAS STENGEL'S WACKIEST STUNT?

It happened in Pittsburgh, and on this occasion Stengel was accepting cheers from the crowd. Naturally, he doffed his cap in appreciation of the crowd's enthusiasm, and as he did so, a bird flew out!

Stories—as to what kind of bird it was and where it had come from—conflict . . .

Casey Stengel (here as Yankees manager) had a sense of humor that was almost as legendary as his fractured English. *(from the collection of Barry Halper)*

WHAT FORMER DETROIT TIGERS OUTFIELDER NEVER PLAYED HIGH SCHOOL OR COLLEGE BASEBALL?

It was Ron LeFlore, who learned how to play baseball in prison. While at the State Prison of Southern Michigan serving a five-to-fifteen-year sentence for robbing a bar in 1970, LeFlore was invited to join the prison baseball team. Although he had never been particularly interested in The Game, Ron proved to be a natural. Word of his ability reached Tiger Stadium and he was invited for a tryout while on a weekend furlough from the penitentiary. LeFlore was signed by the Tigers in 1972.

WHO HOLDS THE RECORD FOR CONSECUTIVE SCORELESS INNINGS PITCHED IN THE WORLD SERIES?

Yankee southpaw Whitey Ford pitched a record 33 2/3 consecutive scoreless innings in the World Series.

EIGHT MANAGERS HAVE WON THE WORLD SERIES IN THEIR FIRST FULL SEASONS. WHO WERE THEY?

The eight rookie managers who managed World-Series Champs were:

Tris Speaker, 1920, Cleveland Indians
Bucky Harris, 1924, Washington Senators
Rogers Hornsby, 1926, St. Louis Cardinals
Bill Terry, 1933, New York Giants
Frankie Frisch, 1934, St. Louis Cardinals
Eddie Dyer, 1946, St. Louis Cardinals
Ralph Houk, 1961, New York Yankees
Dallas Green, 1980, Philadelphia Phillies

WHAT FORMER TEAM OWNER WAS A STAR SCHOOLBOY HOCKEY PLAYER IN NEW YORK?

Longtime Giants owner, Horace Stoneham.

WHAT MANAGERS HAVE WON THE MOST WORLD SERIES?

Joe McCarthy and Casey Stengel each won seven World Championships, a mark unmatched by any others.

HOW MANY BASEBALL PLAYERS HAVE PARTICIPATED IN GAMES IN FOUR DIFFERENT DECADES? WHO WAS THE MOST RECENT?

There are 20 players who have played in four decades. They are: Jim O'Rourke (1887–1910), Dan Brouthers (1879–1904), Jack

O'Connor (1887–1910), Jim "Deacon" McGuire (1884–1912), Kid Gleason (1888–1912), John B. Ryan (1889–1913), Eddie Collins (1906–1930), Nick Altrock (1898–1933), John Picus Quinn (1909–1933), Bobo Newsom (1929–1953), Mickey Vernon (1939–1960), Ted Williams (1939–1960), Early Wynn (1939–1963), Minnie Minoso (1949–1976 and two pinch-hitting appearances in 1980), Tim McCarver (1959–1980), Willie McCovey (1959–1980), Jim Kaat (1959–1983), and most recently Nolan Ryan (1967–1990), Carlton Fisk (1969–1990) and Rick Dempsey (1969–1990).

Minnie Minoso played from 1949 through 1976, spanning four decades. But since he pinch-hit twice in the 1980's, technically he's the only major-leaguer whose career spans *five* decades! *(from the collection of Barry Halper)*

WHAT TWO PITCHERS HAVE WON A TOTAL OF 300 GAMES WHILE PLAYING IN FOUR DIFFERENT DECADES?

Early Wynn and Nolan Ryan are the only two pitchers to win 300 games in the process.

Early Wynn is one of two major-league pitchers who managed to win 300 games while hurling in four different decades. *(from the collection of Barry Halper)*

WHO WAS THE FIRST PLAYER TO HIT THREE HOME RUNS IN ONE GAME AT DODGER STADIUM?
Willie Stargell did it first, on June 24, 1965.

WHAT WERE SATCHEL PAIGE'S "SIX RULES FOR STAYING YOUNG"?
Paige, who was at least sixty-two-years old when he last pitched, and whose career included 2,500 games, attributed his longevity to his rules for staying young. He said, "If you're over six years of age, follow these rules closely:"

1. Avoid fried meats which anger up the blood.
2. If your stomach disputes you, lie down and pacify it with cool thoughts.
3. Keep the juices flowing by jangling around gently as you move.
4. Go very light on the vices, such as carrying on in society— the social ramble ain't restful.
5. Avoid running at all times.
6. Don't look back. Something might be gaining on you.

This last rule became the title of Paige's autobiography.

WHAT BOSTON RED SOX LEGEND IS THE SON OF A POLISH-AMERICAN POTATO FARMER?
Carl Yastrzemski.

SOMETIMES AFTER A BAD DAY AT THE PLATE CARL YASTRZEMSKI HAD A METHOD OF RESTORING HIS CONFIDENCE. WHAT WAS IT?
If Yaz was dissatisfied enough with his batting performance in a game, he would take batting practice immediately after the game.

PHIL RIZZUTO WAS ONE OF THE MORE LIKABLE, EASYGOING GUYS IN BASEBALL, MAKING HIM A SPLENDID TARGET FOR A HOST OF PRACTICAL JOKES. PHIL FOUND FROGS IN HIS BED AND HIS SPIKES NAILED TO THE FLOOR IN SOME PRANKS, BUT HE EVEN SPENT A FEW HOURS IN A JAIL CELL AS A RESULT OF ANOTHER TRICK BY HIS TEAMMATES. WHAT HAPPENED?

It was the old snipe-hunting trick that fooled the gullible Rizzuto, this time at spring training in Florida. A snipe is a long-billed wading bird, and this particular hunt led the adventurers into an orange grove where everyone soon disappeared, as planned, leaving Rizzuto alone. His teammates got the town sheriff into the act, and he quickly joined the scene. Creeping up on the unsuspecting Rizzuto, the sheriff said, "What are you doing here?"

"Nothing," Phil answered, too scared to say anything else.

"Prowling!" blared the sheriff, putting on a convincing act. "We don't like prowlers around here!"

All of a sudden, poor Phil was in handcuffs and on his way to the town jail.

After a couple of dreary hours in the lonely jail cell, Phil was greeted by his teammates and they all had a good, hard laugh.

HOLLYWOOD HAS HAD THE DEVIL AND A GROUP OF INTERDENOMINATIONAL ANGELS TO INTERVENE IN AN AMERICAN LEAGUE AND A NATIONAL LEAGUE PENNANT RACE. CAN YOU NAME THE TWO MOVIES?

In the musical comedy *Damn Yankees,* starring Tab Hunter and Gwen Verdon, the Devil, played by Ray Walston, offers victory to the perennially last place Washington Senators. ("Diamond-gate?")

Angels provided the divine power for a Pittsburgh Pirates pennant in the motion picture *Angels in the Outfield,* starring Paul Douglas and Janet Leigh.

WHAT MAJOR-LEAGUE TEAM HOLDS THE RECORD FOR MOST CONSECUTIVE YEARS PLAYED WITHOUT WINNING A WORLD SERIES?

The Phillies, who else? The National League entry from the City of Brotherly Love did not win a World Series from the time the first one was played in 1903 until 1980. That makes a dreadful total of 76 seasons (no Series was played in 1904) without a Series winner. In their first two appearances in the World Series, the Phillies lost to the Boston Red Sox, 4–1, in 1915, and to the New York Yankees, 4–0, in 1950. Imagine the shock and delirium in Philadelphia when the Phillies took Kansas City four games to two in 1980.

NAME THE THREE OCCASIONS IN BASEBALL HISTORY DURING WHICH BATTING CHAMPIONSHIPS WERE DECIDED BY EXTENDING THE AVERAGES TO FOUR PERCENTAGE POINTS?

The first batting title decided by the mathematicians was in 1931 when the St. Louis Cardinals' Chick Hafey batted .3489 to beat out Bill Terry of the New York Giants, whose average was .3486. In that same season, Hafey's teammate, Jim Bottomley, finished third in batting with a .3482 average. In 1949, the Detroit Tigers' third baseman, George Kell, hit .3429, nosing out Ted Williams, the Boston Red Sox slugger, who batted .3427. In 1970, Alex Johnson of the California Angels won the batting title on the final day of the season, finishing ahead of Red Sox ace Carl Yastrzemski. Johnson hit .3289; Yaz, .3286.

The closest a pair of teammates came to a batting title was 1976 when George Brett and Hal McRae of the Kansas City Royals battled down to the last game. Brett won the title batting .333, while McRae's average was .332.

WHICH TWO BASEBALL PLAYERS HAVE HAD CANDY BARS NAMED FOR THEM?

Hall of Famer Ty Cobb of the Detroit Tigers had a candy bar named for him. It was produced by the Benjamin Candy Company of Detroit, but never caught the sweet tooth of America and quickly passed out of existence. In 1978, Curtiss Candy Company, a unit of Standard Brands, Inc., came out with the "Reggie" bar named for New York Yankees slugger Reggie Jackson.

Contrary to popular belief (according to Curtiss Candy) the "Baby Ruth" bar was not named for Babe Ruth, but rather for President Grover Cleveland's daughter, Ruth, who was born in the White House. In fact, when The Babe sought to endorse another product—"Babe Ruth's Home Run Candy"—Curtiss appealed to the U.S. Patent Office and won an order enjoining the slugger from getting into the candy business.

WHICH MAJOR-LEAGUE MANAGER ONCE CALLED FOR A PINCH HITTER WHO HADN'T BEEN ON THE TEAM ROSTER FOR TWO YEARS?

Leo "The Lip" Durocher. Late in a game in which the Chicago Cubs were trailing by one run, Chicago manager Leo Durocher barked: "Tell Willie Smith to get ready, I'm going to pinch-hit with him." A pregnant silence fell over the Cubs' dugout. Finally, Jim Hickman, who always had a fondness for Durocher, clambered from his seat at the other end of the bench, strode over to Durocher, and whispered: "Skip! Willie Smith hasn't been with us for two years. But if you really want me to, I'll find him and bring him back."

WHAT FIVE MAJOR-LEAGUE MANAGERS EACH WON PENNANTS IN BOTH THE AMERICAN AND NATIONAL LEAGUES?

Joe McCarthy, Alvin Dark, Yogi Berra, Dick Williams and Sparky Anderson. McCarthy won his first with his 1929 Chicago Cubs. The Cubbies lost to the Philadelphia Athletics in the World Series. In the American League, McCarthy won a total of eight championships, all with the New York Yankees. The Yanks won seven world titles under McCarthy. In 1932 they defeated the Chicago Cubs, in 1936 and 1937 the New York Giants, then the Cubs again in 1938, the Cincinnati Reds in 1939, the Brooklyn Dodgers in 1941. The Yanks lost to the St. Louis Cardinals in 1942 but came back to baste the Redbirds in 1943.

Dark's first pennant came as manager of the San Francisco Giants in 1962. The National Leaguers lost to the Yankees in that year's World Series. In 1974, Dark was managing across the Bay in Oakland when the A's won the American League Championship and then the World Series against the Dodgers. Dark came close in 1975 when the A's won the American League West but lost to the Boston Red Sox in the play-off.

Berra not only can claim a pennant in both leagues, he can boast of turning the trick with teams from the same city. In 1964, the lovable Yogi led the Yankees to the pennant, then lost to the Cardinals in the Series. In 1973 he brought the Mets the league championship, only to lose out to the Oakland A's.

Dick Williams was a rookie manager when he took over the Red Sox in 1967. Thanks to good pitching and the MVP performance of Carl Yazstremski, Boston won the American League pennant. They fell short in the World Series, however, thanks to the solid pitching of the Cardinals' right hander Bob Gibson. He was a World Series winner with the Oakland A's in 1972 and 1973. In 1984, Williams managed the San Diego Padres to their first pennant in team history. They lost in the World Series to the Detroit Tigers.

Sparky Anderson won his first pennant with the Cincinnati Reds in 1970. He lost to the Baltimore Orioles. Two years later, he lost to Dick Williams's Oakland A's in a very exciting World Series. In 1975 and 1976, he piloted the Big Red Machine to their first World Series wins since 1940, and in the process the Reds became the first National League team to win consecutive World Series since the 1921–22 New York Giants. In 1984 he got his revenge on Dick Williams, taking his Detroit Tigers to the World Series and winning their first championship since 1968.

**PHIL RIZZUTO AND BILLY MARTIN ONCE
EXCHANGED THEIR BASEBALL SHIRTS FOR A GAME
AGAINST THE BOSTON RED SOX IN FENWAY PARK.
WHAT WAS THE STRANGE REASON BEHIND THIS?**
In 1950 Rizzuto had received a letter from a deranged Red Sox fan who threatened to shoot him the next time the Scooter played in

Fenway Park. While dressing for the game that afternoon, Rizzuto, manager Casey Stengel, and all the Yankees were unusually tense—all except Billy Martin.

"Let's change uniforms," said Martin. "You wear my shirt. I'll wear yours."

Rizzuto looked over at Casey, who shrugged his shoulders.

"Come on," Billy pressed. "I'll wear your number ten. You wear my number one. I'll take the chance, be the target. Anyway, I can run faster than you can."

Billy got what he wanted and on the diamond that day he did a lot of

Phil Rizzuto once gave Billy Martin the shirt off his back. *(from the collection of Barry Halper)*

moving. Martin was not going to be an easy target for the gunman. Fortunately, the man with the gun was apparently not in the park. Martin and Rizzuto escaped without harm while Phil collected his 200th hit that game. Rizzuto went on to win his first and only MVP.

HOW MANY TIMES HAS A PLAYER ACHIEVED 170 RBI'S IN A SEASON?

Nine times a player has reached the 170 RBI plateau; three of those times it was accomplished by Lou Gehrig.

WHO SHARES THE CAREER MARK FOR THE MOST RBI'S PER GAME?

Sam Thompson (1885–1906, with Detroit and Philadelphia), Lou Gehrig, and Hank Greenberg, throughout their careers, averaged 0.92 runs batted in per game.

NAME THE TWO PITCHING BROTHERS, WHO, TOGETHER, OWN THE MOST MAJOR-LEAGUE VICTORIES? WHO ARE THE RUNNERS-UP?

The Niekro brothers, Joe and Phil, surpassed all pitching brothers, with a combined total of 538 wins.

The runners-up are not the Dean boys, though Dizzy and

Daffy did manage to garner 200 wins between them during their major-league careers, but the Perry brothers, Gaylord and Jim, who, between them, accumulated 529 wins. The Mathewsons, Christy and Henry, registered their third-place total of 373 while with the New York Giants in the early 1900's. There's just one small catch: Christy won all of those games! Henry Mathewson pitched for the Giants in 1906 and 1907, appeared in three games, and had one decision—a loss. Not much of a contributor, was he?

WHAT IS THE MAJOR-LEAGUE RECORD FOR MOST YEARS SEPARATING THE DEBUTS OF BASEBALL-PLAYING BROTHERS?

The 'Fowler brothers, Jessie and Art, broke into the majors 30 years apart. Jessie made his big-league debut in 1924 at the age of 24 with the St. Louis Cardinals. Art Fowler was 22 when his career began in 1954 with the Cincinnati Reds.

Jessie's career with St. Louis lasted only 13 games in 1924, whereas his brother was more successful. Art Fowler, 23 years younger than Jessie, pitched nine seasons with Cincinnati and Los Angeles (first the Dodgers and then the Angels). Art's final record was 54–51 with a career ERA of 4.03.

SINCE THE CY YOUNG AWARD WAS FIRST PRESENTED IN 1956, FOUR PITCHERS HAVE WON THE AWARD AT LEAST THREE TIMES DURING THEIR CAREERS. WHO ARE THEY?

Sandy Koufax, Tom Seaver, and Jim Palmer won the coveted Cy Young Award three times and Steve Carlton earned it four times. Koufax, of the Los Angeles Dodgers, won in 1963, 1965, and 1966, when the award was given to only one major-league pitcher. The rule awarding the Cy Young Trophy was changed in 1967, giving it to the best pitcher in each league. Tom Seaver of the New York Mets won it in 1969, 1973, and 1975. Palmer, the Baltimore Orioles righty, won it in 1973, 1975, and 1976. Carlton won in 1972, 1977, 1980, and 1982.

NAME THE TOP HOME-RUN HITTERS FOR EACH LETTER OF THE ALPHABET:

A—Hank Aaron (755)	N—Graig Nettles (389)
B—Ernie Banks (512)	O—Mel Ott (511)

C—Orlando Cepeda (379)
D—Joe DiMaggio (361)
E—Darrell Evans (444)
F—Jimmie Foxx (534)
G—Lou Gehrig (493)
H—Frank Howard (382)
I—Monte Irvin (99)
J—Reggie Jackson (563)
K—Harmon Killebrew (573)
L—Greg Luzinski (307)
M—Willie Mays (660)

P—Tony Perez (379)
Q—Jamie Quirk (37)
R—Babe Ruth (714)
S—Mike Schmidt (548)
T—Frank Thomas (286)
U—Willie Upshaw (123)
V—Mickey Vernon (172)
W—Ted Williams (521)
X—*—
Y—Carl Yastrzemski (452)
Z—Gus Zernial (237)

*There has never been a major-league player whose last name began with X.

Harmon Killebrew is baseball's top home-run hitter for the letter K! *(from the collection of Barry Halper)*

HOW MANY PLAYERS HAVE WON THE MOST VALUABLE PLAYER AWARD IN BACK-TO-BACK YEARS? WHAT YEARS DID THEY ACCOMPLISH THIS FEAT, AND WHO WERE THEY?

Since 1911, only nine players have done it. Here're the elite nine:

1. Jimmie Foxx 1B   1932–33 AL Philadelphia
2. Hal Newhouser P   1944–45 AL Detroit
3. Yogi Berra C   1954–55 AL New York
4. Mickey Mantle OF   1956–57 AL New York
5. Ernie Banks SS   1958–59 NL Chicago
6. Roger Maris OF   1960–61 AL New York
7. Joe Morgan 2B   1975–76 NL Cincinnati
8. Mike Schmidt 3B   1980–81 NL Philadelphia
9. Dale Murphy OF   1982–83 NL Atlanta

EXCLUDING PITCHERS, WHICH THREE MEMBERS OF THE BASEBALL HALL OF FAME ACCUMULATED THE POOREST CAREER BATTING AVERAGES?

Ray Schalk finished his baseball career with a batting average of .253, the lowest career average in Cooperstown. A major-leaguer with the Chicago White Sox from 1912–1928, Schalk led American League catchers in fielding eight times.

Harmon Killebrew batted only .256 over his 22-year career that spanned 1954–1975. The big Washington Senator/Minnesota Twin slugger blasted 573 home runs, good for fifth on the all-time list.

Rabbit Maranville's cumulative average of .258 is the third lowest in the Baseball Hall of Fame. The shortstop played 23 years in the majors, including nine- and six-year stints with Boston of the National League.

Six other enshrined players have career averages below .270. Four are shortstops: Luis Aparicio (.262, 1956–1973), Joe Tinker (.263, 1902–1916), Bobby Wallace (.267, 1894–1918) and Pee Wee Reese (.269, 1940–1958). Third baseman Brooks Robinson batted .267 from 1955–1977. Catcher Johnny Bench had a career average of .267 from 1967–1983.

HOW MANY PLAYERS WITH THE LAST NAME JOHNSON HAVE PLAYED IN THE MAJOR LEAGUES?

74. Abbie, Alex, Abe, Adam Jr., Adam Sr., Art G., Art H., Bart, Ben, Bill C., Bill L., Bill T., Billy, Bob D., Bobby Earl, Bob L., Bob W., Charlie, Chet, Chief, Cliff, Connie, Darrell, Dave, Dave W., Davey, Deron, Dick, Don R., Don S., Earl, Ed, Ellis, Elmer, Ernie R., Ernie T., Frank, Fred, Hank, Howard, Jerry, Jim, Jing, Joe, John, John Henry, Johnny, Ken T., Ken W., Lamar, Lance, Larry, Lloyd, Lou, Mike, Otis, Paul, Randy A., Randy G., Randy S., Ron, Roy C., Roy "Hardrock," Silas, Spud, Stan, Syl, Tim, Tom G., Tom R., Tony, Vic, Wallace, and Walter.

HOW MANY PLAYERS WITH THE LAST NAME OF WILLIAMS HAVE PLAYED IN THE MAJOR LEAGUES?

57. Art, Bernie, Billy (2), Bob, Buff, Cy, Dallas, Davey, Denny, Dewey, Dib, Dick, Earl Baxter, Earl Craig, Eddie, George, Gus (August), Harry, Jim (2), Jimmy, Kenneth Roy, Kenneth Royal, Mark, Matt (Derrick), Otto, Pap, Reggie, Rinaldo, Rip, Ted, Walt,

Wash, and Woody. *Pitchers:* Ace, Albert, Almon, Charlie, Dale, Dave, Donald Fred, Donald Reid, Frank, Gus (Augustine), Johnny, Lefty, Leon, Marsh, Matt Evan, Mitch, Mutt, Pop, Rick, Stan, Steamboat, and Tom.

HOW MANY PLAYERS WITH THE LAST NAME OF SMITH HAVE PLAYED IN THE MAJOR LEAGUES?

122. Alphonse, Al, Bernie, Bill, Billy, Bob, Bobby, Brick, Broadway, Bull, Carr, Charley, Chris, Dick Arthur, Dick Harrison, Dick Kelly, Dwight, Earl C., Earl L., Earl S., Edgar, Edgar Gene, Elmer, Elmer John, Ernie, Frank L., Fred V., George C., Germany, Hal R., Hal W., Hap, Harry T., Harry W., J. Harry, Harvey, Heinie, Jack, Jack J., Jimmy Lawrence, Jimmy Lorne, Joe, John J., John M., Jud, Keith L., Keith P., Ken, Klondike, Leo, Lonnie, Mayo, Mike, Milt, Nate, Ollie, Ozzie, Paul L., Paul S., Paddy, Pop, Ray, Red (James), Red (Marvin), Red (Richard), Red (Willard), Reggie, Skyrocket, Stub, Syd, Tom N., Tommy, Tony, Vinnie, Wally, Wib, and Willie. *Pitchers:* Alfred J., Alfred K., Art, Bill, Bill G., Billy L., Bob A., Bob E., Bob G., Bryn, Charlie, Chick, Clay, Dave M., Dave S., Dave W., Doug, Ed, Eddie, Frank E., Frank T., Fred, Fred C., George A., George S., Hal L., Harry M., Jack H., Jake, Lee, Mark, Mike A., Pete J., Pete L., Phenomenal, Pop (C), Pop Boy, Reginald, Riverboat, Roy, Rufus, Sherry, Tom E., Willie, and Zane.

HOW MANY TEAMS HAVE REBOUNDED TO WIN FOUR CONSECUTIVE WORLD-SERIES GAMES AFTER DROPPING THE FIRST THREE GAMES?

No team in major-league history has come back to win the World Series after losing the first three games.

MAZER'S
MEMORABLE MOMENTS
(AND THE MEN
WHO MADE THEM HAPPEN)

More often than not, when people ask me "trivia" questions, they are actually asking me to remember something that was not trivial at all, but rather, in terms of that particular sport, historic.

There are events that occur in any sport that become legend or myth, and by the time a few years have passed, it would seem that everybody in the world was at that particular event, or their father was! And it is from those events that a wealth of "trivia" arises.

I'm going to give you several examples of such "myths" in baseball history: events that were so striking, so impressive, or so heroic to an audience, that they are discussed even today. After telling you all about the event, I'll then reflect somewhat on the moment.

That is basically the means by which I create the memories that seem to impress so many: I think of an incident (even one at which I wasn't present, but which has been graphically described in print or in photos) that has impacted on my mind, then I "personalize" the incident, that is, add a personal "signpost" to the event that will help me recall it, like what I was doing that day or some idiosyncrasy of the batter or pitcher who performed the feat, and *voilà,* I remember the moment, seemingly forever.

FLOYD BEVENS'S ALMOST NO-HIT GAME
While some baseball fans think about Al Gionfriddo's acrobatic

catch when they remember the 1947 World Series between the Brooklyn Dodgers and New York Yankees, others recollect the remarkable pitching performance that was wasted by Yankee right-hander Floyd Bevens.

On October 3 in Game Four of the Series, Bevens held the Dodgers hitless for eight innings as the Yankees led 2–1. Brooklyn's lone run came on two walks, a sacrifice bunt, and an infield out. The Yankees had a number of opportunities to break the game open, but failed to capitalize. Yet Bevens looked to have all the runs he needed.

In the bottom of the ninth, Bevens's first pitch was hit by Brooklyn's Bruce Edwards deep to the left-field warning track, only to be caught by Johnny Lindell.

Bevens walked the next batter, Carl Furillo—Bevens's ninth free pass of the game. Spider Jorgensen then fouled out, and Bevens was one out away from pitching the first World-Series no-hitter, ever.

Dodgers manager Burt Shotton sent an injured Pete Reiser, recovering from a broken ankle, up to pinch-hit and had Gionfriddo run for Furillo. When the pinch runner stole second, Yankee manager Bucky Harris decided to break one of baseball's unwritten laws by having Bevens intentionally walk Reiser and the potential winning run to first base.

Shotton then sent up Cookie Lavagetto to pinch-hit for Eddie Stanky and put in Eddie Miksis as a pinch runner at first. On the second pitch, Lavagetto lined a double off the right-field wall, scoring two runs—Miksis legging the winning run all the way from first—and the game went to the Dodgers, 3–2.

Ironically, it was Lavagetto's only hit of the Series, and the only ball he hit to right field *all year*. While the joyous Ebbets Field fans celebrated, Bevens stood on the mound in a daze.

"I ordered Reiser put on," said Harris, defending his decision. "And I'd do the same thing tomorrow."

Sure enough, Harris did use a similar strategy the next day. But this time the Yankees prevailed, 2–1, as they moved one step closer to an eventual championship.

●

In a way it's ironic for me to place Bevens's accomplishment as a memorable moment because as a Dodger fan I hated the Yankees and was rooting for the Dodgers all the way. Whether Bevens got his no-hitter or not was of no concern to me that day. I just wanted the Dodgers to win the game, and they did. Bevens's close call with immortality was certainly memorable, but for Dodger fans the most memorable moment of the game was the sight of Cookie Lavagetto's double smacking off the right-field wall and Eddie Miksis crossing home plate with the winning run.

ROBERTO CLEMENTE'S 3,000TH HIT

Roberto Clemente's final hit of the 1972 season was the three thousandth of his career. Due to his untimely death in the off-season, it would be the last hit of his career. On September 29, the Pirates hosted the Mets at Three Rivers Stadium in Pittsburgh. Clemente had already broken the Pirates' records for hits, total bases, RBI's, games played, and at bats. With 2,999 hits, Clemente was on the verge of breaking into baseball's most exclusive hitting club, which boasted members like Ty Cobb, Willie Mays, and Hank Aaron.

In his first at bat, Clemente hit a bouncer over the pitcher's mound, which eventually skipped off second baseman Ken Boswell's glove. The crowd waited to see if it would be ruled a hit or an error. When an *H* was flashed on the scoreboard, the fans went wild. However, the official scorer said it was an error, and the crowd booed when an *E* was flashed on the scoreboard. Clemente said later, "I'm glad they didn't call it a hit. I wanted to get it without any taint."

However, Clemente's double off the wall in the fourth inning of the next night's game was free of any type of taint. The number 3,000 lit up the entire scoreboard, to a standing ovation from the crowd. Jon Matlack, the Mets' pitcher, held back his next pitch for a minute to give Clemente time to soak in the applause.

Clemente was deeply touched. "I give this hit to the fans of Pittsburgh and to the people of Puerto Rico," he said after the game.

Three months later, this superstar and humanitarian died in a plane crash while on a mercy mission to help the victims of an earthquake in Nicaragua. The enormously talented thirty-eight-year-old finished his career with exactly 3,000 hits.

●

I saw Roberto Clemente when he was with the Montreal baseball club of the International League, playing at Offerman Stadium. It was 1954 and he was just a twenty-year-old kid. I remember that he was good-looking and had greyhoundlike speed, but I wish I had taken greater notice of him in Offerman.

Apparently the Dodgers thought no one else would take notice of him either. I'm sure they figured they had him well camouflaged in Montreal, particularly in light of his very modest .257 batting average that season. But, alas, the Pittsburgh Pirates noticed him, and how! They drafted him Number One, November 22, 1954, and the rest, as they say, was history. Obviously, had the Dodgers kept him on their major-league roster, the Pirates wouldn't have been able to touch him; but if a property was on a minor-league roster, a rival major-league club had the right to draft the player. What class —not to mention talent—Roberto would've added to my Bums!

JOE DIMAGGIO'S "COMEBACK"

During Joe DiMaggio's career with the New York Yankees, he proved he was among baseball's all-time elite. His only weakness was his susceptibility to injury, which forced him to miss an average of twenty games a season. Yet in 1949, DiMaggio bounced back from what looked to be a career-threatening injury and led his team past the Boston Red Sox and on to a World Series.

When Joe DiMaggio returned to the lineup, the Yankees surged into first place. *(from the collection of Barry Halper)*

During 1949, he missed all of spring training and half the season because of intolerable pain in his right heel caused by a calcium deposit. The fear that he was through as a player remained with him for half the season as the pain grew worse.

Then a "miracle" happened. One morning DiMaggio got out of bed and stood up painlessly. Two weeks later, he met his teammates in Boston as they were about to battle the first-place Red Sox.

In his first at bat in eight months, the Yankee Clipper singled off lefty Mickey McDermott. His next at bat was more memorable as he hit a two-run homer to spark the Yankees to a 5–4 win.

But DiMaggio was not through. The next night, the Yankee Clipper helped his club erase a 7–1 deficit by hitting a three-run homer and a two-run homer late in the game to spark a 9–7 Yankee victory.

In the final game of the three-game series at Fenway Park, DiMaggio hit a three-run homer to break open a close contest as the Yankees swept their way into first place.

In those three days, DiMaggio hit four homers, drove in nine runs, and batted .455. Later that season, DiMaggio's heroics against the Red Sox at Yankee Stadium on the last day of the regular season boosted the Yankees to the American League pennant.

1949 may have been a painful year for the Yankee Clipper, but it was also a memorable one.

●

If you ever saw Cary Grant in a movie and noted how elegant he was, then you'll know what I mean when I say that to me Joe DiMaggio was the Cary Grant of baseball. He was absolutely the most elegant baseball player I ever saw—not the greatest, but the most elegant. He was a great clutch hitter and could run the bases well, even though he didn't steal many. But the Yankees were never a running ball club.

There was nothing showy about Joe. He didn't have Ruth's power, he didn't have Ruth's charisma, and he didn't have Ruth's composite abilities. Ruth, a home-run hitter, hit .342; DiMaggio had a memorable lifetime batting average of .325. But I will always remember DiMaggio for his total elegance more than anything else.

DODGERS WIN THE 1955 SERIES

The Brooklyn Dodgers consistently had outstanding ball clubs. Gil Hodges, Pee Wee Reese, Duke Snider, and Roy Campanella are only a few of the great players who graced Ebbets Field for the team from Brooklyn. For years the one obstacle that kept the Dodgers from a World Championship was the New York Yankees. The Bronx Bombers had won *five straight* World Series over the Dodgers going into the 1955 fall classic. When the Yankees took the first two games, it looked as though Brooklyn and their loyal, championship-starved fans would finish runners-up to their crosstown rivals once again.

When the Dodgers returned to Ebbets Field, they put a young, bulky left-hander named Johnny Podres on the mound. Podres, who had recorded only a 9–10 regular season, defeated the Yankees in that third game, giving the Dodgers a crucial win in their drive toward the championship. But Podres's work had just begun.

The Series came down to the final game at Yankee Stadium, with the twenty-three-year-old Podres going against thirty-five-year-old Tommy Byrne. Byrne had defeated the Dodgers in Game Two, giving up only five hits.

The Series was to be decided by two basic elements of the game, pitching and defense. Both Byrne and Podres pitched outstanding games, but the Dodgers got the defense. Throughout the game Podres pitched in and out of several tough jams as the Yankees tried valiantly to continue their dominance over the boys from Brooklyn. The Dodgers scored first in the fourth, and then added another run in the sixth. Gil Hodges, who had been struggling at the plate throughout the entire series, drove in both Dodger runs. Two runs were all Podres needed as the Dodgers refused to let this championship slip away.

The Yankees mounted their biggest threat in the sixth inning. Gil McDougald followed Billy Martin's walk with a surprise bunt that put runners on first and second with nobody out. Then came the play that preserved the championship for the Dodgers. As Yogi Berra came to the plate, newly inserted left-fielder Sandy Amoros positioned himself in left-center, giving Berra, generally a right-field hitter, most of left field. Berra slashed a line drive down the left-field line just inside fair territory. Amoros started running toward the ball as the base runners, Martin and McDougald, sure that the ball was a hit, took off. Amoros ran about 100 feet, making a full extension with his glove hand to grab the ball just before colliding with the fence in foul ground. Astonished, both Martin and McDougald had to reverse themselves, but McDougald had already passed second and was doubled up as Reese took Amoros's throw and relayed to Hodges at first.

Podres had to pitch out of another jam in the eighth with two men on base and one out. He induced Berra to pop up and struck out Hank Bauer. The Yankees went down in order in the ninth and there was dancing in the streets—literally—in Brooklyn. There would be no more waiting 'til next year. The Dodgers were the champions of baseball!

●

For me, up until that time in my life, the Dodgers' World-Series win was the greatest thrill of all. I'd watched Dodger teams for years and years and *years*—when they were awful, when they were near-great, then finally when they got to be great. Still, the only team they couldn't beat was the Yankees.

Then in '55 came a miracle worker: Johnny Podres. I vividly recall the last out, sitting in total disbelief—total disbelief because after a while you become convinced that you will never live to see the Dodgers win a World Series. It was quite simply one of the greatest moments I've ever enjoyed in sports.

AL GIONFRIDDO'S CATCH

"Swung on," yelled radio announcer Red Barber. "And belted. It's a long one, deep to left field. Back goes Gionfriddo. Back . . . back . . . back. It may be out of here. No! Gionfriddo makes a one-handed catch against the bull-pen fence. Ohhhhh, *doctor!*"

Forty years later, baseball fans still talk about "The Catch" in the 1947 World Series by Brooklyn Dodger left-fielder Al Gionfriddo at Yankee Stadium.

It was ironic that this catch, which many believe was the best World-Series catch ever, was made by a reserve outfielder, unknowingly playing his final major-league game, at the expense of one of baseball's all-time greats, New York Yankee Joe DiMaggio.

The play occurred in the sixth game of the Series, on October

5, as the Yankees entered the game needing only one more victory to celebrate.

With the Dodgers leading 8–5, Brooklyn manager Burt Shotton installed Gionfriddo as defensive insurance. The strategy paid off in the bottom of the sixth. With Yankee runners at first and second, DiMaggio hit lefty Joe Hatten's first pitch for what looked to be a game-tying homer. Gionfriddo turned and raced back to the deepest area of left field. Literally outrunning the ball, he turned a moment before he reached the 415-foot mark, leaped, and caught the ball just over the bull-pen fence. The crowd roared as DiMaggio stopped, shook his head, and kicked the infield dirt in disbelief.

"The Catch" saved the Dodgers for one more day, as they won the game 8–6, but the Yankees captured the World Series the next day as Gionfriddo was back at his accustomed spot on the bench. The Dodgers sent him to the minors the following year, never to recall him.

Although Gionfriddo did not have a long or great career in baseball, that one play in 1947 immortalized him forever.

●

That was a great World Series in '47, one of the best ever played. It was a young Dodger team against a Yankee team that had already fashioned greatness, and would fashion even more. And above all they had Joe DiMaggio. The thing I remember most about Gionfriddo was not only the catch, but the fact that as DiMaggio neared second base watching the little guy rob him of a home run, he showed an emotion that was very rarely outwardly expressed by DiMaggio: anger. He kicked the dirt. It was a great catch by Gionfriddo. But was it the best catch I have ever seen in the World Series? No.

What was?

There were a number of other unbelievable catches. Willie Mays's catch of Vic Wertz's fly ball in the '54 World Series was a Willie Mays catch, gargantuan, made by a man who made many great catches. But Ron Swoboda made a catch of a Brooks Robinson drive in the '69 World Series that Willie Mays would have been proud to make. Gionfriddo's was a great catch, but when I think of a World-Series catch, the greatest was Willie Mays's.

WILLIE MAYS'S MIRACLE CATCH

Willie Mays made so many great catches that it's hard to pinpoint his greatest. But the play that stands out in most fans' minds when they recollect the "Say Hey" kid's defensive skills was his catch off Vic Wertz in the 1954 World Series that pitted the Giants against the Cleveland Indians.

With the score tied 2–2 in the eighth inning of the first game at the Polo Grounds and runners on first and second with none out, a red-hot Wertz stepped to the plate against Giants southpaw Don Liddle. Wertz hit Liddle's first pitch to deep right-center field as Mays ran toward the bleachers with his back to the plate. With his arms outstretched, he made an astounding over-the-shoulder catch. Later that day, Mays would score the game-winning run in the tenth inning on Dusty Rhodes's pinch-hit three-run homer.

Willie Mays tips his cap after one of his "miracle" catches. *(from the collection of Barry Halper)*

As for the "Say Hey" kid himself, the most satisfying catch occurred in 1952 at Ebbets Field. With the Giants leading by a run in the eighth inning, Brooklyn pinch hitter Bobby Morgan hit a hard liner to the left-center-field wall, which Mays caught, despite running into the wall at full speed and knocking himself unconscious.

The umpire had to run out to Willie Mays and turn the center fielder's body over in order to make the "out" call. It was several minutes before Mays regained consciousness. As he jogged back to the dugout, he passed Dodger Jackie Robinson, who said, "Willie, that was the most amazing catch I ever saw."

●

The Mays catch is memorable for several reasons. First of all, it was vintage Willie. I'm often asked to compare Mays with Joe DiMaggio who played center field for the Yankees. As great as DiMaggio was, he might not have made that catch, at least not in my estimation. To do so, you had to be Kid Lightning and Willie was just that. He often struck me as a human meteor on the field. By contrast DiMaggio was more elegant, a Cary Grant of the diamond. Willie was much more the showman. More often than not when he ran, his cap would go flying off his head and he suffered more than a few spectacular crashes into outfield walls. What I found memorable, in addition, is the fact that most baseball historians have overlooked an important aspect of that particular series game. That is Mays made an even more significant defensive play two innings later.

With the score tied 2–2 in the 10th inning, Wertz came up to the plate and slammed a screwball off righty Marc Grissom. The ball sailed up the left-center slot and looked like a sure inside-the-park home run. As the ball headed for the bleacher wall, the galloping Mays speared it backhanded on a bounce, wheeled and relayed the ball back to the infield so fast that Wertz was held to a double. Grissom eventually got the Indians out without a run and the Giants ultimately took the game. While Mays has received overwhelming acclaim for his over-the-head catch, Willie himself has said that the play he made on Wertz in the 10th inning was considerably more difficult. Whatever the case, they both epitomized wild-running Willie and help explain why he has been one of my all-time favorites.

SANDY KOUFAX'S FOUR NO-HITTERS

Ask a baseball fan today who the best pitcher in baseball is, and you will get a variety of responses: Roger Clemens, Dwight Gooden, and Orel Hershiser are but a few of the answers you might receive. However, had you addressed that question to a baseball fan in the early 1960's, you would receive only one answer: Sandy Koufax. Not only did the overpowering lefty lead the league in ERA's every year from 1962–1966, but he hurled four no-hitters. His fourth no-hitter was of particular note, for it was a perfect game.

On September 9, 1965, Koufax took the mound against the Chicago Cubs. Having already thrown three no-hitters during his career, Koufax would pitch his most masterful game on this day. Koufax recalls, "I didn't have particularly good stuff in the beginning. My control was really good, though. My curve was the best I had all year."

Koufax would strike out fourteen batters in his perfect game. Seven of these would come from the seventh inning on. "In the last three innings, my fastball came alive—as good a fastball as I had all year." The Cubs would certainly have agreed. As it was, they had only three glimmering moments. In the first inning, Glenn Beckert's shot landed just left of the foul line; in the second, Pidge Browne smashed a hard liner to center field, but Willie Davis played him perfectly and made the catch; and in the seventh, after falling behind to Billy Williams, 3–0, Koufax got two strikes and then induced Williams to fly out.

After retiring Williams, Koufax went on to pitch his fourth no-hitter, breaking the record of three, previously held by Bob Feller.

There was yet another interesting facet of Koufax's perfect game. It is the only game in major-league history that produced just one hit. Cubs pitcher Bob Hendley pitched a one-hitter and lost—and the Dodgers' only run came *without* the benefit of this hit! In the fifth inning, Lou Johnson walked, was bunted to second, stole third, and came home on the catcher's bad throw. Two innings later the Dodgers got their only hit, a double by Lou Johnson.

●

My view of Sandy Koufax always was that as a manager if there was one game I had to win, he's the guy I'd want to pitch. I've seen a lot of guys who were great pitchers: Carl Hubbell, Dizzy Dean, Bob Feller. The thing about Koufax—with the only exception being the Orioles game when Jim Palmer beat him, and that was due to terrible outfielding—is that I thought Koufax was the greatest clutch pitcher I ever saw. I mean there are guys who threw a curve ball in the class of Koufax. But Koufax had the incredible ability to rise to that next level when it was a "must" game. He was the best at it.

He had a fastball and a curve ball and he didn't need anything else.

DON LARSEN'S PERFECT GAME

When baseball fans recall great World-Series pitching performances, it is New York Yankee Don Larsen's perfect game against the Brooklyn Dodgers in 1956 that stands out among the rest.

The 64,519 patrons who attended the October 8 game at Yankee Stadium witnessed something that had never been done in World-Series play before when Larsen retired all 27 Dodgers he faced during New York's 2–0 win.

Larsen's perfect game was in jeopardy five times, but his teammates came to his aid by making spectacular defensive plays: Gil McDougald fielded Jackie Robinson's line drive and Mantle made a spectacular catch of Gil Hodges's shot to left center. Sandy Amoros hit a Larsen pitch that would have been a homer, but then it went foul just before going into the seats.

It's hard to tell who's happier: pitcher Don Larsen, who has just completed a perfect World Series pitching effort, or his catcher Yogi Berra, who has just climbed "Mount Larsen" as high as physically possible! *(UPI/Bettmann)*

When the ninth inning arrived, Larsen started to feel the pressure. Only three batters separated him from making baseball history.

"I was weak in the knees out there in the ninth inning," Larsen recalled. "My legs were rubbery and my fingers didn't feel like they were attached to my hand. I said to myself, 'Please help me out, somebody!'"

After Larsen retired Carl Furillo and Campanella, only pinch hitter Dale Mitchell stood between Larsen and the perfect game. The crowd groaned as Larsen's first delivery went wide. But when Larsen came back by throwing two strikes, the fans were on their feet in anticipation.

Larsen threw a fastball, but Mitchell managed to foul it into the stands to prolong the suspense. After mumbling a prayer, "Please help me get out of this," Larsen threw a fastball that catcher Yogi Berra caught on the outside corner as umpire Babe Pinelli yelled, "Yer Out!"

Amazingly enough, this was the same Don Larsen who had been 3–21 two years earlier, and who had been burned by the same Dodger team three days earlier. It has been said that even mediocre ballplayers can become legends in October. Don Larsen is one of the prime examples.

●

The day after the game some newspaper reporter wrote the lead, "The Imperfect Man Pitches the Perfect Game." And he had a point. There are pitchers who have never pitched no-hitters—and Larsen couldn't carry their jocks. But it was Don Larsen who pitched the only no-hitter in the history of the World Series, and not only was it a no-hitter, but it was also a perfect game.

I put this accomplishment in the same category I put Roger Maris's breaking Babe Ruth's record. If you were to choose a man to pitch a perfect game in the World Series, you would pick a Koufax, you would pick a Walter Johnson, or you would pick a Christy Mathewson. Hell, Mathewson pitched three shutouts in *one* World Series, which isn't bad considering that he only pitched three games. There are superstars who will forever remain superstars, even if they didn't pitch perfect games.

THE "LONGEST" WORLD SERIES

In the 1962 World Series the San Francisco Giants almost upset the favored New York Yankees in seven games. In the first game at Candlestick Park, the Yankees disposed of the Giants with business-like dispatch, 6–2, on Clete Boyer's tie-breaking homer in the seventh inning. Whitey Ford outpitched Billy O'Dell, while the Giants contented themselves with breaking Ford's string of consecutive Series scoreless innings at 33⅔.

The Giants won the second game, 2–0, behind their ace, Jack Sanford. A 24-game winner during the regular season, Sanford limited the Yankees to three hits. The Giants nicked Ralph Terry for six, including Willie McCovey's homer.

In New York for Game Three, the teams battled in a scoreless tie for six and a half innings before Roger Maris singled to drive in two runs. He then scored a third that turned out to be the winner. Limiting the Giants to four hits, Bill Stafford bested Billy Pierce, 3–2, despite Ed Bailey's two-run homer in the ninth.

Roger Maris was in the "longest" World Series. *(from the collection of Barry Halper)*

The Giants pulled even the next day. Tied 2–2 in the seventh, they loaded the bases on one hit—Matty Alou's double sandwiched between walks to Jim Davenport and pinch hitter Bob Neiman. Harvey Kuenn popped up for the second out, but light-hitting Chuck Hiller lined one of Marshall Bridges's pitches into the right field stands. Hiller's grand slam, the first in Series history by a National Leaguer, won the game.

The Yankees recovered two days later. In the Terry-Sanford rematch, Tom Tresh's three-run homer broke a late-inning tie. Leading the Series three games to two, the Yankees returned to the West Coast on the verge of victory, only to be forestalled by the weather.

It rained in San Francisco the next three days, delaying the Series and subjecting the Giants' hospitality suite at the Sheraton-Palace Hotel to a horde of restless sportswriters with no sports to write about.

The Series resumed on Monday, October 15. With one out in the fourth inning of a scoreless game, Felipe Alou singled off Whitey Ford and Willie Mays walked. Alou scored on Ford's errant pick-off attempt, Mays came home on Orlando Cepeda's double, and Cepeda tallied on Davenport's single. Roger Maris homered for the Yankees, but the Giants got two more runs in the fifth, leaving them home free on Pierce's three-hitter. Winning 5–2, the Giants evened the Series for the third time.

So, it came down to the final game—Ralph Terry versus Jack Sanford for the third time, each having won once. In the fifth inning the Yanks loaded the bases with none out, on singles by Moose Skowron and Clete Boyer and a walk to Terry. When Sanford got Tony Kubek to hit into a double play, Giants fans gave thanks that the damage had been no worse, not realizing that Skowron's scoring on the double play would prove to be the game's only run.

Trailing by a run in the bottom of the ninth, Giants pinch hitter Matty Alou led off and beat out a drag bunt. But Terry bore down and struck out both Felipe Alou and Hiller. Now only Willie Mays stood between the Giants and defeat. Mays sent Terry's second pitch streaking toward the right-field corner—surely a double, perhaps a triple. Second baseman Richardson took the throw from right fielder Maris and held Alou at third.

With two out, men on second and third, and Willie McCovey at bat, manager Ralph Houk emerged from the Yankees' dugout to talk to Terry. "First base is open," Houk said. "Do you want to walk him and pitch to Cepeda?"

"I want to pitch to McCovey," said Terry. "I can get him out."

Houk told the pitcher to go ahead and returned to the dugout. Terry was facing a team hovering on the verge of a miraculous comeback, but the Yankee pitcher, having been victimized by such miracles before, had fate's sympathy this time. McCovey drilled a one-one fastball on a vicious line toward right field. But second-baseman Bobby Richardson leaped in the air and made a one-handed catch of the ball.

No sooner had the game and Series ended than the "if onlys" began. If only the outfield grass hadn't been soggy, Maris would not have reached Mays's double in time to hold Alou at third. If only McCovey's drive had been a foot to the left or right. The Giants, having achieved the impossible before, could not help but speculate on how close they had come to doing it again.

●

That was a great Series and a spectacular game, one that highlighted the old cliche that baseball is a game of inches. If McCovey's line drive goes one way or another the Giants win the World Series. In those days, the Yankees not only had talent but they had fortune on their side—it was that simple.

And it was a great Series. Jack Sanford pitched very well. And the Giants had Juan Marichal who was a terrific pitcher. But the Yankees were the Yankees. What else can you say? The Yankees had it caught in a bottle and they gave it to nobody else.

Sure, the 1989 Series lasted 14 days because of the earthquake . . . and it went the latest into the year of any World Series— October 28. But it was basically just a four-game sweep by Oakland, not my favorite *long* Series, or anyone else's, I'm sure.

DENNY McLAIN'S 30-WIN SEASON

When Denny McLain strode to the mound in Tiger Stadium in Detroit on the afternoon of Saturday, September 14, 1968, national attention switched from the overriding issues of the day to television's *Game of the Week*—and to Denny McLain. Baseball's Man of the Year was seeking his thirtieth victory of the season.

McLain was a man who was neither shy about opening his mouth nor ruffled by putting his foot in it. Consequently he had been booed by the Detroit fans, ridiculed at times by his teammates, and restrained by the Detroit management. His most enduring nickname was "Mighty Mouth." He once called the Tigers a "country-club" team. Another time he said the Detroit fans were "the worst in the world," a judgment he later tempered by adding that he had meant only some of them. But neither the taunts nor the publicity hampered his pitching in this game against Oakland.

The Athletics reached McLain for two runs in the fourth inning and they forged ahead in the ninth when Reggie Jackson blasted his second homer of the game. McLain's bid for number 30 seemed thwarted as the Tigers trailed 4–3 going into the bottom of the ninth.

Al Kaline gave the Tigers' partisan crowd some hope by coaxing a lead-off walk from Diego Segui. He held first as Dick McAuliffe fouled out, but reached third when Mickey Stanley singled up the middle. The next batter, Jim Northrup, managed only a dribbler toward first baseman Danny Cater, who charged halfway to the plate and fielded the ball. With Kaline coming full tilt from third, Cater's throw on the run sailed past catcher Dave Duncan, and Kaline sprawled over the catcher, gracelessly but emphatically landing on the plate with the tying run.

Stanley raced to third on the error, and Willie Horton stepped to the plate. The Athletics' outfielders, realizing that a sacrifice fly would score the winning run, reluctantly moved in on the powerful Horton. He worked the count to two and two and then drilled a long liner to left that sailed over the head of Jimmy Gosger. Stanley trotted home with the winning run, and the Detroit dugout erupted in a spontaneous celebration for McLain. As soon as Stanley crossed the plate, the Tigers mobbed their garrulous hero and brought him to the dugout steps to receive a standing ovation from the crowd.

One of the 33,688 who cheered was Dizzy Dean, the major-leagues' last 30-game winner, who had come 1,400 miles for the event. With his arms wrapped around McLain, Dean said, "They won't have this much excitement here if they win the World Series."

"I'll never win a bigger one," McLain declared happily. For once, no one disagreed with him.

●

I've gotten to know Denny in recent years and I find him an interesting human being. I guess when you think about McLain you think about guys who live their lives in ways they may later have regrets about.

Winning thirty games is certainly a great accomplishment. Sure, there are guys who won forty games in the major leagues (specifically, two, in 1904 and 1908), but that was in a totally different era. And there are other pitchers you would think of first as possible thirty-game winners. Somebody like a Gibson or a Koufax *should* have been thirty-game winners, but they weren't.

MICKEY MANTLE'S COMEBACK

One of the many wonderful memories that gives Mickey Mantle a big thrill had an inauspicious beginning in 1963 in Baltimore on a rainy June night when Mantle chased a ball hit by Brooks Robinson to the chain-link fence in center field. As the ball went over the fence, Mantle ran right into it and snagged his left foot in the wire mesh. He was carried off the field with a broken bone in his left foot and torn ligaments in his knee. At the hospital, where they put a cast on his foot, doctors told him he'd be lucky if he played again that year. He was on crutches for weeks and as discouraged as he'd ever been in his life. He seriously considered retirement, and thousands of fans anticipated it.

On August 4, eight weeks later, the Yankees were playing at Yankee Stadium against the Orioles. The Birds defeated the Yankees in the opener of the doubleheader and were leading 10–9 in the bottom of the ninth of the second game. With pitcher Steve Hamilton due to bat for New York, manager Ralph Houk motioned for Mantle to pinch-hit. Mickey picked up a bat and to a tremendous ovation strode to the batter's box. He hadn't batted in a regular game in two months.

"I was scared," recalls Mantle. "There were forty thousand people in the stands, and when I came out of the dugout, they all stood up and gave me one of the loudest ovations I'd ever heard. It was the first time in my life I ever got goose pimples. I prayed I wouldn't look bad. I said to myself, 'Just meet the ball. Don't strike out whatever you do.'

"I don't remember stepping in at the plate. George Brunet was the pitcher, so I batted right-handed. I don't remember whether it was the first pitch or the second, but I hit the ball, and it went for a ride. I thought it would be caught, but it kept going and landed in the seats for a home run. As I ran around the bases, I said to myself, 'You lucky stiff!' I hit a lot of balls harder, but I can't say any of them gave me more satisfaction than that one."

●

This moment is memorable largely because it illuminates the fact that often the most important or meaningful moments for an athlete are not necessarily the ones the fans remember. It was also an important moment for another reason. Mickey Mantle often felt the people of New York City weren't always 100 per cent behind him, and that ovation happened at a time Mickey was at one of his most vulnerable points—lame and thinking of retirement. Best of all, the fans gave Mick the hand *before* he'd ever laid wood to hide!

MANTLE'S 370-FOOT "FAILURE"

New York Yankee slugger Mickey Mantle could hit a baseball as far as anyone who put on a uniform. In fact, the era of "tape-measured" home runs did not really begin until Mantle hit a ball 565 feet at old Griffith Stadium in Washington on April 17, 1953. Later that day, Yankee press agent Red Patterson measured the distance and informed the public.

Since Yankee Stadium was built in 1923, no player has hit a fair ball out of the ballpark. A couple of players have hit foul balls out of Yankee Stadium, the last being Dave Kingman, but on Memorial Day in 1956, Mantle just missed being the first player to hit a ball out of the stadium fair.

Batting left-handed against the Washington Senators' Pedro Ramos, the center fielder crushed a fastball high and far that struck near the top of the roof's facade, right above the third deck in right field. Amazingly enough, Mantle's shot traveled against the wind.

The ball struck the facade 370 feet from home plate and 118 feet above the field.

"I didn't believe it myself," Mantle recalls. "Even when I saw it, I couldn't believe it."

●

I often grin when I hear people say today's ballplayer is bigger and stronger than fellows who played thirty or forty years ago. Bigger overall, probably; stronger, I wonder. Strength is not a direct result of size. Mind you, there were plenty of big fellows way back when. I remember the Dodgers having a towering first baseman named Howie "Stretch" Schultz.

Mickey Mantle was six feet tall and weighed about 200 pounds, and there were plenty who were bigger: Dave Kingman and Frank Howard to name just two. But The Mick was about as strong as they come—a *power* hitter in the best sense of the word.

ROGER MARIS'S 61ST HOME RUN

For years, the most coveted record in sports was the single-season home-run record of Babe Ruth, who belted sixty round-trippers in 1927. While hitters such as Hack Wilson, Hank Greenberg, and Jimmie Foxx have come close to Ruth's record, they all fell short. However, in 1961, a twenty-seven-year-old left-hand-hitting slugger named Roger Maris was closing in on The Babe. It wasn't an easy time for Maris, on or off the field. You see, another Yankee slugger by the name of Mickey Mantle was also going for Ruth's record that year.

Maris did not hit a single home run in the Yankees' first ten games of the year. But after that there was no stopping him. By mid-season, both Maris and Mantle, who was the crowd favorite, had a good chance to shatter Ruth's record. Most Yankee fans wanted Mantle, whom they considered a "truer" Yankee than Maris, to break the record, and some actually booed Maris.

You must remember that in 1962 the season lasted for 162 games, compared with the 154-game season Ruth played in 1927. Toward the end of the '62 season, Mantle sustained an injury and would wind up with 54 homers, six short of Ruth's record. With only Maris in the picture, Commissioner Ford Frick decided to get involved. An ardent supporter of Babe Ruth's, Frick stated that Maris would have to break the Ruthian feat in one hundred fifty-four games, otherwise there would be an asterisk placed next to his name in the record book. The asterisk would denote that Maris had eight more games in which to break the record. Maris was understandably bitter toward Frick. "I didn't make the schedule," he said. "Do you know of any other records that have been broken since the hundred-sixty-two game schedule that have an asterisk? I don't. Frick decided on the asterisk after I had about fifty homers and it looked like I'd break Ruth's record."

In Game 155, Maris hit home-run number sixty off Jack Fisher of the Orioles. However, the record-breaking home run would not come until the final game of the season, when it was hit in the fourth inning against Tracy Stallard of the Red Sox. The crowd of 23,154 showed that they didn't care about the asterisk. They cheered the usually reserved Maris until he had taken several "curtain calls" from the dugout steps. "If I never hit another home run," he said, "this is the one they can never take away from me."

●

Talking about Babe Ruth and Maris's 61st home run is like talking about Aaron's 715th. I'm fortunate in that I saw all three play, and, without question, Ruth was the greatest home-run hitter in the history of the game. Somebody will say, "Well, what about the stats?" You can argue stats all day long, but to me Ruth was the greatest—his home-run percentage and slugging average support that contention, incidentally—and I'm not sure I'd rate Maris in the top five or six. But he had one career year, and you've got to give him credit for it. The fact remains that he hit 61 home runs against all odds, and the asterisk that Commissioner Frick placed against the record was a lot of baloney; it was later removed, by the way.

WILLY MAYS'S FOUR-HOME-RUN GAME

All modern ballplayers, who miss games because of the slightest of ailments, should take a cue from Willie Mays and play when their bodies say nay—otherwise they might be missing their greatest games.

In late April, 1961, the Giants arrived in Milwaukee for a three-game set with the Braves. During the first two games, Willie Mays, bothered by a persistent stomachache, went 0 for seven. Warren Spahn, who pitched a no-hitter in the first game, recalls, "I could tell something was bothering Willie. He looked like he was having trouble holding up his bat."

The night before the third game, Mays went out with roommate Willie McCovey for an ill-advised snack of barbecued ribs. Later that night McCovey found Mays unconscious on the floor after falling out of bed. Club trainer Doc Bowman revived him and Mays was feeling slightly better the next day.

During the pregame batting practice, Mays wasn't hitting well, so teammate Joe Amalfitano suggested Mays try his heavier bat. When Mays was at the plate for his first at bat, pitcher Lew Burdette hung a slider that Mays hit 420 feet over the left-center-field fence. So much for the stomach. His next time up, Mays hit another 400-plus-footer.

When Mays came up his third time, there was a different pitcher on the mound—Seth Morehead—but the results were nearly identical: Mays ripped a shot about 450 feet over the center-field fence. But Willie wasn't through yet. After lining out in his fourth at bat, Mays stepped up to the plate in the eighth inning, this time against fireballer Don McMahon. Mays connected on his fourth home run, again to deep-center field.

Mays totaled four homers and eight runs batted in for the game, and the home runs tied the major-league record.

Reflecting on the game, Mays said, "That was easily the greatest day of my life. You're satisfied if you get two in a game, but when you get three, that's something you never expect. Four? That's like reaching for the moon."

After the game, Mays's stomach felt a *lot* better.

●

There have been a grand total of eleven major-leaguers who've hit four homers in a game:

AMERICAN LEAGUE
Rocky Colavito, Clev.,
  6/10/59
Lou Gehrig, N.Y.,
  6/3/32

Extra-Inning Games:
Pat Seerey, Chi.,
  7/18/48

NATIONAL LEAGUE
Joe Adcock, Milw.,
  7/31/54
Ed Delahanty, Phil.,
  7/13/1896
Gil Hodges, Bkn.,
  8/31/50
Bob Horner, Atl.,
  7/6/86
Bobby Low, Bost.,
  5/30/1894
Willie Mays, N.Y.,
  4/30/61

Extra-Inning Games:
Chuck Klein, Phil.,
  7/10/36
Mike Schmidt, Phil.,
  4/17/76

Mays is most memorable to me because I saw more of him than most of the others, and he had such a distinctive style—wonderful exuberance to go with his comprehensive abilities—that appealed to me more than the others (except maybe Gehrig). That's why I remember Willie's quartet more than the others, even though I wasn't an eyewitness to the moment. I have seen the spectacle on tape and film so many times that each swat is imprinted on my mind. Of course, the special "signpost" that always brings the moment to mind is the stomach problems beforehand. The whole story is so representative of what Willie was as a ballplayer: if you knocked Willie down, he'd get up and hit a home run off you—he was that kind of hitter.

BILL MAZEROSKI'S WORLD-SERIES WINNING HOME RUN

The 1960 World Series is a perfect example that statistics, no matter how impressive, don't always tell the whole story. It was the New

York Yankees against the Pittsburgh Pirates and in the Series the Yankees outscored the Buccaneers by 28 runs, outhit them 91–60, and set a World-Series record with a .338 batting average. But the Pirates won the Series.

Going into the seventh game it seemed as though the power and tradition of the Yankees would prevail. The Yankees had been pounding the Pirates' pitching. Only reliever Elroy Face had any success against the ferocious Yankee attack, gaining a save in all three Pirate victories. Those victories were sandwiched between Yankee outbursts of 16 runs in Game Two, 10 runs in Game Three and 12 runs in Game Six. The Bucs were shut out in both Games Three and Six, won by Whitey Ford.

On October 13, 36,683 fans showed up at Forbes Field for the deciding game. Although they tried to remain upbeat, there was an underlying feeling that the Yankees would decimate the Pirates. For five innings Vernon Law gave the fans reason to be optimistic, holding the Bombers to one run. The Pirates meanwhile managed to score two in the first on Rocky Nelson's blast over the right-field fence and two in the second on a couple of hits and a walk. But in the sixth inning the Yankee bats came to life. After a single by Bobby Richardson and a walk to Tony Kubek, Face was inserted into the game. He gave up a soft single to Mantle, allowing Richardson to score and loading the bases for a three-run homer by Yogi Berra. The end seemed even closer when the Yankees scored twice more in the eighth to make the score 7–4.

The resilient Bucs didn't give up. They were helped both by timely hitting and by what must be deemed fate. In the bottom of the eighth, after Gino Cimoli led off with a pinch-hit single, Bill Virdon smacked an apparent double-play ball to Kubek at short, but the ball hit a pebble, bounced up, and hit Kubek in the neck. Kubek went down and the Yankees' descent began.

After a single by Dick Groat, Jim Coates was brought in to relieve Bobby Shantz. Following a sacrifice and a fly out, Coates was late covering first on Roberto Clemente's ground ball, allowing a run to score and keeping the inning alive for reserve catcher Hal Smith, who deposited the ball over the left-field wall, giving the Pirates an improbable lead of 9–7.

But the Yankees didn't fold. Singles by Richardson, Dale Long, and Mantle got the Yankees back to within one. Then Berra hit a smash to first base and it seemed that the Pirates' lead was secure.

But first baseman Nelson, instead of throwing to second to start the double play, stepped on first, allowing Mantle to hustle back to first and pinch runner Gil McDougald to score from third with the tying run.

In the bottom of the ninth, Mazeroski came up with the score tied. The Pirates had waited since 1925 for a World-Series victory and now Mazeroski had the bat to finally do it again for Pittsburgh fans. Maz kept the bat on his shoulder as Ralph Terry's first pitch blurred past him for a ball. Terry was the Yankees' fifth pitcher and Mazeroski figured he could wait for a meatball in the next pitch or two. Sure enough, Terry's next delivery was a letter-high slider. Even though it was fast, Mazeroski got a good read on it and when he swung, his bat connected with the ball at precisely the right moment.

The Pirates' husky second baseman took off for first base as the ball headed for the left-center-field wall. As Maz approached second base he realized what he had accomplished, tossed his cap in the air, jumped in ecstasy, and began wildly waving his arms. Then Bill resumed his sprint to glory, and as he circled third, he was convoyed home by a growing throng of elated well-wishers.

●

I could relate to an underdog team like the Pirates, particularly since I wasn't the biggest Yankees fan in the world. It was a strange Series, one that's easy to remember since the Yankees outscored and outhit Pittsburgh by such a huge margin *and* set a Series batting average record, yet lost the Series.

No, I couldn't feel sorry for the Yanks, but I could delight in Mazeroski's accomplishment. After all, any guy whose name begins with *M-A-Z-E-R* has got to be a good guy!

STAN MUSIAL'S LAST GAME

It was Stan Musial's twenty-second season in the major leagues, 1963. After hitting .330 the previous season, and at age 42, Musial showed only flashes of the brilliant hitting that had made him a legend in St. Louis.

"I hadn't really made up my mind one way or the other whether I would play another year," recalled Musial. "But I found

Stan Musial, shown here with Cardinal teammates early in his career, starred in the majors for 22 seasons. *(from the collection of Barry Halper)*

that I just wasn't able to concentrate at bat as completely as I had previously. My RBI production was good, but my average wasn't. I was taking called third strikes, something I'd rarely done."

By mid-August, 1963, Musial had made his decision. One day he told Cardinal general manager Bing Devine, "This year, Bing, is it."

As the last game of the season, and Stan's last game forever, approached, the pressure on Musial began to build. The expectations of the press and the fans on him to do well were enormous, but Musial seemed at ease, saying, "If I don't get a hit, it's not going to worry me." When Musial took batting practice the crowd went wild with every swing. There was a stirring pregame ceremony in which Musial said to the home fans, "As long as I live, this is a day I'll always remember."

In his first at bat, Musial, perhaps a bit overanxious, struck out on three pitches. After the first pitch the game was stopped and the ball taken out of play to be displayed at the Hall of Fame.

In the fourth inning, with the Cardinals still looking for their first hit, Musial smacked a one-and-one pitch into center field. The fans gave him a standing ovation. In the sixth inning Musial stepped up to the plate with the game still scoreless. Stan Musial drove home Curt Flood from second base with a single to right field, and the stadium erupted. Musial was taken out of the game for a pinch runner as the cheers continued.

●

Stan Musial was one of the greatest baseball players of all time. If he had a failing, it was that he didn't have a great throwing arm, but other than that he was one of the most complete players who ever played the game. He was an incredible hitter on a level with anybody that you could think of, a terrific ballplayer, and as nice a man as he was a ballplayer. Just a super guy!

JACKIE ROBINSON AND THE LAST GAME
OF THE 1951 SEASON

The 1951 baseball season is usually remembered for Giant outfielder Bobby Thomson's dramatic pennant-winning home run off Dodger pitcher Ralph Branca in the final game of the post-season play-off. Yet, it was the heroics of Dodger superstar Jackie Robinson on the last day of the regular season that set up the Dodger-Giant play-off match-up.

On August 12, the Giants were 13½ games behind and looked to be out of the pennant race. But a late-season surge pulled them even with the Dodgers with only one game left.

On September 30, the final day of the regular season, Brooklyn battled the Philadelphia Phillies before a crowd of 31,755 at Shibe Park. The Dodgers quickly fell behind, 6–1, before Jackie Robinson's fifth-inning RBI triple sparked a four-run rally to close the gap to 6–5.

But Brooklyn's pennant hopes were dimmed in the sixth when the Phillies added two more insurance runs and a loud roar went up from the stands as the scoreboard reported that the Giants had defeated the Boston Braves.

After the Dodgers had tied the game with three eighth-inning runs to send the contest into extra innings, it was Robinson's offensive and defensive heroics that would decide the game for Brooklyn.

With two outs and the bases loaded for the Phillies in the bottom of the twelfth, Eddie Waitkus whacked a Don Newcombe fastball up the middle for what appeared to be the game-winning hit. But Robinson sped to his right, dove, and somehow caught the ball.

That play set up Robinson's game-winning, two-out homer in the top of the fourteenth that won the game for the Dodgers.

The 1951 season will always be remembered as the year Brooklyn blew a National League pennant. Yet, it will also be remembered for Jackie Robinson's last-game heroics, which, at least, stretched the Dodgers' season for three more games.

●

Jackie played on a superb baseball team at a time when he was past what you would consider his prime. He was in his thirties by then, yet he could be just unbelievable. Robinson was one of those few who rose to another level. He was an incredible competitor. He wasn't the best hitter, nor the best fielder, nor the fastest man, maybe not even the best base stealer. But he could do *all* of those things exceptionally well: hit, run, steal—and he could make great fielding plays when the situation demanded it. That's what he did on that day in Philadelphia—he made the play.

BOBBY THOMSON'S HOME RUN

Call it "The Shot Heard 'Round the World." Call it "The Miracle of Coogan's Bluff." Call it what you want. But Bobby Thomson's home run in the final game of the 1951 National League play-offs capped the greatest comeback in baseball history.

On August 11, the Giants trailed the Dodgers by 13½ games. But, by winning 36 of their final 43 games, New York salvaged a deadlock with Brooklyn on the last day of the season, forcing a three-game play-off between the two teams.

Today many people forget that it was Thomson's two-run homer off Ralph Branca that won Game One of the play-offs for the Giants. Nor do they remember Thomson's poor base running and two errors that helped lead to a 10–0 Brooklyn win in Game Two. It is the dramatic pennant-winning homer in Game Three that is unforgettable.

The Dodgers seemed in command as they led 4–1 going to the bottom of the ninth and they had 20-game-winner Don Newcombe pitching a strong game. Before the Giants' last at bat, Newcombe complained his arm was tired, yet Brooklyn manager Charlie Dressen left him in.

The Giants opened the ninth with a single by Alvin Dark, then Don Mueller belted another single off Newcombe. The Dodgers got momentary relief when Monte Irvin fouled out. However, Whitey Lockman next whacked a double to left, enabling Dark to score.

The tying runs were on base with one out. It was then that Dressen made his move. Both Clem Labine and Ralph Branca were warming up in the bull pen along with Preacher Roe. Bull-pen Coach Clyde Sukeforth suggested that Branca was the man, and at the time it seemed a good choice. Branca had been one of the best of Brooklyn's pitching staff for years and looked the part as he blazed a fastball over the inside corner for a called strike against Bobby Thomson. Few remembered that only a few days earlier Thomson had hit a game-winning homer off Branca.

The second pitch was a fastball that Thomson lined over the left-field wall.

While the Giants and half their fans tried to embrace Thomson as he touched home plate, the Dodgers stood silently in shock. Later, Branca could be found on the clubhouse steps, crying.

●

Thomson's homer was truly miraculous. It *was* "the shot heard around the baseball world." The only memorable thing I can say about it is that it stands as one of the four or five lowest points in my sports life. I was a big Dodger fan and having that happen was really dismal.

I know that I couldn't possibly have felt as bad as Ralph Branca did, but on a scale of one to ten, if he was ten, then I was eight. And I didn't even throw the pitch.

WARREN SPAHN—VICTORY NO. 300

It was August 11, 1961, when Warren Spahn strolled to the mound at Milwaukee County Stadium with a chance to become the first 300-game winner since Lefty Grove did it in 1941. Spahn had plenty of notable accomplishments over the years, including four World-Series victories, two no-hitters, and 63 shutouts. But for Spahn and the crowd of 40,705 gathered at the game, getting 300 victories would be his greatest feat. The pressure was intense, but Spahn delivered, pitching a solid six-hitter to beat the Chicago Cubs, 2–1.

"That game was even more exciting than the World Series or even the two no-hitters," Spahn told the crowd of reporters and well-wishers that surrounded him after the game. "Beforehand I wasn't too excited about winning my three hundredth because I figured it would come eventually. But a few hours before the game the pressure began to build up. About six o'clock I was wishing we could start the game right then. I wanted to get it over with. I'm relieved that I don't have to go through that again. I've never done anything so tough."

The game itself was a tightly pitched affair that went into the eighth inning tied 1–1, with Milwaukee's run coming off a sacrifice fly hit by Spahn. In the eighth Gino Cimoli hit a home run to make it 2–1, but the seventh-place Cubs put up a fight. Spahn retired the first two batters in the ninth, one on a great catch by Cimoli. But pinch hitter Ernie Banks reached first on Eddie Mathews's wild throw. Then pinch hitter Jim McAnany hit a fly ball to Hank Aaron for the final out. Spahn had his three-hundredth win and his

Warren Spahn, after becoming the greatest strikeout king among left-handers. He was later surpassed by Mickey Lolich and Steve Carlton. *(from the collection of Barry Halper)*

teammates stormed the mound to congratulate him, while the crowd made more noise than it had since the championship days of 1957 and 1958. Spahn left the field to a standing ovation, waving his cap to the crowd. He would go on to gain 63 more victories in his career, still a record for a left-handed pitcher.

●

Warren Spahn was a superb pitcher. He was not the best of his time, yet he wound up as the fifth winningest pitcher of all time. Would you believe that? You have to remember that Spahn was in the service for some time at the beginning of his major-league career. He pitched in only four games of the 1942 season, then didn't return to The Game until the 1946 season. When you talk about Spahn, you talk about a man who didn't have the brilliance of a Koufax and didn't have the brilliance of a Dizzy Dean. But he persevered.

You look at Spahn and you say to yourself, "How did he do it?" He did it with persistence, guts, craft, and guile. He was a pitcher for all seasons. He won when he had great stuff, he won when he had good stuff, and he still won when he merely had adequate stuff. He just knew how to win. Spahn is the perfect proof that to be a winner you don't have to have the *greatest* stuff in the world, just the greatest desire to win.

TED WILLIAMS'S FINAL GAME

Not many baseball players get to choose in which ballpark to end a career, nor do most players hit a dramatic home run on their last at bat. Ted Williams did both and that made his final major-league game most memorable.

Williams remembers September 26, 1960, well. Before the game against the Baltimore Orioles at Fenway Park, he told Boston Red Sox manager Mike Higgins, "This is the last game I'm going to play. I don't want to go to New York."

Before play began, Williams was given a ceremony at home plate as his number was retired. Curt Gowdy introduced him as "the greatest hitter who ever lived."

After walking on four pitches and scoring a run on his first at bat, Williams hit drives deep to the center-field and right-field warning tracks that were caught on his next two times at the plate.

Boston was trailing 4–2, with one out in the eighth inning, as Williams entered the batter's box against Oriole pitcher Jack Fisher. The hard-throwing right-hander knew Williams was looking for a home run, but he felt up to the challenge.

Fisher's first pitch, a fastball, was swung on viciously and missed by Williams. But, on the next pitch, Williams ripped the ball deep over the right-center-field wall for his 29th homer of the year. It was also the forty-two-year-old's 521st of his spectacular career.

The shot closed the gap to 4–3. In the top of the ninth Higgins ordered Carroll Hardy to replace Williams in left. But the fans wanted to see Williams on the field one more time.

"Ted, go out to left field," ordered Higgins. Williams grabbed his glove and ran onto the field as the fans roared. A few moments later, Higgins sent Hardy to replace him and Williams sprinted back to the dugout while the patrons gave him a standing ovation.

Williams left baseball the way all great players should, with "a bang." By the way, his teammates rallied in the ninth inning and won the game 5–4, on what will be remembered as "Ted Williams Day."

●

Whenever you mention Ted Williams to me, I always think that he and Joe DiMaggio are linked. I don't think anybody questions that Williams was the greatest hitter, and a lot of people think that DiMaggio was the greatest all-round ballplayer. I always wondered what would have happened if the Yankee Clipper had played for the Boston Red Sox with that small left-field fence and Williams had played in Yankee Stadium with that short right-field porch. It makes for interesting "hot-stove" conversation.

Williams was not the world's greatest ballplayer. But he was an artist with that bat . . . and one of baseball's all-time greatest hitters.

BASEBALL BRAINTEASERS

As any professor will tell you, there are several ways of acquiring knowledge about particular subjects, be it botany, biology or biochemistry. When I went to college, we spent considerable time answering essay questions that often consumed four or more handwritten pages each. By the same token, we also had to deal with what was known as the "short answer quiz." Like most collegians, I favored the latter because I could handle it quickly and usually with ease. That's why I thought you would get a kick out of this digression from my other tales and more elaborate bits of baseball banter. Herewith, Bill's Brainteasers.

1. ALL-TIME LEADERS (I)

1. Who holds the major-league record for most seasons played?
2. What is the modern seasonal record for most innings pitched?
3. What season strikeout record did Sandy Koufax break with his 382 in 1965 (broken by Nolan Ryan in 1973 with 383)?
4. Who holds the record for the most hits in a single season?
5. What is the longest winning streak by one team over another in history?
6. Who are the only players to strike out 150 or more times in three consecutive seasons?
7. Who is the all-time leader in on-base percentage?

8. What pitcher recorded the most balks in one season?
9. Who is the only pitcher to have two opening-day home runs in his career?
10. Who owns the best career winning percentage among 300-game winners?
11. Who had the most extra-base hits in one season?
12. What shortstop had the highest fielding percentage in one season?
13. How many 40-game hitting streaks have there been in modern baseball history?

(Answers on pages 367–68)

2. ALL-TIME LEADERS (II)

1. What player holds *both* the American League and National League records for season relief appearances?
2. Who collected the most total bases in his career?
3. Who is the all-time game-winning RBI leader?
4. Who had the highest season winning percentage of a 20-game winner?
5. Who holds the highest season average by a pinch hitter?
6. What is the only team in history whose entire starting infield each hit at least 20 home runs?
7. At the end of the 1989 season, what pitcher—with more than 100 career decisions—was baseball's all-time leader in winning percentage?
8. What pitcher allowed the lowest career hits-per-nine-innings ratio in his career (minimum 800 innings pitched)?
9. Who were the only two pitchers to win more than 30 games in a season more than once?
10. Who are the only relievers with four straight 30-save seasons?
11. Who are the only pitchers to win both the Rookie of the Year and Cy Young Awards in their career?
12. What pitcher appeared in the most games in a single season?

(Answers on pages 368–69)

3. ALL-TIME LEADERS (III)

1. Who is the only player in history to accumulate more than 95 but less than 100 RBI's for three years in a row?
2. What player has won the most base-hit titles?
3. What outfielder has the most career assists?
4. Whom did Nolan Ryan overtake to claim the career strikeout record?
5. What National Leaguer owns the most seasonal hitting records?
6. Name the four players who've stolen 100 bases or more in one season.
7. Whose career batting average record did Ty Cobb break with his .367 on retirement?
8. How many players hit 50 or more home runs in a season more than once? Who were they?
9. What pitcher holds the record for the most consecutive seasons with 100-plus strikeouts?
10. Who has the most seasons with 50-plus stolen bases?
11. Who had the fewest strikeouts by a player with 500 or more at bats in a season?
12. What Hall of Fame pitcher had the fewest major-league strikeouts?
13. Name the four pitchers with three or more Cy Young Awards.

(Answers on page 369)

4. ALL-TIME LEADERS (IV)

1. How many players have hit over .400 in one season more than once?
2. What is the record for the most consecutive losses by a team in the modern era?
3. Who has the most career relief wins?
4. Name the only two players to win the Triple Crown twice.
5. Who holds the record for the most strikeouts per nine innings in a single season?

6. Who has the highest batting average in a single season in the modern era?
7. What pitcher won the strikeout title for seven consecutive years?
8. What pitcher holds the record for the most strikeouts over a ten-year span?
9. After Cy Young's immortal total of 7,356, who has the most career innings pitched?
10. Name the two Hall of Fame pitchers with career ERA's below 2.00.
11. Name the pitchers who struck out 300-plus in more than one season.

(Answers on page 370)

5. PITCHERS

1. Who threw the pitch that killed Ray Chapman?
2. Who gave up Hank Aaron's 715th home run, which broke Babe Ruth's all-time home-run record?
3. What is the twentieth-century record for wins by a rookie pitcher?
4. How many relief pitchers have been Cy Young Award winners in the 1980's?
5. How many relievers have won 100 or more career games?
6. What pitcher lost the first official night game at Wrigley Field?
7. At the end of the 1989 season, who was the losingest pitcher of the decade?
8. What Hall of Fame pitcher did Ronald Reagan portray in a Warner Brothers film?
9. What major change in pitching style occurred in 1884?
10. How many left-handed pitchers are there in the Hall of Fame?
11. What pitcher has won the most games in the 1980's?
12. What twentieth-century pitcher won the most consecutive games in a season?
13. What pitcher set a record in 1985 by starting 37 games, and not completing any of them?

14. Who was the oldest pitcher to start a major-league game?
15. In what year did the American League adopt the Designated Hitter rule?
16. Who was the oldest pitcher to win 20 games?

(Answers on pages 370–71)

6. BATTERS

1. What did Ted Williams do in his last career at bat?
2. Everyone knows that Ty Cobb has the highest lifetime batting average, .367. Who has the second highest?
3. Who are the only three players to accumulate 100 or more doubles, triples, home runs, and stolen bases since World War II?
4. What is the highest batting average by a rookie in the twentieth century?
5. Who was the last National Leaguer to hit .400 or better?
6. What player hit the most homers in his first two major-league seasons?
7. Who was the last man to hit 50 home runs or more in a season?
8. Who hit the line drive that hit Cleveland pitcher Herb Score in the eye?
9. How many times did Babe Ruth win 20 games?

(Answers on page 371)

7. LEAGUE LEADERS (I)

1. What National League pitcher won the most games in a season over the last 50 years?
2. Who led the American League in RBI's in 1927, when Babe Ruth hit 60 home runs?
3. How many times did Sandy Koufax lead the National League in ERA's?
4. Who are the only players to lead the league in batting averages and grounding into double plays in the same season?

5. Who is the only 20-game loser in the 1980's?
6. What pitcher holds the National League record for the most wins in one season without a loss?
7. What pitcher is the all-time National League strikeout leader?
8. Who was the first National Leaguer to play in 3,000 games?
9. What player struck out more than any other National Leaguer?
10. Who is the all-time American League at bats leader?

(Answers on page 372–73)

8. LEAGUE LEADERS (II)

1. Who stole the most bases in American League history?
2. Who was the last National Leaguer to win the triple crown?
3. How many National League pitchers have led the league in ERA's with losing records?
4. Who is the National League career save leader?
5. Who led his league in home runs for the most consecutive seasons?
6. Who was the last player to win the American League batting title before the Wade Boggs/Don Mattingly six-year usurpation?
7. Who won the most consecutive batting titles in modern major-league history?
8. Who was the oldest player to win his league's stolen-base crown?
9. Who was the American League's first batting champion?

(Answers on pages 372–73)

9. NEW YORK YANKEES

1. How many homers did Roger Maris hit in Yankee Stadium in 1961?
2. Who gave up Roger Maris's sixty-first home run of 1961?
3. Who was the first Yankee to have his number retired?
4. How many major-league-season batting records does Babe Ruth hold?

5. Who replaced Lou Gehrig at first base for the Yankees after his record 2,130 consecutive games?

6. What is former Yankee great Sparky Lyle's real first name?

7. Who is the only player to finish second in the American League in home runs for four years in a row?

8. In what year did the Yankees have two 50-home-run hitters and who were they?

9. Who was the only Yankee pitcher to go six straight years with double figures in wins, and single figures in losses?

10. What Yankee pitcher had the highest winning percentage in a season for a 20-game winner?

11. Before Hack Wilson drove in 190 runs in 1930, who had the record for the most RBI's in one season?

12. Of the top five slugging percentages in one season, how many does Babe Ruth have?

(Answers on page 373)

10. PLAY-OFFS AND WORLD SERIES

1. Who gave up Bobby Thomson's 1951 "shot heard 'round the world"?

2. Who gave up Babe Ruth's "called shot" in the 1932 World Series?

3. Who gave up Bill Mazeroski's ninth inning tie-breaking home run that gave the Pirates Game Seven of the 1960 World Series?

4. Who gave up Bucky Dent's three-run home run in the 1978 Yankee-Red Sox play-off game at Fenway Park?

5. What manager won the most World Series?

6. Who has pitched in the most World-Series games?

7. Who has the highest batting average, playing every game, in one World Series?

8. Who was the opposing pitcher in Don Larsen's perfect World Series game?

9. Since the beginning of divisional play in 1969, how many times have the teams with the best records in their respective leagues met in the World Series?

(Answers on page 374)

11. BASEBALL FIRSTS

1. Who was the first batting champion of the twentieth century?
2. Who was the first reliever to compile 30 saves in a season?
3. Who was the first reliever to rack up 40 saves in a season?
4. Who was the first player to record 700 at bats in a season?
5. Who was the first player to hit 20 home runs in his rookie year?
6. Who won the first league-sponsored MVP Award?
7. Who was the first rookie to win the Cy Young Award?
8. Who was the first manager elected to the Hall of Fame?
9. What team won the first World Series?
10. Who was the first manager of the Montreal Expos?
11. Who gave up Ted Williams's first hit?
12. Who was the first American League pitcher to win the Cy Young Award?
13. Who was the first million-dollar player?

(Answers on pages 374–75)

12. TEAM LEADERS

1. Who led the 1919 Chicago White Sox in wins?
2. Who was the leading hitter on the 1962 New York Mets?
3. What was the only team with three players who hit 40 or more home runs during a season?
4. Name the three Cy Young Award winners on the Baltimore Oriole pitching staff in the early 1980's.
5. What team has had the most pitchers with 20-win seasons?
6. How many current major-league teams have never had a 20-game winner?
7. What MVP winner's team finished the lowest in the standings?
8. Who was the only player to play for the Braves in Boston, Milwaukee, and Atlanta?
9. Name the four teams that were Division Champions in the first year of divisional play.

(Answers on page 375)

13. MISCELLANEOUS

1. What team did one-armed outfielder Pete Gray play for?
2. Players at which position make the most errors?
3. How many 1–0 All-Star Games have there been?
4. Who broke the color barrier in the American League?
5. Name at least four major-league baseball players who never played a single minor-league game.
6. What was the only team to lose a triple-header, and who were they swept by?
7. Name the only first baseman to play a full season without making an error.
8. Who was the last catcher to win the MVP Award?
9. How many MVP's have won the award unanimously?

(Answers on page 376)

ANSWERS TO
BASEBALL BRAINTEASERS

1. ALL-TIME LEADERS (I)

1. Tommy John entered his 26th season in 1989.
2. Ed Walsh pitched 464 innings in 1908.
3. The previous record was held by Rube Waddell, who struck out 349 in 1904.
4. George Sisler of the St. Louis Browns, who smacked out 257 hits while batting .407 in 1920.
5. The Kansas City Royals lost 23 straight games to the Baltimore Orioles in 1969 and 1970.
6. Pete Incaviglia of the Rangers, and Rob Deer of the Brewers both accomplished this in 1986, 1987, and 1988. Deer made it four in 1989.

	1986	1987	1988	1989
Incaviglia	185	168	153	—
Deer	179	186	153	158

7. The all-time leader is Ted Williams with a career OBP of .482.

8. The record holder is Dave Stewart of the Oakland A's, who had 16 balks in 1988.

9. The two-time power source is Don Drysdale, who hit home runs in 1959 and 1965 on opening day.

10. The best of the 300-game winners is Lefty Grove, who was 300–141 lifetime with a winning percentage of .680.

11. Babe Ruth had 119 in 1921 with 44 doubles, 16 triples, and 59 home runs.

12. Toronto Blue Jay Tony Fernandez compiled a .992 fielding percentage in 1989.

13. There have been only four such streaks in the 20th century. They are Ty Cobb's 40 in 1911, George Sisler's 41 in 1922, Pete Rose's 44 in 1978, and Joe DiMaggio's record-setting 56 in 1941.

2. ALL-TIME LEADERS (II)

1. Mike Marshall appeared in 90 games for the Minnesota Twins in 1979, and 106 games for the Los Angeles Dodgers in 1974.

2. Hank Aaron is the all-time leader with 6,856.

3. Keith Hernandez is the leader of this short-lived stat, with 129.

4. Ron Guidry's .893 (25–3) in 1978 is tops.

5. The most efficient pinch hitter is Ed Kranepool, who hit .486 in 1974 with the Mets.

6. The 1986 Detroit Tigers, with Darrell Evans (29), Lou Whitaker (20), Alan Trammel (21), and Darnell Coles (20).

7. Dwight Gooden, with a .719 percentage.

8. Cleveland Indians great Herb Score holds the distinction with a 6.4 hits allowed per nine innings mark.

9. Christy Mathewson did it four times, in 1903 (30–13), 1904 (33–12), 1905 (31–8), and 1908 (37–11); and Grover "Pete" Alexander three times, in 1915 (31–10), 1916 (33–12), and 1917 (30–13).

10. Three have accomplished this: Jeff Reardon, Dan Quisenberry, and Lee Smith. Reardon made it five years in a row after the 1989 season.

11. Five have won both awards. They are Don Newcombe, Tom Seaver, Fernando Valenzuela, Rick Sutcliffe, and Dwight Gooden.

12. The Dodgers' Mike Marshall appeared in 106 games, all in relief, in 1974.

3. ALL-TIME LEADERS (III)

1. Kevin McReynolds displayed such almost-greatness over 1986, 1987, and 1988 for the Padres and Mets.

2. The legendary Ty Cobb won the most base-hit titles eight times.

3. Hall of Famer Tris Speaker accumulated 448 assists in his career.

4. Walter Johnson held the record of 3,508 career K's before Ryan broke it in 1982.

5. "The Rajah," Rogers Hornsby, owns 11 National League season hitting records.

6. The four are Maury Wills, Lou Brock, Rickey Henderson, and Vince Coleman.

7. Before Ty Cobb came along, the career batting leader was "Shoeless Joe" Jackson, of the Chicago ("Black") White Sox, with a .356 average.

8. Only five players have accomplished this feat. They were: Babe Ruth, in 1920 (54), 1921 (59), 1927 (60), and 1928 (54); Jimmie Foxx in 1932 (58) and 1938 (50); Ralph Kiner in 1947 (51) and 1949 (54); Mickey Mantle in 1956 (52) and 1961 (54); Willie Mays in 1955 (51) and 1965 (52).

9. Right-hander Don Sutton had 21 consecutive seasons with 100-plus K's, playing for the Dodgers, Astros, Brewers, and Angels.

10. All-time stolen-base king Lou Brock stole 50 or more for 12 straight years, from 1965–1976.

11. In 1932, Yankee and Indian Hall of Famer Joe Sewell struck out only three times in 503 at bats.

12. Satchel Paige, in his brief major-league stint, struck out 290 batters.

13. The members of this elite group are Sandy Koufax (1963, 1965, 1966), Tom Seaver (1969, 1973, 1975), Jim Palmer (1973, 1975, 1976), and Steve Carlton, the only four-time winner (1972, 1977, 1980, 1982).

4. ALL-TIME LEADERS (IV)

1. Three players share this distinction. Ty Cobb hit .400-plus three times, in 1911 (.420), 1912 (.410), and 1922 (.401); George Sisler hit .407 in 1920 and .420 in 1922; and Rogers Hornsby hit a record .424 in 1924, and .403 in 1925.
2. The all-time record for team futility is held by the 1961 Philadelphia Phillies, who lost 23 games in a row in August.
3. The most prolific victor out of the bull pen is Hall of Famer Hoyt Wilhelm, with a record 123 wins in relief.
4. The only two players with such productive seasons were Ted Williams, in 1942 and 1947, and Rogers Hornsby, in 1922 and 1925.
5. In 1987, Nolan Ryan struck out 270 batters in 211.2 innings, for a record-setting ratio of 11.5 K's every nine innings.
6. Hall of Famer Rogers Hornsby hit .424 in 1924.
7. Walter Johnson, 1912–1919.
8. Nolan Ryan struck out 2,756 batters from 1972–1981.
9. Pud Galvin had 5,941 career innings pitched.
10. Ed Walsh had a career 1.82 ERA, and Addie Joss's career ERA was 1.88.
11. Five have accomplished this feat. Nolan Ryan did it six times, Sandy Koufax three times, and Sam McDowell, Rube Waddell, and Walter Johnson twice each.

5. PITCHERS

1. Yankee pitcher Carl Mays threw the legendary fatal pitch on August 16, 1920. Ray Chapman died on August 17, the first and only fatality in major-league history.
2. Al Downing, of the Los Angeles Dodgers, April 8, 1974.
3. Grover "Pete" Alexander won 28 games in his rookie year, 1911.
4. Four closers have: Rollie Fingers in 1981, Willie Hernandez in 1984, Steve Bedrosian in 1987, and Mark Davis in 1989.
5. Four relievers have: Hoyt Wilhelm (123), Lindy McDaniel (119), Rollie Fingers (107), and Goose Gossage (102).
6. Sid Fernandez of the Mets took the loss on August 9, 1988.

7. The 1980's most unfortunate was the Houston Astros' and Blue Jays' Jim Clancy, with 126 losses.

8. Reagan portrayed Hall of Famer Grover Cleveland "Pete" Alexander in the 1950 feature, *The Winning Team.*

9. Overhand pitching was legalized.

10. Surprisingly, there are only eleven Hall of Fame southpaws. They are Lefty Grove, Lefty Gomez, Whitey Ford, Carl Hubbell, Rube Marquard, Eddie Plank, Herb Pennock, Sandy Koufax, Warren Spahn, and Rube Waddell.

11. Jack Morris of the Tigers has 173 over the last decade.

12. In 1912, Rube Marquard won 19 consecutive games.

13. The Atlanta Braves' Steve Bedrosian did not complete one of his 37 starts in 1985.

14. Satchel Paige was 60 years old when he started a game for the Kansas City A's in 1965.

15. The DH rule first came into effect in 1973.

16. Warren Spahn was 42 when he went 23–7 in 1963.

6. BATTERS

1. He hit a home run, at Fenway Park, September 26, 1960.

2. Rogers Hornsby, who hit .358 throughout his 23-year career. Rogers played on the Cardinals, the Giants, the Braves, the Cubs, the Reds, and the Browns. He must have been a bad influence on the teams he played with, otherwise he would not have been traded so much.

3. The three are Robin Yount, George Brett, and Mickey Vernon.

4. Shoeless Joe Jackson hit .408 in his rookie year with Cleveland in 1911.

5. The Giants' Bill Terry hit .401 in 1930.

6. Oakland's Mark McGwire hit 81 homers in his first two years, 1987–88.

7. Cecil Fielder hit 51 home runs in 1990.

8. The perpetrator of this tragic hit was veteran Yankee infielder Gil McDougald, May 7, 1957.

9. The Bambino had a 20-game season twice in his brief pitching career, 23 in 1916, and 24 in 1917.

7. LEAGUE LEADERS (I)

1. Philadelphia Phillie Robin Roberts won 28 games in 1952.
2. Surprisingly, it was The Babe's teammate, Lou Gehrig, with 175 ribbies.
3. Koufax was the ERA league leader five times, in consecutive years from 1962–66.
4. The two are Ernie Lombardi of the Reds in 1938 (.342, 30 DP's), and Wade Boggs of the Red Sox in 1988 (.366, 23 DP's).
5. The big loser was the A's Brian Kingman, who went 8–20 in 1980 for Oakland.
6. The record holder is Howie Krist of the Cardinals, who went 10–0 in 1941.
7. Steve Carlton has 4,136 career K's and 4,040 of those were with the National League.
8. Stan Musial was the National League's first iron man.
9. Willie Stargell is the big whiffer, with 1,936 K's.
10. The American League leader is Carl Yastrzemski, with 11,988.

8. LEAGUE LEADERS (II)

1. The American League leader in swipes is Ricky Henderson, with 936.
2. The Cardinals' "Ducky" Medwick won the triple crown in 1937.
3. Six have had such hard luck:

Year	Pitcher	Team	W – L	Pct.	ERA
1893	Ted Breitenstein	St. Louis	9 – 20	.487	3.18
1900	Rube Waddell	Pittsburgh	8 – 13	.381	2.37
1925	Dolf Luque	Cincinnati	6 – 18	.471	2.63
1949	Dave Koslo	N.Y.	1 – 14	.440	2.50
1958	Stu Miller	San. Fran.	6 – 9	.400	2.47
1987	Nolan Ryan	Houston	8 – 16	.333	2.76
1988	Joe Magrane	St. Louis	5 – 9	.354	2.18

4. The top career National League fireman is Bruce Sutter who totaled 300 saves in his 11-year career.
5. For seven years, from 1946 through 1952, Ralph Kiner of the Pirates led the National League in home runs.

6. The last American League batting leader before the Boggs-Mattingly dynasty was Kansas City outfielder Willie Wilson, who hit .332 in 1982.

7. The legendary Ty Cobb won nine straight batting titles from 1907 to 1915.

8. The White Sox's Eddie Collins stole 42 bases in 1924 at the age of 37.

9. Nap Lajoie won the batting title in the league's inaugural season, 1901, with a .422 average.

9. NEW YORK YANKEES

1. Maris hit 30 homers at home in his 61-home-run record-setting campaign.

2. Tracy Stallard, of the Boston Red Sox, on the last day of the season.

3. Lou Gehrig was the first Yankee to have his number, four, retired in 1939. Many people erroneously believe that Ruth had his number three retired before Gehrig's, but in fact Babe's number was retired in 1948.

4. The Bambino holds 13 different single-season records, including total bases, bases on balls and slugging percentage.

5. On May 2, 1939, Gehrig benched himself in favor of Babe Dahlgren, who whacked a home run and a double in a 22–2 Yankee dousing of the Detroit Tigers.

6. Albert.

7. Lou Gehrig finished second in home runs to teammate Babe Ruth from 1927–30.

8. The 1961 Yankees had Roger Maris (61), and Mickey Mantle (54).

9. Whitey Ford was this good from 1953–1958.

10. The Yankees' Ron Guidry, better known as "Louisiana Lightning," went 25–3, with a .893 percentage, in 1978.

11. In 1927, Yankee first baseman Lou Gehrig had 175 ribbies.

12. The Bambino has four of the top five marks, with the only other being Lou Gehrig's fourth-best mark of .765 in 1927.

10. PLAY-OFFS AND WORLD SERIES

1. Ralph Branca, who was hung in effigy all across Brooklyn after he gave up the home run that eliminated the Dodgers from making the World Series.
2. Charlie Root of the Chicago Cubs. The whole team, including Root, had been heckling The Babe, prompting him to point toward center field. He then hit his famous home run to the same spot.
3. Ralph Terry, of the New York Yankees.
4. Mike Torrez, who had been a Yankee the year before and played an integral role in the Yanks' victorious 1977 World Series.
5. It's a tie between Yankee managers Casey Stengel and Joe McCarthy with 7 World-Series wins apiece.
6. Longtime Yankee ace Whitey Ford appeared in 22 World-Series games.
7. In the 1990 Series against the A's that the Reds swept in four games, Billy Hatcher went 9–12, compiling a .750 average.
8. Larsen's mound opponent in the 1956 World-Series classic was the Dodgers' Sal Maglie.
9. This has happened eight times: in 1969, 1970, 1971, 1976, 1978, 1979, 1982, and 1986.

11. BASEBALL FIRSTS

1. Honus Wagner led the National League in hitting with a .381 average, in 1900.
2. Ted Abernathy saved 31 games for the Cubs in 1965.
3. Dan Quisenberry of the Royals saved 45 games in 1983.
4. Willie Wilson of Kansas City recorded 705 official at bats in the 1980 season.
5. Lou Gehrig was first with 20 dingers in 1925.
6. The American League began sponsoring the MVP in 1922, naming St. Louis Browns first baseman George Sisler, who hit .420 that year. The National League started in 1924, naming Brooklyn pitcher Dazzy Vance.
7. Dodger left-hander Fernando Valenzuela was the first rookie to

get the award, going 13–7 with a rookie-record eight shutouts in 1981.

8. In 1937, the second year of operation for the Hall of Fame, three managers were enshrined. They were nineteenth-century legend George Wright, longtime Giants manager John McGraw, and the all-time leader in wins by a manager, the Philadelphia A's Connie Mack.

9. The first World Series, held in 1903, was won by the Boston Red Sox, five games to three, over the Pittsburgh Pirates.

10. Gene Mauch.

11. New York Yankee pitcher Red Ruffing.

12. The Yankees' Bob Turley won the award in 1958, when there was only one pitcher selected from both leagues.

13. Baseball's first one-season millionaire was the Pirates' Dave Parker, in 1978.

12. TEAM LEADERS

1. Ed Cicotte won 29 games for the scandal-ridden American League champs.

2. The Mets leader in their inaugural season was right-fielder Richie Ashburn, who hit .306.

3. The 1973 Atlanta Braves, who featured second baseman Davey Johnson with 43, third baseman Darrell Evans with 41, and right fielder Hank Aaron with 40.

4. Jim Palmer (1973, 1975, and 1976), Mike Flanagan (1979), and Steve Stone (1980).

5. Cleveland Indians pitchers have had 55 20-win seasons.

6. Two teams—the Seattle Mariners and Toronto Blue Jays.

7. Andre Dawson's 1987 Chicago Cubs finished in sixth place in the National League.

8. Hall of Fame third baseman Eddie Mathews visited every home venue of the Braves.

9. In 1969, the National League East champs were the Mets, and the National League West champs were the Braves. The American League East winners were the Orioles, and the American League West winners were the Twins.

13. MISCELLANEOUS

1. Pete Gray played 77 games for the St. Louis Browns in 1945.
2. Major-league third basemen are the most error-prone, averaging 4.9 per 100 chances.
3. Surprisingly, there was only one such midsummers classic, in 1968, with the National League and Don Drysdale beating the American League and Luis Tiant.
4. The second player to cross the color line was Cleveland Indians slugging outfielder Larry Doby.
5. A few major-league players who never played in the minors are Catfish Hunter, Dave Winfield, Bob Horner, Pete Incaviglia, and Eddie Yost.
6. Due to scheduling problems, in June of 1903 the Pirates were swept by the Brooklyn Dodgers, 3–0, in baseball's only triple-header.
7. The Padres' Steve Garvey played 160 games of errorless ball at first base in 1984.
8. Thurman Munson of the Yankees, who won the award in 1976.
9. There have been eight unanimous MVP's. They were Hank Greenberg in 1935, Al Rosen in 1953, Mickey Mantle in 1956, Frank Robinson in 1966, Denny McLain in 1968, Reggie Jackson in 1973, and Mike Schmidt in 1980.

EPILOGUE

WHO SAYS IT'S TRIVIA?

As for Bill Mazer, the job at NBC turned into a bonanza. My audience liked the homey style (which was real) and my knowledge, which had come from so many years of being exposed to sports. By 1964 there weren't many broadcasters in New York who could say that they had been to Ebbets Field when Casey Stengel was still managing the Dodgers. And here old Casey had been the first leader of those crazy Mets—it was almost like the good old days in Brooklyn. To my amazement, the interest in sports trivia was growing bigger and bigger. I found that I had not only made it on radio but was being sought to do other jobs—and there is no more satisfying feeling than this in my business.

Because of the successful telephone talk show, NBC thought it would be a good idea if I branched out. My new vehicle was a game show called *Reach for the Stars*. I was the host. Well, I reached for the stars, all right, and fell right on my keister. The program ran thirteen weeks and died.

Then there was talk that I might become the next host of the *Today* show, but that became one of those "close-but-no-cigar" stories, because the show was switched from the entertainment program department to the news department. In the news producers' eyes, I wasn't a newsperson. Instead, they picked Frank McGee.

Naturally I was discouraged. But, having established a foothold in New York, I was able to move around without fear of returning to Buffalo. I left NBC and worked for a time at WOR Radio. Soon afterward, I received a call from CBS. That network had gotten the National Hockey League contract and they wanted me to be their hockey analyst along with Dan Kelly, who was doing play-by-play.

Hockey rapidly became my broadcasting bread, if not my butter. I became color analyst for the Rangers, with Tim Ryan, and did the same for New York Knickerbocker basketball games with Jim Gordon. For a time I also handled the New York Islanders' games on radio. At one point I worked both the Knicks and New York Nets games as color commentator and thanked Heaven for the experience I got in Buffalo doing the Canisius and Saint Bonaventure games. I'm the only guy who did both those teams as analyst, although Marv Albert handled them for play-by-play.

Meanwhile WHN (I never forgot the time when Bert Lee, Jr., beat me out for that job) paid me a handsome sum to do a talk show from the Plaza Hotel. It was while I worked the Plaza that I received what would be my biggest break up to this point. The call came from WNEW-TV, Channel Five in New York, now Fox Five. They liked my radio work and came up with the idea of producing the first-ever, half-hour all-sports news show. It would run on Sunday evenings, after the regular hour of news, and be called *Sports Extra*.

This was the challenge of my career. First of all, I had to make good on it, after flopping with the game show. I knew it was a gamble, because many people figured a half-hour devoted only to sports wouldn't sell, and we were on a limited budget.

At first they teamed me up with Lee Leonard, an amiable

fellow but one who was not nearly as steeped in the sports business as I was. Still, we complemented each other and managed to get the show off the ground and keep it aloft. In time my co-host changed. John Dockery, a former football player, would come aboard. He remained until the producers decided that *Sports Extra* should simply have Bill Mazer as a solo act.

My success on *Sports Extra* had nothing to do, however, with my trivia expertise. This remained a relatively insignificant adjunct to my on-camera persona until someone got the bright idea to add me to Channel Five's nightly newscast as the regular sports commentator. The exposure on the weeknight shows put me over the top. Now I was being seen not only by the sports nuts but by the casual fan and the non-fan as well. I may not have become a household word in Forest Hills and Canarsie, but I was getting there. The move in the trivia direction was accelerated by a staff reporter who had become familiar with my retentive memory and keen knowledge of past events.

Bob O'Brien suggested to our news director that it would be a nice twist to the hour-long show to have a segment in which the fans tried to stump me by sending in questions about sports. The idea fascinated me and I decided to question some friends, to get their opinions. One of them who was representative of the typical response put it this way: "Bill, don't do it. Either way, you lose. If you miss the question, you look like a fool. If you get it right, the skeptics will say you had been tipped off to the answer."

I could see their point, but I decided to go ahead with the idea anyway. Despite the warnings I received from well-meaning friends, none of the negative predictions came to pass. I had little trouble fielding the majority of questions, and those I missed merely revealed to the viewers that I was "amazin' " as billed, but not perfect and therefore phony. We also hoped it would be apparent that the questions were not fixed, since they certainly were not rigged in advance. My anchor, John Roland, would get them a few seconds before our segment began and I never had any idea what was inside the envelope.

Undoubtedly, the best testimonial to the success of the new trivia format came in the public response. It was overwhelming, both in the growing numbers of trivia questions received and in the growing number of those who watched the segment. People began tuning in just to see how I would fare in the night's trivia test and they began reacting as John Roland had when he dubbed me "The Amazin'." I was rapidly developing an image as the king of trivia, and, while I never liked the term, I was quite willing to accept my new position of "royalty."

Sometimes I'm taken aback by the trivia phenomenon, because I see it as an *adjunct* to a totality, not the totality itself. For example, there are times when I hear questions and think, "Gee, that's a really good question, something I never thought of." But if you think I sit around all day thinking of trivia questions, you are mistaken. I would call this mass of sports facts I've retained general knowledge—information—and I'm always happy to discover new information. But I don't ever think up questions I wish people would ask me.

In any given year, two dozen books on baseball alone will be published, with a ton of new information, or new ways to look at old information. And, I've talked to thousands of people over the years who impart even more information, people like a Ted Williams or a Joe DiMaggio. Since I've now been around for more than a few years, I can speak firsthand about characters today's sportswriters have only heard about.

For example, when the wonderful boxer, Ray Robinson, died early in 1989, many writers wrote columns about Robinson. But in truth, what did they really know about Ray? Did they ever meet him in his prime, as I had? To me the great Sugar Ray Robinson wasn't a picture on the wall, or a series of numbers on a page. I *knew* the man, broadcast his fights. My first broadcast in Buffalo was a Robinson fight.

Another example: A movie called *Eight Men Out* made the rounds in 1989 and caused a lot of talk. It was about the infamous Black Sox Scandal of 1919. I'd say about 99.9 percent of the sportswriters knew about it through secondhand sources—and even though I may be getting gray around the muzzle, I wasn't there then, either! But I got the firsthand information. How? When I was in Buffalo, the manager of the Bisons one year was Ray Schalk, who also happened to be the "clean" catcher on the White Sox the year they dumped the World Series to Cincinnati. Schalk gave me the inside story, person-to-person, so it wasn't as if I had just read about it.

I have always tried to move behind the numbers, the trivia, to the story. To me, there is a universality that traces its way through broadcasting through the forties, fifties, sixties, seventies, eighties, and hopefully into the nineties. That is, people want to know the story and they want to know the players in the story.

Face it, if you came down from Mars and saw nine guys contesting nine other guys in a game where they swung a piece of wood at a horsehide ball, you'd wonder what the hell was going on. Now there are those who compare the home run "escaping" from the arena to the Greek concept of the soul escaping from the body, and there's no doubt that watching that soaring ball can be a heart-stopping experience. But to me, the people playing the game are far more important. Who are they? What are they? How do they perform the game? Uppermost in the Mazer scheme of broadcasting is the individual ballplayer who is usually the story. And the story is often not the superstar.

For instance, when Babe Ruth and Joe DiMaggio were the greatest players who ever stepped on a diamond, I attached myself to a guy named Van Lingle Mungo. Why? Because it was a constant struggle for Mungo. He had all the equipment, but he was like Sisyphus in the Greek myth: he kept rolling the stone uphill and it kept rolling back. Ruth rolled the stone up the hill and over it. It was the same with my attachment to the Brooklyn Dodgers. Like Sisyphus, they rolled the stone up to winning the pennant but never could win that World Series, at least not until I was well into adulthood.

My goal as a sportscaster has been to bring alive the struggles of the Van Mungos of the world. I was inspired by Red Barber, who brought players like Whitlow Wyatt and Dolf Camilli alive for me. It was thanks to Barber that I learned that Camilli's brother, Frankie Campbell, who was a heavyweight fighter, had been killed in a fight with Max Baer. Thanks to Barber, I learned about Hugh Casey, who, by the way, had a bar under his name outside the BMT Prospect Park subway station at Ebbets Field. Do you remember the trivia question I posed about how Casey and Ernest Hemingway once got into a boxing bout? Even more interesting, in a morbid kind of way, is the fact that both men would end up committing suicide.

Sports is fascinating because it provides an instance where man transcends his existential life. When you see people rise to the heights of a Babe Ruth, Carl Hubbell, Mickey Mantle, Reggie Jackson, it lets you think that maybe you, too, can transcend mundane life. Maybe *you* can succeed. We all want to live with our feet on the ground but our heads in the sky, and that's one thing sports—maybe baseball in particular— lets us do. When you see someone beat the odds, then life isn't simple existence anymore. Sports helps make a human being something more than just a piece of movable clay on the planet.

Somebody who works a nine-to-five job can vicariously perform the feats of a ballplayer, live his life. What the hell, that's what movies are all about. That's what books are about and that's what art is about. The artists who enliven the canvas that is sports give us a sense of transcending mere living.

At any rate, I must have done a fair job of telling the stories about sports, because *Sports Extra* is now more than halfway through its second decade and I've long passed the decade-mark with the ten o'clock news. To make life even more fun, I was invited back to a prominent radio slot when WFAN, the first all-sports station in the country, hired me to host a daily interview program on weekday afternoons from Mickey Mantle's Restaurant in Manhattan. Within weeks of my starting the new slot, the ratings shot up. It became difficult for me to walk down the street after finishing the afternoon show without doormen, cabbies, and pedestrians stopping me, mostly to recommence a discussion I might have been having that day, or to dispute something I had said on the news the night before. What seemed to amaze acquaintances who occasionally walked with me after the show was how accessible the general public assumed I was. Lots of times when television people walk down the street, their admirers are afraid to say anything; they feel the personality is untouchable, not real. But not the fans in New York City—they just march right up and start talking.

Truth is, I love it. Not just because of the recognition, but because they *do* feel that I'm accessible. After all, that's exactly the sense I've been trying to get across all these years: I really am talking to *you* when I address the camera. It's you and I having a talk about what happened in the game today, or who got hurt or who's too big for his britches. I'm just another working stiff who is lucky enough to be doing what I love and getting paid for it. The greatest sense of accomplishment comes from seeing that people feel that they know me, not just that they know who I am.

Another great satisfaction I've had was knowing that, before he died, my father began to see that choosing a life in sports and broadcasting wasn't as petty as it had looked on Minna Street. He actually became a sports fan. That's right, my dad, who never knew Joe DiMaggio from his brother Dom, would call me up and have endless discussions about baseball, football, whatever. It really tickled me. One night, when Dad was giving me his opinions about the Twins' chances that season, the thought flicked through my mind, "Even *Zayde* would have been proud!"

Besides, who said it was trivia?

INDEX

H

I

J

S

T

Y

Z